Railway conversion

- the impractical dream

by   E. A. Gibbins

M.C.I.L.T.

Published by

Leisure Products
11 Bedford Grove
Alsager
Stoke on Trent ST7 2SR

British Library Cataloguing in Publication Data

A catalogue record of this book is available from the British Library

0 9535225 1 2

Dedicated to Irene with all my love and gratitude
for her continued encouragement in my research

oooooooooo

The author wishes to thank those who assisted his research:

Public Record Office, House of Lords Record Office,
Chartered Institute of Transport Library, Keele University,
British Library & Newspaper Library

libraries with railway collections
National Railway Museum, Newton Abbott, Widnes, Winchester

other libraries:
Alsager, Birmingham, Bishopsgate Institute, Bradford, Crewe,
Hanley, Inverness, John O' Groats, Liverpool, Manchester,
Oban, Somerset, Sunderland, Wick

organisations which generously supplied copies of media reports
and local authorities which sent data and maps,

Carl Defebo of the Pennsylvania Turnpike Commission,
Jerry Quelch of the New York Port Transit Authority,
Michael Leppard,

those who provided photographs
Bishopsgate Institute, David Hibbert, Basil Jeuda, Jamie Orr, Carl Tart, Mark Watson

and many others

oooooooooo

Written in memory of
the many BR managers who tried to make railways viable,
despite inequitable Government policies which favoured road transport,
and a scale of unwarranted and unqualified interference
never experienced in any other industry.

Preface

I came across the idea of converting railways into roads in 1958, whilst researching for material to use in a debate between the Station Masters & Goods Agents Discussion Groups based at Sunderland and Newcastle on Tyne. I was, then, Assistant Goods Agent at Sunderland. These groups met on one evening per month, and were addressed by someone from outside businesses or by senior BR managers. At least one of the latter would attend our meetings. As a change, the Newcastle secretary came up with the idea of a debate. The motion he proposed was: *That it is in the national interest to restrict the carriage of passengers & freight by road.* Sunderland had to speak against the motion. Not surprisingly, our secretary had difficulty finding someone to take on this task and eventually asked me to be the lead speaker for our side, despite me telling him that I had no experience of public speaking or debates. To try to prepare a case, I wrote to every road organisation that I could trace. A directory in Sunderland library listing their names, mentioned Brigadier T.I. Lloyd - author of a concept of converting railways into roads. I did not tell him - nor the road organisations - that I was a railwayman, they may have been less helpful. He sent me a copy of his booklet and a transcript of proceedings of the Institution of Civil Engineers, inviting me to make full use of these items. They were useless for the subject being debated, but, having a tendency to hoard papers, I kept them. The material supplied by the other organisations - BRF, AA, RAC, British Road Services, Road Haulage Association, Municipal Bus Operators and Private Bus Operators proved to be of some use. The seconder against the motion was Len Wright.

The debate was attended by Norman Payton, the Divisional Operating Superintendent covering Newcastle and Sunderland Control areas. Afterwards, he told Len and I: '*You won the debate, but lost the vote - as you would expect among railwaymen*'. The irony is, that those who proposed the motion - to place legal restrictions on road transport - had history on their side, although the full scale of restrictive railway legislation was not catalogued. It would not have been easy to collect in a short time. I later discovered that railways were deliberately impeded, over many decades, by government, from competing on a level playing field with road transport. The facts gleaned from post-retirement research proved this beyond doubt, and were brought out in my book: *Square Deal Denied*

The impression that I gained of many critics of railways, was that they were trying to demonstrate the railway skills that they had learned on the playroom floor. It was my belief then, and still is, that had railways been treated on a comparable basis as road transport, no special favours were needed for railways to be successful. However, I was to learn that politicians had never had any intention of giving railways equal commercial freedom as that enjoyed by other businesses, including other transport and nationalised industries. The evidence of this is recorded in my books *Square Deal Denied* and *Britain's Railways - The Reality*. Ministers claimed that they knew how to run businesses, but enforced policies on BR which would have bankrupted *any* company, however skilled their management. However, playing to the gallery, by interfering in pricing and other management decisions, had major electoral advantages. Anyone who reads recent critiques by leading historians, of political blundering in other fields, over the last 90 years or so, should see how railways came to be decimated by political incompetence. Had that not happened, the basic premise for conversion would never have arisen.

My book *Blueprints for Bankruptcy* - which demonstrated how government policies had bankrupted BR - included a Chapter on the subject of conversion. This included the text of an unpublished letter to the Daily Telegraph which - using publicly available data - destroyed the basis of an advert by the Railway Conversion Campaign. Material from that book and some new sources was used for an article for *Focus* - journal of the Institute of Transport & Logistics - in October 2001, which was prompted by an article in the *Sunday Telegraph* urging conversion. I wrote to tell the editor that it had been put forward 50 years ago and demolished by road experts. He thanked me, but made no correction, but pursued the idea again in two subsequent articles.

The article in *Focus* prompted Frank Paterson, (former General Manager, Eastern Region, BR), to suggest to me that the subject required a wider audience. Hence this book, which contains a few facts and statistics included in my original draft article - but which being too long for publication, were left out by - together with a wealth of new material. When I began to research for this book, I discovered that Brigadier Lloyd's proposal had first appeared in the Royal Engineers Journal in June 1954, under the pen name *Monstroviam*, literally, *I show the way*. I fear that he was showing the way to catastrophe in terms of finance, fatalities and congestion. He certainly demonstrated that he knew precious little about commercial road transport - never mind railways! Having managed cartage operations at three railway goods depots, my experience embraced both road and rail transport. My job entailed a good knowledge of the law of inland transport relating to both rail and road - the principles of which we, in BR, adhered to, in marked contrast to the attitude and behaviour of our competitors. Little has changed, in that regard, since then.

This discovery led me to investigate what had been written or published since Brigadier Lloyd's book. This turned up a number of other papers, reports, media articles, etc., which are covered in this book. All have something in common with the Lloyd thinking - all are impractical and, where they venture into finance, it is proved - with their own figures, that they would be disastrous.

When researching for a previous book: *The Railway Closure Controversy*, I visited the offices of the Transport Users Consultative Committees in England & Wales and those of the Central Transport Users Committee. Among hundreds of files on closure cases examined by me, not one contained a representation that closure be approved and the line converted to a road. Why these opportunities were missed, when every case was advertised in the media, with the address of the Consultative Committee which would conduct a public hearing, is not clear. It may have been a fear of public ridicule or worse.

In my first book on railways, published in 1993, on the eve of the privatisation, in a Chapter on the external misinterpretation of complaints statistics, I coined the phrase: *If you are criticised on statistical grounds you must first check the source data*. That proved even more relevant and important for this study. This book reveals that statistics quoted to prove the alleged cheapness of conversion have no basis in fact, as costs claimed have been dismissed by the local authorities involved in 'conversion' of invariably small lengths of railway into part of a much longer section of new road. No separate costs were prepared for the railway section, since there was no need to do so. All other statistical claims made by the conversion campaign have been closely examined and shown to be wrong.

My investigation into conversion theory led to the discovery of the unreliability of road traffic statistics used by the road and conversion lobbies. I have learned that the impressive volumes of traffic: billions of tonne miles/km and billions of passenger miles/km prepared by the DfT - copied dutifully by ONS and freely quoted by the road and conversion lobbies - are really valueless, when making comparisons between road and rail. They may be adequate for other less accuracy sensitive matters. The second discovery is to find how different are the objectives of the road and conversion lobbies. The true self-centred road lobby counts every tonne and every passenger originating on every road whether rural or residential. Conversion campaigners count only motorways and trunk roads in comparisons of highway mileage and accidents. Perversely, they then seek to count all road traffic wherever it flows, including that originating on rural and residential roads. They ignore that no traffic originates on motorways, and relatively little on trunk roads. Most fatalities occur on those roads, whose existence the conversion campaign endeavours to air brush out of any comparison with railways. Thus claims that using converted railways for express buses would cut accidents caused by buses, overlooks that those causing most accidents - i.e. in residential and business areas - will remain there because otherwise they will be virtually empty! They keep losing the plot. Their endeavours to beef up road traffic volumes, and downplay rail volumes, led me to research the reliability of their data. It opened a can of worms. Road traffic volume is based on little more than crude estimates.

So obsessed are the conversion theorists with the desire to prove that railways can be converted to *good* roads, they are willing to accept sub-standard width roads - really no better than tens of thousands of miles of existing roads. At the same time, they decry the inadequacy of those tens of thousands of miles of similar width roads as having been built in the horse era, and air-brush them out of any comparison with rail.

Ted Gibbins

Contents

Photographs   from the Author's collection except where shown

From 1555, road maintenance was, by law, carried out by local men who had to devote four days pa to the task; 'roads', such as they were, being mainly for local traffic. A local 'surveyor' was responsible for seeing each man performed the required number of days, which was later increased to six days. Surveyors were not qualified as we understand them today. Many roads were usable only by packhorse. Inadequate transport limited potential markets and increased prices. Rising industrial output taxed the existing means of water transport and seriously worsened the condition of 'roads', especially those leading to ports or rivers.

As traffic increased, parishes were unable to cope with increased maintenance. This led to the concept of Turnpike roads, whereby the users of roads could be charged for their use of roads and the funds devoted to maintaining and improving them. Turnpike Trusts were established by Act of Parliament which specified the tolls which could be charged. The earliest Turnpike was in 1663.[1]

As more turnpikes were developed, there was opposition by road users and from owners of other turnpikes who may lose their own traffic. The top surface of the better turnpike roads consisted of small stones, which were progressively crushed by coach and waggon wheels, thereby compressing the surface.

By 1706 the Turnpike system embraced all main roads - 22,000 miles; 100,000 miles of secondary and minor roads remained the responsibility of parishes. There was little overall improvement - if some roads were better, others were noticeably worse. Many users were critical of turnpikes - due to the frequency of having to stop to pay tolls at gatehouses, and to the condition of surfaces, some of which were not as good as users considered they had a right to expect for their tolls.[2]

Trusts were profitable, with returns which usually exceeded those from other available investments. By the end of the 18th century, new development had passed its peak, although measures to improve existing turnpikes continued.[3]

The original idea of turnpikes was that a Trust would borrow money, needed to repair a road, against security of future tolls, and when the income had paid off the debt, the road would revert to the parish, so Trusts were set up for a limited period, usually 21 years. In practice they seldom, if ever, succeeded in paying off debts, and were renewed by Parliament as a matter of course. After the 1870's, Parliament ceased to renew Turnpike Acts, and Trusts were gradually extinguished.[4]

A Commission of Inquiry in 1843 was told that in Swansea they cannot go 100 yards from their doors without paying a toll. Even a short journey could involve passing from the ambit of one trust to another. Users referred to exorbitant tolls demanded, whilst many glaring defects persisted. In 1835, before railways came to Wales, visitors found roads in a bad and insecure state.[5]

---

[1] *The Turnpike System in England*, by Wm Albert, Page 17.
[2] *Turnpike to Iron Road*, by HCB Rogers, Page 26.
[3] *The Turnpike System in England*, by Wm Albert, Page 114 & Appendix C.
[4] *The Archaeology of the Transport Revolution* by PJG Ransom Pages 22 & 195.
[5] Stage Coaches in Wales, by H Williams, Page 72

In its 3rd Report [Cmd 3751] in 1930, the Royal Commission on Transport noted: Between 1760 and 1774, over 450 Turnpike Acts were passed. Between 1785 and 1809, 1062 Acts were passed. Turnpikes were never popular, and were a source of resentment. In the mid 19th century, Parliament embarked on a policy of disturnpiking, reverting the liability to parishes. [Paras 24, 25, 33]. The turnpikes were set up for routes between towns. Roads that served industrial premises continued to be of a very poor standard. Industrial and population expansion also placed an excessive load on turnpikes.

As a direct consequence of the poor condition of what were loosely described as roads, the concept of 'railways' came into existence nearly 200 years ago - initially by laying timber or iron plates on those roads. On these, horses could haul much greater loads. Initially, this technique was confined to short distances from collieries or industries to the nearest waterway - river or later canal - over which minerals and goods could be conveyed at lower cost, and greater speed, than what passed for roads. This, in turn, led to the construction of purpose designed railways on land that had not hitherto been in use as roads, and horse-power was replaced by steam locomotives. The loads hauled progressively increased.

This new development led to vast profits being made by landowners for the sale of their land to railway promoters, which far exceeded the return they had been able to get from any other use of land. After the principal towns and cities had been connected by railways, the contractors had to promote lines elsewhere to maintain their business, and these tended to be rural with little prospect of viability. Landowners were keen to foster such lines, because of the assured profits from land sales. Unfortunately, many investors, sucked in by reports of huge dividends on lines sitting on coal, lost their capital.[6]

As a direct consequence of this greed, posterity became lumbered with railway lines in rural areas which always struggled to compete profitably with horse-drawn loads on roads which were gradually improving. Many minor railways were taken over at a fraction of their construction costs by bigger, profitable railways. Often, take-overs were motivated to block a possible route for competitors into intensively trafficked industrial areas. A classic example was the Wensleydale line from Northallerton to Hawes which was taken over, at an early stage by the NER, which enjoyed a virtual railway monopoly in the North East of England, and thereby sought to block other companies such as the Midland Railway and the LNWR from developing a route into the mineral rich North East.

---

[6] See *The Railway Closure Controversy*, Chapter 1

The conversion proposal initiated by Brigadier Lloyd[1] was founded on the premise that railways were declining, were losing money and would, in any circumstances, continue to lose money, whilst road transport was expanding and making profits. His paper[2] contained not *one* sentence to prove that he had endeavoured to research the causes of loss of rail traffic and deficits, by referring to the Annual Reports of the British Transport Commission and other publicly available data, including media reports.[3] Nor does he give *any* indication that he was aware of factors such as the excessive hours worked by road transport drivers nor reports of overloaded lorries, poor maintenance and dangerous speeding, which undermine any meaningful comparison.[4]

Factors affecting railway viability
The First World War

On the outbreak of 'The Great War', (later called World War 1), in 1914, the government which had not put a penny into railway construction or operation, seized the railways[5] under an Act of 1871. This Act empowered Government so to do during an 'Emergency'. Actual running and maintenance of the railways was left in the hands of professionals. An Executive Committee composed of twelve of the General Managers of the 123 railway companies was formed - on the advice of Railway Chairmen before war broke out - to undertake the task of running the whole railway system as one co-ordinated body. The Act specified that the railways would be entitled to compensation for use of railways, wear and tear from conveying war traffic and any injury, etc., arising from this sequestration.

Throughout the War, all conveyance connected to the war - munitions, materials, industrial purchases, soldiers, sailors, etc., - took place without a single penny changing hands. The Government interpreted its assumed power to use railways without charge very liberally, and it soon came to include allied military personnel, nurses, munitions workers, refugees, relatives visiting wounded soldiers in hospital, and many others on 'Government business.' As if this were not enough, Government transferred railway assets - locos, wagons, coaches, track - and manpower to the war zones to build and operate military railways to move masses of materials piling up on the docks! Eric Geddes, Assistant General Manager of the NER. was charged with the task of organising military railway transport in France and resolving the transport congestion on the docks.[6] Uniquely, he was given the rank of Major General to give him the required muscle with army top brass. The C-in-C of British Forces in France approved of this and

---

[1] He was Deputy Engineer-in-Charge at the War Office.

[2] See chapters 3,4,5.

[3] Informed reports in the *Economist*, *Times*, *Financial Times* and *Guardian* clearly identified that the causes of BR problems lay with inept political policies, not management, nor were they inherent of railways as such. See *Britain's Railways - The Reality*, Pages 167,170,171,173,174.

[4] See *Britain's Railways - The Reality*, Pages 186-189.

[5] Canals - except those owned by the railway companies - were not brought under government direction until late in the war, and then only at the suggestion of railway managers. Ships were never brought under central control.

[6] Responsibility for organising rail and road movements for the army was that of the Royal Engineers - the regiment of Brigadier Lloyd. This regiment included its own railway battalion.

acknowledged that this help by a professional railway manager was vital in pursuing the war.

During the control period, government directed increases in rail wages to match inflation - to be paid by the railway companies, not government, whilst the cost of all materials purchased by the railways also increased. Government froze rail fares and freight charges throughout the war, except for changes designed to discourage civilian travel. They turned to road transport. Employees in government and private sector munitions factories - among the best paid in the UK - were given free tickets or vouchers for half price rail tickets for travel at bank holidays and other times by government. Other government departments joined the band wagon, and the total vouchers quickly topped 1m pa. This was an outrageous action to take with the income of a private company. No other company was required to provide cut price products to anyone during the war.

At the end of the war, inflation had risen 200%, whilst rail fares and charges were largely at pre-war levels. When government was due to return railways to their owners, many faced serious financial problems not faced by other industry which had worked for government on a cost-plus basis, and whose prices to all customers - including railways - had increased without hindrance.[7] Thus, railways had income at pre-war levels, despite a traffic growth, whilst costs had rocketed. Before handing back control, and without consulting the owners, government granted the workforce an eight hour day, and further increased wages. The effect was calamitous on many railways, despite post-war increases in fares and charges being permitted by a series of government Inquiries.

Government then welshed on the provisions of its own Act and its undertakings to put railway compensation claims for excessive wear and tear, and free use of railways for government and military traffic, to arbitration by a Court of Law. Instead it set up a political Committee under Lord Colwyn[8] to decide what was due. Railways were not even allowed to be present to set out their claims nor to cross examine government witnesses. It took only 17 days to decide on the complex records for seven years sequestration. The media reported that the claim would amount to about £400m, the biased Committee said it should be £150m. They criticised railways for 'a tenacious insistence on Documentary Rights', which were *contracts* between railways and government! The Minister of Transport, who had appointed the members of the Committee, reduced the figure to £60m to be paid over two years - and then deducted tax from it![9]

The threat of nationalisation of railways was openly voiced after the war - notably by Winston Churchill. This was a threat the railways could not ignore, and left them with no choice, but to accept the pittance offered. Many railways - especially in Scotland, Wales and other rural areas faced bankruptcy. The traffic of these smaller companies had risen during the war - but it was government traffic free of charge, and revenue had been cut by loss of profitable civilian traffic. Their costs were increased by government decisions on wages and industry fuelled inflation, and they faced heavy maintenance arrears. The prospect of widespread closure of thousands of miles of lines could not be tolerated by government. It would be electorally and economically disastrous, and would lead to de-population. With fear of nationalisation as a backdrop, the government passed an Act

---

[7] Government contractors were amassing vast fortunes from the war. (*Realities of War* by Phillip Gibbs, Page 437)

[8] See *Britain's Railways - The Reality*, Page 5.

[9] See *Square Deal Denied* for a full account.

4

forcing 123 railway companies into four groups - each embracing profitable and unprofit-able railways, the former subsidising the latter. Initially, Ministers envisaged more than four groups, one of which would have comprised all railways in Scotland, but were dis-suaded when it became apparent that widespread closure in Scotland would be inevitable.

Inter-War Period

Railways have been criticised retrospectively, for not closing more rural lines during the inter-war years. There is no doubt that government would not have allowed railway companies to seriously undermine government policy which was intended to keep uneconomic rural lines open - at no cost to the taxpayer. The threat of nationalisation was always in the background.

As a sop to the public and industry, both of which had waxed fat on higher earnings whilst paying pre-war prices to use railways, but would have to face substantial increases in rail charges to bring income above costs, government legislated for a permanent control of railway charges by a Court of Law created for the purpose. Its duty was to peg total railway profits - *in perpetuity* and without adjustment for inflation at 1913 levels! No other industry in war nor peace has ever faced such commercial restraint and interference. The essence of this law remained until 1957, when the Court's powers were reduced - but not abolished until 1968.

Whilst this was taking place, government deliberately fostered the growth of the infant road transport industry, (see pages 7,8,12). An Act of Parliament gave *anyone* the right to inspect railway rate books to find out what charges applied between any two points. This was exploited by hauliers to undercut railway rates. If railways wished to cut their rates to compete for one firm's business which had come under threat of transfer to road, the railway had to also cut the freight rate for every other customer with like traffic, whether or not their traffic was at risk to poaching by hauliers. There was no similar constraint on hauliers. Railways had to apply to the Court to alter its standard rates. Hauliers were not interested in traffic carried - by law - at very low rail rates to help inefficient industry, but only in that at higher rates, which was supposed, under the law, to cross subsidise rail traffic at low rates. It was not long before the financial balance was under strain.

Railways tried repeatedly to get government to change the law so that both forms of transport competed on an equal basis - both controlled by the same regulations. Government set up a series of Public Inquiries to consider ways of regulating road transport. Sir William Wood [Vice President of the LMSR], in a lecture to the Institute of Transport in April 1936, said either road transport must be regulated like railways or railways must be given comparable freedom from controls. (Times 7.4.36). He overlooked the third option, viz. government inertia.

The Inquiries proved ineffective[10] so railways asked to be given the same complete freedom as hauliers. Their campaign was called the 'Square Deal Campaign'. Ministers made sympathetic noises - in public - but in private, they were adamant that they would

---

[10] Although they led to licensing of road passenger and freight transport, there was no comparable limit on working hours. Hauliers retained complete charging freedom, and were free to select which traffics they would convey, whilst rejecting anything potentially uneconomic. Licences designed to limit the number of lorries on the road, ostensibly to avoid over capacity, were easily thwarted by the widespread use of trailers - whose numbers were uncontrolled - and the overloading of lorries beyond their design capacities. The Inquiries were given evidence of serious malpractice in road transport of overloading, speeding and excessive hours.

not concede such freedom[11]. Government papers reveal that Ministers were well aware that if they did, the burden of subsidising inefficient industry would transfer from railways to the Exchequer. They also feared closure of many rural lines which were becoming important - serving new airfields, military camps and munitions factories in rural areas - for the war which was imminent. As will be seen, railways - but no other industries - were to be prevented from gaining any profit from the increased war traffic. Private sector industry reaped huge profits in the lead up to war. Government played 'pass the parcel' until, war came - as it had been forecast by a government committee five years earlier.[12] It has been claimed that the outbreak of war in 1939, blocked the conceding of equality. Public Record Office files of government and privately owned railways show that Ministers had no intention of conceding equality, and used the war as an excuse. During the War, Ministers stated, that after the War, there would be no Square Deal[13].

The road transport industry launched an advertisement campaign to try to block the equality of commercial freedom for railways, which hauliers enjoyed. They decried the relevance of this lack of basic managerial and commercial freedom, to the loss of rail traffic to road. They did not, of course, offer to prove this - by putting their money where their mouth was - and exchanging their freedom for the legal constraints on railways!

Government set up an ostensibly independent Inquiry into the railways' claim for freedom, but Public Record Office files show that Ministers and civil servants interfered secretly with the Advisory Council's findings, and had the draft Report altered before it saw the light of day[14]. The duplicity of Whitehall warriors fooled many[15] into believing that the railways were going to get their freedom eventually. They did not fool top executives of the Big Four railway companies. However, nationalisation ensured that railway views remained under wraps for 50 years, along with Whitehall memoranda which would have given the game away.

The Second World War

Once again, Government seized control of railways - but not shipping, road transport or canals - to subsidise the war, and did very nicely out of it, to the tune of £1 billion. Once again they froze railway charges, whilst the rest of industry - including other transport - was free to increase prices to match inflation. Road transport was slapped on the wrist for outrageous increases in charges - which went way beyond inflation - but did not end the malpractice.[16]

Masses of traffic diverted from coastwise shipping and road was carried by railways, effectively free of charge, due to the profits ceiling imposed on railways. The railway companies protested and had support from the media which described the arrangements as unfair, and made comparisons with industry which was working for government on

---

[11] Recorded in papers held under lock and key for up to 50 years - see *Square Deal Denied*.

[12] See *Inland Transport* by C.I. Savage, Page 51.

[13] HoL Hansard, vol. 129, col. 384.

[14] See *Square Deal Denied.*, Pages 110,112.

[15] Most of the media was misled, only *Modern Transport* saw the writing on the wall. Professor Gilbert Walker was misled for, in his book *Road & Rail*, he implied that long sought freedom was imminent. The book's second edition three years later, left out any reference to the Square Deal. He never lived to see the damning government papers released, so he would not know how he had been misled. Others, who read Walker's book were misled to this day.

[16] See *Square Deal Denied*, Chapter 13, & *Britain's Railways - The Reality*.

cost-plus contracts.[17] Again, the dreaded word 'nationalisation' was voiced in Whitehall, and railway companies had to accede to government flouting legislation that it had passed in 1921, designed to limit profits to the level of 1913, which they were still below, entirely as a result of Government's iniquitous and discriminatory transport policies.

Politicians of both parties concluded, during the war, that, after the war, nationalisation of railways would take place, to avoid the electorally unpalatable but inevitable alternative of increasing railway fares and charges after the war to catch up on inflation created by other industry and government - as had happened after the First War.

After the war, railways were not allowed, even, to restore to pre-war standards, much less modernise, whilst road transport was allowed free licence.[18]

Nationalisation

In 1948, three years after the war, railways were nationalised and a re-named and more powerful Court of Law - The Court of the Transport Tribunal - was created to control fares and charges. Despite industry in both private and public sectors having increased prices to match rising costs during the war, whilst rail prices were frozen, BR was not allowed to increase any charges to catch up on seven years of under inflation pricing. In 1948, railway charges were at 1941 levels, and suppliers' prices at 1948 - in some cases. 1949 - levels! Rulings of this Court of Law and Directions of Ministers held fares below inflation for 40 years, and freight charges for 14 years. During this time, the Court reduced proposed increases which were below inflation and delayed those reduced increases by an aggregate $12^3/_4$ years.[19] By the time of privatisation in the mid 1990s, BR had been denied £11.6bn in fares alone as a result of fares falling behind inflation.[20] BR was obliged, unlike competitors, to carry military personnel, and families at half fares. In March 1951, the Chancellor told the Cabinet that this cost BR £3m pa - 3.3% of income.

Losses soared as a direct result of this and other interference including, the inability to cut the dead wood of rural lines without external approval and Ministers directing BR to pay higher wages than they could afford, after managers had declined claims.[21] Interest had to be paid on loans taken out to cover deficits created by these policies.[22]

A Draft Bill in April 1952 proposed total freedom for the BTC and BR, but Prime Minister, Winston Churchill told Cabinet: he *would not accept they should be free even with the approval of the Transport Tribunal to adjust rail rates without intervention by Government or Parliament*. This was not surprising, as government had a few days earlier overturned a *legal* judgement by the Tribunal. The DoT file on the Draft Bill states: 'The main principle is that road haulage should be allowed to expand to the extent that may be justified by demand and BR should effect economies to offset the loss of traffic'. (PRO: MT62/138). That was only valid if Ministers foresaw that BR could not avoid

---

[17] The Times 16.8.40.

[18] See *Britain's Railways - The Reality*, Page 54, 55.

[19] See *Britain's Railways - The Reality*, Appendix B.

[20] Some economists illogically focussed on fare increases above the *current* RPI in the early 1970s, ignoring the long term effects. BR was formed in 1948, not 1972 and was still carrying deficits created by 25 years of serious underpricing and interference. These increases did not recover earlier losses. See *Britain's Railways - The Reality*.

[21] See *Blueprints for Bankruptcy*, Page 38 and *Britain's Railways - The Reality*, Page 131.

[22] Referring to railway problems, the Times editor wrote (25.1.55): government influence on railways has been far reaching, and they cannot escape the lion's share of responsibility.

traffic loss, due to statutory rates control. For someone with Churchill's command of the English language, the phrase *'free even with the approval of the Transport Tribunal'* is astonishing. It is clearly a contradiction of freedom.

'Charges Schemes would provide for maximum charges giving flexibility'.[23] They would *'contain provisions precluding unduly low BR charges designed to undercut competitors and drive them out of business'*. Road charges designed to drive BR out of business were not precluded! To match cost increases, *'the BTC would have power to make temporary increases up to 10%, which must be across the board, not discriminatory'*, and seek approval of the Transport Tribunal to those increases which were needed to catch up on inflation.[24] Hauliers did discriminate. The BTC drew attention to 19th century laws from which competitors are free - while a new disability is introduced giving hauliers power to object to lower charges, whilst they undercut rail charges as they please.

Reporting on Tory Government's proposed legislation, *The Economist* warned (29.11.51) that the Bill was flawed and that flexibility of charges would be blocked by traders' objections. It further stated, (10.5.52): If road haulage is to be freed on those terms [i.e. free of public obligation and free to choose traffics and name its own charges], and railways left under the present forms of control, there will be no competition between the two that will serve the public good in the long run. Railways would be left with public obligations as common carriers, subject to close political control, required to provide some services below cost and impeded from altering those charges as their costs change. If the railways are to have a chance of competing with road haulage, let it be on terms that leave them less hampered by restriction applying to them alone and more free to run their affairs as an independent business. If railways can be given the chance to act less as public carriers and more as providers of such transport as can be made to yield a reasonable return over the cost of carrying, there is no reason to suppose that they would necessarily come off worse in competition with road transport. These are broadly the terms on which long distance road passenger services pay so well. They have not been the conditions under which railways have ever been allowed to operate in this country. But they are the only conditions under which competition between the two different forms of transport has any meaning. The result would be a pruning, which might not be to the public's liking.

Until 1957, BR was compelled to hang onto the deadly rates system forced on railways in 1921, requiring BR to seek legal permission from the special Court of Law to increase freight rates to match inflation and rising costs. From then until 1962, this Court of Law still exercised control on about a third of all freight rates, and even directed the reduction of some existing rates. Suppliers' prices continued to rise unchecked.[25]

Of all transport and industry, only BR was required to accept all business offered whether profitable or not.[26] A fraudulent practice of UK industry and businesses, encouraged by hauliers, was the despatch by rail of empty crates and boxes as 'returned empties', which had been used on the outward journey to convey goods by road. Boxes and containers returned empty by rail attracted a very cheap rate to reflect that railways had benefited from an outward profitable transit. Those who worked in parcels offices and

---

[23] Flexibility demands no maxima - as applied in any industry except railways, even when privately owned.

[24] They never succeeded in catching up - see Appendix A.

[25] Trade rings operating in the UK electrical industry pushed prices up. (*On & off the rails*, by Sir John Elliot).

[26] Freight traffic until 1962; unprofitable passenger traffic until 1969, when subsidies for rural trains began.

goods depots were warned to look out for such fraudulent practice, but among hundreds of thousands of items, they were not easy to detect. The task was made more difficult when senders of empty containers fraudulently signed a consignment note declaring that the items were actually *returned* empties. Some were discovered because the item was unusual in some way and stood out, and staff could be certain it had not arrived by rail. Such discoveries were attributed to human error on the part of the sender's staff. The malpractice was known in Whitehall.[27]

In addition to the financial burden arising from government policies, the cost of acquiring the assets of the former railway companies fell not on the Exchequer, but on BR, which had to buy itself out of a restricted revenue, and eventually donate the assets free of charge to the State. BR had to pay annual interest on the loan stock forced on owners by the government, and to redeem a portion of the capital each year.[28] These sums averaged £32m pa. No other industry redeems all its capital. All losses had to be funded by loans from the City or government. By the end of 1962, despite government interference in prices and wages, their inertia on closures, indifference to soaring materials' prices, and directions to BR to subsidise bus companies following closures, BR managers contained the *cumulative* deficit before interest to £147m at 1963 prices, but were denied £1115m revenue,[29] by prices held below inflation and traffic lost to road by the archaic rates structure.[30] By the end of 1962 - before Beeching took over - BR would have had a substantial surplus instead of a loss had there been no interference.

Deficits created by government and the Court of Law [The Transport Tribunal] and escalated by interest on government loans, by 1963, created a debt of £1,560m. Until 1969, BR had also to fund the ideological Transport Tribunal, CTCC and TUCCs. [31]

In addition to losses caused by government and its agents, BR suffered further losses, arising from its inability to offer an adequate service to passengers and freight customers because government refused to permit them to restore assets to the excellent pre-war condition in which government took them over, although the privately owned companies had the resources to do much between 1945 and 1948, and nationalised railways were making good earnings for several years, from a buoyant post-war traffic. In contrast, the road transport industry took delivery of new vehicles in much bigger numbers than the government had decreed that the availability of steel and other resources permitted.[32]

At the same time, government threw taxpayers' money at the fragmented and infant aircraft industry in a futile endeavour to make it an effective competitor to the USA which was decades ahead. Not content with that, it could afford to throw taxpayers' money at UK industry - notably textiles, cotton, and shipping - and to *give* industry - *free of charge* - wartime factories built at government expense, whilst throwing money - it could ill afford - at the former Empire and the military. Despite this, when the crunch came, the military were unable to defend British assets abroad in the Middle and Far East. And finally, it shovelled out massive sums in compensation to shipping companies to replace

---

[27] The MoT told the Cabinet of this malpractice. (see *Britain's Railways - The Reality*, Page 9)

[28] See *Britain's Railways - The Reality*, Table 13.

[29] See *Britain's Railways - The Reality*, Page 176.

[30] See *Britain's Railways - The Reality*, Table 12.

[31] See *Britain's Railways - The Reality*.

[32] See *Britain's Railways - The Reality*, Pages 54, 55.

ships lost in the war - with the notable exception of railway companies which owned over 100 ships pre-war, and lost many from enemy action whilst in government service.

Government also carried out a promise to refund 20% of wartime Excess Profits tax to industry - but not to railways, which had not only paid this and other taxes, but had had a large percentage of its wartime profits seized by government - before tax! To facilitate diversions in the event of track and bridge damage by enemy bombers - which due to government parsimony were likely to have a free hand over the UK, government had funded some minor provision of track, bridges and sidings[33] before and during the war. After railways were nationalised, a parsimonious and grasping Treasury demanded that BR pay for these paltry well worn assets. Negotiations took place between civil servants at the Treasury and DoT on the one hand and ex-civil servant Reginald Wilson on behalf of the BTC speaking for railways. He was backed by Sir Cyril Hurcomb, chairman of the BTC, another ex-civil servant. Had more astute professional railway managers been negotiating, they would have told government what to do with its few well worn assets! Big Four management had told government during the war, that these assets would not be required post-war[34]. Had government been so told by BR, they would have been given BR's bill for removing and dumping these 'assets' elsewhere for government's disposal.

BR's suppliers played a part in increasing BR losses, by supplying unreliable equipment at inflated prices and subject to unreliable delivery dates[35]. This, of course, was par for the industrial scene in the UK, which is why UK manufacturers lost a world lead in *every* field since the war, despite Europe's industries being in worse physical shape at the end of the war. In addition, industrial customers of railways falsely attributed blame to BR for delays and phantom losses in transit, that were part of a smoke screen created to conceal industrial failures[36] in the face of overwhelming consumer demand, in the post-war era.

In cataloguing these external causes of financial decline, it is not intended to imply that BR managers made no errors, nor that their staff did not cause traffic loss. There is *no* evidence that they made more - nor even as many - errors as industry. It is certain that BR managers were more committed[37] to their industry than much of the rest of UK industry. Had the private sector been half as good as the media and they themselves appear to believe,[38] the UK would still be in the First Division on the world stage, and transfer of production to the Eastern Hemisphere would not have been necessary. There is clear evidence that UK industrial managers were lacking in imagination and afraid to implement productivity improvements that BR implemented without disputes. [39]

In 1961, MoT Ernest Marples appointed the Stedeford Committee of top businessmen, to report on the causes of railway deficits. Obviously, he expected them to expose BR

---

[33] £13m (see *Britain's Railways - The Reality*, Page 12), and in contrast with the assets of railways which were over £1bn, and with the £129m capital investment plus £1bn in working expenses spent by railways between the wars.
[34] See PRO: AN3/7.
[35] See *Britain's Railways - The Reality*, Chapter 14.
[36] See *Blueprints for Bankruptcy*, Page 162 et seq, & *Britain's Railways - The Reality*, Page 120 et seq.
[37] The Monopolies Commission found BR managers totally committed to the railway with a high degree of pride in the service which come before financial reward in importance and were impressed by managers they met at all levels. (BRB Rail Policy for 1980s, Para. 6.1)
[38] The author's personal files bulge with complaints to UK companies and businesses, with little redress. They believe they have put matters right, if they deign to apologise. Getting redress is often like trying to get blood from a stone.
[39] See *Britain's Railways - The Reality*, Chapters 9 & 14.

failings, as it was a political belief that state industries were, by definition, inefficient, but they said political ineptitude was the main problem. He expected advice on how to make BR run like a private sector industry, but these involved freedom to decide prices, freedom to cut dead wood, freedom to invest and freedom to develop surplus lands as carparks and other purposes. All were vote losers. The Committee criticised interference in fares and charges which were below inflation, which should be left for professionals to determine, and said that the Law Court deciding rail charges, should be abolished. They said that closure of uneconomic lines should not be delayed, or if they were, government should overtly subsidise them. They stated that railways should be run by professionals, not, as hitherto, by outsiders such as Civil Servants and Generals.

The MoT prudently refused calls by MPs to publish the Report and did not disclose it to MPs. Only the MoT and Prime Minister would know the conclusions of the Report. The revelations may have brought down a Government that had been in power for nine years - too long to blame Labour. The Tories would quickly be reminded of the scale of their interference by the media and the Opposition. It may well explain why Marples remained MoT for five years - among the longest period that any politician remained as MoT - to ensure that the findings were buried.

Contrary to popular opinion, the Government did *not* implement the major recommendations of this body of private sector businessmen, which the MoT had wrongly assumed would be critical of nationalised BR, not of politicians! The Report[40] was not released by the Public Record Office until 1991, when it was virtually ignored by the media. It would have undermined much media criticism of railways, and may well have scuppered the ill-conceived, badly designed and costly privatisation of railways.

Some politicians have been misinformed with regard to railway history:
'Railways only got investment by borrowing £26m at 2.5% from government'. (Hansard, 17.12.46, vol. 431, col. 1832). The loans were Treasury guaranteed Bonds, not loans from government, and were to help reduce unemployment, rather than help railways. Meanwhile, government spent £130m on roads and told railways to spend their own money to make bridges stronger to help road transport. The railway loans were repaid in full. Railways invested over £129m of their own money on new capital projects between the wars, plus £1bn in asset renewal and working expenses. 'After World War 1, government gave railways a subsidy of almost £30m'. A more knowledgeable MP stated that it was 'in payment[41] for free war services'. (Hansard, 7.11.51, vol. 493, col. 306).

Contrary to political belief, railways did not consider themselves 'lucky when government took them over in World War I'. They accepted it as part of the war effort, although they must have been dismayed when they found that this action was not mirrored for other transport and industry, which were allowed to increase prices *and* profits. It could not have been considered lucky when government decreed that all war and government traffic would be carried free of charge, whilst they paid top dollar to other transport and industry. They did not consider it lucky when government forced the eight hour day on railways but not on road transport. They did not 'panic when

---

[40] See *Blueprints for Bankruptcy*, Page 41 & *Britain's Railways - The Reality*, Pages 29-30.
[41] They were seriously underpaid. (See page 4).

government let them have their industry back' after that War,[42] despite the most iniquitous treatment by government during and after that War. They were angry when they discovered that government intended to welsh on its contractual obligations to pay retrospectively for their free use of railways, and compensate them for abnormal wear and tear, and to ignore the 1871 Act under which they were seized.

If railways were *on the brink of collapse at the start of World War 2* as some claimed,[43] it was entirely due to government's anti-rail, pro-road policies.[44] Despite those policies, pre-war railways were 'not begging to be taken over by the State', nor did they fail to make investments,[45] nor did they get investment money from the Government,[46] nor were they 'saved by the war'.[47] Railways were *seriously* run down during that war because government unjustifiably sequestrated them - but not road transport - ruined their assets by over-use and under maintenance and siphoned off £1bn railway revenue.[48]

No other industry has ever suffered such interference in its competitive position - either in peace or war - as that experienced by railways, both when in the private and public sectors. The effect on railway finances must have been easily predictable to the most obtuse and biased mind. No industry - other than railways - has been legally required to incur costs which benefit a competitor - e.g. strengthening bridges to facilitate use by heavier road vehicles.[49]

Factors benefiting road haulage

Inter War Period

After the First World War, ex-soldiers and others were able to buy ex-military vehicles at knock down prices - many were in mint condition, direct from manufacturers, had not left the UK, nor turned a wheel in military service. Some changed hands in minutes at higher prices. For many years, new hauliers used roads - financed by local ratepayers, of whom railways figured large - without paying a penny for their use, and were able to work hours considerably in excess of those forced on railway companies by politicians for electoral gain in 1919. All hauliers and many bus operators could be - and were - completely selective in the traffic they conveyed, unlike railways, which were prevented by law from exercising similar practices.

It was an open secret that hauliers exercised their legal right to inspect railway freight charges books, and to offer a small discount on those charges to carefully selected railway customers to switch to road. If conveyance of such traffic at such charges proved uneconomic, the haulier could push the rate up, or abandon the traffic, and the customer would be *legally* entitled to revert to rail without penalty or facing higher charges than before. Railways were hampered in retaliating by a legal requirement to seek the

---

[42] Hansard, 2.2.93, vol 218, col 199/200.

[43] Hansard, 2.2.93, vol 218, cols 181/185.

[44] See *Square Deal Denied*.

[45] Hansard, 29.10.92, vol 212, cols 1173/4. Railways invested over £129.6m in that period.

[46] Hansard, 29.10.92 vol. 212, col 1174/7. Government provided interest bearing loans, which were repaid. (See *Britain's Railways - The Reality*, Page 11).

[47] Hansard, 2.2.93, vol 218, col 181/5.

[48] See *Britain's Railways - The Reality*, Page 18.

[49] See *Britain's Railways - The Reality*, Pages 128-129. Unlike other transport, hauliers introduced bigger transport without taking steps to ensure that the infrastructure was improved. Railways picked up the tab for the consequences.

permission of the law court to reduce rail freight charges. Moreover, if they did so for the one customer whose traffic was - at that moment - being poached, they had to make equal reduction in charges to all other customers who may be of no interest to hauliers.

The 1930s Public Inquiries by the Transport Advisory Council into competition between rail and road uncovered a mass of evidence of irregular and dangerous practice by road hauliers. No action followed.[50]

The Second World War

There were half-hearted and unsuccessful attempts to bring road haulage under government control in the interests of the war effort. Government took over the Big Four railways, because it could not liaise and lay down priorities with four companies, but would liaise with 300,000 hauliers! Hauliers' charges were uncontrolled, despite being warned several times that increases were unreasonable and unjustified.[51] They made huge profits.

Modern Transport reported (28.2.42): the Minister of War Transport said 'road haulage pools have not hesitated to push up rates to an undesirable degree. In October 1941 he again drew attention of the tendency of road rates to increase. In November 1941, increases in road rates were approved to reflect Sunday working costs for drivers.[52] 'The rise in road rates was out of all proportion to increased costs'.

Government's Road Haulage Scheme was announced January 1941. *Modern Transport* pointed out, that 'not until March 1942, did the first chartered vehicle turn a wheel under the *compromise* partnership scheme, evolved between Ministry and Road Haulage' which was intended to embrace 2,500 vehicles - a fraction of the road fleet.[53]

A Select Committee reported in April 1944 of complaints by industry of unexplained increases in road rates. 'Protesting firms said charges were absolutely ridiculous'. (Report Para. 32 f).

Post-War Developments

After the war, road transport was given a head start, with a blind eye turned to an excessive increase in fleets over pre-war, in contravention of government controls of resources, whilst railways were directed not to restore railways to pre-war standards.[54] Hauliers were again able to obtain ex-military lorries, many in mint condition, at knock down prices, and to buy brand new post-war built lorries. Two years after the war, privately owned road haulage industry had a fleet nearly 50% bigger than before the war. In contrast, railways were blocked from restoring assets even to pre-war numbers and condition[55] - much less modernising - for ten years after the war.

Marketing Ploys

One popular claim, made by hauliers to gain traffic was that a sender's goods would always be secure, as the driver was always with the vehicle. We now know that to be nonsense. If they cannot prevent a dozen illegal immigrants climbing into a lorry, they cannot prevent one person getting in and removing a package. Moreover, the security of

---

[50] See *Square Deal Denied*.

[51] See page 6 & *Britain's Railways - The Reality*, Page 17.

[52] No allowance was made for railways' increased Sunday working and overtime to handle their traffic increase.

[53] Three years after sequestrating railways, Government was compromising with hauliers over 1.6% of the fleet.

[54] See Government Economic Surveys 1947 to 1951 inclusive. These Surveys are summarised in *Britain's Railways - The Reality*, Page 54-55.

[55] Government Economic Surveys Cmd 7647, 7915, 8509 & *Britain's Railways - The Reality*.

goods by road is diminished by the scale of overturned lorries, shed loads, spillage of liquids, especially of chemicals and fuel into watercourses.[56]

In the 50s and 60s, BR sales staff reported that some hauliers were giving Christmas gifts to the person who decided whether goods would go by rail or road. BR sales staff were unable to do so - there were no BR funds for this purpose.

Road transport drivers were permitted - by law - to work for 50% longer each day than all railway staff - not merely engine drivers. The hours of all railway staff had been pegged at eight per day since 1919 by the government, against the wishes of railway companies. It was an open secret that even the excessive hours permitted for road transport, were routinely exceeded. Indeed, a White Paper stated as much: 'Many bus and coach drivers are working hours substantially in excess of their limits'.[57]

In *British Railways after Beeching*, W. Freeman Allen quoted from *Sunday Times* articles that revealed examples of road transport malpractice which made their use economically appealing to commerce and industry. It was clear that the hopes of BR that the, then new Freightliners may attract substantial freight traffic from road, would be limited by these practices which held road freight prices artificially low. This situation still prevails[58]

Articles by John Barry were published on 23 & 30 August 1964, headlined: *Scandal of 'cowboy' lorries* and *Phantom drivers who mock the law*. 'Such is the cut-throat rivalry, that in practice a substantial proportion of hauliers - not solely cowboys - infringe the law'. 'At least 65% of firms on the road are fiddling in some way or other'. He had interviewed three drivers who had slept for a few hours in their lorries.[59] One from Shropshire had delivered a load, and was waiting orders from the office when it opened, for a return load. Another from Sunderland would deliver that morning in Luton and London after two nights on Tower Hill, and then return loaded to Sunderland. A third had left Newcastle in the early hours for Slough, was awaiting a load to Avonmouth, where he would load back to Newcastle. By law, a driver should work no more than 11 hours daily. (*Clearly these were breaking the law*). Mr. Barry refers to queues of lorries with sleeping drivers at Covent Garden and Billingsgate, waiting for markets to open. He drew attention to the staggering scale of defective vehicles discovered in roadside checks. One driver drew into a checkpoint and asked for a check, as he hadn't had one for a year! His vehicle had four serious defects and was ordered off the road. Over 12% of vehicles were found seriously defective in 1963. The 'phantom driver' is a name of another person, entered on a fresh log-sheet when the legal hours of the original driver have expired. A different set of log-sheets were prepared for the purpose of calculating wages.

BR was criticised if unstaffed stations were vandalised. By contrast, vandalism of bus shelters does not produce criticism of bus companies nor the councils who provide shelters, but is acknowledged to be the fault of vandals, who in all probability are the ones who vandalise stations. Vandalised bus shelters are restored at public expense, not, as applies with rail [bus-type] shelters, at the expense of passengers or operators.

---

[56] There should be an annual report entitled Road Accidents to compare to the analogous one prepared by the HMRI on railways, with detailed analysis of individual road calamities, which usually only grace the media for one day.
[57] MoT Paper: Public Transport & Traffic, (Cmnd 3481, Pages 23-24).
[58] See *Juggernaut* by John Wardroper. There are references to some of his findings in chapter 12.
[59] By law, rest was required to be taken away from the vehicle.

Since the last war, proposals have occasionally been made to reverse the process of replacing roads by railways and convert railways into roads. The first conversion proposal appears to be that advanced by Brigadier T.I. Lloyd[1] in an article, under the pen name *Monstroviam* in the Royal Engineers Journal of June 1954. The word literally means 'I show the way'. He was showing the way to chaos and catastrophe. Whilst his approach to the task of assessing vehicle needs might have been adequate for the non-commercial basis of military assessments, they were never going to be the basis for any self respecting road transport operator. In a wartime scenario, the top military brass can probably pressure their political masters to make up deficiencies in their assessments of manpower and resources, without worrying about cost, by giving warnings of impending disaster. Anyone who has read military histories of the two World Wars, will find that they abound with accounts of planning, transport and logistical failures by the British. They do not have to justify a penny spent during a war. Everything that goes wrong and requires more resources and cannon fodder can be attributed to matters beyond the ken of those without military experience, especially politicians. The principle that *commercial* transport matters may - for like reasons - be beyond the ken of those of a *military* background, clearly escaped Brigadier Lloyd.

The period of which Lloyd was critical was when the BTC - which ran railways - was under the direct leadership of a retired general[2], who brought in others from the military with no commercial railway background. It was marked by increasing deficits. Railway professionals were not allowed to make decisions affecting day to day matters which would have increased revenue to supplement gains they made in increasing productivity.[3] It is not without significance, that the highly secret Stedeford Committee[4] were particularly critical that fares[5] had lagged behind inflation, were especially critical of government and external interference, and said that railways should be run by professional railwaymen. It was eight years later, that Henry Johnson became BR's first professional chairman - twenty years after nationalisation. Only two of the ten chairmen throughout the nationalised period, were professionals.[6] Their tenure was marked by significant improvement in running railways: modernisation, new traffic and more economies.

In his article, which appeared under the title: 'BR or BM?[7] An imaginative solution of the Transport Problem', he argued that, as the voice of the scientist is heeded increasingly in national affairs, a plea is made for the adding to it, the voice of the engineer. Whilst

---

[1] He was a professional soldier, joining the army at age 20 until age 55. He served in the Royal Engineers in the chemical warfare company and in the bridging company. He had no industrial nor commercial transport experience. Hence, his approach to the subject of commercial railways and road transport is impractical, a deficiency exposed on the following pages.

[2] Sir Brian Robertson who was also from the Royal Engineers.

[3] See *Britain's Railways - The Reality.*

[4] This was the name by which it became known in the media. Officially, it was the Special Advisory Group, composed of four top businessmen, the Chairman was Sir Ivan Stedeford, chairman of Tube Investments. Richard Beeching - who later became chairman of British Railways after Robertson was dismissed by the Government - was also a member. Their secret reports were withheld, even from Parliament, and not released for 30 years.

[5] Fares applications to the Transport Tribunal were made by non-railway professionals at the BTC, not BR managers.

[6] Johnson & Robert Reid. Raymond was not a railwayman as some have said. See *Britain's Railways - The Reality.*

[7] British Railways or British Motorways.

the scientist has clearly much to offer to business and industry,[8] and indeed did so on railways, being more than one step removed from contact with the customer, they share the same *commercial* limitations as engineers.[9]

He let his imagination run away with him, and ignored the realities of conflicting demand and supply from widespread areas, which contrast with military experience of supplying the demands of the front line - if the requirements of cannon fodder at the front can be termed a demand.

In advancing his theory for the conversion of railways to roads, his approach to assessing the number of road vehicles required to replace rail transport was one that will never gain a following in the *commercial* road transport world. No self respecting operator would order a fleet on the basis he uses. He began by taking an average attainable speed of a bus on the converted railway route of 60 mph and then related to it, the volume of rail passenger miles - some 20,000, pa. He concluded that 1,250 buses of 30-seat capacity could convey this passenger volume,[10] employing perpetual motion. He then went on to multiply it by 20 to arrive at what he said was a *practical* fleet of 25,000 buses. He gave no rational explanation for his method, nor did he explain why he selected 20 as a multiplier. It is pertinent to point out that this method of calculating transport fleets is still not in use. He then turned to railway freight traffic - some 22,400m ton miles - and said that this could be transported by 4,250 lorries of 10-ton capacity travelling at 60 mph. This was then turned into a *practical* fleet of 85,000 lorries. Having made these calculations, which will never be used by road operators as a basis for capital investment, he compared his 110,000 road fleet[11] with BR's rolling stock: locos, coaches, wagons, road motor vehicles and horse drawn vehicles. This came to a total of 1,242,000. From this, he claimed, the case was made at once for converting British Railways into British Motorways - and disposed of any argument that the present railway traffic could not be handled by his miniature fleet.

It is unfortunate that he did not really study BR statistics properly, nor worse to study road transport statistics at all. In the first place, he would have discovered wagons and locos involved in renewal and maintenance of track and infrastructure. These should be excluded in any comparison, in common with the vehicles required for highway maintenance, as neither are involved in moving revenue earning business.

He would also have discovered that BR had to maintain a fleet of some 6,000 coaches[12], plus locos, to carry industrial workers on their annual holidays. He was clearly unaware - as he spread freight and passengers around the 24 hours and across the four seasons - that entire industries shut down for two weeks each summer, and that their workers went by

---

[8] Railways had their own scientists who made an invaluable contribution to improvements on BR. (see *Britain's Railways - The Reality*, Chapter 9).

[9] When the author was Divisional Operating Superintendent, his colleague, Ken Brown, a highly respected Engineer told the author: 'my role is to help you to run the railway.' The author replied, 'mine is to respond to what our commercial and marketing colleagues ascertain that the customer wants.'

[10] See his book, Page 80. He ignored evidence that when railway lines closed, buses provided in lieu and subsidised by BR, did not survive. Passengers switched to car as soon as they could. Published data shows that whereas, rail volume fell slightly, bus volume plunged like a stone.

[11] Within a year, his fleet had fallen to 10,300, with little change in traffic level!

[12] See *The Reshaping of British Railways*, Page 15.

train en masse to traditional holiday resorts. In effect, a big percentage of the population of many industrial towns went on holiday at the same time. Dr. Beeching argued that the large number of coaches devoted to industrial holidays was uneconomic. Prior to that, it was always expected that BR would handle this peak seasonal traffic as a matter of public duty. It would have been uneconomic for *any* road operator. Of course, UK industry has obligingly removed the comparable problem which would have arisen for road operators, because they have shut down, and transferred to the Far East!

BR ton miles were the miles that freight was moved by rail. They specifically exclude the miles, traffic was moved by BR road vehicles. Hence 44,000 BR owned road vehicles were completely irrelevant to ton mile comparisons for a start. Moreover, he would have found that the bulk of BR's freight traffic was one-direction with no prospect at all for a return load.[13] Even lorries conveying merchandise would not all have return loads. Those delivering to wholesalers would not - except possibly returned empty crates, which take up a lot of space for negligible weight - as wholesalers use their own vehicles for distribution. In addition, he would have found - had he studied published data - that a large proportion of BR merchandise traffic consisted of consignments of under one ton each - Sundries traffic. Depots - and manpower - would be needed to combine these into 10 ton lots to one similar depot elsewhere. By definition, they did not go to one consignee. These depots would have to have a separate fleet of vehicles to collect and distribute this traffic in surrounding areas.

Why he took this convoluted route via a completely theoretical and dubious calculation, and then clutched an adjustment figure from thin air, defies comprehension. There was data available from which to assess the relationship between theoretical capacity of road vehicles and the volume of traffic actually moved.

MoT studies[14] revealed that 1,271,340 lorries moved 23,000m ton miles. True, this may include deliveries of coal, etc., in towns. However, he and the road lobby have never shirked from counting every last ton carried by road to prove it was much more than that carried by rail. They cannot, now, have it both ways. Elsewhere, Lloyd stated that four fifths of traffic is by road. He neglected to convert originating tonnage into ton miles when the volumes by road and rail became almost the same, and much less did he consider the much greater road mileage capacity needed for this equal volume of traffic. Moreover, of the 22,000m ton miles by rail, over 70% was mineral and coal traffic[15] that had no return load, and no possible return load. In contrast, most road vehicles probably had a return load, even if not fully loaded. He ignores the reality that senders of freight traffic will not - indeed cannot - always provide a consignment to a single customer in nice round lots of 10 tons weight, much less one that will always fit into one lorry.[16]

In the real transport world, operators know that weight and volume rarely synchronise to produce economical loads. True, he expected his new roads would permit higher speeds - although this would be constrained by the retention of the contra flows of road traffic at thousands of level crossings. He should have started his calculations from available not imaginary data. Even so, assumed higher speeds would have no effect on

---

[13] Particularly with millions of tons of coal to power stations, gasworks, ports and steelworks; also ore & aggregates.

[14] *The Transport of Goods by Road.*

[15] See BR Annual Accounts.

[16] This problem is exacerbated when he later changed his lorry size to 20 tons, and then 40 tons. (see pages 22,36,42)

average loads. His calculations ignore empty, and part-loaded journeys between customers to get a full load.

Likewise, there was available data to show what was being achieved by road passenger transport. In 1954, 80,643 PSVs handled 50,000m passenger miles. On that basis, to handle 20,712m rail passenger miles[17] by PSV would require 33,400 PSVs. This contrasts with Lloyd's figure of 25,000 vehicles required.

He claimed that the converted railways would be free of cross roads and accident black spots. He went on to say that the railway permanent way was consolidated by a century of rail traffic.[18] In fact, BR's civil engineers were constantly engaged in renewal and maintenance of the permanent way - restoration of landslips, replacement of ballast, maintenance of earthworks, bridges, cutting walls, embankments etc. - to maintain a good standard. One can only marvel that an *engineer* could be unaware of the ongoing magnitude of the railway engineer's task, not least because one would have expected a Royal Engineer officer to have had close contact with railway engineering staff called into the armed forces and serving in the Royal Engineers' own railway and transportation companies.

He expected that fares would fall, but the evidence is that when branch lines closed, hitherto competing bus fares *rose*.[19] Moreover, at the time of his paper and for the ensuing decades, the evidence is that BR fares were held below inflation[20] whilst bus fares were not. Both rail fares and rail freight charges were controlled at that time by a court of law, which both delayed increases and held them below inflation. It is not without irony, that he wrote in his article: *'This article must not be overloaded with known and knowable facts'*. It was not!

An example of the naiveté of his thinking is contained in his perception of how commuters would travel. To cater for those used to catching the 8.21, he imagined a number of buses lined up in station A ready to depart for station B at 8.21. Passengers would fill the front bus first, and it would probably move off at 8.18, when full, without objection. This is a misconception of commuter practice. They time their journey to a station to the second, and will not arrive 3-4 minutes early. Moreover, their door to door journey is based on the timetable. They allow themselves the minimum time possible to embrace their different modes of travel - including walking - for the throughout journey. If a train was late, they blamed BR. Indeed, commuters were masters at blaming BR when trains were *not* late, but they had arisen late after a bad night.[21]

He went on to postulate a late passenger arriving at 8.22, finding the last bus had left full at 8.21. This assumes a utopian world in which the number of passengers for a given train is divisible precisely by 60 - or 20, 40, or such other number as represents the size of his buses - so that every bus will depart full, without a prolonged wait for the last bus of a group to fill to 100%.

---

[17] The volume recorded in audited BR accounts, not the down sized 20,000m used by Brig Lloyd.

[18] Inquiries of local authorities involved in using the formation of closed railway lines, reveal that the railway foundations were not all so sound. (see pages 188,190).

[19] See Hansard, vol 590, col. 202.

[20] See *Britain's Railways - The Reality*, Appendix A.

[21] The author replied to a letter in the Liverpool Echo which attributed lateness at work to unpunctual trains, denying that it was the cause, and inviting employers to check with BR as to the record of any train blamed by employees. No letters were received, nor were there further letters in the Echo. see *Blueprints for Bankruptcy*, Page 177.

He said that there would be no timetables, buses would be employed as required, hence a full load factor of 100%. He ignores that not all passengers would be going to B, but to C, D, etc. in the same direction as B, and sundry destinations in the opposite direction. How many buses would be needed at any one time at this one station, is a matter that he ignores. Elsewhere, he dispenses with the need for signal boxes and sees no requirement for staff other than bus and lorry drivers. He ignores those who are to liaise and control his 25,000 buses to make sure that they are at the bus stations that need them today, which may well be vastly different from yesterday's requirements.

He saw traffic standing in wagons as something not wanted by the sender or consignee. Unfortunately, the century old habit of using wagons as warehouses to avoid double handling, and to provide a buffer against the all too frequent occurrence of a suspension of production due to strikes, manufacturing breakdowns, goods produced in blocks, will not be ended merely to make this theorist happy.

Nevertheless, he was certain that his new system would end the practice of BR providing free warehousing for industry, holding wagons in sidings and yards for days. To achieve that, UK industry would certainly have to change dramatically. It would need additional warehouses, machinery and staff to unload arriving traffic without delay. Loudest among the complaints would be that from UK's tens of thousands of coal merchants who could not function economically if they had to unload coal and coke at once. The ensuing double handling would cause the cost of solid fuel to soar, and would ensure that the political party which presided over this change would never enjoy government office again. The effect on UK industry would also be a sharp rise in prices which would have accelerated their evacuation to the Far East. UK industry was production led, which meant that materials were produced in volume runs that kept down production costs, whilst leaving customers to double handle and store as materials arrived, mitigated only by the extent to which they could coerce BR to provide free storage for them, to call in as required.

He casually notes that railways are fenced in throughout, but was unaware - or ignored - the reality that BR paid for the fencing and the frequent repairs resulting from vandalism and general wear and tear.

His scheme specifies that there will be no [common carrier] obligation to accept any traffic. This would be a major change and restraint on trade, as BR was the only form of transport that could not refuse to carry any freight - with the exception of dangerous goods, which were subject to stringent packing conditions. BR still carried large volumes of dangerous goods, but under stringent safety conditions. The article notes that nowhere does there exist well disciplined traffic, such as he expected would be that which would use the new roads. It is a matter of record, that, even with the current motorways - whose constructional and design eclipse those of the converted railways into roads that he envisaged - that well-disciplined is the last phrase that springs to mind when observing driver conduct in action today.

It was his belief that widening the railway to provide lanes to match MoT standards was unnecessary, even given greater speeds. There would be a few simple rules:-
• No dawdling - a standard *minimum* speed of perhaps 60 mph
• No halting, except in a lay-by, or shunt lane in a station.
• No overtaking at all on a two lane motorway.

- Only uni-directional overtaking on a three-lane motorway, e.g. for 5 miles in one direction, then for the next 5 miles in the other direction, or varied throughout the day to suit rush-hour traffic.
- On multi-lane motorways, a strict keep in lane rule, except at clearly marked places where transfer to the adjacent lane is permitted.

Finally, he stated that if the motorway were formed from a double track railway, probably no very great engineering problem would be met in adding a fourth lane.[22] He totally ignores the cost, which may prove to be a major problem, especially where compulsory purchase of adjoining property arises. As proof of the adequate width of rail routes to convert to roads, he instanced the Mersey Tunnel - 36 foot wide between kerbs, but did not mention its 30 mph speed limit! Later, he and his successors dispensed with kerbs or verges - a standard part of road construction - to prove railways were wide enough!

One benefit claimed was that tons of exportable coal would be replaced by a *few gallons* of imported petrol. Clearly, he had not seen the poor quality of coal being supplied to BR, since the post-war spread of coal cutting machinery. Export markets for this would have been hard to find, even for skilled marketing experts - of which, even he, could not have claimed to be one. In contrast, export markets for motor vehicles - even of the basic quality of those produced in the UK - abounded after the war. Modernising railways to effectively reduce home market demand for motor vehicles was a simple option that Ministers overlooked, when they directed that BR must not restore railways to pre-war standards for ten years, and burdened the nationalised industry with the clapped out coal wagons of the pre-war wagon owning companies. Those companies gained from nationalisation, being given cash with which some of them created very profitable hire purchase companies, which helped to fund motor vehicle purchases.

One or two throwaway lines in his article include: there would be heating of roads to deal with frost, lighting of roads, and 'the cost - forget it.' That may be a policy that the army could follow, but railways and industry had to follow strict principles to determine the financial viability of investment. Heating of roads can now be discounted as even a long term possibility. As a general rule, lighting of roads may be said to be uncommon, especially on single carriageway roads which Brigadier Lloyd saw as being the norm of converted railways.

A year later, he had modified his proposal to try to make it *sound* credible, followed by further modifications in the book that he published thereafter. Events proved that he failed to convince road engineers, commercial road transport operators, parliament and the public.

---

[22] He is supposing that he can get three road lanes out of one double track railway. Their comparative widths are set out on page 198. His successor - Angus Dalgleish disagreed with him, (see page 85).

Brigadier Lloyd delivered a Paper to the Institution of Civil Engineers in April 1955. It had many changes from that in the Royal Engineers' Journal.

He began by saying that he made no proposals for financing of conversion, since their relevance is a matter for individual judgement! He described the characteristics of new roadways - being on a permanent way, which runs *straight and true* - which showed how little he knew of UK railways!

He stated that:

- Rail gradients seldom exceed 1 in 100, and the steepest is 1 in 38.
- Converted railways would be reserved for fast free-running vehicles.[1]
- They would form a reserved toll road with no dangerous bends, having single carriageways, which professionals now favoured[2] as being safer than dual carriageways because drivers would have to remain alert!
- MoT requirements on new roads are for lane widths of ten feet, or eleven feet if on a single carriageway. Double track railways are never less than 24 feet, and often 30 feet at formation level.[3] The 30 foot tracks would form roads of three lanes, with intermittent two lane widths. Often at little extra cost, a fourth lane could be added. Single track railways could be converted to sub-standard roads which would compare favourably with minor public roads.[4] The expense of raising them to a full standard would no doubt be justified in some places.[5]
- It seemed reasonable to expect that road surfaces can be laid with an evenness comparable to railways - with the added advantage of being without joints.[6]
- He could not 'discern any factor that would impair the theoretical lane capacity, that he estimated at 1,000 vehicles per hour, corresponding to a vehicle spacing of 100 yards, travelling at a *minimum* acceptable speed of 60 mph, users achieving that voluntarily over the entire system, round the clock and over the four seasons'.[7]
- There would be enough points of access - stations, level crossings and junctions, their average distance - he said - was about $3^1/_2$ miles. The passage through these places would be easily regulated by automatic lights, especially conflicting traffic at existing road level crossings.[8]
- The most significant factor is that railway alignments often provide the shortest route between places.[9]

---

[1] He later decided that these new roads would be used by cars and other existing vehicles.

[2] He did not identify these professionals.

[3] For DoT standards - see page 198.

[4] Obviously, these would not be suitable for his utopian new vehicles - but he doesn't say so.

[5] These examples of the facile assumption that routes could easily be widened at unspecified places at low cost, and other presumptions, clearly demonstrate the superficiality of the paper.

[6] Under BR's 1955 Modernisation Plan, BR began to lay jointless continuous welded rail. Roads and motorways today often have noticeable joints at bridges or where they have been resurfaced.

[7] This is incompatible with having no passenger timetable. Buses setting off at will and trying to insert between vehicles travelling sufficiently far apart as to preserve the 100 yard spacing, was a pipe dream. A sophisticated signalling system would be required and he had dispensed with it. Moreover, the acute seasonal peak for coal would prevent evenly balanced seasonal flows.

[8] Hopefully, without disturbing that nice regular flow of vehicles at 100 yard intervals!

[9] That illusion is not borne out by an examination of maps, and a study of the historical records of objections to direct routes by landowners. He was soon disabused of this belief by road experts. See example of Bourne End - page 125.

- The new roads would be used by eight foot wide vehicles.
- Roads will never maltreat vehicles, and vice versa.
- His plan required that there would be a strict wheel load limit which would be lower than that permitted on existing roads.
- Only fast vehicles, regularly inspected for road-worthiness would be allowed. Drivers would have to pass stringent tests, and have special driving licences.[10]
- BR's 20,000m passenger miles and 22,000m freight ton miles can be equated to 10,300 fully laden vehicles at 60 mph for eight hours daily, six days per week. One third would be 40-seater buses and two-thirds 20 ton lorries[11] supplemented by an abundance of trailers.[12]
- There would be no problem with the Waterloo rush hour[13] daily passengers are no more than 200,000. Sixty-seater bus-trailers at $1\frac{1}{2}$ minute intervals from each of Waterloo's 21 platforms [*one every 4.2 seconds*] - redesignated bus lanes - will be able to carry 50,000 passengers per hour. The rush hour flow of 840 vehicles per hour, would not amount to the capacity of one lane - so there would be no bottlenecks beyond the station due to the great multiplicity of lanes at Clapham Junction.[14]
- To reduce injuries in accidents, seats would be rear facing on all vehicles permitted on these roads.[15]
- There would be no timetables, as soon as a bus was 100% full, it would go.[16]
- Buses would have one or two trailers, which could be discarded in the non-rush hours[17] and could also be used as slip coaches.[18]
- With screened drivers, accidents would almost cease. A Table compared rail fatalities in 1952, the worst year since 1915 - due to the Harrow & Wealdstone crash[19] in thick fog - with road fatalities in August 1954, when, in all probability, there was no fog.

---

[10] Both would have been a first, now - much less then! He made no allowance at all for the out-of-service time of these vehicles during these *regular road worthiness checks*.

[11] Having increased his bus size by a third and doubled his lorry size, he claimed to cut his earlier forecast of fleet size by 86%. He had carefully flattened the daily and seasonal peaks of both freight and passenger to spread the load over 24 hours, six days per week. The 10,300 vehicles split into 6,866 lorries and 3,434 buses.

[12] Thrown in as if they came free from manufacturers and incurred zero maintenance and running costs. They would have to be available at every factory, unless lorries always had one attached! It was a catch-all throwaway line to cover up any deficiency in his *calculations*.

[13] He seemed unaware that there were major rush hours at several other London and Provincial stations.

[14] Overlooking that they were largely on one level.

[15] They would be very unpopular. No one has succeeded in doing so in aircraft, where the passengers cannot see where they are going anyway. It would rule out existing PSVs and cars.

[16] Involving long delays for non-peak passengers. Balancing vehicle provision would be chaotic. Without a timetable, the end of a driver's 8 hour shift could find him at the wrong end.

[17] Probably discarded at the wrong end!

[18] Slipping a trailer at 60 mph, with another bus 100 yards behind beggars belief. Unlike rail coaches, they would require steering and power to park clear of other traffic.

[19] Government directives blocking renewals were a major factor in the accident (see *Britain's Railways - The Reality*, Pages 52-55). He claimed 1952 rail accidents were the most recent. It is nonsense. The 1953 HMRI Report published October 1954 shows a decrease on 1952. The 1954 Report was published September 1955, but the DoT would have had all data by February. Lloyd, at the War Office, should have been able to get it from HMRI, who were also ex-Royal Engineers. Moreover, the MoT quoted 1954 rail & road fatalities in March 1954, (Hansard vol. 539, col. *27*) to which Lloyd and all civil servants had daily access. 1954 rail fatalities had **fallen 75%** from 1952, road fatalities had **risen 6%**. Clearly, that was unhelpful. In 1954, no rail fatalities were in collisions, but were at level crossings - as would be likely to happen after conversion - or were falls on stations - which might happen in converted carparks or bus-stations. Had 1954 been worse than 1952, he would, doubtless, have used it.

- A hire-car service, including self drive, would be an equivalent replacement for first class.[20] He envisaged Epicurean dining cars.
- Demurrage on freight trailers would be low, encouraging clients to make up complete trailer loads.[21]
- If drivers slowed excessively at 24 foot bridges and tunnels, the question of widening should be taken up.[22] Most of the interesting engineering problems arise at these points!
- There would be prompt sanding and snow clearance, and radar would be fitted to all vehicles to enable them to operate safely in fog. [23]
- New traffic rules would apply: keep strictly in lane, except at clearly marked places of transfer to adjacent lanes; no overtaking at all on two lane stretches of roadway; no dawdling; special driving licences would be forfeited for breaking the rules.[24]
- A re-named BR would be responsible for mobile traffic police, an efficient breakdown service, maintaining roads, telecommunications, controlling access and ensuring that vehicles and drivers had the required high standards.[25]
- There would be ample room for toll traffic. Present traffic on BR amounts to one-fifth of the whole, that on public roads to four-fifths.[26]
- BR 'were now to be given an injection of £1200m to modernise'.[27]

The Lloyd scheme stated that 'BR will undertake the upkeep of the entire system: patrols, police, breakdown service, telecommunications, control of admission to the system, including initial and periodical testing of authorised drivers and vehicles'. Why this road system - connected to the rest of the network - required a highway authority and had to provide telecommunications, when no such provision existed on any other road, he did not explain. Nor was their purpose defined. No costs were estimated.

He ignored the delay element in gaining access to the system implicit in producing proof of driver and vehicle worthiness, and what happens when a dispute occurs, not least the effect on following vehicles. A breakdown service implies that the nice regimented flow of vehicles at 60 mph, 100 yards apart, coming to an abrupt stand in one direction, whilst they await arrival of the *high speed* breakdown service from the nearest point. He didn't say how many the system could afford, hence we cannot work out the distance to

---

[20] These would have to slot into the 100 yard gaps, reducing the headway.

[21] Unless the demurrage equated to cost provision, it would be a financially ruinous plan. It may take weeks to assemble a full load. Given BR experience, clients would detain trailers to suit their convenience.

[22] Closing, after conversion, for alterations would be crazy. No professional would entertain it. No estimate was made of costs. Tunnel widths were as little as 11 foot, e.g. Glenfield, near Leicester. Because of their limited clearance, and narrow cess, tunnels had refuges in both walls to enable staff to move to a position of safety when a train approached.

[23] The latter has not yet been achieved on our motorways - witness the typical pile-ups. There have been failures to sand in good time, and snow clearance has been subject to failure. Hauliers will not fit safety devices at their cost.

[24] There is one indisputable aspect of road transport and that is a tendency for most drivers to ignore the Highway Code today. Few fear the risk of losing a licence or having it endorsed

[25] This was ingenious, as, when the system proved unworkable, politicians, the media, comedians and, of course, Brigadier Lloyd would have a handy whipping boy! Decades later, 100% checks on vehicles could not be achieved on 2,500 miles of motorway, (see *Juggernaut* by John Wardroper).

[26] This comparison ignores that road route mileage was 22 times as much as railway route mileage. The figure quoted was preferable to the road lobby, and ignores distance. Passenger miles and ton miles were about equal on road and rail, despite the greater capacity of roads, (see page 88,173). Road traffic data is unreliable, (see page 153).

[27] This was, and still is, a popular myth. The government had made it quite clear that BR must raise this sum from its own sources or from interest bearing loans. It did. Accounts show that BR was repaying the loans and the interest thereon, (see *Britain's Railways - The Reality*, Page 61).

the nearest, and therefore the average time to clear the offending obstruction. It will be noted that he had tacitly admitted that his regularly inspected high standard of road worthiness vehicles with their saint-like drivers were not going to be immune to breakdown and accident, in contrast to more recent claims (see chapter 10).

Operators would possess vehicles which spent their entire life on the new system, never using existing public roads. They would certainly have been prohibited from existing roads, as he envisaged 63 foot long vehicles with no springing, and a body slung a few inches from the ground, with 'wheels fore and aft - not under the vehicle'. The consequential problems and cost of transhipment were glossed over. BR would be able, he said, to restore equity of competition by varying its contracts with the tied operators and its scale of toll charges levied on others. In effect, this would have allowed BR - as owners of the new motor road - to discriminate between users - a practice they were specifically forbidden to do in respect of rail customers. It was to be the responsibility of local authorities to encourage motorists to park cars in new carparks, and travel on these new roads using tied buses. Local authorities are still struggling to achieve that end, with buses which are not restricted to a limited route.

As to who would buy the special lorries and buses which would be confined to the converted system, he remained silent. No research was presented at all. There was no evidence that even one operator would do so. Then what? Doubtless, another ready made excuse was ready for when the concept goes belly up.

He claimed that dismantling the track would not be a problem, 'it would more than pay for itself in scrap value'. Neither, he claimed would the civil engineering task be a problem, because the civil engineering industry was able to do far more. He added that rail engineering staff could easily switch from rail to road construction. He may have been right - but it has become very clear that the reverse - road engineers switching to rail has been fraught with problems. BR engineers would never have tolerated deferment of track renewal for months as applied at Hatfield. The prospect of a railway Operator successfully demanding deferment to avoid delays was unheard of. Operating managers certainly pleaded with engineers for short term relief - a temporary speed restriction for a few days or perhaps a week, or a less severe speed restriction.

Lloyd argued for narrower lanes than the 12 foot envisaged by the DoT, on the grounds that 'the narrower the lane, the more conscientiously, do drivers observe the lane markings. Traffic will *never* swing out to overtake'. He must be turning in his grave, at the incidence of overtaking in the most dangerous places which prevails today. He claimed that 'because railways have no hills, there will be no need to overtake'. Experience shows that the more level, or more straight a road, the *greater* the incidence of overtaking.

He believed that two cars could pass in a single track rail tunnel - at 60 mph. The author would not be in either of them! Unlike BR, 'British Motorways would be under no obligation to accept any traffic that does not conform to their own standards'. That would put some firms in difficulty, with no means of moving traffic that road hauliers have previously rejected as uneconomic and left to BR, who still had a common carrier obligation. Conversion of BR to 'British Motorways' would end that.

He gave no thought to repairs, when his single carriageway roads had a half of their width closed for a mile or so. He believed that 'within towns railways are already multi-track'. There were thousands of towns where that did not apply, and there was no room to remedy it. Having said that the railway formation was perfect, he then introduced the need for super-elevation. Overtaking in a centre nine foot lane, with a 60 mph vehicle approaching in daylight, much less with glaring headlights at night, would not be performed by anyone without Formula One experience!

After the Paper had been presented, 22 people spoke.

His proposal was demolished by ten road experts:

Dr. W.H. Glanville, Director of Road Research, Department of Scientific & Industrial Research - forerunner of the Transport Research Laboratory: Could not see how buses could run, fully loaded for eight hours a day, six days a week, and if this did not happen, the financial basis for conversion was affected most seriously. The Minister of Transport had stated that traffic lanes on motorways would be twelve foot wide, further affecting the proposals which were based on ten foot lanes. The vehicles would remain on the concreted ways, with all the terminal difficulties that would involve in the transport of goods and people. Dr. Glanville did not accept, that 'higher standards of driving, would be sufficient to overcome the dangers of high speed traffic on the same carriageway'.

S. Mehew, County Surveyor, Derbyshire: On road widths and the necessity for dual carriageways, he entirely agreed with Dr. Glanville. He recalled that, during the war, the proprietor of a very large road haulage business, was in charge of coal traffic by road and rail, and was amazed at the ease of moving large quantities of materials such as coal by rail. Rail transport was less affected by fog and snow than road.

Major H.E.Aldington, Technical Adviser, BRF: Knew no one who believed that a single 22 foot or 24 foot carriageway was adequate for heavy volumes of traffic and said it was quite preposterous. He viewed with alarm the prospect of travelling at 60 mph on single carriageways against opposing traffic, particularly at night with glaring headlights. Driving from London to Birmingham, [in 1955], at night was quite terrifying. It was impossible to get a 20 foot carriageway through an ordinary double-line rail tunnel.[28] There was considerable curvature on some lines. He pointed to one route running over a sharply curved viaduct with 25 feet between parapets. It would be costly to alter.

J.B. Burnell, London Transport Buses: It was totally impracticable to ask staff to drive on a road 22-24 feet wide at such speeds. They would rightly refuse. He postulated a driver handing over to a relief driver saying: Engine pulling well, there is ice and snow and fog, but the radar is all right. In the USA, there was a tremendous number of head-on collisions on roads below 15 foot width.

Brigadier C.C. Parkman, partner in a firm of Consulting Engineers: The incidence of accidents was bound to increase, especially when visibility was impaired by rain, fog or darkness. He forecast a reduction in signal boxes by modernisation[29] which would enhance railway safety. Two causes of accidents were human and mechanical failure; both would be magnified by using a smaller trackless vehicle. Where unremunerative and redundant lines closed, they may be suitable for conversion. Retention of railways would offer the prospect of using electric power.

---

[28] British Railways 1963 Year Book shows 1,050 tunnels, which included single bore tunnels.
[29] He was far sighted. There were 9,800 in 1955, and 900 when BR was privatised. The network had halved.

Lt-Col S.M. Lovell, County Engineer & Surveyor, Yorkshire West Riding: suggested building roads above railways was the best solution to co-ordinate road and rail transport.

A.A. Osborne, Resident Engineer, Wilson & Mason: Highway width must be 88-93 foot with dual 22 foot carriageways and 15 foot verges. Double track rail formation is 39 foot reduced to 19-22 foot in tunnels and deep cuttings with retaining walls; quadruple track was only 55 foot wide. Gradients are a serious problem; less than 1 in 200 is inadequate[30] for water drainage on roads, hence a completely new drainage system would be necessary. He contradicted Brigadier Lloyd who said there were *no dangerous bends*, pointing out that railways had curves of 660-1,320 foot radius[31] often on viaducts, bridges or through tunnels, against a motorway standard of 2,865 foot, and said conversion had no potential and was economically impossible. Rail services would be completely withdrawn long before roads were laid on which replacement services would operate.

Dr. A.W.T. Daniel, Lecturer in Civil Engineering, London University: Proposed speeds were a step back. Rail speeds were above those envisaged, and the world stood on the threshold of another great railway era.[32]

N. Seymer, Editor of International Road Safety & Traffic Review, opposed abandonment of railways and suggested that in some cities, railways should be put underground and roads built on the rail route.

W.K. Taylor, City Engineer's Dept., Exeter: Tracks could not provide the required dimensions for motorways carrying traffic at minimum speeds of 60 mph. Some 500 trains carried 300,000 passengers on the Southern Region in London's rush hour, requiring about 5,000 buses - about a half of the proposed 10,300 for the *whole country*. Only 840 buses were allowed for Waterloo traffic.

> *He misunderstood. Of the 10,300 vehicles for the whole country, only one third were buses: 3,433; two-thirds - 6,867 - were lorries. Moving every bus from and to rural extremities for London's morning and evening peaks would be an interesting logistical problem. Noticeably, his error was not corrected by Brigadier Lloyd. Later, Lloyd postulated a line of buses waiting at a station for the morning commuters. As there were nearly 5,600 passenger stations, there would not be enough buses to provide each station with one!*

The proposal was opposed by four railway experts:-

D. Blee, Traffic Advisor, who, 'not being an engineer' expressed no opinion on technical matters, but was sufficiently experienced in traffic matters to argue that the proposed vehicle numbers would be totally inadequate, and suggested near half a million would be required.[33] He pointed out that Lloyd had ignored the problem of peaks. No vehicular provision would be available for seasonal peaks, nor for sporting events.

J. Ratter, Technical Advisor: 30,000 bridges would need new floors to make them suitable for road vehicles, because rails were laid on longitudinal girders which could not carry a roadway. Driving a vehicle at 60 mph would certainly require the driver to be alert on a 24 foot road - he would also be frightened. Roads would then have to be

---

[30] Quadruple tracks had the heaviest flows, gradients of less than 1 in 200 are commonplace.
[31] Hall-Smith (Page 12) claimed that they were rarely less than 800m (2500 ft). See also page 168 of this book.
[32] He displayed uncanny foresight - far more than the few supporters of conversion.
[33] See author's assessments - pages 18,48-49.

widened at great cost, as railways were built on embankments and viaducts. Heavy earthworks would result. Trains would soon be travelling at 100 mph on jointless track. Converted terminal stations would need a huge area for turning buses.

R.C. Bond, Chief Mechanical Engineer: Nearly all principal junctions were laid out on one level, and flyovers and a very elaborate form of cloverleaf constructions would be essential to allow traffic to keep moving.

S.B. Warder, Chief Electrical Engineer drew attention to the higher speeds and lower costs which would accrue from electrification.

Five gave qualified support for conversion:

Professor Bondi, Kings College, London: A twin tracked railway was wide enough for one carriageway, without a parking strip. A ten foot lane was adequate, more than eleven was positively dangerous in encouraging small cars[34] to pass. The Marylebone-Sheffield line could be made a north-bound road, and Sheffield-St. Pancras a southbound road.

Contraflows would be difficult. Wisely, he did not mention Birmingham-Norwich, London-Scotland, York-Manchester, Sheffield-Manchester or many other routes. Commuters would be inconvenienced by routes converted to a one-way system.

Major Carter of the School of Military Engineering said that conversion would start at the coast, taking out a section of 30 miles. A transfer station would be created at the change point for passengers and freight.

They would involve track and signalling alterations to enable trains to turn back. Some would require carriage cleaning, fuelling and maintenance facilities. Dust from coal and aggregates being transferred between rail and road would be unpopular.

A. Goode, Deputy Director of Works, Air Ministry: double handling would be eliminated.[35] He favoured the development of steam powered road vehicles. 'The *comparatively few* tunnels (see page 29), would have to be enlarged or uncovered'. He advanced a theory on the cost of conversion - but not for tunnels, (see page 31).

F.W. Davey, Consulting Engineer, even if the proposals were not adopted in their entirety, railways around London, and other large cities might be made suitable for electric traction, and main railway terminals sited thereon, leaving railways within the ring to be replaced by roads.

F.P. Dath, CEA Engineer, referred to the problems raised by transport needs in war.[36] He thought passengers would approve of motorisation.

Logistical reservations:

Lt-Col. H. Cartwright-Taylor, School of Military Engineering: nervousness was no more likely to attack drivers of trucks and buses than drivers of French trains approaching at [a combined speed] of 400 mph.[37] He did not accept that the number of vehicles envisaged would be sufficient.

---

[34] He assumed that there would be capacity for them. He wrote to *The Times* (7.7.54), that the railway was generally wide enough for four lanes, but where widening was expensive it could narrow to two - a recipe for delay & accidents

[35] Not with 63 ft 20-40 ton lorries which were confined to the converted network, (see page 38).

[36] Transport needs were almost wholly met by railways, with huge diversions to rail from coastwise ships and road transport, to add to vastly increased imports & output of mines and industry, and the needs of the military, see page 6.

[37] French train drivers were confident that an oncoming train would not swerve into it. How bus passengers on the converted system would react should have been of more concern!

Two were non-committal, neither for, nor against:

W.P. Andrews, Roads Consultant, spoke only of the standards required for road surfaces, but expressed no opinion on the scheme.

H.J.B. Harding, Director of John Mowlem: believed that the railway tunnels were likely to fall down as most were 100 years old.[38] A simple by-pass could be built allowing cars on the converted system, to climb out of cuttings and skirt the tunnels.[39] In 30 years time, locos built under the Modernisation Plan would be obsolete.[40] The railways had killed the canals for gain, and the country had suffered in time of war.[41]

Having been warned of the impracticability and dangers of vehicles at 60 mph on single carriageways, especially in the dark, Lloyd, after the debate, said that 60 mph was an estimate of the average speed[42] that would be achieved, but 40 mph might render it worthwhile. He overlooked the increase in vehicles, manpower and road occupancy by 50%.

Other Weaknesses & Problem Areas

Surprisingly, no attention focused, in the debate, on level crossings.[43] Brigadier Lloyd claimed that 'junctions and level crossings were relatively infrequent.' In the Royal Engineers Journal, he had said that the 20,000 miles of railway[44] are 'free of cross-roads'. He overlooked over 24,000 level crossings, not including public footpaths across railways. He had not said how many crossings there were, although the statistic was publicly available. In addition to 4,670 public level crossings, there were 19,700 unmanned Accommodation and Occupation crossings providing access to farmer's fields or other property, plus 2,500 public footpath crossings.[45]

The attendant dangers and delays from slow moving tractors and animals on farm crossings would be a very serious problem, which he had completely overlooked. The opportunity for them to cross between vehicles travelling 100 yards apart at 60 mph would be virtually zero. Their speed of crossing would be much slower than that for cars at a public crossing. New bridges would be necessary at all such points.

No one observed that his plan for traffic lights at public level crossings meant that his concept of traffic flowing at 60 mph with 100 yard intervals, would be subject to frequent stoppages. Vehicles travelling on his new road system at 60 mph, 100 yard apart would leave a maximum 'window' of only 3.4 seconds - if vehicles from opposite directions passed each other *precisely* on a level crossing. This would reduce to 1.7 seconds in the more probable scenario of vehicles in opposite directions passing over the level crossing, at an aggregate opposing gap of 50 yards. A car on an existing road, starting over the

---

[38] Events have proved him hopelessly wrong.

[39] The cost could be horrendous, as experience in the USA reveals, see page 168.

[40] Events proved him wrong. Moreover the life of a loco totally eclipses that of a lorry or PSV.

[41] Canals lost to rail without help. They were too narrow and locks too short and too frequent to make any real contribution to the war. Railways had to cope with diversion from road, canal and coastwise shipping - and gained not a penny from it. (See *Square Deal Denied*).

[42] Elsewhere, he had envisaged standard 60 mph and minimum 60 mph, (see pages 16,19,22,23.36,40).

[43] Weaknesses listed in these pages would have been highlighted by a BR Operating Manager, had one been present.

[44] His theory - based on spreading rail traffic, mostly, carried on main lines across all lines including 1000s of miles of rural branch lines going to the wrong places - was ludicrous.

[45] Report to the MoT on the Safety of BR for 1957 by HMRI (the MoT's Railway Inspectors). Level crossing data can also be found in *Facts & Figures about BR*, which Lloyd's paper records that he had seen.

level crossing; from a stand would take 4 seconds, lorries and tractor drawn trailers much longer. Even if the headway on the converted road could be doubled, the synchronisation of conflicting movements would put the RAF Regiment Colour Squadron or the Royal Signals motor cycle display team to shame! At a typical 'B' road over a level crossing, in the morning peak, and, in some cases, throughout the day, the backlog of waiting traffic on the existing road would never clear. An even worse situation would arise at the many locations where an 'A' road crossed a line on a level crossing, of which there were many in 1955, and still some in 1970.

His 100 yard intervals was, of course, an average. Given that there was much more traffic on some lines than others, meant some would have a wider gap, and some none at all. It was a nonsensical and naive approach, when what was needed was a route by route analysis. If he had persuaded the MoT that such a study was merited, BR would have been told to provide it, and it would not have cost the conversion league a penny.

There were thousands of junctions on the flat, and, worse, railway routes crossing each other at right angles on the flat, such as at Retford, Newark, Darlington. Negotiating flat junctions in and around cities, against conflicting flows would demand skills far in excess of those prevailing then, or now. Traffic signals would be essential at these locations

The concept of lorries and buses travelling at 100 yard headways at 60 mph would also have been shattered by the existence of swing bridges over rivers, canals and estuaries, at several locations on BR.

All these would pose serious problems for road vehicles having to maintain a minimum speed of 60 mph. The inevitable increase in accidents would keep garages, hospitals, emergency services and lawyers very busy. Delays would be horrendous.

There was no challenge to the idea of 60 mph buses slipping trailers without stopping on a single carriageway - with another vehicle 100 yards behind.

Attention had been drawn to inadequate clearance in tunnels, but the issue was not pursued with sufficient vigour. *The BR Yearbook* shows 1050 tunnels. *British Railway Tunnels* by Alan Blower lists 52 over a mile long, including 8 over 3 miles, 5 of 2-3 miles; and 56 between half and one mile long. (UK's longest road tunnel is 0.9 miles and has costly ventilation and lighting). The book mentions tunnels of less than 15 feet wide, down to just over 11 feet. Even where a tunnel was 24 feet wide, which some were, it would be very dangerous having vehicles hurtling through at 60 mph with a tunnel wall inches away from road vehicles. Costly ventilation was ignored, as was lighting, which would be costly to provide in their mostly remote rural locations. Neither this, nor other conversion proposals allocated a penny for this purpose. He had not considered the implications of a vehicle that was too wide or too high to pass through a tunnel or, too wide or too heavy to pass over a viaduct or bridge, having to stop, turn round and return to a diversionary point - with hundreds of vehicles pressing closely behind

The debate overlooked that collieries, quarries, industry, docks and ports - dependent on a large pool of wagons would have to turn to three shift working from single or double shifts and a six-day instead of five-day week. The flow of imports from ports was irregular and unpredictable in the 1950s, and little improved even twenty years later. The arrival of ships was affected by weather, different routes, ship types, cargoes, etc. Serious problems would arise in making deliveries round the clock to wholesalers and retailers

No one drew attention to the special needs of collieries, coke ovens, quarries and ports, which were unable to function without a pool of wagons - the first three required them in hundreds per location and the latter in thousands. In 1955, there were 850 collieries. Collieries loaded coal of different grades by gravity from screens above the sidings. A colliery with six screens[46] had to have a wagon standing under each screen as coal was poured non-stop into it, and wagons immediately behind ready to lower by gravity from empty wagon sidings, down the gradient of the sidings as each wagon under a screen became full. Each wagon was then lowered by gravity down over the weighbridge into loaded wagon sidings to await labelling and allocation to a customer. With 850 collieries needing at least twelve lorries, even with the most expeditious weighing, invoicing, etc., arrangements, and lorry turnround, collieries alone would need 10,200 lorries, working a five day week. Lloyd envisaged 6,867 lorries to move all existing rail freight! (See page 26). Any failure to replace a lorry on each road beneath the screens, after it was loaded, would result in costly diversion of coal to stock. Prolonged failure would stop production.

Conversionists may argue collieries would be served by that 'abundance of trailers'. That would require the collieries to work three shifts - instead of one or two per weekday, which was then, and remained, the norm. They would also have to invest in tractor units and drivers to move trailers under the screens, and from screens to weighbridge and thence to a lorry park to await allocation of load to a customer. Some form of control would be needed to enable lorry drivers to be told where to find a trailer with the requisite consignment in a constantly changing parking area.

The Coal Board would have been faced by mass resignations of colliery managers who were expected to meet production targets. There may have been one or two who would carry on, if given a personal guarantee by Brigadier Lloyd of financial recompense if the concept failed.

A substantial volume of coal was conveyed by rail from collieries in Northumberland, Durham, Yorkshire and the Midlands to ports to go by coastwise shipping to London and south coast power stations, built to receive coal by sea. Some coal went to ports for export. Much of this was carried in hopper wagons which were unsuitable for any imports, hence they returned empty. Many docks were designed for discharging coal from hopper wagons on high level staithes direct to ships' holds. The staithes would require complete reconstruction to render them usable by lorries. Ports and docks, therefore, had a two way flow of empty wagons of varying kinds for which there was no suitable alternative load.

The coking industry presented another problem. In 1955, some 84 locations received 30m tons of coal for converting to coke.[47] Wagons in which coal was received at coking ovens were not suitable for despatching coke. Coke is lighter than coal, and filled wagons to their cubic capacity, with a tonnage less than the plated weight capacity. Therefore, it was despatched in higher sided wagons. Hence, there were two one-way flows of loaded wagons inward and outward, with balancing movements of empty wagons.

Brigadier Lloyd and his friends could have learned of the existence and nature of these problems by reading a few good books on railway operating and commercial practice.

---

[46] See photograph of colliery screens at Burley in Staffs, (Wm Jack collection, Keele University).
[47] Coke Oven Managers' Association Year Book.

Bus Company conditions of service[48] suggest they would have had difficulty complying with his standards, typically reserving *the right to alter, cancel or withdraw services without notice.*

Converting Waterloo station into a bus station based on Lloyd's figures, required a bus departing every four seconds to move the evening peak. One ignition key turned twice and the peak would be in chaos. His estimated 50,000 rush-hour commuters finding their way to the correct bus would be a sight to behold. One ticket-less passenger lacking change to pay would risk lynching by impatient season ticket holders, as the plan was based on buses without conductors. A driver attending a call of nature would create a riot.

The conversion process was virtually ignored, except for a suggestion of using transfer stations. Using transfer stations on commuter lines, whilst conversion progressed, each one for many months, would create chaos. To build one *every 30 miles* would be a significant cost factor, requiring 700 for the 20,000 mile system, and their use - and staffing - would extend over the ten years envisaged for conversion.

His quaint method of calculating vehicle fleets overlook that lorries and buses working eight hours non stop - include provision for re-fuelling, meal breaks, empty running from garage to loading point and back. His figures depended on every sender having 20 ton loads (later revised to 40 ton consignments) and these vehicles would never leave the special roads, so they would need tranship depots and smaller vehicles to enter towns.

He dismissed fears that fatalities would increase by setting out to prove that the entire community was at risk on roads, whilst only passengers and staff were at risk on railways. This theory is deeply flawed, (see pages 46,62,63).

Costs

The cost of his *mobile police and efficient breakdown service* was not brought into the equation. Indeed many costs were not brought into the equation: the capital cost of vehicles, the unquantified number of trailers, and the cost of 20,000 new bridges for agricultural use. Despite advancing no capital costs for building the yet-to-be-designed super lorries and buses, nor, therefore, to know what their working life would be, he felt able to quote depreciation figures for them, which he used to 'calculate' the viability of his proposals! This specialised fleet would all have to be built before the railways were closed down, to enable the displaced rail traffic to be moved. Thereafter, the manufacturers could mothball their production line, and lay off their workforce, until, at the end of the yet-to-be-established working life, vehicles needed to be replaced. Among other unspecified expenditure, he planned telecommunications to control the vehicle fleets. No manpower was envisaged for this purpose. Mechanical handling of freight and radar were both stated to be essential, but again no cost came into the equation!

During the debate, A. Goode [Deputy Director of Works, Air Ministry], came to his rescue on costs, by relating railway track mileage to the area of 300 airfields. How he arrived at the ground area occupied by Britain's railways, he did not state - it was not a published figure. He took recent costs of building airfields and, *then,* reduced them on the grounds that axle loads would be less and arrived at a cost of £1,000m spread over ten years. He ignored the fact that construction costs for 300 sites would, acre for acre, be less

---

[48] National Express Timetable 1996/7 - see also page 180.

than when spread over 20,000 miles, and that the former were built on land clear of activity, whilst the latter involved the temporary displacement of existing traffic. The financial consequences of temporary diversion would not be insignificant. Brigadier Lloyd seized on this life-line and promptly set about reducing it to £600m by arguing that existing railway ballast would be incorporated into the road structure. Mr. Goode advocated the development of steam powered road vehicles for use on the converted system. It is highly improbable that steam powered road vehicles, stopping for water, would achieve the 60 mph that was essential for conversion to be, even theoretically, practical in logistical terms. Surprisingly, no one pointed this out, least of all Lloyd, who could not afford to alienate one of his few supporters!

Following the debate, Brigadier Lloyd conceded the use of the new roads by private transport - i.e. existing non-specially designed vehicles, but ignored the mechanics and costs of proving they conformed to his reliability standards, and that their drivers held special driving licences. He said that 'possibly, tolls would cover the cost of upkeep, and make some contribution towards interest on capital'.

He made a new claim that a converted two track railway could cope with 20 times as much traffic as railway trains. He argued that if any piece of a converted double track railway was overtaxed, it ought to have been triple track originally, and it would no doubt have been scheduled for tripling under the railway modernisation plan! This was an incredible argument.[49]

His naive belief in the capacity of roads ignores the reality that 22 times as much road length was required to handle 10 times as much traffic, (see pages 88,173).

The crude and unsupported figures - masquerading as statistics - used by Brigadier Lloyd to justify his theory, were subject to frequent change, and appear to have been clutched out of thin air.

The following pages will reveal how 'facts' have been 'interpreted' to try to prove the conversionist case. The founding father of the pipe dream was especially guilty in this respect. In 1968, he wrote an article for *Municipal Engineering*. In it, he made the astonishing claim that, when his scheme was debated at the ICE, 'BR took part, and now, 13 years later, its successful opposition reads as amusingly as the opposition to the construction of railways a century or so earlier'. This falsely implies that the only opposition was from BR representatives who were, in fact, a minority of those present. Secondly, as will be seen from the preceding pages, most opposition was from those in the road transport camp: operators, engineers and the BRF itself. He went on to refer to 'the, by no means negligible support for the proposition'. Ten non-BR speakers were opposed to his plan, and highlighted its weaknesses. Of four BR representatives, one would not express an engineering opinion, as he was not an engineer, but drew attention to errors in assessing the number of road vehicles required. Three BR engineers expressed engineering opinions, pointing to impending modernisation which would undermine his comparisons and to the problems of converting bridges, etc., which non-BR engineers also highlighted. Of

---

[49] The author was deeply involved in modernisation on the West Coast main line in the 1960s, and recalls no location where this happened. Indeed, the reverse was more often the case, when it was realised that multiple aspect colour light signals and faster trains so increased line capacity, that sections of track could be removed.

the five who supported Lloyd, one envisaged using some railways as one-way roads and one wished to introduce steam powered road vehicles. One was partly in favour, but said that vehicle numbers were under-estimated, and two were completely non-committal. By no stretch of imagination could it be said that his scheme was opposed by BR alone - the main opposition was from road experts! Of all the misrepresentations, the greatest was the remark that he attributed to Dr, Glanville (see page 25), who he claimed had merely said that the *economics of the matter deserved detailed examination.* Lloyd had air brushed out, the first part of the sentence, which read: 'the Paper did not prove that people would be saved time and money, but ....'. Moreover, Dr. Glanville had said that 'the costs, were at the least, very optimistic, that it did not seem to him likely that buses would run 100% full, 8 hours per day [round the clock], 6 days per week, and if not, the whole argument was affected most seriously.' Finally, Dr. Glanville said that 'the proposed road lane widths were inadequate, which higher driving standards would not overcome' (see page 25).

Lloyd - being in Whitehall - should have known that the opinions of BR's professionals as to such matters counted for nought. The main decisions were taken by Government and its appointed Agents, to guard against electoral disaster which may be expected if BR were free to act like a private sector business.[50] BR fares and charges were decided by a court of law acting under Government directions, and were often subject to further direct interference by Ministers. Disposal of dead wood - in the form of uneconomic branch lines - was in the hands of Government appointed Committees, with the last word being with Ministers. Investment plans were second - and third guessed - by the DoT and Treasury, who knew zilch about railway operating, marketing, engineering and technology. The top decisions, within the industry, were taken by imported chiefs: retired Generals, and retired Civil Servants, at the British Transport Commission.

Lloyd's article was published as the 1955 Rail Modernisation Plan was bearing fruit. London-Birmingham-Manchester/Liverpool 100mph electric trains had increased revenue by 66%, without fare increases. Other main lines had good traffic increases as new 100 mph trains and jointless track (even today only pipe-dreams on roads) came into operation. MGR 1,000 ton coal trains were running, whilst freightliner and HST were just around the corner. Had he returned to the ICE to make these announcements in a new pitch for glory, he would have been laughed out of court.

He also moaned in his article, the inability of the conversion league to get its hands on railways to convert to roads. But, BR was obliged by government directive to give first refusal on closed lines and surplus land to them or local authorities for the very purpose of using them as roads and carparks. The land often stood empty and increasingly derelict waiting a use. Many hundreds of miles had been closed by 1968, and Lloyd must - like anyone else who read a newspaper - have been aware of it. All this was happening in the watch of the most road minded MoT to hold office - and that is saying something, when one realises that there had only been one rail minded MoT, and that was in 1919!

Another of Lloyd's throw-away lines was that economists had concluded that buses can pay *given* the same kind of route, but failed to identify the source of this statement, nor note the significance of the words *'given* the same route', i.e. infrastructure free of cost. Almost anyone could make a profit on any project, given assets free of cost!

---

[50] See *Britain's Railways - The Reality.*

Chapter 5

In 1957, Brigadier Lloyd published his much revised plan in a booklet: *The Twilight of the Railways*. In it, he tried to cater for criticisms of the weaknesses of his scheme, arising from the ICE debate and elsewhere, and other oversights.

- 'On the converted system, apart from a few[1] level crossings where traffic lights will normally give priority, there will be no conflict.'

  Cross traffic would have very limited opportunities to cross between 60 mph vehicles travelling 100 yards apart. Effectively, opposing direction flows would cut gaps to 50 yards apart. Among cross flows, of which he is so dismissive, were many on main roads which crossed railways throughout the country.

- 'The permanent way having been constructed by many companies includes numerous ready made flyovers. Route junctions occur on average scarcely once in ten miles.'

  In fact, by far the majority of railway junctions did not have flyovers. Such remarks suggest that he had never been near the railway.

- 'Transfer from the existing road system will be provided only at existing stations to or from the permanent way, left handed invariably so as never to interfere with through traffic.'

  This would involve some vehicles making detours to approach only from the left. Their journey times would increase accordingly. Likewise, vehicles leaving the system would have to turn left, and make similar detours to get to the right hand side of the network.

- 'A strict traffic code will be enforced by helpful patrolmen. Parking will be forbidden except in plentiful sidings with their service stations, etc.; there will be a prompt breakdown service.'

  Vehicles would leave to the left, which would extend journey times.

- 'A million rail vehicles will be replaced by 30,000 vehicles of a type already existing in Britain to the number of seven million and being manufactured at a rate of one million pa.'

  He gave no indication where the 7m vehicles - 63 foot long, capable of carrying 60 passengers or 20 tons or more of freight - could be seen. He ignored that some existing rail rolling stock were required specifically for maintenance and breakdown, and they would need replacement by suitable road vehicles. Needless to say, he ignored the reduction forecast under the Rail Modernisation Plan.

- 'Sixty road employees will always be more productive than sixty rail employees.[2] A high proportion of railwaymen are specialists, requiring years of training and experience, leading to a strategical aspect, for in war, manpower rules national strategy and specialists are a nuisance.'

  This is typical of the superficiality, generalisation and ignorance of railways which underlies his concept. Many grades of rail staff were trained in weeks. To gain promotion, many advanced their knowledge by attending training courses in their own time.

---

[1] He still ignored publicly available data. There were 24,000, which hardly constitutes *a few*. His paper to the ICE shows he referred to *BR Facts & Figures* which included this data.

[2] This claim - also made by a MoT - was demolished in *Britain's Railways - The Reality*, Page 148, (see page 181)

Brigadier Lloyd claimed in his book: 'The subject of railway conversion provokes a multitude of facile objections. At heart, we humans are great know-alls on transport, and understandably so, for are we all not the experts? - expert passengers'![3] This remark is, itself, facile. By the same token, all can claim to be as expert as the Royal Engineers at building bridges, because they have all walked over one! What he overlooked in trying to make what he saw as a clever point, was that having convinced the reader that every rail passenger was a railway expert, this would equip them to become expert in road building and road transport operations!

The book states that 'in ten years, railways have worsened. BR was always bankrupt.' They were not bankrupt in the first years before inept government policies kicked in.[4] Lloyd claimed that *an increasing number of thoughtful people* point out that railways might be converted very simply into superb roads. Typically, he failed to quote figures or a source for his sweeping claim. In comparing the number of railway wagons with road vehicles, his lack of railway knowledge shielded him from the facts. Government had long manoeuvred to get railways to take on the liability of the 0.5m decrepit colliery owned railway wagons,[5] had finally forced it on BR by the 1948 Transport Act. Over the next 10-15 years, BR had to devote precious capital to build new wagons. Had they not been so burdened, and permitted to exercise the freedom of commercial decision enjoyed by competitors they would have remained profitable.

He claimed that railways 'now receive extra capital freely.' In fact, the capital being advanced was solely interest bearing loans. Clearly, he had not studied published and independently audited accounts.[6]

Traffic speed

He invited readers to 'imagine cross-roads, junctions and other bottle-necks eliminated or much reduced in number so that traffic goes three times as fast.' Even with his ingenious arithmetic, (see below), he could do no better than claim that the speed of his yet-to-be-designed vehicles would be double. Their purchase, maintenance and running costs had yet to be established. No self-respecting planner could make comparisons between this non existent transport and existing rail transport, nor higher speed trains already coming on stream, for which costed plans were set out in the 1955 Railway Modernisation and Re-Equipment Plan, published December 1954. Its ultimate cost was increased by industry fuelled inflation. Equally important, he made no allowance for the cost of flyovers and bridges to enable the conflicting cross routes to be eliminated.

He stated that a road freight vehicle, carrying 40 tons already existed on an open-cast coal site in Northumberland. He advanced no data on its cost and speed, no data on the

---

[3] This is an unsound theory as the author explained, in October 1982, to a councillor, who knew more of what [all] passengers wanted than BR managers, *because* he travelled by rail. The author's journeys, had topped a million miles, he conversed regularly with passengers (see *Blueprints for Bankruptcy*, Pages 171-2,174,181) and read letters of complaint. By analogy, that the author could drive and maintain a car didn't qualify him to run General Motors

[4] See *Britain's Railways - The Reality*.

[5] The Railway Clauses Consolidation Act, 1845, compelled railways to accept them from collieries and industry and haul them to destination and back. Known as private owner wagons (POWs), they were of a lower standard than railway owned wagons and were not as well maintained, see *Britain's Railways - The Reality*, Page 50.

[6] For details of the source of capital and repayments by BR see *Britain's Railways - The Reality*.

cost of converting it for high speed use on the new roadway system shared by other users, and, of course, no assessment of how these lorries could form a design for a bus. It is a safe bet that they had a very restricted speed. No assessment was made of the higher fuel consumption which is a known consequence of higher speeds.

He claimed that the [better] reliability of rail travel in bad weather and lower reliability of road travel are largely a measure of gradients, corners and intersections on their routes. In fact, the reason is due to not having to steer on icy surfaces, having signalling, a control office system and good organisation in tackling problems.

Lloyd arrived at his 60 mph figure by forecasting an improvement on existing average speed, (Page 10) - said to be 28 mph - by up to 7 mph for each of seven different 'benefits', and when this reached 56 mph - double the current speed - he rounded it up to 60! Every item was speculation. He advanced no data to prove that any *one* of the changes would produce such an improvement. This basis was not explained in his original 1954 paper nor to the Institution of Civil Engineers in 1955. With pseudo-scientific accuracy, his seven benefits were allocated 7, 6, 5, 4, 3, 2, 1 mph improvement respectively, totalling 28 mph! The seven 'benefits' were:-

1. Cross-roads, particularly in towns, are the chief source of delay. On the converted system, the driver will meet none - apart from a *few* level-crossings where the traffic lights will *normally* give him priority.

2. There are *numerous* flyovers. Junctions occur on average once every ten miles.[7] Connection will be provided only at existing stations[8] where vehicles will transfer to/from the new system left handed[9] - entry being controlled so as never to interfere with through traffic.

3. Slow vehicles will not be allowed, admission being restricted to fast road-worthy vehicles competently driven.[10] Patrols will enforce a traffic code and penalise dawdling, unauthorised lane quitting or parking.

4. Delays caused by uneven surfaces will be avoided, as the new roads will be brand new, built to the latest standards, will be uniformly perfect and will remain so.[11]

5. Trespassers, such as pedestrians, children, cattle, dogs and non vehicular users of public roads will be banned.[12]

6. There will be no corners which reduce speeds.[13]

7. Gradients are easier, and coupled with improved design, buses and lorries will be able to keep up with cars on the converted system.[14]

Having laid great stress on 60 mph, and made all calculations as to the number of buses and lorries required to move ex-rail traffic on the basis of that *minimum* speed, he then

---

[7] As an example, on the busy 158 miles Euston-Crewe line there were 2 flyovers in 1957 & over 30 flat junctions - one every 5 miles - excluding junctions into collieries and industrial premises.

[8] There were 8,000 passenger & freight stations, (see BR Facts & Figures), one every 2.5 miles

[9] At many locations, they would use a station level crossing *twice* to turn left. Where a road at a station is bridged, a new route would be needed, leading to compulsory property purchases

[10] The labour, equipment and buildings required to undertake this monitoring task were ignored.

[11] He must be turning in his grave. Fifty years on, contraflows are endemic! Lane blockages destroy his *60 mph traffic, 100 yards apart round the clock and throughout the four seasons.*

[12] Railway Bye-laws and fines have not stopped trespassers, (see also page 76), pedestrians have a legal right to use public level crossings. Farmers have a legal right to take animals across thousands of farm level crossings.

[13] Except when they exit sharp left at a level crossing.

[14] They are unable to do so today, despite advances in vehicle design.

says that 'no particular speed is essential for conversion: 40 mph would be ample because rail speeds are so abysmally slow at present.' The prevailing rail speed was irrelevant to calculation of the number of buses and lorries required, and their impact on converted route capacity. Clearly, lowering the speed, increases the number of road vehicles, requiring a review of costs and the adequacy of route capacity.

He claimed that when 'a motor vehicle breaks down, it does not block the route.' Unfortunately, it sometimes does block the route. It always blocks the lane concerned. As he would ban overtaking, traffic would be delayed. With no 'U' turns nor right hand turns permitted, the approach of a breakdown vehicle would not be swift.

Capacity of the new road system

Lloyd claimed that four track routes would be wide enough for six road lanes[15] and that three track routes would convert to a 40 foot motorway adequate for four lanes. He asked whether any converted three-track route would be required to carry more traffic than the 8m vehicles pa of the 36 foot wide four-lane[16] Mersey Tunnel, which had adequate width - but gave no answer. He posed a similar rhetorical question of the converted double track rail routes which were - he said - between 26 and 30 feet wide, narrowing to 24 feet. He compared these to the projected Dartford-Purfleet road tunnel, which was to be 21 feet wide. He ignored that the latter, unlike converted tracks, would be used at 30 mph, later raised to 40 mph and still unchanged! It took six years to build. The 44 foot wide Mersey Tunnel opened in 1934 had - and still has - a 30 mph limit, which any prudent person would consider essential with such narrow lanes. Hence, neither can be prayed in aid of a plan which depends on a 60 mph average!

The best width of lane, he said 'is a controversial subject. The Mersey Tunnel shows that 9 foot lanes are adequate, but only just.' As it is used at 30 mph, not 60 mph, that would destroy his theories. He was dismissive of the MoT decision to increase lane width standards from the existing 11 foot to 12 foot, arguing that the narrower the lane, the more conscientiously do drivers observe lane markings! He appears to have forgotten that, to achieve the utilisation and productivity that he envisages, two vehicles - buses or lorries - will approach each other at a combined 120 mph, with inches to spare between them.[17] 'The precise width to be adopted is unimportant', he added. Such a statement is incredible. The viability cannot be assessed without a decision on it. The narrower the width, the lower speeds *must* be. The wider it is, the more costly it will be.

He claimed that there was 24 foot clear width at bridges and tunnels, (see photos). In fact, most viaducts and many long bridges were so restrictive between abutments or parapets that electrification masts had to mounted on the outside face, (see photo). He was certain that 'a single line railway is immediately convertible into a road of 14 foot minimum clear width',[18] (see footnote, page 23). Enlargement to 22 foot where required for two-way traffic will possibly be the most costly type of conversion.[19]

---

[15] This is ridiculous, see diagram on page 199.

[16] He seems to have lost the plot. One would expect four lanes to carry more traffic than three.

[17] His plan was based on rail traffic being carried on such vehicles, built to high standards and checked - at an unspecified cost. The use of the converted routes for cars was a reluctant afterthought.

[18] Seven foot lanes were bound to cause delays to his eight foot wide vehicles, requiring light controlled contra flows.

[19] Single lines would be useless for road traffic unless widened to two lanes. One way streets of the length of typical branch lines do not exist for obvious reasons. This is stating the obvious, and exposes the unreality of the plan.

'The railway system is so abundant that there is scope for organising extra-fast one-way routes.' So now, the double lines would become one-way. This idea was advanced at the debate in November 1955, (see page 27). The original proposer overlooked - as did Brigadier Lloyd - the effect on journey mileages and contra-flow during road maintenance.

Lloyd was making comparisons between futuristic road transport and existing - already being displaced - rail transport. This is the classic error of comparing chalk and cheese. Once, government gave authority for BR to spend its *own* money - from its depreciation funds and loans it negotiated - improved signalling, new traction and improved rolling stock would rapidly increase line capacity well above prevailing levels. This is what should have been compared with his implausible road transport figures. Railway modernisation had been deliberately held back by government to release maximum materials and resources into what it believed were the key industries. Many began to lose market share long ago, and some have vanished. Manufacturers of road vehicles and the road transport industry ignored less stringent government limits on vehicle production for the home market, thereby giving them an advantage.

He intended that operators' new vehicles will spend their entire life on the converted system, never using public roads and never becoming subject to normal laws and taxes. They will be 63 foot long, able to turn in their own length, very low tyre pressure and no springing. Terminal facilities - bus stations - will be provided by BR. Coal, coke and minerals will be in the new large vehicles. Other rail freight will be in conventional road-licensed vehicles or trailers to eliminate or minimise transhipment.[20]

'Hire car services, corresponding to rail first class, using **tied** vehicles will range from conventional cars to special motor coaches which may be equipped as multi-seaters, diners or sleepers. These will pay tolls.' These vehicles were not costed.

'Unlike the railbound vehicle, the free running vehicle can overtake and be overtaken,' he stated. This contradicts his traffic rule that there will be no overtaking, (see page 23). He was making up the rules, altering them and altering his figures as he went along!

He stated that 'although the public road system is 186,261 miles, the greater part of the traffic is carried on 8,254 miles of trunk roads and 19,551 miles of Class 1 roads. Those roads will be outclassed by railway conversion's 20,000 miles. The extra roads will be 4-8 times[21] as useful.' This is another chalk and cheese comparison. He sought to compare traffic moved on 15% of existing roads with that moved on 100% of the existing rail network! Again, he had not been studying available data, or he would have realised that thousands of miles of rural railways faced closure under the Modernisation Plan, due to low traffic potential. Even if they were not, many of these railways running from the back-of-beyond to the outback were useless for existing trunk rail flows, and hence for use by new road vehicles carrying that ex-rail trunk traffic. Indeed, they would run mostly empty on such routes Major coal and mineral flows and most of the merchandise never went near these minor lines. Some mineral traffic originated on a short branch line, but most branches carried very little as the Beeching Reshaping Plan indicated.[22]

---

[20] This is another afterthought to resolve another overlooked problem. Hitherto, all traffic would be in the new ultra large vehicles.

[21] Yet another figure pulled from thin air to justify his theory.

[22] The Plan showed that 99% of traffic was carried on two thirds of the system.

He forecast that 'much of the fast traffic using public roads will transfer to converted railways, lessening congestion and accidents on public roads. The public will become free to use it [the converted system] as and when they - being reasonable - will.' A *reasonable* motoring public and *reasonable* professional drivers - are still a distant dream. Driving standards have fallen. It is almost endemic for drivers of commercial vehicles and cars to pass red lights. The amber light, which in Lloyd's day was regarded as one at which to *stop*, unless it was dangerous to do so, is passed routinely. The consequences of this conduct at the traffic lights that Lloyd planned to have at the 24,000 level crossings, given a main route flow at 100 yard headways at 60 mph would be disastrous. However, road users will not switch from dual carriageways to converted roads, which would have thousands of traffic lights.

Costs of conversion

He claimed road making would amount to 320m square yards, without naming a source of this figure. Despite the mass of statistics required by the bureaucratic DoT, BR did not supply *this* figure. Aided by a crystal ball, he foresaw 'as work progresses, better machines will be developed[23] and the cost of the last mile will be very much less than the first.' Given the time to design, build and test one, conversion would take many years.

He went on to postulate[24] conversion costs of the whole 20,000 miles of railway route, based on an estimate of converting the rural Inverness-Wick line to a fast all-weather motor road. The conversion cost of £2.25 per square yard [of surface] was attributed, in Lloyd's book, to Sir David Robertson, MP (see page 49): £29,000 per mile for converting the 155 mile Inverness-Wick single line[25] into a 22 foot road. The first traceable reference to the conversion of this particular railway line was in a debate in the Commons: 'Robertson was the author of a scheme to lift the Inverness-Wick railway line and replace it with a motor roadway,' (Hansard 11.7.55, vol. 543, col. 1682). Sir David died on 3rd June 1970. He was still alive when the opportunity arose to fulfil his dream, when BR proposed to rationalise, and later to completely close the line, (see chapter 6). Newspapers carry no record of his support for closure, rather they record his opposition to closure! Railway closures were a vote loser.

That estimate did not mention the cost of acquiring adjoining land to make the single track line wide enough, nor make any mention of the wild terrain and hillsides into which some of that railway is built. Nor does it mention narrow high viaducts and bridges - all of single line width,[26] nor level crossings, especially those used by farmers, which would represent a special hazard to high speed road traffic.

Claiming that the task of conversion 'in its most difficult form would cost £2.25 per square yard,' he concluded that 'the total cost of conversion would be £600m for the whole of BR'.

He said costs of 'platform removal, illumination, drainage, traffic lights, land marking and tunnel ventilation' were 'incidentals' - 'something of little significance'. *Tunnel ventilation would be a major and costly task.*

---

[23] This *pie in the sky - jam tomorrow* - basis is typical of his superficial plan. Better machines would cut BR costs.

[24] By no means could the word *calculate* be used.

[25] The BR timetable shows the distance as 161 miles.

[26] Illustrated in various books on this line.

His book states that 'inland transport used annually only some 32m coal-equivalent tons [1954]. Of that 15m tons was debitable to railways. Other transport on a consumption of 17m tons does an amount of useful work that has been *variously estimated* at 5-10 times that done by railways.[27] That other transport is mainly road transport. If road transport were to take over from rail transport there would be a considerable saving, because on converted roads, road transport will require even less fuel per journey than rail.' Given the higher speeds he envisaged, that was pure conjecture.

Passenger traffic

His 'buses will be *presumed* to be 60-seaters, consisting of a 20-seat motive unit, 20-seat semi-trailer and 20-seat trailer. Internally, they will resemble air liners.' This was a further modification. In 1954, buses had 30 seats, then, in 1955, 40 seats with a 20 seat trailer. The working life of a bus - which has a major bearing on depreciation costs - was not mentioned. The greater the annual mileage, the shorter is its working life. He also claimed that with the journey time halved, each bus seat would be worth two train seats. Given impending InterCity 100 mph speeds, halving journeys would be a challenge.

His previous and subsequent estimates of the size of his bus fleet were based on there being no daily nor seasonal peaks - which created high demand on a few summer Saturdays only - nor major events such as football matches. Buses would travel at a *minimum* 60 mph.

In trying to make his case, Lloyd argued that rail passenger speeds of 60 mph were rare. The underlying reason was that government. had skimmed-off £1bn of railway profits in the war, and had prevented fares being linked to inflation, despite rocketing industrial-fuelled inflation which pushed up costs of materials bought by railways. Worse, BR was compelled to provide below cost services for UK industry to enable them to compete with more efficient foreign industry, and continue to retain under-utilised resources on branch lines - without subsidy - to keep the electorate happy.

'Buses will not be railbound like trains' *forgetting that he has decided to have 63 foot vehicles with no springs, etc., on the grounds that they will not leave the converted system,* (see page 24). 'These buses will be equipped with two-way radio between driver and owner.' Another hidden cost, which would also require the 'owner' who would have no intention of personally working a 24 hr day, to employ control staff.

His plan - previously outlined to the Institution of Civil Engineers - for dining facilities on sixty-seat buses, without regard for the ensuing higher costs, scale of take-up, nor staffing and equipment costs was typical of his superficiality.

'The services need not run to a timetable. Passengers would arrive at any terminal and find a bus waiting for them, which will depart as soon as it is [100%] full.' Unfortunately, the prospect of every bus starting from or calling at different towns and villages, and slipping into a slot 100 yards behind one vehicle and 100 yards in front of a following one from different towns and villages, so that each could run at 60 mph, was nil. In which event, his theoretical calculations - as to the number of buses and lorries required to move existing rail traffic - simply disintegrates. The idea of a bus waiting at a rural station until it was 100% full is completely ludicrous.

---

[27] Estimated by whom, he did not say. The road lobby juggle between originating tons on *all* roads and on *trunk* roads, and studiously avoid the crucially important ton-miles figure on all roads.

'Every city and large town will be given an express service to London. These need not run to a timetable. As soon as one is [100%] full, it pulls off, and another pulls into the bay.' The time that could elapse before a bus is full is unknown, so departure and arrival times will be a complete mystery.[28] Yet, he forecasts twelve 60-seat buses departing every two hours from each city or large town - each would stand two hours [see above] before leaving. A friend or relative waiting at the destination would have no information as to arrival time, because the actual bus concerned out of the twelve would be unknown, even if they retained a railway-style control organisation to know the whereabouts of buses.[29]

'A bus would be continuously employed on a long and busy route such as London-Glasgow, covering the 402 miles in 7 hours' (pity the poor driver needing a legal break), 'with a full load of 60, but might fall to a load of 66%.[30] It would manage 21 hours running in 24, though maintenance time *might* reduce its effective working year to 330 days.' It would run 12,000 miles between service, even assuming no breakdowns, which Lloyd expected - or else why have a breakdown service? If these mileages are not achieved, the whole basis of his superficial 'costs' collapse. One factor which would affect his working year would be the time taken for a bus to be loaded and unloaded. No reference had been made previously to this aspect, but in his book, he envisages that loading a coach and stowing luggage would take 5-10 minutes. Most people who have travelled by coach with luggage would probably argue that the time required has been underestimated. He made no reference to any allowance for time to load and unload at intermediate points.

Having first envisaged a 21 hour day for buses, later in the book he opts for 22 hours as the norm. From this he arrived at 6450 buses,[31] saying it would not be beyond the wit of man to control a fleet that size. *One man? If not how many working round the clock, at how many locations, and with how many staff on the ground reporting passenger numbers.*

'It will be possible to resurrect the slip-coach principle. On the London-Bristol service, the 20-seat trailer might be slipped off and on at Bath.' A coach may be slipped-off, but *never* on. His unwritten schedule would be in chaos as some buses stopped at Bath to attach a trailer. How that would be organised is a discreet mystery.

'The first class hire car (see page 38), will provide express service from any station to any station. Travel in a hire car with all seats occupied, need not be as expensive as railway first class.' It is not stated how many seats there would be in a hire car. It is overlooked that each first class businessman would need to find others to fill a car, as no provision is made for a sales organisation for hire cars. The time lapses at each end, whilst someone tries to find the next remunerative job for such a car, not to mention empty running to the next pickup will eat into his fantasy headways, and the economics and reliability of *first class* services. No vehicle nor manpower costs are disclosed for this service.

In earlier versions, he overlooked that commuter trains run lightly loaded in one direction. In his book, he introduces a 50% load factor on rush hour services, when trying to assess costs and revenue, but his fleet was premised on 100% loads and remained

---

[28] 'Meet me at Euston bus station some time this evening'.
[29] It would be worse than any military cock-up in either World War.
[30] If a bus only departs when it has a full load, how can it get a 66% load factor?
[31] His fourth figure for bus fleet size: see chapter 3 (1,250 & 25,000), chapter 4 (3,434).

unaltered. How commuters could decide which bus to catch to ensure keeping their jobs, without a timetable, is not explained. It would not be long before buses would be scrapped as commuters became redundant through unreliability, or used cars. This may have led him to say that private cars would be allowed on the system in exchange for tolls, although, he did not accept that they would drive into city centres. 'Railway yards and sidings and other railway land will form vast car parks'.[32] How they would complete their journey was not explained. Moreover, there was no prospect of private cars and other non-specially designed vehicles slipping into the traffic stream on converted railways, in such a way as to preserve the crucial 100 yard headway.

Freight traffic

Throughout, he assumes that all traffic - bulk material or otherwise - will fill a lorry to its maximum *weight* capacity. A considerable amount of traffic - coke is one example - will fill a vehicle's *cubic* capacity long before it reaches the weight capacity. A significant proportion of BR merchandise traffic was Sundries - consignments of less than one ton. These included returned empties - some of which were not *returned* - which meant having arrived by rail - but had arrived by road, and the hauliers did not want the trouble of handling such unprofitable flows.[33] These would still need depots to amalgamate them and would involve much mileage in making multiple calls. His theories on freight show that he has no real comprehension of the diverse nature of freight. His book refers to an open-cast in Northumberland which built a private $1^1/_2$ mile road to convey coal in special 40-ton lorries *to a railhead* instead of extending the railway or using an available public road. Under no circumstances was a local authority likely to permit 3,000 tons of coal per day - 75 juggernauts, with coal dust blowing everywhere on public roads. It made economic sense to build such a road for a seven-year project, when rail life for such a low volume would have been more like 50 years, and required that use to be economic.

Initially, however, he was less ambitious than 40tonners. He envisaged that rail freight will be in fully-laden 20ton freighters. The average number of freighters in motion on the 20,000 mile[34] network will be no more than 1,480. He goes on to say that: 'at the worst, an equal number of freighters would travel empty.' It is not 'at the worst', which implies that it may not be that bad. That the vehicles would return empty after carrying coal and minerals is a cast iron certainty. There are no - nor can there be - return loads. Wagons conveying petroleum products will return empty for obvious reasons - as they do on roads. Even the vehicles conveying merchandise will have some empty running between unloading and re-loading points. There are no return loads, with the possible exception of returned empty crates - full of air - from wholesalers who distribute their own traffic.

He claimed it was '*an arithmetical fact that 1,452 freighters, of 20-ton capacity, running at 60 mph were needed to move existing rail traffic, but it has to followed by a*

---

[32] By definition, these will allow access in one direction only to avoid right turns. How far they would travel in the wrong direction, before being able to make an off-system 'U' turn, Lloyd did not consider.

[33] See *Britain's Railways - The Reality*, Page 118.

[34] Unfortunately for his arithmetic, they would never travel over more than one half of that route mileage, (see *Reshaping Plan*, Page 10). Branch lines had very little traffic and were kept open for electoral reasons, and were mostly remote from points of origin and destination of bulk mineral and coal loads! Elsewhere, in making comparisons to try to prove that road utilisation isn't as bad as it is, he claims that road freight only travels over 15% of the road network, whilst deliberately concealing that an analogous disparity applies on railways.

certain amount of speculation'![35] He concludes that with one running under load, one running empty, one loading *or* unloading, and one under repair or maintenance - would give a total of 7,260. He then cut the figure to 5,000 because of improved efficiency!

Unfortunately, he forgot to ask the collieries for an opinion. Engineering and steel industries would have to get their finger out and double handle raw materials. Instead of discharging as convenient direct from BR owned wagons. They would have to unload, stockpile, lift and move again. All these non-transport costs are left out of the equation - although equation is too precise a word to use for his figures.

Given his basic lack of railway knowledge, which led him to overlook the more obvious seasonal peaks for passengers, it is no surprise that he was unaware of a seasonal peak - and a corresponding deep trough for freight, especially coal. Colliery output fell during the summer due to holidays.[36] Despite this, during an extended summer, collieries had to stockpile coal in the order of millions of tons. This arose because, during the summer, when consumer demand for heat and light plummeted, power stations, the gas industry and coal merchants[37] slashed their orders. Likewise, industries that closed down for summer holidays, cancelled their orders. In the winter, all was reversed and above average levels of movement were required. Collieries used BR wagons, supplemented by a small number of their own wagons to move surplus coal to stacking areas. When demand lifted, they required extra wagons to lift coal direct from stacking areas. If this traffic transferred to road, and lorries and their drivers were not wanted for several months - what would happen to them? and where would the extra be found in the winter?

During the hours when they were open - which were mostly not around the clock nor at weekends - collieries needed a pool of wagons, usually in terms of hundreds per location. Their method of production and handling, conveyed coal through overhead screens, which sorted coal according to size and dropped it through the screens into BR wagons below. Typically, the screens at a colliery would span six or more tracks, on each of which there would be a string of wagons. As a wagon was filled, a worker would release a wagon's brakes and let it run by gravity over a weighbridge and into the departure sidings. If a track had no wagon under the screens - due to a colliery, not a BR failing, as sidings were kept well supplied - conveyors would stop or coal be diverted to stock. If that did not happen, a growing pile of coal would end on the tracks below. The idea of a colliery organising its output to the forecast arrival of one lorry to cope with coal from one screen, much less five is laughable. NCB management would not be laughing!

He must have been unaware that the height of a railway wagon was dictated by the headroom of screens, and its other dimensions by the space between vertical supports of colliery screens. These would impose the same limit on the size of lorries. Attempts to manoeuvre 63 ft long 8 ft wide lorries under screens would be slow, if not impossible.

His lorries would have had some problems with coal merchants, who were unwilling to unload a 16 ton wagon at once. Their standard practice[38] was to shovel coal into sacks

---

[35] That his subsequent figures are so unrealistic, clearly stems from speculating instead of studying detailed point to point flows and working out requirements as any operator - road or rail - would do.

[36] As an example of the effect on wagon use, BR's Sheffield Division - one of ten with collieries - had to store upwards of 7,000 wagons from summer to Christmas in the 1960s, (see *Britain's Railways - The Reality*, Page 123).

[37] A director of Coalite, producers of patent fuel, told the author in 1966 that they stock surplus production each year, which only cleared when a very bad winter came about every seven years.

[38] There were, nationally, only a handful of merchants who had hopper discharge to ground level compounds.

direct from wagons. Tipping to ground from a lorry would be unacceptable, because it breaks coal, degrading its value and use. No inducement that Brigadier Lloyd could think of - short of carrying coal free of charge - would have induced them to even consider changing.[39] A 63 foot lorry would only be one-third filled for a coal merchant's order.

Ore and other mineral quarries did not work round the clock nor week-ends. They required a large pool of wagons to maintain a smooth loading pattern. Halting conveyors to await a lorry delayed by a breakdown, or hold-up at the destination of the last load or other problems would create chaos.

Steel, coal and the engineering industries used BR wagons for internal movements - often keeping wagons under load for weeks, whilst waiting for an order. They were required to pay a hire charge for BR wagons, but that depended on them reporting the user. Often, it was a question of paying if caught. Obviously, Lloyd was unaware of the practice, never having been involved in day-to-day rail or industrial management. Keeping thousands of lorries on the premises for days or weeks would be a non-runner. Excluding wagons kept under load by inefficient industry and consumers would severely reduce the BR fleet with which Lloyd made comparisons.

The Lloyd plan envisaged that road freight operators who make use of the converted railway will have a great advantage in respect of port traffic - because rails would be replaced by roads. In fact, beginning in wartime, many ports had set their rails in concrete allowing access to both means of transport. However, road hauliers being highly selective did not want the traffic which created vehicle detention - of which there was much[40]. BR had no choice. Ports required a pool of thousands of wagons to await an incoming ship, whose arrival was not subject to reliable prediction. Conversely, they required thousands of wagons loaded with exports to ensure that ships were loaded quickly. Port authorities and shipowners believed that ships must be turned round quickly - not wagons. They would take the same attitude to lorries. The change in recent years to containerisation - which was initiated by BR through the Freightliner train system - will have reduced the problem. Lloyd could not have foreseen that.[41]

The fact that UK industry did not work round the clock, and enjoyed a five-day week, would scupper that even and Utopian flow of freight around-the-24-hours-and-around-the-four-seasons. His lack of appreciation of how railways and commercial road transport operate was truly staggering. Apart from these examples of the industrial limitations on the scope for the most productive handling of freight, one could not pass industrial premises without seeing a queue of lorries waiting to unload or load.

To try to reduce the volume of traffic which would be transferred to the new freight vehicles, he reiterated the comparison of one-fifth traffic only being by rail. This, of course, counts all traffic over every road, including domestic deliveries in residential streets. Elsewhere, he tries to argue that only 15% of roads should be considered in any comparison, (see page 38). It is also expressed in originating tons, regardless of whether it is

---

[39] When BR tried to introduce mechanised handling at coal depots, with lower freight charges and a contribution to mechanisation costs by the NCB, it was like trying to draw blood from a stone.

[40] An example was loose loaded timber. (See *Britain's Railways - The Reality*, Page 121).

[41] In 1957, South Yorkshire Woodworking Coy told BR, which tried to deliver timber in part-packaged loads, that timber had never been packaged and never would be! (See *Blueprints for Bankruptcy*, Page 167). They were wrong.

conveyed one mile or fifty. For all practical purposes, and for a meaningful comparison, it was irrelevant, and made less so, by current revelations of unreliable data, (see page 153).

He claimed that 'the swelling volume of 'C' licensed vehicles will have whittled away BR's obligations as common carriers'. These were licensed only to carry a trader's own goods. They would not, in any way, affect volume, but would increase empty mileage, being predominantly employed in one directional flows. BR would still be obliged to carry any traffic from firms not having such vehicles, and even from 'C' Licence owners who tried to avoid sending vehicles to rural backwaters with one package..

He tried to hedge his bets on vehicles required and route capacity, by remarking 'if a rigid eight-hour day is worked ....' If it isn't, manpower comparisons are invalid. Railway staff had an eight-hour day imposed by government in 1919 against the wishes of railway companies, whilst road transport for the next fourteen years could work a 24-hour day - and some may have got close to it, and do so now.[42] Thereafter, an undemanding limit of 11 hours was imposed by government on road transport, which was largely ignored. Although, the limit has been trimmed, the law is still ignored.

A properly policed lower limit on drivers' hours is long overdue. One thing was certain, if BR ceased to exist, the lid on road prices which are held down by low haulage wages and long hours to maintain pricing competition with BR will disappear, and secret cartels will push prices through the ceiling to meet demands for shorter hours, higher wages and bigger profits. With BR as an alternative, senders could threaten diversion if road operators hinted at price increases. Now, there is less of a problem, because UK heavy industry has thrown in the towel. They left the railways with redundant freight resources.

To prove what could be conveyed by road, he took the average BRS lorry in 1954, which, he said earned £2380 and cost £2100 to operate. Its load totalled 1100 tons, it ran 16,200 miles laden or partly laden and produced 142,800 ton-miles. 'Those ton-miles are one-eighth of the theoretical[43] maximum a vehicle could have produced in a year, running fully laden at its customary 15 mph'. (The source for that speed is not identified. It was not in BRS Accounts). 'Theoretically, [at 60 mph] one vehicle will do the work of four'.[44] He says that 'an increase in productivity will be fully attainable provided techniques of mechanical handling result in a speeding up of loading and unloading'. Assuming that UK industry could have dragged its workforce and methods into the 20th century by 1960, which it failed to do, unlike BR which introduced mechanisation without disputes.[45] It depended on whether industry was willing to invest to expedite loading, which was very often performed unaided by the lorry driver. Had UK industry been willing to modernise, BR productivity would have been likewise improved as wagons in private sidings and BR delivery lorries were loaded or unloaded quicker.

The Lloyd plan specified that 'sources and destinations that are rail served will be incorporated into the converted system'. What he was - perhaps unwittingly saying,

---

[42] A driver was killed when his lorry left the road, after he had worked 22 hours, (see *Juggernaut*, Page 55).

[43] A theory originated by him and recognised by no one else.

[44] Subject to a willingness of industrial labour to give up their 8-hour, 5-day week, and falling over themselves with unaccustomed anxiety to take immediate delivery of traffic. Lloyd overlooks, that outside any UK factory, would be a queue of lorries waiting to load or unload, and woe betide the driver who arrives at break time! He made no provision for time waiting access to premises, to load, unload, sheet and rope, deal with documentation and pull out onto a public road

[45] See *Britain's Railways - The Reality*.

without a by-your-leave, was that he would sequestrate and convert privately owned sidings into roads. This meant that collieries would have to replace *their* locos and wagons which are used to stockpile unsold coal, with road vehicles, and provide bunkers to hold coal waiting for lorries, which expect to arrive, load and depart in seconds. It will come as a shock, when power stations and coal merchants slash coal intake for six months of the year, and then call for above average quantities in the winter.

A suggestion that large consumers may run their own transport is made. It would not take the capital and operating costs of *their* new lorries out of the equation. The task of synchronising lorry provision, whoever is the owner, between the different collieries over a wide area, which suddenly, and with little warning take, on the role of current supplier to the CEA, on a day-to-day basis, will open many eyes, and create more empty mileage.

Safety
In an endeavour to prove that road safety was as good - or better than rail safety - Lloyd took the *whole* population of UK as being at risk of accident on roads and related it to total road fatalities, whilst relating rail fatalities to the total of passengers and railway staff. In fact the whole population was just as likely to get killed walking or driving over level crossings or using footpaths across railways or as trespassers crossing elsewhere - the incidence of which was, and is, unknown (see page 62,63). Hence, railways could also count the whole population, making the scale of rail fatalities even lower than appears, further widening the gap to road. Moreover, he overlooks, that part of the population are house bound, in hospital, in prison, live on remote unmotorised islands, are abroad, etc.

Conversion task
'The alignment of the first London-Yorkshire motorway provoked 126 objections'. Seeing problems with securing wayleaves for this motorway, he argues for exploiting existing wayleaves of BR. What he fails to comprehend is that those wayleaves for railways are just that. Conversion to another purpose, indeed any significant change in rail user terms provokes public inquiries. Anyone who has ever lived near a road heavily used by lorries, would gladly exchange their location for one next to a railway.

Brigadier Lloyd claimed: 'Conversion will be far simpler than ordinary new construction on virgin land. The railway permanent-way has a ready made formation compacted by trains. It is no more than re-surfacing an existing road'. Anyone who believes that a skimming of tarmac on the formation would support the weight and withstand the wear of a heavy lorry is completely out of touch with reality. Not one complete route of railway formation has ever been reported as being so converted for such a purpose. Such conversions as there have been - mostly short lengths and needing widening - involved excavation, new drainage, etc. No engineer should have advanced such a proposal without field studies and test borings.

He claimed that on converted roads, due to strict limits on wheel load [perhaps 9,000 lbs], and tyre pressure of the authorised vehicles, conversion would be easy and cheap. However, elsewhere he plans to permit conventional vehicles to use the converted roads, so the roads would need to be constructed to conventional strengths.

Lloyd referred to a critic who 'sought to appal others with the difficulties and cost of re -decking 30,000 bridges. An [unnamed] contracting engineer commented that Stephenson,

Brunel, etc. remained undaunted at the prospect of 30,000 bridges to build'. It is almost too obvious to point out - except to the conversion league - that:

1. They did not foresee the prospect of building so many bridges. Wherever possible, they created level crossings rather than costly bridges.
2. The 30,000 were built over a period of 70 years by hundreds of railway companies.
3. They built these bridges before there was any railway traffic, i.e. they did not face the problem of diverting traffic in order to build them.

He gave little thought to what would happen to millions of commuters, not to mention Intercity routes. 'There will be localised dislocation of traffic wherever conversion is in progress, but that need not be serious! Work will start at the coast and proceed inland, the roadhead advancing from station to station[46] as the conversion progresses'. This would include passengers and commuters, mixed with coal traffic. They would find it prudent to wear wellingtons as they tramped between platforms and bus through work in progress! He envisaged temporary links between the existing roads and the converted system, but made no financial allowance for them. There would be thousands of such temporary roadheads to create. He said 'the whole operation lends itself to pre-planning' as though it may be merely *useful* to pre-plan, when it was absolutely vital.

He claimed 'BR staff will readily switch from rail to road engineering; it is far less complex and specialised'.[47] apparently without training, as he didn't mention it. He said that 1,255 local authorities with highway responsibilities would pitch in and convert an average 16 miles each. He had not consulted them.

Management of the system

His plan envisaged that 'BR would remain as proprietors and controllers of the new network - not local authorities.' He advanced no reason for this proposal. BR had no experience of managing, maintaining nor policing long distance roads. In the task of converting railways to roads, he had not originally envisaged work being done by BR, but by contractors and local authorities. Quite clearly, logic demanded that the new trunk roads be under the MoT or County Councils as was the prevailing practice. There can only be one reason. If his master plan failed, he would have a handy whipping boy in the form of those whom he assumed had made railways financially unviable. Given that BR was already a useful whipping boy for many industrial failures, that would be a logical course for him to pursue! BR was to ensure all users, including one-off use by conventional vehicles, were highly competent and their vehicles of the highest road-worthy standards. Perhaps realising that this task would have caused delays whoever was running the system, he came up with a face-saving solution:

It is possible that by the time conversion has taken place, the entire motor vehicle driving fraternity - professional and amateur - will have become so responsible, law-abiding and considerate of one another that the converted railway system will scarcely need organising in the accepted meaning of the word. The reservation of these new fast roads would be observed voluntarily without need of enforcement.

---

[46] This idea was fed to him at the ICE meeting, (see page 27).

[47] We have discovered, to our cost, how true this is, now that road engineers have become involved in the converse task!

Under ideal conditions, without gates or barriers, appropriate vehicles will pass freely from one road system to the other. That is a picture for a remote period when the standard of living perhaps may have doubled, with the number of cars doubled.[48]

A mysterious concept was for 'BR to be able to restore equity of competition by varying its contracts with the tied operators and its scale of toll charges with others'. How and why operators should have contracts with BR to use this road system, and what represented equity is not explained, nor who will decide if the contracts or tolls are fair.

No provision was made for disruption to his 100 yard headway round-the-clock-and-over-the-four-seasons by road maintenance and renewal. Speeds could not be maintained at 60 mph when cars are admitted. Inevitably, some drive slower. This will create jams.

His theories conveniently ignore manpower, machinery, vehicles and other costs arising from managing, maintaining and operating the system. He fails even to throw in figures of the same inexactitude as those forming the basis of his capacity or conversion costs, etc. The book and his whole plan were based on random figures without any scientific basis of selection, which masqueraded as comparative statistics. 'If', 'perhaps', 'possibly' occur in his book with such frequency that one assumes this book was not widely sold.[49] He coined a new word in his book: 'carpmanship' for all who dared to disagree with him. Anyone arguing against his grand design was carping. That this could be applied to his criticisms of BR escaped him.

Harold Watkinson, a noted anti-rail MoT, did not agree with Lloyd. He said that conversion would cost 4 times the cost of a motorway of identical length, *(The Times, 15.10.58)*

Fleet sizes

The approach used by Brigadier Lloyd to estimate the numbers of vehicles that would be required to move existing rail traffic defies belief. There is no logic or value in estimating the number required on the basis with which he began - i.e. perpetual motion - nor in the selecting an arbitrary percentage increase on it, (see page 16). Alternative data was publicly available that would have enabled a more credible figure to be assessed.

Taking first, his estimate of the number of lorries required. In his paper in the Royal Engineers Journal, he stated that 22,400m ton miles of rail freight could be transported by 4,250 lorries of 10-ton capacity travelling at 60 mph. This was then turned into a *practical* fleet of 85,000 lorries, based on a 5% reality factor.

In his paper to the Institution of Civil Engineers, he replaced it by 6,866 lorries of 20 ton capacity, operating in 'eight-hour shifts, round the clock, and over the four seasons' without explaining why he had changed. The doubling of vehicle capacity, whilst the speed remained at 60 mph, would, at best, even assuming his earlier figure was right, only halve the fleet to 42,250, if all were *always* fully loaded.

In his book,[50] he changed the fleet size to 1,480, which he then said would be doubled 'at the worst'. He had reverted to 20 ton vehicles still at 60 mph, and the volume of rail freight he used was the same. His second guestimate of 6,867 20-ton lorries involved

---

[48] There are now six times as many cars - and drivers are, if anything, less considerate than ever.

[49] It was sent free to the author (see Preface), who quickly perused it, and found it valueless for his purpose. Had he read it at the time, it would have been dumped, and would not have been exposed for the fantasy that it is.

[50] See pages 16,31 of this book.

3.2m ton miles per vehicle pa. This equates to 10,256 ton-miles per vehicle per day, with all vehicles loaded to 100% capacity, and gives 512 miles per day, which at 60 mph requires 8.5 hours. The 24 hour day would have to become a $25^{1}/_{2}$ hour day!

The number of lorries required could have been more logically derived by examining data[51] on work performed by existing road transport. At the time the biggest lorry on public roads was a 5 ton u.l.w., with an average capacity of 13.7 tons. There were 12,170 such vehicles out of the total lorry fleet of 1.27m. The average ton miles *claimed* to be performed by these larger vehicles equated to 1,051 per day. They were recorded as being fully loaded on 74% occasions, although for some traffics it was said to be based on volume not weight. Allowing 46% increase in this workload, to compensate for higher capacity lorries envisaged, brings ton miles per day to 1,534 and allowing for a doubling of vehicle speed brings it to 3,068. It will be seen that this figure is less than one third of Lloyd's figure. On this basis, 40,683 lorries would be required. This does not reflect that instead of 74% vehicles fully loaded, as the whole of the coal and mineral traffic on rail cannot secure a return load, the incidence of full loads would be less, and hence, the fleet larger, (see page 30). Moreover, some of the other rail traffic was in consignments of less than one ton, whilst some was in the range one to ten tons. The effect would be to increase the vehicles from 40,683 to 70-80,000. That does not mean that this figure would apply, merely that is a minimum, as DoT published data is unreliable, (see page 153).

Turning to buses, Lloyd postulated in the Royal Engineers Journal that 1,250 of 30-seat capacity would convey BR's existing 22,000m passenger miles employing perpetual motion. He then went on to multiply it by 20 to arrive at what he said was a *practical* fleet of 25,000 buses. He told the Civil Engineers that 3,434 bus/trailer combinations carrying 60 passengers were required. A doubling of capacity would, at best, have led to a halving of his initial guestimate. His book quotes 6,450 of 60 seats still at 60 mph. A more logical method would be to base fleets on the utilisation achieved by existing fleets. The MoT publication *Passenger Transport In Great Britain* shows, in 1955, 80,000 PSVs carried 50,000 passenger miles. On that basis, 33,400 extra PSVs would be required to cater for displaced rail traffic. Allowing for new buses being twice as big would cut it to 16,700. Against this, commuter flows would produce a lower average load than existing bus services. On the other hand, the higher speed postulated should reduce the number. A better guestimate than the Lloyd figures would be at least 15,000.

The effect on the headway of there being, say 87,000 vehicles on the converted network, instead of Lloyd's 10,300 buses and lorries would be to reduce his theoretical headway from 100 yards to about 12 yards, considerably below the braking distance for vehicles travelling at 60 mph, which is about 60 yards. One consequence would be to completely destroy any chance of cross traffic at level crossings of any kind, and even of pedestrians using public footpaths across the existing infrastructure. Clearly, it would have been totally impractical to move the BR traffic by road vehicles, even of larger and faster types, much less provide space for traffic to transfer from existing roads.[52] Whilst there has been a decline in freight traffic, passenger traffic has grown on main routes, and at speeds which the most ardent conversionist could not envisage on a converted system.

---

[51] *The Transport of Goods by Road,* published by the MoT
[52] See also statistics on page 88,173.

Chapter 6   Conversion opportunities missed!

Several opportunities to prove conversion theories were missed.

Inverness-Wick

Sir David Robertson MP [Caithness & Sutherland] was the author of a scheme to replace the Inverness-Wick line by a road, (Hansard 11.7.55, vol. 543, col. 1682). Scottish newspapers reported that his plan to convert the line into an autobahn[1] had been explained to constituents, gained wide support and was backed by influential Scottish Unionist MPs, who intend rousing public interest. It was believed that it would open the way to converting unremunerative lines[2] in other parts of Britain, at far less cost than the construction of new roads.[3] He said that an estimate of the cost was prepared by civil engineers Balfour, Beatty & Co. 'On the assumption that the BTC would lift the rails or permit them to be covered, the cost was estimated at £4.5m.' It was not explained how they made the estimate of nearly £30,000 per mile. Surveying a line needed special arrangements with BR, including lookoutmen for which payment would have been required.

It would provide 'a road 22 foot wide, with existing overbridges altered as necessary to give additional headroom. It was to be an all-weather motorway.[4] It would be restricted to fast motor vehicles, entering at existing terminals and stations. Pedestrians, cycles, horse drawn vehicles and tractors would be excluded. BR would continue to operate passenger and goods services using fast motor coaches and lorries'. He stated that 'signals and track would be recovered to serve more populous areas,' (*John O'Groats Journal* 15.7.55).[5]

He did not explain what would happen to farm traffic - animals, horse drawn vehicles and tractors - which crossed the railway line on farm and public level crossings. Nor did he explain what provision would be made for pedestrians using level crossings and statutory footpaths across the line. Nor did he mention how much land was needed to widen the formation and widen or duplicate under-bridges on this predominantly single line! No mention was made of the cost of drainage, that experts raised, (see pages 25-27).

He did not say whether BR delivery drivers would remain the only ones obeying the law on driving hours, as it was widely acknowledged that that law was *routinely* flouted by lorry and coach drivers.[6] If not, BR wouldn't be competing on cost for very long. The estimated cost covered 'provision of a 22 foot wide roadway and widening of over bridges' but ignored the widening of *under* bridges and other aspects, such as the cost to BR of scrapping rolling stock and buying new motor vehicles to carry traffic which was already known to be uneconomic. Locos and coaches on this line would certainly not be regarded as suitable on 'more populous areas', and the number of wagons effectively released for general use would represent an infinitesimal change in availability.

---

[1] This was the German name for their pre-war built motorways - built with military use in mind.

[2] It will be noted that they advocated replacing *unremunerative lines* by roads, not all lines including busy trunk routes which Brigadier Lloyd envisaged. His costings are therefore suspect.

[3] This proved to be a pious hope.

[4] In the 1970s, objectors to closure of the Alston-Haltwhistle branch ridiculed the idea that it be replaced by an all-weather road, and *that* line was 350 miles nearer the equator.

[5] The track and signalling would have been of a minimum [rural] standard, unsuitable for busy routes. It only serves to emphasise the superficiality of knowledge of politicians and others on railways.

[6] See pages 14,171,176; also *Square Deal Denied & Britain's Railways - The Reality.*

Obviously, the motive for proposing that BR provide a road service was that it was the only way to guarantee that the remote Highlands would still have a transport service. If the traffic had been profitable for private sector road transport, it would long ago have transferred from rail to road, given past and prevailing government policy which was focused on facilitating expansion of road transport to the detriment of railways.[7] However, the statutory control of fares and charges, coupled with Ministerial interference to keep them below inflation, and the common carrier obligation which applied only to railways, meant that road operators were disinterested. Without the provision for a BR road service, the area would have been deprived of transport for existing rail traffic.

The estimated cost of conversion, did not include the cost of providing new road vehicles to carry displaced rail traffic, nor the costs of diverting the traffic via existing roads whilst conversion took place.

1959 - station & branch closures

Details of the proposed closures and the £41,200 pa savings were sent to local authorities and the TUCC, (*Inverness Courier* 15.5.59). The editorial called for 'a reduction in fares and freight charges which were prohibitive.' Both had trailed inflation since 1948.[8] As inflation was created and fuelled by UK industry, one wonders why the media did not wake up to the need to call for a reduction in prices across the private sector.

The closures of stations and changes to train working on the Inverness-Wick line would make 120 staff redundant, (*Inverness Courier* 30.6.59). Staff redundancy always affected attitudes of local authorities and local MPs to proposed railway economies. At other times, they would be calling on BR to cut costs. When it fell on local labour - which was 66% of costs - critics shouted foul !

'Local authorities and others were urged to object to closure of stations and lines north of Inverness. A deputation of eight authorities was to put the case against closure to the TUCC in Edinburgh on 17th July. A letter from the MoT to a local MP does not suggest any appreciation in Government of the anxiety in the Highlands. It was claimed that the BTC had no right to say that the public must do without a railway because it doesn't pay! The closure would conflict with Government policy in *protecting industry and employment* in the North. The MoT said the TUCC conclusions will be sent to him and the BTC, and he could not anticipate their findings. The facts had been set out in a Parliamentary debate on 17th June.[9] Objectors said regard must be paid to the White Paper *Review of Highland Policy* recently issued. The BTC say there is no case for retention of northern railway lines, and bus companies say that they could not run economic services on that route',[10] (*Inverness Courier* 21.7.59).

Councillor Mr. Thompson said we all realise that railways north of Perth are uneconomic, but they are socially necessary, (*Inverness Courier* 10.7.59).

When BR announced its station closure plans, there should have been dancing in the streets, and demands to close the line *completely,* thereby opening the door for the conversion to a road which was said to be so keenly supported by MPs, constituents and others. This was the time for Sir David Robertson, the road construction lobby and the

---

[7] See *Square Deal Denied & Britain's Railways - The Reality.*

[8] See *Britain's Railways - The Reality*, Tables 4,8).

[9] There had also been a debate on the services on 3rd June, (see Hansard, vol. 624, col. 1786)

[10] This unwelcome truth was ignored by Lloyd and other BR critics.

conversion theorists to seize the opportunity. They did not even poke their heads above the parapet. Instead it was 'to the barricades.'

The TUCC for Scotland approved the station closures and reorganisation of the railway services at a meeting on 17th July. However, some members of the TUCC expressed concern about the possible effect on the economic and social effects of the changes.

A press conference was told that the TUCC had recommended acceptance of the closure proposals. Caithness County Council is objecting to the decision, (*Inverness Courier* 11.8.59). A plan was put forward for a summit meeting between Inverness Town council and the Prime Minister, and a deputation to the MoT, (*Inverness Courier* 18.8.59).

The TUCC for Scotland again reviewed the proposal in September 1959 following further objections, relating specifically to an apparent contradiction between Government policy for the Highlands and the railway station closures, (Hansard, vol. 624, col. 1812).

A reader's letter (*Inverness Courier* 25.9.59) argued that as trains were ill used, what was needed was road improvements. This was the first such view in the newspaper since closures were first disclosed in the paper. It fell on deaf ears.

The MoT said that there will be no closures until he has met a deputation of Inverness Town councillors, (*Inverness Courier* 9.10.59). The deputation met the MoT on 3rd December, and were told that he had no power to act, as closures were a matter for the BTC to decide. The editor asked why the MoT had not told them that, when they asked for a meeting, instead of wasting the time of twelve representatives? (*Inverness Courier* 4.12.59).

The Town council had noted that the BTC expected to save £40,000 pa by closing 22 of the 39 stations, and save £20,000 pa by introducing diesels. They were concerned about unemployment. The editor regarded it as 'shocking that forty staff were being made redundant at Aviemore as a result of diesel modernisation,' (*Inverness Courier* 8.12.59). This is incredible. Critics had opposed closure and called for modernisation - the objective of which must be to cut costs, whilst, hopefully, increasing business. Clearly what they sought was infinite capital to modernise beyond the wildest dreams, whilst not reducing employment!

A reader, who claimed to be a trained railway engineer, had a plan - presumably to avoid closures and redundancies - details of which were not revealed, (*Inverness Courier* 15.12.59). The precise nature and extent of knowledge of this engineer was not disclosed. Even an anonymous reader could have summarised his CV.

Lord Forbes attacked the BTC plan in the Lords last week, (*Inverness Courier* 22.12.59).

In March 1960, the Highland Fund offered to fund retention of a short branch line off the Inverness-Wick line and may be able to help financially in other directions, if need be, (*Inverness Courier* 18.3.60). Closure of 24 stations north of Inverness was approved by the TUCC, and were to take effect from 13th June, (*Inverness Courier* 3.5.60).

In May 1960, Sir David Robertson asked the Secretary of State for Scotland if he was aware that government policy for development of Highland tourism conflicts with the decision to close, and asked if he will consult with the BTC to remove the difficulty. The response was: 'No'. He then asked what was government policy with regard to subsidising railways in the Highlands as an essential public service. The MoT replied that the future of railways as a whole were under study, and that he could not add to the statement of the Prime Minister[11] on 10th March. Robertson asked in view of representations from a Highlands deputation, will the Minister postpone closure of stations and services north of Inverness for three months. The Minister refused, neither would he ask the TUCC to re-consider the matter, (Hansard vol. 624, cols. 30,47,73). It is astonishing that the man who had advocated replacing the tracks on *this* railway line with tarmac was objecting to rail closure on *any* grounds - much less that they were essential !

On 3rd June 1960, the proposed closure of some stations on the Inverness to Wick line was debated at length in Parliament, (Hansard, vol. 624, cols. 1786-1815). Sir David Robertson was the lead speaker calling for the proposal to be postponed. He spoke for half an hour. He literally begged the House to support him in securing a three months deferment, (col. 1797). He was very critical of the composition of the Transport Users Consultative Committee - which had conducted the public hearing into the closure. In accordance with the 1953 Act - passed by *his* Party - the members of these Committees were selected by the MoT from names submitted by various industrial, trade, voluntary and consumer bodies. Neither he, nor any other MP, had objected to the composition of this Committee prior to the Hearing. He was critical of the presence at the Committee meetings of BR representatives, suggesting that they would have been an effective bloc on that Committee - overlooking that they had no vote, and could be asked to retire whilst a vote was taken.

He was completely confused by the appointment of a member of this Committee to the BR Area Board, which he thought 'should not be a natural ground for promotion of that kind.' Members of the Committee and the Area Board were from similar non railway backgrounds - the former in order to be independent, and the latter, ostensibly, to bring external expertise to railways.[12] Appointments to both were for fixed periods. He was concerned about the loss of employment for 79 railwaymen. Converting the line to a road - his original plan would have sacked many more. This tendency of MPs to object to closures in their own backyard, whilst applauding economies elsewhere, had been remarked on by another MP on a previous occasion.[13] He admitted that he had supported the *general* plan to cut services - until it became clear it was going to hit this line's handful of passengers. He argued that the way to make the line profitable was to cut prices - a policy noticeably ignored by British industry as it went into terminal decline by failing to match the lower prices of foreign competitors. Of course, with the private sector, it was different - their policy was to charge as much as they could get away with. Even so, he went on to call for the line to be subsidised, indicating that he accepted - as other MPs accepted - that the line was bound to be uneconomic, (Hansard col. 1804). He foresaw that replacement bus services would lose money. This was from an arch-priest of conversion, and an advocate of an industry - road transport - which would not have to pay for conversion. He was impressed by the savings which could accrue from diesels, but lost sight of the source of the capital required. He reminded MPs that railways were managed 'in other days - in competition.' What he had lost sight of, was that his Party had been driving pre-war privately owned railways towards bankruptcy by anti-rail, pro-road policies which left

---

[11] The PM said that services would be cut to the size of current demands, but named no routes, (*The Times*, 11.3.60)

[12] Dr. Beeching - as a member of the secret Stedeford Committee - had argued that railways should be run by professionals, and on becoming Chairman, sacked most external members of Area Boards and replaced them with career railway executives. All Board chairmen were replaced by managers, see *Britain's Railways - The Reality*.

[13] See *The Railway Closure Controversy*, Page 13 and Hansard vol. 547, col. 711.

road free to compete but tied railways to archaic rates structures controlled by a court of law, which were relevant to an era when there was no competition.[14] Those rates were specifically designed and controlled to protect inefficient UK industry from imports.[15] When railways sought equality of opportunity to compete, the pre-war Tory Government rejected their claim. Likewise, in 1952, the Tory Government decided that railways should not be free to pursue 'cut-throat competition, which might drive hauliers out of business.' It was happy to permit the converse situation in which railways could be driven out of business by hauliers, and ignored media warnings to that effect.[16]

Tory MP John MacLeod supported Sir David and was critical that BR had made up its mind to close this [grossly uneconomic, very ultra-rural] line. What he ignored was that any losses had to be made good from elsewhere - main line passengers' fares or cuts in staff costs on other lines - not from taxpayers. He said closure was a negative approach. This contrasts with private sector industry which is presumably positive when it throws in the towel.[17] He said that BR had failed to make services more attractive, overlooking that post-war governments of both Parties had prevented BR from restoring the system to pre-war standards for ten years, much less modernising whilst free rein was given to road transport to increase and modernise their fleets.[18]

MP, G.M. Thomas chided that it was unreasonable to criticise BR for making losses and simultaneously attack it for not running services at a loss to meet local needs. He blamed the government.

On 13th June 1960, passenger services were withdrawn between Inverness and Bonar Bridge except for Dingwall, Invergordon, Feran, and Tain. On the north part of the line, 7 stations closed. The elimination of a total of twenty stops permitted a substantial saving in journey time between Inverness and Wick. In April 1961, another station closed.

1963 - total closure of the line

Complete closure of the Inverness-Wick line was included in the Reshaping Plan in 1963. This should have brought the advocates of conversion onto the streets. It didn't. Again it was to the barricades. Lord Cameron, Chairman of the Highland Panel and the Highlands & Islands Development Consultative Council said that the Highland Transport Board could not develop a plan if there was a possibility of rail closures, (*The Times* 29.2.64).

A TUCC hearing began in Inverness on 9th March into the proposed closure of Inverness-Wick/Thurso. There were 1000 objections from local authorities and others, (*The Times* 10.3.64). Objectors included Inverness Town Council, County and other Councils involved, some of whom were represented by QCs,[19] organisations and individuals. One objector travelled four times a year from Dingwall to Inverness. One objecting business-man said that rail was the only all-weather transport link in north Scotland. They all stressed the hardship that would be caused by closure. The TUCC Annual Report for 1964 said that the proposal aroused heated public criticism. Neither the TUCC Report, nor media reports mention any support for closure by the Conversion League.

---

[14] See *Square Deal Denied*, Chapter 7.
[15] See *Britain's Railways - The Reality*, Pages 6,7.
[16] See *Economist*, 10.5.52. This article was seen by the MoT who told the PM of it, (PRO: MT62/138)
[17] Thousands of companies are wound up annually - none due to political interference. For statistics on industrial decline see *The Railway Closure Controversy*, Page 49 and *Britain's Railways - The Reality*, Chapter 14.
[18] See *Britain's Railways - The Reality*, Pages 54-55.
[19] Local authorities could find cash for legal fees to oppose closures, but none to support uneconomic lines.

Sir David Robertson MP,[20] wrote to the TUCC that the 'gravest hardship would beset the people in the northern counties if the line was closed. Industries could not be introduced to the towns and villages without railways. New light industry, land reclamation and other things had to go hand-in-hand with the retention of railway services. Any Government that insisted on closing down a life-line used in both world wars[21] would have a short life'. MP Neil McLean was present at the TUCC Hearing and spoke of the great hardship that would be caused by closure.

The TUCC also held a Hearing into the BR proposal to close the Inverness to Kyle of Lochalsh line. It heard that objectors would face severe hardship if this line closed. MPs and councillors were prominent in making objections to closure. One councillor said 'I tremble to think what will happen if there is no rail service.' The county road surveyor said that improving the [55 mile] road from Garve to Kyle of Lochalsh up to a suitable standard would cost £5-6m, (*Inverness Courier* 10.3.64). On that basis, to create a *new* road using the formation of the 161 mile Inverness-Wick line, (of which less than ten miles was double track), would cost considerably more than the £4.5m envisaged by Sir David Robertson. There would also be a need to lay road foundations and drainage. Well over the pro rata £15-18m would be needed. Noticeably, there was no call to replace either railway formation by a road.

The Tourist Board said that hoteliers would suffer enormously from closure. Inverness County Council pointed out that closure negated government's own plan as set out in a White Paper: *Review of Highland Policy*, which stated that government would promote economic growth and provide suitable amenities and social services. Other objectors said that a bus, having no toilets nor room for luggage, from Thurso to Inverness would be unacceptable. It was unrealistic to expect children to remain seated for a nine hour bus journey, without access to toilets. Others focused on the closure of roads by snowdrifts, and the even greater danger of accidents caused by black ice. If railways closed, there will be no further development in North Scotland. There were fears of staffing problems at Dounreay power station if rail services were removed. Many communities would become unviable, and depopulation would accelerate. 70% of patients travelling long distances to hospitals go by rail rather than ambulance which leave them sick and exhausted. A proposed new boarding school near Dunrobin would not proceed if the line closed. A supplier of poultry, who supplied the House of Commons said there would be hardship there [at the House of Commons] if the rail service was withdrawn! (*Inverness Courier* 10.3.64, 13.3.64).

BR's representative at the TUCC Inquiry said that if all objectors used rail there would be no need for closure. Objectors who asked the TUCC for an early decision to end anxiety were told that their MPs had quicker access to the Minister, (*Inverness Courier* 10.3.64).

Mr. E. Popplewell, MP had no doubt that the line could not be made to pay, but closure would leave many people hundreds of miles from a railhead, (Hansard vol. 621, col. 1261). He made no suggestion as to the source of funds to cover deficits. Government did not begin to do so for such lines until 1969.[22]

---

[20] He had advocated ripping the route up in 1955. His plan had been praised by Lloyd and used by Lloyd as the basis for his *costing* of the total conversion proposal. It was his golden opportunity to realise his dream.

[21] This was a common ploy to try to undermine closure.

[22] See *Britain's Railways - The Reality*, Page 178.

Young Scottish Tories called for subsidies for uneconomic railway lines in Scotland, (*The Times* 4.3.63). The Tory government ignored them.

1964 - the line is reprieved

MoT, Ernest Marples[23] reprieved lines north of Inverness: the line to Kyle of Lochalsh was losing £120,000 and that to Wick £240,000, (*The Times* 17.4.64). The Minister said that the TUCC had reported that closures would cause extreme hardship, (Hansard, 16.4.64 vol. 693 col. 687, and vol. 688 col. 169). The *Inverness Courier* stated that the TUCC had reported that 'closure would cause extreme and widespread hardship.' The paper added that 'there was great satisfaction throughout the North when news of the reprieve became known.' A Scottish Unionist[24] conference earlier in the day had passed a resolution expressing anxiety at the threat of the proposed closure.

In common with other loss making services which BR had been prevented from closing over the past sixteen years, no subsidy was to be paid by Government or local authorities to retain the services.[25] Mr. Marples did not undertake to provide Government funds to keep these lines open. The continuing losses would appear in the Accounts - as hitherto - to be due to BR inefficiency, rather than Government interference in business decisions for political reasons and a failure to fund its own social policies.

Dr. Beeching, BR Chairman said that the figures quoted by the Minister were the minimum savings expected. BR called on objectors to make full use of the services. This was a reasonable request, in view of the low level of existing user.

A TUCC meeting on 15th May, responded to a request by the MoT to examine the effect of closing some intermediate stations and agreed that no hardship would arise from closing five, including Dunrobin, the location for the proposed new school, (TUCC 1964 Report). It had earlier been said that the school would not be viable without a station.

Objectors had emphasised the effect on tourism

Objectors to closures - of either selected stations as in 1960 or complete closure as in 1964 - stressed the effect on tourism and hence the economy of the area. It did no harm to their case that the Loch Ness monster was seen round about the time of each closure announcement, and when TUCC Hearings, to consider objections, were taking place.

The *Inverness Courier* reported 'two sightings of the monster' and 'Objections made to railway closures,' (7.7.59). 'The monster was seen again on Wednesday by more than 40 tourists, and was visible for fifteen minutes,' (*Inverness Courier* 24.7.59). A reader has put forward a plan to capture the Loch Ness monster, (*Inverness Courier* 25.8.59).

The newspaper carried a further report of a 'hunt for the monster,' (*Inverness Courier* 13.10.59). At the most crucial time - when closure was threatened, they carried another report that the monster had been seen, (*Inverness Courier*, 20.3.64). Whether these reports led to more tourists is not known, much less whether more tourists used the railway.

Other good opportunities for conversion theorists

The proposed closure of the Inverness-Wick line was the golden opportunity for the advocates of conversion to stand up and be counted, there were several other opportunities

---

[23] Marples was a partner in Marples, Ridgeway, a road construction company. *The Great Railway Conspiracy* claimed Marples pursued railway closures whilst facilitating road construction, because he favoured road transport.
[24] This body had supported the Robertson plan to convert the line to a road! (see page 50).
[25] See *The Railway Closure Controversy* and *Britain's Railways - The Reality*.

M&GN

The earliest long line conversion opportunity was that of the M&GN, which was proposed for closure in 1958, and closed in 1959. This line from the East Midlands across to Norwich and the East Anglian coast, was 174 miles long. As with all closures, there was a deathly silence from the conversion league. One or two minor sections much later formed part of a new road after, as was, invariably the case, being substantially widened to give the minimum width adequate for a modest road. The costs of widening were concealed in the total cost of building the new section of road. The M&GN was basically single line, and had a level crossing about every $1^1/_2$ miles to accommodate hundreds of main and minor roads and farm level crossings. The cross flow at these crossings would have hampered the free flow envisaged by Brigadier Lloyd.

Barnard Castle-Penrith/Tebay

Closure of the Barnard Castle-Penrith & Tebay line was proposed in 1959. It was 55 miles long, of which half was double and half single track. It had some high bridges and viaducts, the widening of which would not have been practical. They would have to have been duplicated to give required road widths. It ran over the Pennines through some inhospitable terrain. Weather could be very bad in the winter. The line closed in 1962.

Somerset & Dorset Railway

The S&DR - from Bath to Poole, some 100 miles, of which less than half was double track, the rest was single - was proposed for closure in 1962. The terrain was hilly, but gradients would not be a serious challenge to motor vehicles. Widening throughout to give a reasonable road width would have been a costly challenge. It closed in 1966.

Great Central line

The closure of the GCR, from Nottingham to London Marylebone, which took place in sections, in the mid/late 1960s was a great opportunity for the conversion league. It was about 125 miles long, largely double track. However, it had some daunting engineering features: viaducts, tunnels and embankments. Where it passed through towns, and especially the outskirts of London and into the terminus at Marylebone, widening would have been costly, as houses and business premises hemmed the line in. Its construction in the late 19th century proved very costly due to the volume of closely built workmens' houses and workshops or factories. The railway company was obliged to build replacement housing in London. Widening to create a decent road would have been equally costly. The London end of the line was subject to a financial and technical appraisal by an independent body some twenty years later.[26]

Waverley line

The closure of the 98 mile long double track Waverley route in 1969, was another superb opportunity. The route is largely still intact today, and there are vigorous moves to, at least, partially re-open it as a rail route, so the opportunity to convert to road has not yet vanished. But the conversionists have wasted 35 years. It would have been a difficult task - narrow viaducts, embankments, and difficult terrain.

---

[26] Consultants, Coopers & Lybrand examined ten routes - including Marylebone-Northolt - comprising 200 km of rail route. 'In all cases, it proved uneconomic to meet design standards laid down by the DoT highway engineers because of the very large capital sums needed to reconstruct bridges, enlarge tunnels and widen rights of way. The Marylebone-Northolt line would have been 5.9 to 6.7 metres in width compared to the 7.3 metres required by the DoT. It would have been suitable only for cars and would have fed into the already heavily congested Baker Street.'

Isle of Wight

An early opportunity was on the Isle of Wight, some 56 miles of railway, mostly single line. The inhabitants of the Isle of Wight were not enthusiastic about the prospect of losing their railways, and none voiced the idea of conversion. All routes except one were closed over a period of years in the early 1950s, after being delayed by objectors.

Wensleydale line

Another chance for glory was the Wensleydale line, about 40 miles long from Northallerton to Garsdale, which closed in the mid 1950s. Helpfully, the route passed outside most of the towns and villages, making it an ideal route for a road. Part has now been re-opened for a rail service of sorts, although it cannot be regarded as a commercial railway, being dependent on free labour. It may yet be abandoned a second time, when reality sets in, when the conversion theorists may have a second chance.

Hull & Barnsley

Still another opportunity was the Hull & Barnsley, which had 71 miles of route, excluding joint lines. It could have been converted and creamed off traffic from the coalfields to the docks at Hull. The line closed in sections over several years, with the final closure being in 1964.

Opportunities on shorter routes

Some short lines longer than the average 1.5 miles achieved, (see page 65) were:-

Potteries Loop line

The Potteries Loop ran 7.25 miles from Kidsgrove via Hanley to Stoke on Trent. Construction required over 1,000 properties being bought. When it closed, the area was densely packed with housing, workshops and other premises close to the line. Over-bridges had noticeably tight widths and headroom. The cost of land and property acquisition to provide a reasonable width would have been high. This situation was a common factor to be faced with railway lines in urban areas, so as to preclude scope for widening to accommodate suitable roads. It closed in 1964. Most has been converted to footpaths.

Haltwhistle to Alston

The 13 mile single Haltwhistle to Alston line, with its daunting Lambton viaduct, near the Scottish border, would have been particularly difficult to convert. Closure was opposed by residents and infrequent users, who knew there would be serious problems in winter. That was when users of road transport turned to railways in this area as in many others. Objectors scoffed at promises of the provision of 'an all-weather road.' That was the prospect held out by Sir David Robertson for the conversion of the Inverness-Wick line to a new fast road. The Alston branch was 350 miles nearer the equator than the Inverness line! No conversionist dared to voice support for closure. It closed in 1976.

Yelverton-Princetown

The branch in Dartmoor was about 400 miles further south than Alston and objectors there were opposed to losing their infrequently used railway, because the existing roads became impassable during winter. This was also a single line, about six miles long. The terrain was inhospitable and would have proved a challenge to convert.

Wivenhoe-Brightlingsea

This route was closed in 1952 as a result of severe damage by the sea. It was re-opened, despite there being no financial justification nor economic demand for it, and at BR expense. This increased deficits for which government's brilliant solution was not a subsidy for this line to a fishing-village-cum-minor-seaside-resort[27] which enjoyed fishing subsidies, but interest bearing loans! Regrettably, this was in 1952 before Brigadier Lloyd had his brainstorm. He might have had the support of BR management, but not that of the local community, who were convinced that the line could be made viable and sat back waiting for others to pay for it, whilst making occasional use when other transport was unavailable. It closed after a delay of ten years. It is not without significance that among objections was included evidence that bus fares were higher than rail!

Among other lines closed, there have been hundreds of miles which were taken over by amateurs, to run an infrequent tourist attraction service for periods varying from a few bank holidays to half the year, or, in a isolated cases, longer. They do not operate at night, and are under no pressure to run trains, if the unforeseen happens. Why the road lobby did not jump in quickly in these cases, and put some quick cash on the table, whilst enthusiasts were trying to drum up funds, is a mystery. In all, to date, about ten thousand miles of railway routes have been closed. By 1980, the total was already about 7,000. For all practical purposes, the conversion league did not seize the initiative and get these routes converted to roads. The league - in its publication, (see page 65), extolling the success of conversions - tabulated only 43 miles 'converted', and these were in lengths varying from 109 yards to six miles, with an average of 1.5 miles. Whilst the conversionists have been dithering, several railway routes that had been closed, have been re-opened as part of BR, in recent years, invariably with local authority funds.

A favourable political climate

From 1954 to 1964, when the conversion campaign was at its height, Britain was governed by the Tories who were firmly anti-rail. They favoured road transport between the wars, ignored the failure of hauliers to conform to wartime pricing Acts, and protected them from open competition from BR.[28] With such open support for road transport, if the league could not convince Ministers of the practicality of conversion, it must have been seen to be deeply flawed. During this period, hundreds of miles closed, offering opportunities for trials. If Lloyd could have persuaded some in the City to put up the cash, his scheme could have been tested.

Further opportunities arose when Tories were in power in 1970 - when the League published a new plan. What stopped them from funding a trial scheme to convert one full length line? They claimed to have massive support. After 1969, when the State began for the first time to subsidise loss making routes, they could have asked the anti-rail Tory government to give them the proposed subsidy for a line less say 10%, even 50% given their arrogant boasts. Putting their money where their mouth was would have convinced all doubters. They could have negotiated a deal to charge tolls to use their new roads.

An opportunity for the League to convince the Tory government recurred from 1979 to 1992. Another thirteen wasted years. In 1993, the unconvinced Tories opted to keep railways, and to privatise them.

---

[27] Brightlingsea. See *The Railway Closure Controversy*, Chapter 6
[28] See *Britain's Railways - The Reality*, Pages 8,9,20,21,26,27,28,112,114.

In 1957, Brigadier Lloyd sponsored the formation of what he called the Railway Conversion League, (*Commercial Motor*, 6 December 1957).

Submission to the Special Advisory Group

In 1960, the Conversion League submitted a paper to the Stedeford Committee - the MoT's Special Advisory Group,[1] (PRO: MT124/559). It claimed that the railways belonged to the nation. Unfortunately they didn't, as the nation had not put down a penny piece to buy them. The railways were acquired compulsorily from their owners, *without* arbitration, at a price dictated by government, in contrast to the purchase of the coal industry which had been subject to prolonged negotiations and arbitration. No money changed hands to acquire the railways and other assets - canals, road transport, ships, ports, etc., - owned by the Big Four railway companies. The shareholders were given IOUs in the form of British Transport Stock, to be redeemed over 30 years or so, of which, at least, eighteen years remained, when the Conversion League submitted its letter to the Committee. Under the 1947 and 1953 Transport Acts, the cost of capital redemption and the annual interest on the Stock was to be paid out of BR revenue.[2] Arguably, the railways were acquired through hire-purchase, and if the payment was not completed, were the original owners not entitled - like a retailer - to repossess their goods? Moreover, most land - on which railways had been built - had been acquired by compulsory purchase under the railway company's Enabling Act of Parliament. Some Acts contained provisions that, if the land was not used to operate a railway, or ceased to be used to operate a railway, the land must be returned to the original owner. In some cases, the property was to be returned *free of charge*, in some cases at the original selling price.[3]

The final payments to redeem the Stock were not made until 1988. The State could only *then* claim to have bought, and, therefore owned the railways. The intention was that the railways would buy themselves out of revenue, and then donate the assets free of charge to the Nation. Unfortunately, government decided that a unique form of operation would be introduced for BR, which had never been tried out in any other business, in the private or public sector. It required BR *alone* to seek the permission of a court of law to vary its prices, whilst the cost of everything BR purchased from outside was increasing without let or hindrance. No court was more dilatory than this one.[4] Had BR been allowed to determine its prices, decide which traffic to accept, decide which routes had no prospect of profitability, decide its wages without interference by ministers who were *pushing wages up*, then it could have succeeded in doing what no other industry does, and that is to redeem its entire capital. In 1956, Tory MoT Harold Watkinson stated that 'by applying the ordinary principles of enlightened private enterprise, we are going to show how BR can make a profit'. He did not identify *one* role model in the private or public

---

[1] It was expected to prove that BR was inefficient and badly run, but instead concluded that the problems were caused by the MoT and statutory bodies such as the Transport Tribunal which controlled fares & freight charges, and held them below inflation. It said BR ought to be run by professional railway managers - not outsiders - and freed from all political and other external interference in pricing, investment and closures. See *Britain's Railways - The Reality*.

[2] BR made these payments until 1963 - see *Britain's Railways - The Reality*, Page 176.

[3] The Countryside Commission also mentioned this fact, (see page 193).

[4] Se *Blueprints for Bankruptcy*, Chapter 3, and *Britain's Railways - The Reality*, Appendix B.

sector, which had to accept political interference in its business decisions, much less one which was doing so and making a profit. To make matters worse, he promptly froze BR fares, then trailing inflation by 43 points[5] for a year! A year later, the inflation rate had risen, clearly proving that inflation was industry led. The lesson was lost on politicians. Road transport, which had complete freedom to make the decisions denied to BR, and was allowed to have staff work 50% longer by law, than rail staff, was *not* a role model.

Conversions claimed

The paper from the League referred to the conversion of parts of the M&GR [sic] Railway in Norfolk and Lincs. This would be the M&GN. They said that 21.9 miles[6] of the 174 mile single track line had been converted to a 24 foot road, albeit they admitted that it had been necessary to buy land alongside to secure the requisite width. Duplicate routes, they said, could be used one-way. In addition to segregation of pedestrians and cyclists, there would be strict access and control. By 1960, 1,261 miles of route had been closed, and the sum total of their claim was 21.9 miles!

Costs

They claimed that the cost of conversion would be low. They referred to the estimated conversion cost of the 155 mile Inverness-Wick railway to a 22 foot[7] road of £36,000 per mile or £2.8 per square yard. They prayed in aid the cost of conversion of an M&GN section of single track to a 24 foot road of £40,000 or £2.84 per square yard.[8] The latter - they said - included the cost of purchase of additional land at £200 per mile.[9] They said that it did not include sections in cuttings as the cost would have been considerably more. They stated that the area occupied by the entire BR system was 320,000,000 square yards - but gave no source for this figure[10] - and to convert at £3 per square yard would cost £960m. *Costs would be slightly higher at junctions*! Such a codicil in a plan to a Board of any self respecting business would lead to its prompt disposal in the nearest waste paper basket. They claimed there would be considerable credits from scrap sales and the sale of land. They had yet to learn that scrap value was variable and falls when supply expands.

It would still cost £1 bn. There was no mention of the cost of land for widening, nor of the implications for compulsory purchase powers to acquire adjoining property needed for widening. They stated that the cost of 100 miles of motorway built in mid 1959 was £0.32m per mile, or £7.6 per square yard.[11] On this basis, they claimed, conversion would be £2.24 per square yard in open country and £13 in urban areas.

They did not include any costs for the provision of tens of thousands of new road vehicles to convey displaced rail traffic, nor any costs that would be incurred during the conversion period, including transfer stations, (see page 27).

---

[5] See *Britain's Railways - The Reality*, Appendix A

[6] Their 1970 booklet (see page 64), shows under eight miles in that geographical area, comprised of small different sections. The costs are not accepted by local authorities, (see chapter 13). The MoT told Parliament, in 1960, that 23 miles had been converted, (see page 186).

[7] Which would be below DoT standards

[8] The M&GN ran through some of the flattest terrain in the country, in contrast to the Inverness-Wick line, which indicates that the cost of converting the latter was under estimated.

[9] But didn't say what the width was over this mile.

[10] This figure will not be found in BR Annual Accounts nor published statistics.

[11] The original estimate to build the M1 was exceeded. It cost £0.4m per mile, excluding bridges and acquisition of land, (*BR Study of Rail & Road Costs*, 1964).

The League said that the system would be managed by a body which would have no powers to put vehicles on the system except for maintenance and breakdowns. They did not specify how it would be funded to maintain and police the system.

They went on to compare the profitability of road transport against BR, showing a failure to study the facts.[12] They ignored that: BR was a common carrier unable to refuse uneconomic traffic, unlike hauliers who were highly selective; BR charges were published preventing the discrimination prevalent in haulage; Transport Acts were designed to block BR from undercutting hauliers on profitable flows by giving hauliers a one-sided legal right to challenge low rail charges in a dilatory court of law.[13]

Safety

On safety, they sought to compare the whole 50m [sic] population as being at risk on roads compared to 3m on railways, reduced to 1.5m on the basis that they were the same people making a return journey. They did not, of course, halve the journeys of bus and car passengers who were also making return journeys. They assessed highway fatalities at 5,970 in 1958, and railway fatalities at 454 [including suicides and trespassers]. They included 147 suicides on railways - 'an evil characteristic of railways' and 103 trespassers - 'as they are a characteristic of railways' - to inflate railway fatalities.[14]

This desperate attempt to prove that the whole population was at risk on the roads, ignored those confined to prisons, hospitals, nursing homes or away abroad on holiday or business. They assumed that not *one* member of the whole non-rail using population ever crosses a railway on foot - at level crossings or designated public footpaths.

They assumed that no one ever went onto a line intent on suicide, but changed their mind and omitted to tell the media, or HMRI. To suggest that suicides are an evil characteristic of railways, implies that without railways these 147 suicides would not have taken place, which is patently absurd. In the absence of speeding trains, speeding juggernauts will probably prove an acceptable alternative!

They assumed that all trespassers were killed, i.e. none trespassed without being killed - which is clearly complete nonsense. They speculated on the safety of road transport on a railway system converted to roads. These figures - they cannot be graced with the word *statistics* - were not worth the paper they were written on.

They claimed that motor patrols would prevent trespass on the converted roads, and that, in any case, trespassing is not dangerous as there is no electricity on roads and vehicles can steer to avoid trespassers! This assumed that the roads will always be free of other vehicles, at the precise moment when trespass occurs, or otherwise there would be a risk of collision for the swerving vehicle! Given that an approaching vehicle, would, under Brigadier Lloyd's concept, be within the braking distance, swerving would be disastrous. Sadly, too many vehicles steer *into* pedestrians on pavements.

They overlook that these motor patrols would have to be very frequent to be effective, and would thereby eat heavily into the 100 yard headway around the clock envisaged in the Lloyd plan, and would require a virtually continuous hard shoulder to enable the patrol to pull off and deal with offenders. The loss of headway would destroy any prospect of cross traffic at level crossings, which Lloyd had belittled.

---

[12] See *Britain's Railways - The Reality*, Chapter 15.
[13] See *Britain's Railways - The Reality*, Pages 25, 26-27, 112-116, 168.
[14] In 1958, a total of 53 passengers were killed on railways, (see *Britain's Railways - The Reality*).

To claim that trespassing is an evil characteristic of railways is total nonsense and merely exposes their ignorance as to the objective of trespassers. The aim of almost all is to get from A to B in the shortest possible time. The railway line is in the way, so they damage fencing to create an entry, or climb over or through it. If a road replaces a railway, they will be still determined to get from A to B in the shortest possible time, and will do so whether or not there is still a fence - which, the conversion league seemed to envisage there would be. The replacement of difficult-to-walk-on ballast by easy-to-walk-on tarmac will make trespassing easier! The shorter headways of motor vehicles will render it even more dangerous. Whether such people will cease to be classified as trespassers, but simply be pedestrians is irrelevant - some will still be killed in the process. A few trespassers are 'playing chicken'. This is also a practice on motorways, hence, it is likely to continue on converted railways. Trespassers who are less likely to transfer their interest, are trainspotters, who by and large, have to remain at a distance from the track, or otherwise would be unable to read the numbers of locos as they streak past at 100-125 mph. From observation, they tend to sit on a fence, parapet of an underbridge or something similar.

The League claimed that 'existing roads will lose much of their traffic to the converted roads, making existing roads much safer'. The assumption of surplus capacity on converted roads is completely destroyed by their motor patrols, and by new statistics, (see page 88,173). The cost of these patrols and the cost of acquiring extra land for a hard shoulder was totally ignored. They claimed that accident rates on the converted single carriageway system with no central reservation would be at the level of those on three lane motorways with a central reservation. There is no evidence to justify such a claim.

The Stedeford Group sought the comments of the MoT, who at that time, was likely to be even more road biased than his predecessors or successors, being a partner in one of the biggest road construction companies in the country. They should have been preaching to the converted. If they could not convince the most road minded MoT the country has ever had, clearly their case was full of holes. His advisors in the road dominated Department of Transport did not give any credence to the proposal.

The MoT replied to the Group: 'The idea is open to insuperable objections. The most serious is that most double track widths are sufficient for only one traffic lane in each direction with clearances as narrow as 3 feet over bridges. This is below the standard we set for *any* main road and far below motorways. The Department believes that the estimated cost is much too low and does not take account of construction of junctions. Unless all over-bridges and tunnels are rebuilt, it would be unusable by large vans or double deck buses. New type vehicles would have to be constructed to carry required loads at the speeds contemplated. It would require a very high capital investment for very doubtful advantage. The possibility is not ruled out of conversion of disused lines *where the necessary widening can be arranged.*'

This statement was from the MoT, Ernest Marples - partner of one of the biggest road construction companies in the UK - who, opponents of railway closures claimed, was keen to close branches so that his former business could benefit.[15] A theory that he was

---

[15] 'A Minister of Transport, who was not only road biased, but a successful road contractor into the bargain'. 'Some, like Marples, had positive personal and financial incentives to see railways close', (Henshaw - *The Great Railway Conspiracy*, Pages 110,234). He was advised by road-biased civil servants.

closing branch lines to facilitate motorway construction is absurd. If all displaced rural rail freight had been brought together from thousands of miles closed, it would not have taxed one short motorway. No government cash would have been released by closures for road building, as they did not subsidise railways until long after Marples left office.

It is significant that after 1958, the League dropped all references and estimates to the number of lorries and buses, and of manpower, that would be required to move displaced rail traffic. No proper comparison of the costs can be made without such data.

The 1970s campaign

Little was heard of the Conversion League from 1960 to 1970 aside from occasional letters in the media, which were often countered by others.

In 1970, the League published a 29 page book[16] endeavouring to prove the advantages of conversion, and to claim that - based on very limited evidence of closed railways 'converted' to roads - complete conversion of the whole railway system was practical.

Re-using a closed railway is irrelevant to the League's objective of converting all railways. Using a closed route as part of a road is not conversion in the sense that it would apply to an operating railway. There is no displacement of rail traffic, with its consequential costs of thousands of new road vehicles to new designs, nor transfer stations, nor diversions over existing roads whilst conversion took place. Ex-rail traffic is already on existing roads.

It said that over the past fifteen years, railway conversion had received a great deal of attention. No evidence was produced in support. A survey of the media will find only scattered evidence of their activities, and will also find dismissals of their ideas by opponents. This is, despite the fact that the media has published regular criticisms of BR, which certainly destroys the claim that there had been 'years of anti-road, pro-rail propaganda', as quoted in the book as an extract from the Daily Telegraph in 1974.[17]

They refer to a 'failure of BR's modernisation plan'. They ignore as others - who failed to carry out basic research - have done that the cause of the poor return on the railfreight investment was the unforecast decline of major UK industry.[18] No one in industry, government or media foresaw the 1958-60 decline of industry, nor its later emigration to the Far East. It is remarkable, that those in industry and government always believe that economic and trade upturns result from imaginative leadership, whilst declines are due to unforeseen developments in the world economy! Only BR was criticised for failing to foresee the prospect of industrial decline which was not obvious to *anyone* else.

They claim that 'railways are supposed to cause less environmental disruption, because their track is not shared by pedestrians'. It is not usually related to that factor. It is arguable that, as pedestrians preceded motor vehicles in using roads, it is the *latter* who share roads with the former. Moreover, railway track is shared by pedestrians: at level crossings and when taking a short cut elsewhere [trespassers]. Both categories will continue unabated after conversion, should that catastrophe ever occur.

---

[16] *Conversion of Railways into Roads.* It was later re-issued to include post-1970 comments, see pages 73-77.

[17] The author believes that the Daily Telegraph, if anything, tended to be anti-*rail*. His failure to have one pro-rail, research-backed letter published in response to criticisms of BR, led him to write to the Editor suggesting that the paper was anti-rail. He disagreed. True, the views in their columns seem to be mirrored in some other newspapers. A few examples of his 90 unpublished letters may be seen in his previous books on railways.

[18] Government departments and industry had been forecasting expansion! See *Britain's Railways - The Reality.*

Scale of conversion claimed

They claimed that 'more than a hundred lines had been converted' when the figure was just over 20 and stated that there were 'many instances of similar conversions abroad'. Not *one* foreign instance[19] is mentioned in the Report. They claim that the conversion of railways to modern motor roads has now been demonstrated. They define a motor road as 'one formed by *straight conversion with no widening* of the [railway] formation of two-track railways into a single carriageway road with two lanes 24 foot wide. They would have no frontage access, no standing vehicles and negligible cross traffic'.[20] In fact, of their list of schemes implemented, *not one* is defined as a motor road! Of their *maybe* list of 112 schemes, eleven were forecast to become motor roads, of which three were single lines. Only five were converted into roads totalling 5.9 miles. All required widening, (see chapter 13). On the grounds that these *motor roads* would have limited access, they claim that their capacity would be a third higher than normal. They 'assume 25% of commercial traffic consisting of equal numbers of light and heavy vehicles'. They claim that new roads would accommodate more traffic than existing urban trunk roads, whose capacity is quoted as 1,500 PCUs [passenger-car-units] per hour in an MoT Report.[21] There are no grounds for the assumptions - not least because of limitations imposed by bridge, viaduct and tunnel widths. Neither are there grounds for clutching a figure of one-third increased capacity from thin air. Having conjured up an *imaginary* figure, they compare it to a *known* rail capacity figure, to try to prove that a converted system would have greater capacity! No self-respecting statistician would accept the validity of such a comparison. It does not compare chalk with cheese, but compares chalk with nothing.

They add that the scale of conversion 'depends on the extent and placing of railway lines which become available for conversion'. This clearly implies acceptance that not all lines are suitable for conversion. They repeat the claim that BR land was owned by the nation, (see page 60).

The book lists 29 instances, totalling 43.7 miles, of closed railways in England, Scotland & Wales converted into roads, including *five single lines converted into dual carriageways*. One of these was recorded for posterity.[22] Photographs show this line at Barton, which 'passed through a 12 foot cutting, and was *opened out to a minimum motorway width of 102 feet*!' This brings a whole new meaning to the word conversion! Engulfed would be more appropriate. The new motorway is shown to be a dual carriageway, with a wide central reservation, wide hard shoulders, verges and embankments - within the boundary fence[23] - varying from wide to extremely wide. This *conversion* accounts for 5.5 miles of the total. Three other sections of single line totalling ten miles in length, were shown as being converted to dual lane carriageways, with hard shoulders, verges, central reservations, to a total width of 190 feet! Eight other single lines were widened to 36, 36, 40, 40, 60, 75, 80 and 103 feet respectively. The extent of

---

[19] A letter to *The Times* identified some in very minor countries, (see page 203).

[20] There is no evidence that the volume of cross traffic flows had been evaluated.

[21] *Urban Traffic Engineering Techniques*, published by DoT. In 1978, DoT dropped PCUs, (*Juggernaut* Page 132)

[22] Robinson & Groundwater in *Past & Present in the North East*.

[23] Fence costs do not fall on road transport, but on owners of adjoining land. Railways have always had to bear fencing costs. This is another disparity in road-rail comparisons ignored by the road lobby, (see *Britain's Railways - The Reality*, Pages 38, 130). The photo did not include the next interchange, whose width - as revealed in a map supplied by the local authority to the author - would have eclipsed the 102 feet shown in the photo!

widening of the three remaining single lines was not shown. Single line railways had low traffic prospects, and hence limited capital could be raised. Minimum land purchase was usually unavoidable.

Fifteen of the conversions listed were less than a mile in length, one was 109 yards. This shows a measure of desperation in scraping the barrel for anything that can - in the League's judgement - be remotely termed a conversion. From 1948 to 1970, the rate of conversion was 1.9 miles pa. Closures had averaged 355 miles pa.

A 1970 study for the Countryside Commission (see page 193), *shows that, by 1968, 1037 miles of closed railway had been sold. As the League identify only 43 miles of railway converted to road by 1970, this suggests that most closed lines were unsuitable for roads, since the lines were first offered to central and local government who would consider that option. Most lines were converted to footpaths or farm use.*

Their list of 'conversions' was expanded to 29 from 25, by entering, as if they were separate schemes, short sections of the same railway line and the same road. Thus, '500 yards Flood Lane to Combens site' was merely an extension of '109 yards Crown hotel to Flood Lane'. There were three separate entries for the B4567 in Radnorshire, totalling 1.62 miles - two were in the same month, one was a year earlier. They were set out among a list of five Radnorshire schemes, in such a way as to distract from their common link, by separating them by two other unrelated schemes. There was no logic in this. Had they been entered chronologically, the three B4567 schemes would have been entered first, followed by the other two unconnected schemes. Similarly, two items relating to the same piece of road in Monmouthshire were entered separately. The reality, therefore, is that there were only 25 separate railway to road 'conversions'.

They highlight the conversion of 4.5 miles of closed railway into a 24 foot motor road at Southport[24] and quote a *recent* statement[25] by Mr. N.E. Tovey, the Borough Engineer responsible for the task. It states that 'the road has a very good safety record'. It doesn't now, according to the media.[26] They go on: 'the roads previously used by this traffic did not have a good safety record, which means that there are people alive today who would not have been but for the conversion of this stretch of railway'. It doesn't mean that, at all. It is pure conjecture. There is not one statistic to prove that there were fewer fatalities. There is no evidence that the roads previously used by motorists were identified so that a comparison could be made. Their lack of skill in making valid comparisons, is exposed in the book. An example is that 'it is interesting to note that the length of six-lane motorway, which could have been built elsewhere for the same cost as this 4.5 mile road is roughly 125 yards'. It is uninteresting and irrelevant, given the different speeds and capacities. In stressing the cheapness of this conversion, the League neglected to mention its' construction benefited from 'free tipped material', a fact revealed in a report of the

---

[24] The use of this term *motor road*, appears frequently throughout conversion proposals from 1955 onwards. It seems to be trying to imply that a 24 foot wide road is just one step below a six lane motorway. Of course, it isn't. Without a central reservation and barriers, collisions are as likely as ever.

[25] They do not quote the location of this statement, in which they insert an ellipsis, which experience shows excludes facts which undermine their claims, (see pages 74-6). None of the professional bodies of which he was a member, can trace this statement in a Paper, Lecture or letter. Reports in the technical media, including his address to the League, do not refer to safety, (*Municipal Engineering* 20.12.68; *Civil Engineering & Public Works Review* April 1968).

[26] e.g., see Daily Post 7.4.04, which refers to 'a notorious blackspot on Southport's coast road. This is believed to be the seventh death in three years on the coast road'.

retirement of Mr. Tovey[27]. They neglect to mention that the majority of the 20 mile closed Southport railway route was converted to form part of a long distance Walkway, rather than a road.

Clearly recognising that their two page list of 'successful' conversions after 22 years was unconvincing, they looked for another barrel to scrape. Nine more pages, with wide margins, list *proposed* conversions which were implied to be almost certain. These pages list 112 different sections of mostly single line, in 45 different local authority areas and totalling 211 miles. It equates to a monumental average of 1.8 miles per scheme, which is not breathtaking, even if they were fully implemented, which they weren't, (see chapter 13). The list included a reference to an already completed conversion in Glamorgan[28] with 'a very satisfactory safety record'. Again, no facts were given to enable a comparison to be made to safety on the roads hitherto used by the traffic. This sort of claim, unsupported by proper statistical data, demonstrates the amateurism of the League. Tucked away in the text of this 'maybe' list the diligent reader will find 'West Sussex: the new road - converted from a single track railway - will be 100 foot in width, and will involve considerable acquisition of land on both sides'. Also, 'a single track in Buckinghamshire will be part converted to a three-lane carriageway, with [two] 12 ft verges'. The verges would be wider than the track. In fact, it was not used for a road at all, (see page 125).

In 17 instances, their 'maybe' list was vague and unhelpful in enabling a researcher to trace the railway that it was claimed may be converted. Descriptions such as 'a section of disused railway' - with no clear geographical pointer as to their location - proliferate. Some 37 schemes had no precise information regarding the length of the railway line to be converted. Schemes were peppered with 'proposal', 'possibility', 'consideration is being given to the feasibility', 'no decisions have been reached', 'the Council has no proposals, but has declared an interest'. As with the list of 'conversions achieved' they append cases in Northern Ireland. These were never part of BR, nor its 20,000 mile network, to which Brigadier Lloyd and the League had laid claim.

A reference to a revival in public [road] transport identifies West Riding as dependent on conversion of a rail to a bus route. In fact these schemes listed in the Report have not been progressed by the local authority, which is expanding rail travel, (see page 192).

Practicality

The league claimed that conversion was a straightforward engineering job, quick and inexpensive compared to new road construction. Their naiveté was breath-taking. New road construction involves little or no disruption to existing traffic; conversion would involve 100% disruption to existing rail traffic, and as it moves over existing roads, interference with that as well. How it could be organised without bringing cities to a stand, is not addressed. This traffic problem during conversion of operational lines was ignored. Traffic would have had, at least, temporarily, to go onto existing roads.

Traffic on existing major roads could not be diverted onto converted closed rural railways, which were nowhere near the major route, nor between the same towns.

They state 'normally, land in railway ownership is of such width that vehicles using it are substantially from inhabited buildings than in existing roads' [sic]. This is completely meaningless. They add that 'railway property comprises a network of routes clear of older

---

[27] Southport Visitor, 26.7.78.

[28] This anonymous line was probably the Heads of the Valley road, whose safety record is poor, (see page 105).

town centres and shopping areas'. A more erroneous claim is difficult to imagine. Railway construction in urban areas required property demolition, leaving other buildings close to the line, whilst in other areas, industry and houses were built close to the railway to reduce journey times on foot, by horse or horse drawn vehicles.

They claimed that railways as roads are vastly superior in width and alignment to present highways. This proves a failure to study maps, which prove that railways have neither of those attributes. The inclusion in their conversion list of 12 foot wide railways widened to 102 feet or more, should have cautioned them to avoid such claims. They were confident that motor transport would be able to perform, better and more cheaply[29] and with greater safety, every task performed by railways. This would exclude prevailing 100 mph safe running applying on railways, as the League plan was for 60 mph.

Their argument proceeds 'in places, construction of verges and hard shoulders would require the acquisition of additional land, but over most of their length these routes have ample additional room between fences[30] for whatever provision of this nature might be deemed desirable'. Any planner or manager submitting an investment plan on this vague basis would promptly be shown the door! It is, as with the generality of their theory, pure speculation. In a serious study, each route would be surveyed.

They refer to the 'average four track rail width' without saying what it is, so that reader can judge whether it is practical or not. They claim that these can be converted to a four lane *motor road*. [31] An *average* width is no help in a below-average location!

They add that routes with three to ten tracks account for nearly 2,000 miles and they are the predominant constituent of the inter-city network. On the contrary, the very much wider formations are on heavy commuter routes into big cities.

They claim that double line rail routes are of sufficient width for a standard two-lane 24 foot carriageway road.[32] It is based, not on any proper survey but on speculation. They claim that such a conversion '*can* show a very large saving'.[33] Stating that a motorway costs £1m per mile, whilst 'it is difficult to give an accurate assessment of the saving which would result from substituting conversion for new construction, they claim that a reasonable expectation of saving might be a quarter'. Where this figure originates is a complete mystery. Elsewhere, they refer to 'studies conducted by them'. Unfortunately, no data is produced for examination, nor is the reader directed to the location of these *studies*. In trying to compare costs, they completely ignore speed in any comparison. They try to compare the cost of building a six-lane 70 mph road with 'converting' a 100 mph railway line to a 60 mph single carriageway road. Clearly, the capacity of the former will be higher, even if users keep strictly to 70 mph.

They state that 'a fair proportion of these [7,000 miles of single line track] could be classed with two-track routes since their formations were constructed with sufficient width to allow for a second track'. Possibly, some were so planned, but whether that was a fair proportion, in the absence, once again - of any detailed appraisal by the League, is pure guesswork. To emphasise their amateurish approach, they then insult the reader

---

[29] There are no figures and no field study to substantiate this sweeping claim.

[30] This uncompacted 'room' would be *soft* shoulders, that proved disastrous on the original M1.

[31] This implies something more important than a mere *road*, and just below a motorway. Local authorities asked by the author could not define it. The League dreamed up a definition, but did not adhere to it, (see page 65)

[32] Brigadier Lloyd had said he would get three lanes onto a two-track formation, (see page 21).

[33] A scheme that *can* be profitable - i.e. with luck, could show a profit - is not one for the wise investor.

further, by adding that 'the remaining formations are too narrow for a 24 foot width, but the width between fences would over much of their length allow widening without acquiring more land'. This envisaged tarmac laid up to existing lineside fencing to provide the necessary width. Such a road would be dangerous. This area would not have the *compacted formation* upon which Lloyd depended to provide a cheap sound sub structure for a road, on which he would lay *concrete*, not *tarmac*. This is another example of speculation and comparing chalk and cheese. Every new motorway and road has a substantial verge, and many roads have a pavement as well. But to try to prove the adequacy of rail formations, they ignore that, and propose roads without verges. It would not permit *one* extra vehicle to pass through a bridge or tunnel, most built to minimum width with a narrow cess. Again and again, they fail to compare like with like. Rail histories record that some rural companies were under funded, had questionable traffic prospects, and consequently, bought minimum land to meet their needs. Lineside fences often run in ditches or natural hollows, the filling in, or culverting of which, would add to costs of creating adequate road width. They had not surveyed the actual widths of a main line route.

They state that problems associated with widening narrow routes are irrelevant, because, single line routes have been actually converted to new four lane dual carriageways. They quoted in support five cases of genuine single lines so converted, that are listed in their book. Their book shows that every one was significantly widened, up to widths of 190 feet. Some members of the public may become convinced - had the League produced detailed drawings and costings of every such individual case.[34] After all their attempts to prove that the railway is wide enough already, they later admit that 'much of the length would involve widening'. With complete abandon, they continue: 'If the actual formation is not wide enough, this fact is comparatively unimportant; it can be widened as necessary!' Just like that - destroying homes, businesses and livelihoods.

With wild abandon, and not a penny allocated, they state that 'intersections - where not eliminated by under or over passes - would occur only at existing level crossings'. The cost of providing such bridges was not even crudely estimated.

They argue that the alternative to converting railways to roads, was to displace occupied property, but that arises with conversion of closed routes, because the width of railways is inadequate for a road. Inquiries of local authorities reveal that this was often the case, (see chapter 13). As there are no verges under bridges or in tunnels, their use is restricted.

They focus on 'narrow roads, steep gradients, sharp bends, many junctions and limited sight lines as the sole cause of road transport having failed to take over all rail traffic', despite the helping hand given by government.[35] The League will not let its mind swerve from the little picture, whilst wilfully ignoring that the premises of sender and consignee are often found on such roads, as are some haulage contractors! Widening them could well work out cheaper than purchase of land to widen rail routes - an aspect that any serious study would have covered in depth. Nowhere do they show that this has been fleetingly considered, much less evaluated. How, then, can their proposal be taken seriously? In believing that sight lines on railways are better, they overlook that train driver sight lines are at 2.75m above *rail level*, not 0.5m above as would be required by car drivers. Bridge abutments, retaining walls, etc. could obscure the sight line of a motorist.

---

[34] The author had long experience of working on single lines, from which he can say that widths were inadequate.
[35] See *Square Deal Denied & Britain's Railways - the Reality*

They do not address the objections and criticisms to conversion of members of the Institution of Civil Engineers, (see chapter 4). Instead they say: 'In this report, it is not possible to go into particular aspects of the adaptation of railways to roads, as for methods of dealing with tunnels, embankments, viaducts and suchlike'. Resolving the problems and costs arising from these structures, is *fundamental* to the whole issue. If it hadn't been addressed after fifteen years of study, when did they intend to get around to it? One imagines, it would be after conversion has begun of the easy bits - should that catastrophe ever be visited upon the public! They claim - without proof - that 'all such problems have been overcome in actual conversions which have been carried out'. Even assuming that this claim were true, no data is produced to prove that the *unconverted* structures would pose exactly the same problems. The conclusion is that the sole reason for not converting thousands of miles of closed and unused lines is the insuperable engineering task associated with such structures and the costs of acquiring additional land, and the fact, that rail routes are often *not* the shortest between two towns.

Neither had they addressed the problem of the turning circle of a juggernaut leaving a converted railway to turn onto an existing road at a converted level crossing to make a delivery in a town or to a farm.

Costs

According to the League: conversions so far carried out by local authorities suggest a final cost per square yard of surface could be as little as one eighth or less than the current cost of motorway construction. Local authorities concerned stated that they were unable to separate costs for conversion of the ex-rail element of such new roads from the total costs, (see chapter 13).

They claim that 'in railway costings, no account is taken of the opportunity costing of land occupied'. The same, of course, would apply to road accounts, if governments were ever to publish any.

The book claims that freight has switched to road because it provides the most economic and efficient means of moving goods. As the late Professor Joad used to remark: *It all depends what you mean* by economic and efficient. If delays caused by road haulage, and lorry-initiated accidents involving other users, and costs arising therefrom are excluded, one might be deluded into believing that it is more economic and efficient. Likewise, if the dangerous hours that road transport drivers are allowed to work are ignored, then a different perspective of economic is perceived.

Capacity

They claim that *one tenth of the new capacity would be utilised for existing rail traffic,* without explaining why 22 times as much road route was required for ten times as much traffic, (see page 88,173). At least 60% of the existing road system should have been closed to bring its utilisation up to prevailing BR levels. No spare capacity would arise unless they could force all existing rail users to spread their demands equally around the clock and across the four seasons, as Brigadier Lloyd envisaged in 1955, and spread it across the entire railway system. Even then there is no certainty until every flow is studied and rescheduled. They ignore that two thirds of the rail system carried 99% of rail traffic.[36] There can be no doubt that if the rural routes which are under-utilised were converted to

---

[36] *British Railways Board Report & Accounts*, 1963, Para 4

roads, the buses on them would require subsidies, and fares would *also* rise, (see pages 72,98,179). This fact has been confirmed by bus operators and others when rail closures were proposed or had actually been implemented.[37] The idea of frequent buses on such routes is laughable. Regrettably, this issue was not raised by road experts at the Debate in 1955 (see chapter 4), who concentrated on the problems on busy routes. Buses on these rural routes would *not* have been 100% loaded, undermining League arithmetic

Traffic

The League's book claims that 75% of ton-mileage and over 90% of passenger-miles are by road.[38] No breakdown is advanced which would expose that a massive proportion is over short distances, in or near towns which has no relevance. Every passenger-mile by an urban bus, every passenger-mile to a village that never had a railway, every car mile to a supermarket, local shops, schools, etc.,[39] is completely irrelevant, along with deliveries to houses from shops, farms, milk suppliers. etc. When the League begin to reflect these aspects, and provide the aforementioned ignored data, will be time to study their proposal. It is pertinent to point out that the road lobby and the League try to downplay the excessive road mileage in use for its market share, and to claim that what is relevant is the length of trunk roads. Thus they count all traffic, but only part of the road system! They switch from argument to argument at will.

They claimed that *'commuters would leap at the chance of a high speed bus route to their place of work'*. Unfortunately very few work on terminal stations, so buses would add to town and city congestion to get commuters to their *place of work*. The parking of the extra vehicles was not seen as a problem. They said that *'The line into Marylebone would be an ideal stretch.'* It has very severe restrictions as a consultant's report showed.[40] Traffic would have to feed into the heavily congested Baker Street

They allege that conversion would reverse rural depopulation[41] and industrial decline, but do not support it with any data. By 1970, thousands of miles of rural railway had closed, and it is doubtful that county councils would have missed the opportunity to reverse these rural trends. The fact is that the League are preaching revolution, but failing to advance their own money to finance it. Any rural conversion of a full length rural line which takes place, without reversing de-population can be attributed to incompetence of the local authority concerned in overlooking some important elements, rather than the fallacy of the theory itself.

They also claim, without evidence, that conversion would produce a revival of public road passenger transport. In this context, they take a tilt at windmills, by saying that the prospective 'comparison between rail and road transport has been obscured by meaningless comparisons between rail and the private car'. However, it is the League itself and its founder who argued that these converted roads would be open to cars. Indeed, the restrictive nature of tunnels, viaducts, earthworks and other features of railways would render it necessary to maximise the use of converted railways by cars, and free up space on trunk roads and motorways for juggernauts and PSVs carrying displaced

---

[37] See *The Railway Closure Controversy*, Pages 16,95,169,170.

[38] Inquiries by the author have established that official statistics of road traffic are unreliable, (see page 153).

[39] 73% of car journeys are less than five miles, 47% less than two miles, (see TRL Report N° 104)

[40] See page 168.

[41] Objectors to the Inverness-Wick closure held precisely the opposite view, (see page 55).

rail traffic. Moreover, the reality is that when railway lines closed, despite alternative bus services being subsidised by BR until 1968, many of these services were subsequently withdrawn.[42] The reality is that whereas bus patronage has declined, it is car travel that has expanded. It is complete nonsense for the League to argue that displaced rail passengers would all transfer to buses and not cars. They claim that 'a satisfactory solution of future commuter traffic is possible, however, it is a subject which cannot be treated at depth in this report!' How did they expect to be taken seriously? Providing detailed assurance on the adequacy of proposed road transport arrangements is merely a *first* essential step in selling the theory of conversion to commuters.

Subsidies

They stress rail subsidies, but ignore hidden and overt subsidies to road transport. Road transport employees subsidise operations by virtue of their long hours, a practice that will be brought to an abrupt end if there is no rail benchmark with which to compare pricing, and which can be used as a threat by senders to hold down charges. As if the legally permitted long hours were not enough subsidy, exceeding legal hours is almost endemic,[43] as is the failure to take proper rest - a practice which the MoT urges on ordinary motorists. Overloading freight transport is common. Judging by blown out tyres and vehicle parts to be seen on roadsides, maintenance leaves much to be desired. Reports of court cases into accidents arising from badly maintained vehicles do not instil confidence that the problem is being tackled vigorously. Some involved may be 'cowboys', but their existence makes road transport more competitive. Bad design which permits lethal spray to be thrown up by LGVs to blind motorists, should have been resolved long ago, the method of doing so was known years ago. All these are hidden subsidies, which have been ignored in the equation. In the near future, the UK is going to be compelled by Brussels to bring road transport up to scratch and reduce drivers' hours. Operators will feel the pinch.

In addition to these hidden subsidies, are costs borne by the emergency services and NHS arising from accidents, and the knock on effect of insurance premiums for motorists resulting from accidents precipitated by LGVs and PSVs. They ignore all these issues. It would be interesting to know by how much, car insurance premiums would fall if cars were driven only on roads bereft of LGVs and PSVs. They claim that railways would no longer survive the removal of artificial supports. A brief consideration of the above, would reveal, that neither would road transport.

The road lobby places great emphasis on the *subsidy* paid to keep open rural branch lines, which BR was prevented from closing by the government.[44] They focus on the subsidy, paid in 1969 for the first time. Hitherto, BR had to carry rural line losses. Prior to 1969 when BR closed a line, it usually had to subsidise a bus company to provide alternative services. Not infrequently, they then went on to increase bus fares as well.

The 1968 Act belatedly accepted that retention of loss making lines for social reasons was a state - not a BR responsibility. Government did not undertake to pay retrospective subsidies. The League alleged that InterCity passengers were subsidised. Once again, they ignored publicly available data. The Annual Reports of the BRB show - *quite clearly* - where the subsidy was allocated, by listing every unremunerative line or service which the

---

[42] See *The Railway Closure Controversy.*

[43] See White Paper CMD 3481 set out in *Britain's Railways - The Reality*, Page 186.

[44] No road operator would have provided a below cost rural service without a subsidy.

government was subsidising for social reasons. It shows the amount each service was allocated by government, and the total for the year. No Inter City services were listed.[45]

They focus on subsidies to rail passengers, but air-brush out reference to subsidies for bus passengers. For example, their 1970 book lists quotes from *experts* - who were nearly all journalists or academics. In these quotes, an ellipsis is frequently used, apparently to abbreviate a quote. Investigation reveals embarrassing phrases have been left out, which undermine the picture they try to depict of profitable buses competing with subsidised rail. For example, a quote from the *Economist* of 22.6.74, inserts an ellipsis in place of

> '*and subsidies for bus fares could cost even more in a few years. More costly and wasteful [than rail subsidies] in the long run, are the operating subsidies provided for buses, just to prevent fares from rising*'.

By juxtaposing railways and subsidies, and leaving out the damning reference to bus subsidies in their quote, gives credence to their criticism of rail subsidies, and lends strength to conversion. They also left out a statement from the same article that

> '*building more roads helps the rich more than the poor*'.

Their chairman made the same claim with regard to *rail* travel! (see page 80).

Grants of 25% of the cost of one-man buses were given to operators in 1968. It was later increased to 50%.[46] Operators were given subsidies of £40m over three years to support rural buses. Support and grants for local bus services [concessionary fares, support and rebate] totalled £351m in 1978.[47]

Other claims

The book would have caught few eyes. Hence, its meagre six pages of unconvincing text was expanded with a list of 'maybe' conversions, four photos[48] and appendices:

- A claim of traffic capacity, that fails to explain why roads are 22 times as long as rail for ten times as much traffic. They fail to see that a rural line with capacity for 1,500 PCUs is never going to see that volume. To arrive at undreamed-of capacities on a converted system, they said there would be negligible cross-traffic. That means thousands of roads crossing railways on the level, would become cul-de-sacs.
- A statement of passenger carrying capacity, which claims that displaced passengers would transfer to buses - rather than as experience proves - to cars, which would destroy their claims of a surplus of route capacity for existing road traffic to transfer onto.
- Statistics, which lump private and public road passenger transport, thereby concealing the decline of bus usage, but excludes data which would show the improved productivity of BR staff and assets.[49]
- A claim of one seventh increase in tax revenue, without any mathematical proof. It ignores the capital cost of conversion, renewals and interest thereon, and maintenance costs of the converted system. They assume all income and no expenditure. Whilst rail subsidies - paid only for rural services - that would be ended are shown, increased subsidies for rural buses are ignored. The postulated savings are invalid.

---

[45] When privatised, InterCity could not run without subsidy, (see *Britain's Railways - The Reality*).

[46] Buses Yearbook, SJ Brown.

[47] Transport Retort 2001.

[48] Covering about $\frac{1}{2}$ mile of open and $1\frac{1}{2}$ mile of closed railway against 11,000 open and 7,000 closed at that time. One closed line was so distant as to make impossible, an assessment of width, another featured *one* small car unrealistically close to a bridge abutment, a photo of an open line had a train loaded with Minis, not HGVs!

[49] See *Britain's Railways - The Reality*.

- A statement of 'expert views', which transpire to be mainly the views of journalists or academics, for whom no evidence is catalogued that they have ever managed any transport activity.[50]
- A *two* page response to a *seventy* page thoroughly argued Paper by the Civic Trust[51] on heavy lorries and their hidden costs.

In this brief response to the Civic Trust, the League claimed that 'most old villages have rail routes which could act as bypasses, keeping lorries away from the awkward corners found in them, and their historic buildings and bridges'. It is a claim *entirely* without foundation. It is beyond dispute that most villages *never* had a railway. It should be perfectly obvious that if 220,000 miles of roads are needed to link all villages and towns, the original 20,000 miles of railway had, by definition, left the majority without railways. Any serious study on the subject, would have listed every such village where they proposed a bypass. The League's report didn't. They ignored the fact that many offending vehicles enter such towns and villages to make deliveries because government had allowed the building of juggernauts despite the fact that they would have to leave motorways, to enter towns and villages to make deliveries, as hauliers did not intend to have tranship depots to transfer goods to smaller lorries. The road lobby focused listener's minds only on the evident capacity of motorways to accept such large vehicles, and concealed the necessity to enter towns. The Civic Trust Report stated that HGVs entering towns for deliveries had increased, causing vibrational damage. The Report over-looked that these vehicles also delay other traffic.

Not content with sweeping inaccurate generalisations about village bypasses, they proceed to another: 'Often rail bridges would require only the decking to be replaced'. Clearly, they have not had the tens of thousands of railway bridges inspected by a qualified engineer, or they would have tabulated fact and figure. The absence of any £ sign in this connection merely confirms the superficiality of their proposals. The Civic Trust Paper, in contrast, abounds with financial data, which the League ignored. The Trust draws attention to the underpayment by road haulage for roads and damage and the consequent overpayment by car owners.

In seeking to dismiss the views of the Civic Trust on safety they claim that roads are twice as safe as railways, praying in aid - not an independent analysis - but a document prepared by that most biased transport theorist - Brigadier Lloyd himself. They claim that J.J. Leeming in his book[52] has 'shown that the way to prevent road accidents is to provide good roads', and - the League claims - the only way to do so is to convert railways to roads. As, even the League does not claim that existing *bad roads* would be closed and replaced by converted railways, the Leeming policy would still require all roads to be re-

---

[50] They neglected to draw attention to views in the *Economist* in 1952 which called for BR to be given equal freedom with road transport, (see *Blueprints for Bankruptcy*, Page 35). Long experience as an accountant, banker, architect, engineer, doctor, journalist, or any profession is a definition of expertise. In only *one* profession is it dismissed, by critics - that of railway manager.

[51] *Heavy Lorries*, 1970.

[52] *Road Accidents - Prevent or Punish?*. In seeking to show that accidents caused by motor vehicles have not risen when compared to pre-motor age travel accidents, he has included, drownings on the basis that river, canal and sea transport were involved. There is no indication how many drownings occurred during recreation, or were due to accidentally falling into water or tomfoolery, nor those arising from a water based employment - e.g. fishing.

designed to create safer conditions. Moreover, he does not say that good roads would eliminate accidents - but only forecasts a reduction. The cover of his book states that 'the first essential in preventing accidents is the investigation of causes and *the financing of road improvements which must inevitably follow.*' This implies that no accident is caused by driver error, poor vehicle maintenance, bad vehicle design or assembly!

They dismiss a comment by the Civic Trust that there is 'irresponsibility to the point of madness' in the conduct of road users, on grounds that the irresponsibility lies with those who have failed to make adequate provision of roads for road users. The reality is that the creation of more roads has not ended the madness of tailgating, not even on motorways.

They likewise dismiss the issue of parking nuisance by lorries on the grounds that there is plenty of railway land that could be converted to lorry parking. No money, of course, would change hands to tip the illusory balance of the economics of road transport. Again, they ignore the reality, which is that lorry drivers park where it is convenient to them - in streets and lay-bys, often close to their homes or lodging place.

'Modern road transport is much more economical in its demands on space' is another claim by the League without a single figure in support.[53] They dismiss another statement by the Trust regarding the cost of building roads on the grounds that they claim that a railway line can be converted for £15,000 per mile. Replies from local authorities demonstrate that the cost of widening and provision of drainage have been ignored, and there is no confirmation by local authorities of the claimed conversion costs.

It is not without significance that the League comments on *selected* parts of the Civic Trust Report. These relate to seven Sections of the Report, namely: IV, V, VI, IX, XIII, XIV, XV. Without explanation, they ignore the intervening eight sections, namely: I, II, III, VII. VIII, X, XI, XII.

Edited 'expert' opinions

Their selected quotes from the *Economist* excludes a letter from an academic disputing claimed benefits from conversion set out in an earlier *Economist* article[54] which is extensively quoted in the book. They exclude reference to an *Economist* article (10.5.52) warning against government policy which prevented BR from competing with hauliers on a level playing field, and another (24.11.73), revealing that rail was cheaper than road, (see page 211).

One report claims that there is no transport corridor in Britain where demand would exceed the capacity of a bus lane, and refers to the cost of rural rail subsidies. (*Economist*, 6.5.72). No entrepreneur put money forward to test the validity of that claim. That report overlooked that when BR closed a line - which were unsubsidised until 1969 - BR had to subsidise an alternative bus service, which invariably raised fares destroying the illusion that bus fares were cheaper.[55]

Quotes attributed to experts include an extract from *Municipal Engineering* (2.2.73). It states that the 'turning point was a report by the Countryside Commission, (see page 193), which showed that disused rural railway lines could be put to a wide variety of amenity uses ...... however, many authorities are making roads out of disused lines'. This implies

---

[53] See page 199 and the diagram illustrating comparable headways.

[54] Anti-conversion letters, which the League ignore, in the media include one challenging the facts in respect of the USA Pennsylvania Turnpike, which had been claimed as proof of the practicability and benefits of conversion, (see *Railway Magazine*, January 1965 referred to in footnote, page 167).

[55] See *Blueprints for Bankruptcy*, Pages 80,109, *The Railway Closure Controversy*, Page 37,75, 95,109,134,179; and *Britain's Railways - The Reality*, Page 93.

that the whole article was extolling the practicality and advantages of conversion to roads. In fact, their quote represents only 16% of the article in that journal. Their prolific use of the ellipsis, air brushes out 84% including: 'Cheshire CC's chief landscape architect, like many other planning officers, discourages suggestions that lines can be used as roads. He says the track is too narrow'. More damning is the excluded sentence: 'It [the Commission] encouraged the growth of the planning school of thought which rejected the argument that the only thing to do with disused railway lines was to convert them into roads!' Also left out are references to West Sussex County Council using 26 miles of closed railway to extend footpaths, Cheshire County Council doing likewise with 12.5 miles of closed lines, and 'the most exciting footpath scheme in Stoke' [on Trent]. The latter is about 7 miles long. These together exceed the 43 miles of railway converted to roads. The article mentions that West Sussex has sold parts to farmers.

The League book says that the Commission's Report (see page 193), recognises that 'it is difficult to put railway land to other uses'. The League claim it is 'ideal for transport purposes, provided that the necessary adaptation can be carried out'. The inference is that there is no other realistic use, except roads, whereas the Commission's Report itemises several other uses, which significantly outnumber conversions to roads.

An ellipsis in another article they pray in aid (*Economist*, 18.5.74), air brushes out the words: 'the railway route is not ideal', and 'the benefit may not justify the cost'.

An extract of the views of another of the League's experts was stated to be in *The Times* of 15.4.74, but was found after much effort to be in the edition of 29.4.74. It made no reference at all to conversion, but was merely a letter about relative fuel consumption of bus and train, which are but one element in costs. An important cost is the depreciation of vehicles. The life of rail coaches is much longer than buses

Another highly selective extract from an article (17.10.72), by *The Times* transport correspondent, leaves out the statement by a road haulage operator: 'Nothing I have said should be taken to mean that I am against railways - which I am not'. The extract also judiciously ignores a comment by the transport correspondent, regarding a government plan to slash the railways: 'It has been difficult to find anyone speaking out intelligently and openly against the view that railways should be retained at their present size, even if that means a large and growing contribution from the taxpayer'.

Experts' views includes one by academic Peter Hall[56] (*New Society*, 23.11.72), on the use of railways as roads - but he was advocating replacing *lightly used rural lines* by roads. He envisages reserving a new road for buses if it becomes congested. No figures are quoted in this article, except to repeat the erroneous claim that hundreds of lines had been converted. In praying the opinion of this academic in aid of their campaign, the League airbrushes out from its book anything inconvenient: 'though many of these conversions are short', 'in these areas, traffic densities are seldom high'; 'overbridges pose a minor problem, either they can be raised[57] or be replaced by grade [i.e. level] crossings'; 'where a new road met the *remaining track system*, buses would run into the railway station. Rural areas would get an integrated system'.

The League ignores an article on the *same* page of New Society which points out that rural bus services are declining, and that even urban bus services frequently fail to

---

[56] Professor Peter Hall was co-author of the East Anglian main line conversion study, (see chapter 10).

[57] A requirement consistently dismissed by the League.

generate an adequate surplus. This article states that the NBC has instructed abandonment or drastic reduction of buses, including on routes of closed railways. 'A public service confers benefits to car users in event of breakdown or bad weather. A bus service provides insurance to car users. Is it not reasonable to ask society to pay a premium for such services? The premium will be paid either by the state or regular bus users, not solely by motorists who gain the benefit.' It is an incredible proposition and analogous to the attitude of objectors to proposed rail closures.

They also ignore letters in the next edition of New Society which rubbish the idea: 'A slightly more detailed examination of his [Hall's] argument will reveal many absurdities. Most of the rural routes he envisages disappeared years ago, What remains are provincial urban commuter with loads that labour intensive buses cannot cope with, and Inter City lines with freight and local services on them'. 'Hall's scheme has validity for lines already closed, but for existing lines it would be wasteful and futile. As an example, the East Suffolk line has fifty level crossings to replace by bridges in a flat landscape or by dangerous grade-crossings which constitute a *mild problem* for Hall'.[58]

Land Use Inquiry

Their book admits that 'thousands of miles of railway route have already become redundant', but do not explain why only 43 miles had - by then - been converted. In the light of their admission of the paucity of conversion, there is no evidence - as they claim - that 'the conversion of railway routes to modern motor roads has now been demonstrated as a practicable proposition'.[59] They called for an inquiry into the uses to which all railway land could beneficially be put to provide the UK with an adequate road system. Anyone *genuinely* interested in UK transport needs and claiming the moral high ground, should advocate a wide ranging inquiry, which would look at *all land used for transport*. This would consider airports and roads. The latter then using 22 times as much as rail for ten times as much traffic, should be item one on the agenda. The use of airports for short haul flights should be item two. It was long ago obvious to inquiring minds that the Channel Tunnel would increase rail traffic, whilst reducing air, sea and road traffic. Of course, NIMBYs could and did obstruct BR attempts to create a fast route from the coast. BR prepared five separate route plans - all rejected by government following orchestrated objections supported by MPs and councillors. NIMBYs objected in vain to the M2, M25, and airport expansion. Having peppered their document heavily with 'assuming', 'maybe', 'possibly', the League arrived at a precise conclusion!

The Chairman of the League wrote to *The Times*: There would be difficulty if railways closed, and traffic was thrown onto existing roads, but no problem if government changed its attitude and permitted closed railways to be converted into roads, (*The Times* 6.4.72). It is unclear what changes were sought. No attitude problem seemed to arise in 'converting' closed rural railways into roads, if there was - in the eyes of central and local government any merit and benefit therefrom. It will be seen that this represented a climb down from the objective of replacing all railways by roads.

---

[58] Jointly with Edward Smith, he produced a later plan to convert a railway route, (see page 97).
[59] Thirteen years later, the author drew the attention of the British Road Federation to the tardiness of conversion, which had left the country with thousands of miles of closed railway route *begging to be converted*, (see page 92).

Other contemporary supportive views

A consultant told the Conversion League that it would be wasteful to apply modern railway techniques to Britain. He said that the future of European railways was to develop long freight hauls with Russia. *(The Times, 13.12.72)*. He may have been unaware that the Russian gauge is wider than its European neighbours, specifically to impede invasion. A change of gauge would be very costly. He overlooked the plan for the Channel Tunnel to link BR to the European network, which was the same gauge as that in the UK.

An article *(The Times, 21.1.74)*, stated that an American study had shown that buses are cheaper than trains for moving urban commuters.[60] It states that the conclusion was based on certain assumptions. The principal ones were that buses would have reserved lanes and that it was assumed that all train passengers would be collected by feeder buses perambulating around residential streets, whilst Express buses would pick up in the same streets and run direct to cities where they would discharge at several points. These assumptions make the study invalid for UK purposes because, here, the claim has been that the converted railway would be used jointly by bus, car and freight. UK railways are not wide enough to provide reserved lanes. In the UK, thousands of commuters walk to stations, thousands are taken by car and dropped off, and thousands leave cars in station carparks. Moreover, thousands of UK commuters do not go into the city, but alight at various stations en route. If Express buses did not make similar stops, then there would be tailgating buses going round streets picking up for different destinations. Moreover, many travel from suburban areas *away from the city*. The article mentions that 'the capacity of the two systems is roughly the same!' The inference is missed, viz., that there would be no spare capacity for cars, nor for other public transport freight or passenger, which the Conversion League has always claimed there would be!

It is noticeable that the conversion league focuses on this particular American study - because it appears to suit their case - but blatantly ignores the more widely known American research into the cost of road haulage wear on roads, (see pages 170,181,182).

---

[60] The article fails to mention that American trains carry more staff than BR trains, (see page 202).

In 1975, the League made a minor change to its title - adding 'Ltd.' This limited company [registered N° 605059] was dissolved at the end of 1981. It later changed its name again from the Railway Conversion League to the Railway Conversion Campaign.

Other than occasional letters to the media, little was heard from them. Their chairman wrote to *The Times* occasionally, and his views were invariably demolished by others, (see chapter 15). A search of *The Times* produced the following from the League's chairman:

- Prof. Hall's study of expected benefits of conversion at last puts authoritative figure to them. When Lloyd propounded this revolutionary idea, it is doubtful if sufficient information was available on transport economics and busway capacity for a definitive study.[1] It has long been obvious there is no role for railways in a small crowded island surrounded by all-weather ports,[2] (19.12.75).

- It is not true, as claimed in a previous letter, that heavy lorries were not paying a full share of road costs. They pay more in tax than the cost of maintaining and building roads, and, as taxpayers, help to subsidise railways[3]. Government received no return on its rail investment, (19.4.77).

  Government received a return from keeping open uneconomic lines in rural areas, providing commuting and other services below cost, holding down wages - especially of its 2.55m employees[4] - and helping to subsidise inefficient industry and the electorate, through fares and freight charges held below industry-fuelled inflation. Moreover, some UK industry benefited from sales to BR, and this led to some foreign contracts.

  Plowden & Buchan state that DoT calculations show that lorries account for 43% of the maintenance bill, compared to their 7% share of vehicle mileage.

- The Transport Studies Group[5] took costings mainly from one scheme to build a wide new road on poor subsoil on the alignment of a disused railway. This is not conversion as the Railway Conversion League defines it.[6] We advocate using rail formations as they stand. Transferring traffic to routes with no pedestrians and no frontage access[7] will cut accidents by a factor of 20. He referred to railways being fenced off, whilst road transport *has* to operate without fencing.[8] Transferring all long distance traffic to a segregated route will save 3,000 lives pa, (4.5.77).

No basis was quoted for this dramatic reduction in road deaths. In 1977, 6,614 were killed on 220,000 miles of roads, of whom 2,313 were pedestrians. If pedestrian deaths

---

[1] That is not the impression that his predecessors had given, as they publicised their objectives.
[2] Ports are *not* all-weather, (see page 159). The author was on a ship held outside port in rough seas in the late 1970s.
[3] Independent studies including the 1980 *Armitage Report* prove lorries do not pay their full road costs. The road lobby never relates lorry taxes to the extra cost of building & maintaining roads suited to HGVs. BR freight was not subsidised from 1977, (Hansard 2.2.93, vol. 218; col. 165/7)
[4] See *Britain's Railways - The Reality*, Page 92.
[5] See page 123.
[6] This was news. There was no previous definition. They were not slow to exploit a case if subsoil was favourable. Tovey's Report on the Southport conversion referred to favourable subsoil. In their 1970 Report, the League claimed this case proved the validity of conversion, but did not mention the soil. It deplored a BR requirement to raise bridges, ignoring that this was standard policy to cater for later electrification and would avoid subsequent disruption.
[7] Collieries and industries had private siding - frontage - access directly on main lines. Conversion will not eliminate thousands of pedestrians - trespassers - using level crossings nor taking short cuts.
[8] They do not have to do so. That is easily remedied. These deaths could be slashed by fencing roads now!

were cut by diverting existing road traffic to converted railways, given that the railway route is only available for one tenth of existing traffic flows, at best, perhaps one tenth of 2,313 *might* be claimed. Even this would, in the absence of case studies, be speculative. Moreover, this might well be swamped by an increase in deaths from pedestrians continuing to cross between more closely spaced road vehicles at traditional points: level crossings, and unauthorised trespassing points.

The solution to our problems (?)

In 1979, Dalgleish issued a new missive[9] to solve road problems. He claimed that mechanical road transport - steam carriages - had been discouraged by penal road tolls, and that many main roads had scarcely changed since horse days. He was wrong. Horse traffic had modest effect on road surfaces, steam carriages ruined them, and alarmed horses, needing an extra man to warn riders and waggoners of their approach. They were slow and needed frequent water and fuel supplies. From then to 1979, there were vast improvements in roads:

• Loose stone and cobbled surfaces had disappeared.
• Bridges replaced thousands of level crossings for which road transport did not pay.
• Hundreds of railway over-bridges were strengthened at railway expense.
• Many bends were eased to improve safety and permit higher speeds.
• Thousands of miles had been made into dual carriageways.
• Bypasses had been built around many towns.[10]

He stated that BR freight track costs were charged to passenger services, when they were not. In contrast, extra costs created by heavy lorries are effectively charged to motorists, who pay more than their fair share. He claimed that those who travel by rail are mainly the well-off;[11] a third being business travellers who don't pay their own fares. If it was true, it would be precisely analogous to motorists in company cars. Only since 1980, have they paid tax on motoring as a benefit in kind. He tried to make a big deal about the time taken to get to or from a station. He should, of course, compare it with the time required to find parking space in London or other cities, or walking to and waiting at a bus stop in the rain for a bus that never comes. Whether business travellers use rail, air, bus or car, the cost comes out of the company, and is tax deductible.

He referred to the legal power for BR to object to the provision of new bus licences. He completely ignores the equal legal power of existing bus operators to object to new applications, and they were doing so on a much bigger scale. He would be oblivious of the classic case in which the independent Licensing Authority rejected an application for a licence for a new operator who had mischievously accepted bookings from holidaymakers before getting a licence, to which BR *and* bus operators objected. Churchill personally called for the licence to be granted, (Cabinet minutes, 7.4.52).

He said that the HGV is regarded as a villain, but only as it is forced to run on unsuitable roads. That is complete nonsense. Motorists frequently curse HGVs for pulling out with inadequate warning, only to grind along 0.5mph faster than the preceding HGV.

---

[9] It mentioned that he also, had been in the Royal Engineers for 22 years. He was chairman of the Campaign.
[10] New by-passes have increased mileage. Average length of haul has increased since 1970, (Plowden & Buchan)
[11] The League quoted the Economist, but left out a reference to road users being rich, (see page 73).

He reiterated the fallacious claim that the same bus or coach would take people from residential areas, direct to city centre destinations. It is clearly absolute nonsense. If they went round every street, it would take for ever to get a full load all going to the same street in the same city. If the vehicle went around the destination city - or worse, around several cities - the journey time for some would be quite intolerable.

He claimed that the problem of overtaking is insoluble on railways. He overlooks doing so at stations, or where there is multi track, and the provision for one train to propel a failed train to a suitable passing point ahead. The comparable facility on roads is provided for by lay-bys, which are funded by non users, and by manhandling broken down vehicles clear, assuming that other drivers are willing to risk cardiac arrest. He stated that the breakdown of a motor vehicle would not - 'as it does on railways' - cause long delays, revealing his ignorance of the aforementioned railway practice, which is especially surprising as the Royal Engineers were responsible for railway operations in war zones.

He claimed a gain from fewer accidents, as pedestrians and cyclists - who account for a high proportion of fatal injuries - would not be allowed to use converted routes. He claimed that the transfer of traffic *could* well halve the total number of deaths, giving no reason for selecting this fraction. Perhaps it wouldn't cut deaths. It all depends on the fallibility of a crystal ball. The reality is that if traffic fell on existing roads as a result of diversion to converted routes, remaining traffic would travel faster, and there is a strong possibility that this would more than wipe out the theoretical assumption of fewer deaths.

He argued that 'now is the time to start *trial conversions*[12] to demonstrate the benefits of converted railways with necessary priority for high occupancy vehicles including carpools, *where appropriate*. PSVs will never take up more than a small proportion of the available capacity.' He makes no reference to endless convoys needed to carry coal to power stations. If PSVs did take up only a small proportion of available capacity, it would be because new roads were packed with nose-to-tail cars, whose owners turned up their noses at PSVs. Those cars are not likely to be car pools, of which the conversion league has dreamed since 1955. They are still largely conspicuous by their absence, as the average load in cars has not changed in several decades. Incredibly for a soldier, who would be taught to consider the strong possibility that Plan A may not work, he has no plan B if the *trial* proves to be the disaster which experienced road engineers and operators have forecast. The concept of trials in business leaves open the option to revert to previous practice. Reverting to railway would prove extremely costly, if not impossible.

The truth about transport (?)

'A fresh study on conversion was prepared by A. Dalgleish, transport engineer[13] and chairman of the conversion league, claiming that political objection to conversion springs from ignorance. He claims that road carries $9/_{10}$ths of UK freight and passengers on 2,500 km of custom built roads compared to 18,000 km of railway[14] and that other roads were a

---

[12] A proving trial should convert a dual carriageway road to the modest dimensions envisaged for a converted railway: reduced bridge headroom, shorter deceleration lanes and more right turns. It would be easily reversed when it proved unpopular, caused deaths and bridge bashing. It should, of course, be funded by the conversion campaign.

[13] *The Times* Careers A-Z defines it as someone concerned with managing the best use of roads and related facilities, working mainly with road transport.

[14] This is a desperate attempt to prove the unprovable - that roads are more intensively used than rail. See pages 88 & 173 for a meaningful comparison of road and rail network productivity. For validity of traffic share, see page 153.

network of centuries old paths. He argued that asphalted railways would make good roads. The Centre for Policy Studies - which circulated the report - said it was not committed to the conclusions. The report claimed that £1bn pa could be saved immediately, 2,500 lives would be saved[15] and juggernauts would be removed from residential streets', (*The Times*, 24.3.82).

By no stretch of imagination can it be claimed that 90% of UK traffic is carried on 2,500 km of roads. Nor can it be claimed - as Dalgleish does - that traffic on relatively narrow single carriageway roads on converted railways could attain the safety of motorways. Juggernauts would not be transfer from other roads because of the limitations of bridges, tunnels, viaducts, cuttings and embankments[16] - an irrefutable factor which the League has consistently tried to dismiss. Even were juggernauts able to use a converted system, that would not remove them from residential streets, because drivers have a habit of parking there overnight, near to their homes or lodgings.

Principal claims in the Dalgleish Study

The 43 page booklet entitled *The Truth about Transport*, by Angus Dalgleish, was published March 1982, by the Centre for Policy Studies [CPS], who distanced themselves from it, (see above). It was peppered with inaccuracies and assumptions, which destroy the claims and conclusions. The booklet begins with what is described as the historical background, ostensibly to lead to a clear understanding of the present position. As it contains errors and assumptions, it could only lead to false conclusions.

- Telford said that all rail traffic would be handled by the company which owned the line, breaking a rule that they should be open to anyone wishing to pay a toll.

  All Acts which gave powers to build railways, empowered anyone to put their wagons on the line on payment of controlled tolls. This right was exercised by those industries which owned wagons - mainly collieries, quarries, etc., - until 1948.[17] Although the practice was severely curtailed by Government decision in 1948, (see page 164), the facility never ended. Initially, anyone could provide their own locomotive power, but this was soon ended on safety grounds.

- In 1831, Telford stated that those who embark on constructing railroads will be great losers. He must have had a vision of deficits to come.

  He must have foreseen two World Wars, in which government would siphon-off billions of railway revenue, whilst allowing industry and other transport to profit handsomely; that government would impose a unique limit on rail profits; would create courts of law to hold only railway prices below inflation; and would deliberately prevent them from competing with road haulage.[18]

- Promoters realised that railways would give monopoly control on routes and traffic.

  They were quickly disabused. Early railways were built to break a canal monopoly, which delayed traffic and charged high rates. That canals would fail to modernise to compete was not foreseen; they had to cut rates. Railway Acts enforced companies to provide junctions with other railways, to allow through traffic from other lines, and controlled rates and tolls.

- Because of cheap labour, double handling of rail traffic [in the 1800s] was not a problem.

---

[15] N.B. The saving in lives has fallen, but is still above actual pedestrian deaths which numbered 1869 in 1982.

[16] See page 100 which refers in the Hall/Smith conversion to 25 miles of line abandoned which has these limitations.

[17] This gave BR a burden rather than a benefit and was done to force replacement of the decrepit wagons favoured by industry, thereby creating employment. At that time, half of all wagons were owned by collieries and other industry, (see *Britain's Railways - The Reality*, Pages 50-51).

[18] See *Square Deal Denied* and *Britain's Railways - The Reality*

Except over short distance, road transport did not then carry throughout, but only to rivers, ports, canals, so that traffic was already being double and triple handled.

- The explosion in road transport was not matched by road improvements.

  For decades, road transport did not pay for roads. There were many improvements: by-passes, dual carriageways, easier bends, safer junctions, bridges strengthened, (see page 80).

Having got basic claims on railway history wrong, he then proceeded to do so with the current position.

- Bridges and viaducts are crumbling due to inadequate attention.

  Not a scrap of evidence was advanced to support this wild claim. Reduction in expenditure on the infrastructure by Railtrack after privatisation shows that is nonsense.

- He refers to BR's monopoly position as supplier of one mode of transport.

  As the road lobby has sought to prove that road handles more traffic than rail, obviously, there is no monopoly. Ministers repeatedly said that BR had no monopoly.[19] Any company could create a railway by promoting an Act of Parliament as others have done, or could have bought up closed lines.

- By road it is possible to make a journey without change.

  No bus route caters for every direct journey. Only by car is it possible, and he tries to put cars out of the equation - except for using its volume to 'pay' for conversion. People walk, from their homes, or go by car, to bus-stops as to stations. He ignores a steep decline in bus travel, whilst rail share fell only slightly.

- A rail traveller cannot go when or where he wishes, but must join others.

  The same is true of bus travel, with the added inconvenience that buses are cancelled, and those at bus stops remain uninformed. No data is published - unlike railways - to show the incidence of cancellation.

- Roads without traffic on routes crossing at flat junctions can provide flow-type transport. This flow, provided that the traffic stream consists mainly of high occupancy vehicles [from a car with three in, to an articulated bus with 80], will have no difficulty matching flows of seated passengers carried by railways provided an appropriate vehicle is used. He envisaged an important role for car-pools.

  Converted railways will have thousands of flat junctions at which traffic crosses. The premise depends on assumption and if. The car load will have to almost double. It would be unwise to try to pass an articulated bus turning at a junction. There will still be standing commuters - left behind at the bus stop! Car pools are still a rarity.

- On railways, one disabled vehicle disrupts the whole line; on road a broken down vehicle can be pulled onto a verge. If a bus breaks down, it can be pushed to the side.

  As conversion envisages no verges to create the required road width, there will be nowhere to move it. A disabled train is pushed forward by the next train. A broken down road vehicle may block both lanes if a bus or lorry is involved. Any pulling or pushing of a bus would have to be done by the passengers. On rail, they never have to do that.

- Claims that fuel duty paid for buses more than covers their track costs.

  His historical review forgot to mention buses and coaches had been paying the same road tax as a mini for decades. Bus track costs have never been established, so it is impossible to say whether they pay their share or not. Clearly their effect on road wear will be substantially greater than a car, and they should have paid far more.

- Park and ride [by train] is a wasteful and expensive use of a car.

---

[19] See *Blueprints for Bankruptcy*, Pages 48, 50, 84.

Obviously, motorists disagree, and in the absence of a change in the law, they will continue to do so. If park and ride by train is wasteful, so it must be by bus.

- Reference was made to the rapidly rising cost of rail travel.

  Fares had just caught up with the RPI for the first time since 1948, having been 47 points behind. By 1982, passengers had benefited by £11bn.[20] For two-thirds of that time, there was no subsidy, although fares were held down by a law court and Ministers.

- Rail supporters claim that heavy lorries do not pay a proper share of road costs. This argument should be used with caution. If they pay too little, it means that cars pay too much. BR would not wish to see car taxes cut thus increasing competition.

  Rail supporters quote TRL figures. The Highways Agency states[21] that the costs of building a motorway for cars only would be 35% less than one allowing heavy vehicles. Car tax has little bearing on competition. Competitive use is based on the marginal cost of fuel or convenience.

- The lorry has come to the rescue of towns.

  That is not the opinion of residents nor of motorists when lorries double park, take up the whole road when turning a corner, and damage pavements or verges.

- He compares the alleged average energy consumption of a train: 410 kcal per passenger km; with 430 kcal average for all cars.

  No source is quoted. This is a typical chalk and cheese comparison used by the road lobby. 73% of cars make journeys of under five miles, where speed is unlikely to be high, often in the 30 mph zone, against a train at 100-125mph.

- There is nowhere on the railway system where present passenger loadings in express buses on a converted route will use more than fraction of the capacity.

  He did not take the busiest route and prove it with fact and figure based on a timetable which all operators would require. He spread all traffic, including the peak over 16 hours and over the whole system. These valueless global estimates have always been used by the League.

- Delays caused by points, signals and train failures will end.

  Daily experience shows that they would be replaced by longer delays caused by traffic light failures, accidents, jack-knifed lorries, shed loads and slow lorries preventing overtaking.

- A £775m electrification project may save 9,600 barrels of oil daily, but for the same cost, plants could make 38,000 barrels oil daily from coal.

  No source was given for the cost of building plants, nor is it said how much coal would be required, nor whether that tonnage would be available. A few years later, coal production fell as hundreds of mines were closed.

- Trains were only allowed to run on fenced-off property for safety reasons. Entry is prohibited to the public.

  Fences were not enforced for safety reasons but to prevent trespass from railroads to adjoining land. Roads could be fenced-off, costs being paid by transport operators. Many European railways are not fenced-off. Entry to stations, goods depots or level crossings is not prohibited.

- He claimed that, to prove rail was safer, BR splits train deaths from others which are due, he theorises 'to the stupidity of passengers'.

  The split is made - not by BR - but by HMRI, in their Annual Reports[22] for their own reasons. No BR manager ever called a dead passenger stupid. Pedestrians killed trying to cross busy roads are more likely to be called stupid by selfish car, HGV and PSV drivers

---

[20] See *Britain's Railways - The Reality*, Appendix A.

[21] Letter to the author.

[22] These Reports contain a synopsis of HMRI Inquiries into railway accidents. If a similar body carried out detailed investigations into road accidents, the death toll may fall.

- He states that a misty morning means fog with half of trains cancelled, whilst road traffic moves with extra care!

  Where has he been? Massive pile-ups on roads are clear evidence of lack of care. When road users exercise care in fog, road accidents will plummet, and the diligent will see the proverbial animal flying. Fog has caused no cancellations on railways since the 1960s and the advent of new signalling. The only impact of fog on train running arises when railway staff are delayed on fog-bound roads en route to work !

- BR adverts in 1981 on the benefit of electrification ignored essential costs of improving track and signalling.

  In fact all main line track was relatively new by 1981, and signalling on main lines had been largely modernised to meet speeds of 100-125 mph.

- His most pathetic claim was that 'BR has a corps of 500 letter writers protesting to editors against criticism of railways'.

  The reality is that most letters or articles in the national media are anti-rail.[23] It is impossible to take seriously a 'Study' which descends to such trivia which clearly is without foundation.

- A claim is made that many working in the road transport field - as economists, planners or highway engineers - had worked for, and had a sentimental attachment to railways'.

  This is an own goal, showing up a lack of management skills in the road transport industry.

- Segregating cyclists and pedestrians could save 2,500 lives.

  There were 2153 deaths in 1982, so 2500 could not be saved, not least as they were spread over 200,000 miles of road, most of which could not possibly lose traffic to an 11,000 mile system.

- Refers to short distance road traffic: milk, furniture, building materials, post, domestic rubbish.

  This lets the cat out of bag and undermines claims as to the disparity between rail and road traffic, and cuts road traffic in competition with rail at a stroke.

- He says that existing roads are blocked by people stopping to pick blackberries, inferring that on converted roads this would not happen.

  This is clutching at straws. If converted roads can have laws to stop this - so can existing roads. The road lobby hasn't tried to improve traffic flow.

- Figure 1 in the booklet claims to split traffic between road types - tonne km; passenger km.

  The DfT say that such data does not exist. Moreover, even tonnes carried by road transport is of questionable reliability, (see page 153).

- It is claimed that juggernauts cause less vibration than trains.

  Not a word of proof, nor a reference to an independent study is made. Where railways are separated from property by verges, juggernauts will be close as converted railways would be tarmaced up to the fence.

- He states that two-track railways should not be converted into dual carriageway roads as the cost would make it impractical.

  This is a complete reversal of long standing Conversion League claims. They have repeatedly claimed that there is plenty of space to convert both two-track and single track railways into dual carriageways, and even into motorways! This destroys the whole basis of the claims made, in the past and since.

---

[23] Over 90 letters from the author to the national media. replying - with researched fact and figure - to inaccuracies in anti-rail letters or articles were not published, including one demolishing the 97% spare capacity claim originated in Dalgleish's book and repeated in an advert, (see pages 88,173).

- Under-powered vehicles and standing vehicles would be banned.

  Vehicles waiting to make right turns would have to be banned. Under powered vehicles would need to be legally defined. It would end daily cross-railway movement of tens of thousands of farm tractors. These measures could be taken now on existing roads.

- Additional land would only be essential at junctions to which no valid objections could be made.

  It is usually claimed that no extra land is required. It defies belief to suggest that no objections would come from those whose land is to be taken.

- The plan depends on assuming reasonable average loadings for buses and trucks.

  Yet another assumption is made. The whole concept is built on assumptions, for which no independent justification is advanced.

- A 300 day year is taken to allow for lower weekend and holiday loadings, giving 11m vehicle-km daily, 3.3% of available capacity of a converted network. As much rail freight moves by night, 3% is probably a truer figure. 97% of capacity[24] is available for traffic on local roads

  Except on commuter routes, passengers are not lower at weekends or holidays, and on some routes are higher. He spread peak, weekend and holiday traffic when passengers don't want to travel and customers do not want freight to move. Most coal - the biggest flow - moved by day, when collieries were manned. The theory assumed no empty return lorries and none under loaded due to cubic capacity limitations. With 220,000 miles of roads, and 11,000 miles of railway, traffic on 210,000 of them will have to stay exactly where it is.

- Figure 2 claims to show the spare capacity of railways converted to motor roads (the diagram is clearly dual carriageway throughout, with bridges and no junctions.[25] It claims the system 'could carry 219bn passenger km + 50bn tonne km. All purpose roads would then need only to carry 178bn passenger km + 41bn tonne km'.

  The reality is that the rail system did not have that spare capacity, and moreover, the idea that 220,000 miles of road could transfer 40% of its traffic to an 11,000 mile network is patently absurd. It is noticeable that no one offered to back these wild ideas with their own money.

- He claimed that few villages are not near to a railway.

  This ignores the geographical reality outlined above.[26]

- Drivers would transfer from old roads, linked with converted roads at stations. Motorists may even desert motorways which are longer routes. The two systems must be connected at as many points as possible.

  By definition, 210,000 miles of old roads have no railway anywhere near. It would create flat junctions at stations, which do not have level crossings. Hitherto, conversionists had envisaged fewer, not more, junctions. It was absurd to claim that motorists would desert motorways.

- Figure 3 claims to illustrate the likely effect of conversion on accidents.

  It has no foundation in serious study. It assumes much and proves nothing. It ignores the reality that most existing road traffic is on roads remote from railways and travelling very short distances, (see page 77). *Plowden & Buchan quote 'that 35% of those treated for minor road accident injuries in hospitals do not appear in official road statistics'.[27] This indicates that road accidents are understated, hence Dalgleish was starting from the wrong premise.*

---

[24] This mysterious figure appeared in an advert in 1989 (see page 88). As it was unchallenged, the figure would be assumed to be accurate. The author's letter would have demolished it - had it been published.

[25] By definition, that means building thousands of new bridges.

[26] Railway staff had a gazetteer listing thousands of villages which had no railway station, and indicating which was the nearest. Many were several miles distant from a station.

[27] From a comparison of police and hospital information by Ball & Roberts.

- The plan invents single carriageway motorways with flat junctions, claiming they would have the same accident rate as 3-lane motorways, and quotes the A465 Heads of the Valleys road 'built along the line of an old railway.'

    The A465 is unsafe (see page 105). Only part of the road was built on a railway, (see page 166)

- He concedes that private capital is required, and advocates toll roads for which government would pay road owners, based on axle counts.

    Why have there been no offers to fund roads? Doubtless, because owners would demand government guarantees of a good return on capital.

- Conversion must start in the cities.

    The rest of the system would be immediately useless and all traffic will be diverted to existing roads.[28] Operators will have to buy vehicles well in advance of moving any traffic. The previous idea was to start at the coast, (see page 27).

- He claims that land sold to local authorities for roads was at a high value, and claims that railway land is already owned by nation.

    Land is sold before a use is decided. BR needed to get rid of liabilities: bridges, fences, drainage. There was an option to use closed lines as roads, but most have become footpaths. The nation hadn't then repaid previous owners, (see page 60).

- Mention is made a book [29] which alleges that members of the BTC were either fools or knaves, and tries to make a big deal of the absence of any consequential libel actions.

    No libel action ensued because he named no one. The matter is irrelevant to railways or to conversion. It is yet another straw which desperate people will cling to, when other arguments fail. Senior civil servants at the DoT should have sued that author, (see footnote page 164).

- It is claimed the DoT specification for converted roads is needlessly elaborate, as they can be paved as they stand. However, after experience, improvement may be needed!

    By inference, motorways are needlessly elaborate with hard shoulders, verges, huge junctions, vast services areas and expensive signalling equipment. Inevitably, experience will prove a need for hard shoulders, extra lanes and improved junctions. Only someone out of touch with reality would claim otherwise, and plan to close those roads after conversion, to make improvements, creating massive delays. Motorists would soon vote with their feet - or wheels.

- There is no reason to insist on 5m height *initially*, as existing roads are littered with sub standard bridges; 4.5m would be adequate *initially.*

    Roads are littered with damage caused by lorries bashing into them - a problem so widespread it led to a special investigation by HMRI. Warning signs are often ignored, (see pages 184-185 & photos). Lorries would be diverted back to old roads. His inference is that - after experience - bridges would be lifted. This unprofessional approach would create horrendous delays

- Refers to BR's propaganda machine which influences the DoT, which merely rubber stamps BR plans and passes them to the Cabinet. He claims that there is no road lobby to counter the powerful rail lobby!

    No DfT source is mentioned. Propaganda is information issued by the opposing side, information is propaganda issued by your own side. The road lobby was headed - according to John Wardroper[30] - by the DoT, which was opposed to transfer of traffic to rail. There was

---

[28] Angus Dalgleish had already written to *The Times* that: 'There would be difficulty if railways closed, and traffic was thrown onto existing roads, but no problem if government changed its attitude and permitted closed railways to be converted into roads', (see page 78). The government *did* permit closed railways to be converted if practicable.

[29] *The train that ran away*, by Stewart Joy. Many of his criticisms were demolished in *Blueprints for Bankruptcy* & also *Britain's Railways - The Reality.* (See also page 164).

[30] See his book *Juggernaut*, and references to it in this book, chapter 12.

also the BRF, comprising 100 industrial and commercial bodies. It is ridiculous to claim there is no road lobby, which is the most powerful transport lobby. The rail lobby was powerless to prevent closure of half of the system, nor prevent outside interference in its management. No comparable interference of road transport has ever existed.

- Professor Alan Day (*The Times*, 17.6.81) said BR schemes are laundered until they give the 'right' answers.

  The conversion league clearly manipulated figures until they got the right answer, as changes of figures by Lloyd reveal, (see pages 16,22,34). *Assumptions by Dalgleish are a way of laundering. An answer which was published in The Times (18.6.81) to Professor Day* (see page 204) *was ignored by Mr Dalgleish.*

A 1984 study, ignored by the conversion theorists shows that the cost of road accidents was £2.4 bn pa, and refers to £1.5 bn of other hidden subsidies. Another by the same body[31] draws attention to £2.8 bn for sound-proofing against HGV noise which is going to have to be funded, and a further £100m for damage to gas mains, whilst the cost of damage to sewers by HGVs delivering in towns had yet to be quantified. A further £100m for repairs to bridges caused by heavy lorries is not funded by road transport.

In 1989, the Railway Conversion Campaign took out a full page advertisement to reiterate the discredited conversion theory[32] :

  '*The railway system is only working at 3% of its potential. A Department with such poor utilisation ought to be sacked*' and expressed concern for '*our precious green land*'. *Conversion would keep heavy freight away from people and homes.*

The advert called on readers who agree with their theories, to send this advert to their MP. It must have fallen on stony ground, because Parliament took no action.

The author's unpublished response to the Daily Telegraph pointed out:-

- Due to the poor utilisation achieved on roads,[33] converted railways would not accommodate existing rail traffic, leaving no space for traffic to be transferred from existing roads. In addition to converting 10,400 miles of railway, it would be necessary to build 10,000 miles of new roads merely to cope with traffic displaced from rail.
- If the League is concerned about '*our precious green land*', 60% of roads should be closed to bring road utilisation up to British Rail's level.
- Under-utilised lines are mainly in rural areas, kept open by government, without subsidy for the first 20 years of nationalisation. BR had to fund them from interest bearing Treasury loans which, with fares held below inflation, caused the deficit.[34]
- 6,940 miles closed since the 1960s was available for conversion, but remained unused.

---

[31] Wrexham-Birkenhead Rail Users Association newsletters January and March 1984.

[32] *Daily Telegraph*, 26.7.89; also in *The Times, Guardian & Independent*. This was *propaganda*. They continued to have themselves listed in the *Directory of British Associations* as the Railway Conversion League until 1996.

[33] Based on the common practice of adding freight tonne miles/km to passenger miles/km to produce total traffic, and comparing the totals to road & rail route mileage. (See CSO Annual Abstract of Statistics for traffic data and route length). On the basis of published DoT road traffic data in 1986 - the author's last year with BR - road transport required 22 times as much road mileage, and vastly more acreage, for 10 times the traffic. The disparity is really likely to be much worse, due to the unreliability of road traffic data, (see page 153). Studies published by Transport 2000 and others reveal a substantial element of empty running by road haulage, further wasting road space

[34] See *The Railway Closure Controversy*.

- To be proved fatally wrong, anyone believing that rail utilisation is 3%, need only sit on a main line for a few minutes, not 58 minutes in an hour, which is the 97% that they claim is unused.
- Rail track widths were almost invariably inadequate even for single carriageway roads, whilst limited bridge heights would restrict use to cars and small commercial vehicles.
- Roads are built on the basis of social benefit, an ingenuous formula based on the time road users *may* save by using new roads. British Rail in contrast, had to justify investment in cash terms with reduced costs or higher revenue.
- They said that a Department with such poor utilisation ought to be sacked. On the contrary, anyone who produced such mis-aimed, error-ridden statistics as theirs, should be sacked.

The author asked for the source of the 'published statistics which claim only 3% utilisation'. There was no response to the letter, other than another acknowledgement card to add to a growing collection. It is now apparent that the source was not independent as implied, but some creative arithmetic by the chairman of the Conversion Campaign. (see page 86).

How to get the roads we need

An undated[35] leaflet entitled *How to get the roads we need - and keep traffic away from people* by RM Bale was published by the Railway Conversion Campaign. It begins by asserting that 'almost every village had a passenger and goods station'. *Not so.* In 1946, BR staff used a gazetteer *listing thousands of locations with no station*. A reference is made to lorries in villages, but ignores that many must start, end or call there. The author states 'we need a road system that separates lorries from people'. If a road system is created purely for lorries, taxes they currently pay will not scratch the surface of the cost, and haulage prices would soar. They are not paying a fair share of road costs now, but hide behind car taxes.[36] Fenced-off pavements would achieve separation of people and lorries.

It refers to *BR still being allowed to sell off land*. They were *obliged* to do so, to re-pay loans, when government refused a subsidy for an uneconomic service, despite BR being required to subsidise replacement bus services.[37] Such land must first be offered to central or local government, who have the option to use it for roads. The evidence of this book is that the routes were unsuitable or too costly to convert. They opted instead for separating pedestrians and cyclists from motor vehicles by converting closed railways into footpaths and cycleways. The option to acquire some routes was rejected, even for this purpose, and therefore sold to adjoining farmers, industry or householders.

It claims that rail freight is uneconomic for short hauls. That cannot include 1,000 ton MGR trains. It stated that the 'outcome of the miners' strike showed that even bulk mineral traffic by road is cheaper'. Power stations were over-stocking for a year to prepare for this strike, hence less transport was needed during the strike. In the year before the strike, BR carried 77% of total coal production, in the strike year, 88%, and the year after the strike, 83%. Coal by sea - coastwise and export - was 8%, 9.7% and 8.9% respectively.

---

[35] It includes photographs of a road opened at Blackpool in 1986.
[36] The Hall/Smith study envisages that conversion costs would be funded mainly by motorists (see page 104,139)
[37] See BTC/BRB Annual Accounts and *Britain's Railways - The Reality*, Page 128, 137, 138.

Coal by canal was 1.6%, 1.3% and 1.6% respectively[38]. In the strike year, that left 1%, of which some was on direct conveyor belts from collieries to adjacent power stations, and some was sold to local merchants or delivered to miners' homes. The road element didn't register on the Richter scale. Post-strike, the non-rail share was lower than pre-strike! The average distance of railfreight in 1974 - strike year - was 79.5 miles, above 1973. Rail traffic is based on paid invoices, unlike road traffic, which is based on estimates.

A photo of an under-used road with *one lorry and two cars* is captioned 'East Grinstead bypass is a converted rail route'. This road is *Beeching Way*, not the bypass which failed to get planning approval. Less than a mile of the 16 mile Three Bridges-East Grinstead-Groombridge line was used as part of a road. A narrow tunnel had to be opened out, and 34,000 tons of stone used to raise the formation to secure adequate width. It cost £2.75m and took *over two years to build*.[39] Having no pavements, it does not separate people from traffic! 15 miles form Forest Way and Worth Way bridleways/cycleways/footpaths.

A reference is made to the conversion of a closed railway line near Blackpool. It states that it was 'built on an old two-track railway embankment'. Other land had to be acquired to build part of the road, whilst bridges had to be rebuilt, and the width of *hard strip* in lieu of a proper hard shoulder on the rail route, was less than the width of the smallest car. An article in *Highways*, (February 1986), reports that part of a new highway constructed on the disused Blackpool Central Railway track was opened in January, connecting the M55 to Blackpool. Contracts included an advance of £148,000 in July 1984 for reconstruction and strengthening of the bridges which carried the railway over various side roads, and a main works contract of £3.5m covering construction of 4.9km road, of which 0.7 km was dual carriageway, with hard strips varying between 0.5m and 1.0m. 'Land acquisition, main earthworks and main drainage had already been carried out.[40] The part on the disused line was 3.1km of single carriageway with 450mm wide hard strips. Two bridges had steel girder decks replaced by pre-cast reinforced concrete beams and slab concrete decks. Brick abutments were strengthened by reinforced concrete backing. Two other bridges had brick arches strengthened by reinforced concrete. A fifth bridge was completely rebuilt, including a pre-cast concrete safety/noise barrier on the edge of an embankment. The £3.65m cost for 4.9km of mainly single carriageway, with sub standard hard strips in place of hard shoulders, works out at £0.75m per km', (£0.47m per mile). Track, reusable signals and equipment had been removed. In contrast, conversion of East Anglian lines proposed in 1975, from which track, signalling, other structures and OLE would have to be removed, was costed at £40,000 per km (see chapter 10). Inflation[41] would have increased this to only £0.14m per km by 1984, clear confirmation that it was too low

The leaflet included a photo of the closed GC line to illustrate the width of a skewed arch overbridge in relation to a *small* car. The implication on height restriction of this skewed arch for lorries and double-deck PSVs is overlooked. Replace the car with two trucks similar to the one passing under a 9 foot 9 inch arch bridge, in the adjoining photo, and a different impression is gained. The road under this latter bridge leads to a trading estate. The bridge has a railway on it, so conversion to road would leave the tight arch

---

[38] The statistics are drawn from published records by BR and the Office of National Statistics.

[39] *A History of East Grinstead*, Page 181, by M.J. Leppard.

[40] These costs were not included in either contract.

[41] A new base year was begun in 1974 (= 100), by 1984, when the Blackpool contract was let, it was 352

completely unaltered. If there was an attempt to build a new road link from the top of the rather high embankment, after conversion, it would take up valuable space occupied by industrial premises. The trading estate has been identified as the Brooklands Industrial Park, sometimes referred to as the Wintersells Road Business Park. The road under the tight bridge is not the only entrance to the estate. There is another which is wider. The estate was built in the 1950s. To build a trading estate beyond this restricted access bridge was - to put it kindly - imprudent and short-sighted. Nevertheless, there is no reason why the bridge could not have been widened if the local authority, the owner of the trading estate or users of the estate had put their hands into their pockets and provided the cash. However, it is typical of the road transport industry to wait for others to subsidise them, whilst they increase vehicle sizes, so that, eventually, someone else is pressured to pick up the tab and pay for suitable roads and bridges.[42] It should also be remembered that the photo of the lorry and the tight bridge represents $^1/_{250}$th of a second in 365 days.

One can equally find railway overbridges with similar restrictions as the latter, and far more road overbridges as wide and even higher than that on the closed GC railway line.

Another $^1/_{250}$th of a second photo shows Chelsea railway bridge empty. There is no date. It may have been Christmas Day: sparse road traffic confirms it was not a weekday in the off-peak, never mind the peak! One could take a similar photo of the M1 on Christmas Day or many roads on other days.[43] A photo of a conversion in Edinburgh has an under-whelming nine cars, carrying perhaps 15 people, in a space that would take four trains carrying thousands or 50 cars carrying 75, illustrating the wastefulness of road utilisation.

The leaflet contains quotes by two *experts*. One is Professor Hall, a geographer at Reading University, co-author of a scheme (see chapter 10), to convert railways into busways. The other is a *competitor*! It would be surprise indeed if a haulier praised railways! The validity of *his* criticism must be related to the *damning* indictment of the road haulage industry and its sponsors - the DoT - by John Wardroper, in *Juggernaut*. It reveals the dangers from lorries to which other road users and the public are exposed. They are a greater danger to motorists than to pedestrians and cyclists, who seem to be the only risk groups which register with the conversionists. Separating lorries from pedestrians would not cut deaths caused by cars, nor by lorries to motorists, but the conversion campaign ignores that, by trying to claim that all pedestrian deaths would be avoided.

The leaflet conclusion that 'the DoT recognises the great value of disused railways in providing land for new roads', is not borne out by the reality of 10,000 miles closed in relation to the 200 miles used as *part* of a road. It claims that the 'DoT has refused to carry out studies', that would lead, by inference, to converting all railways to roads. This seems to overlook the study carried out at DoE expense in 1975, (see chapter 10), but goes on to mention it, without asking why that study did not lead to conversion. The reason claimed for DoT inaction, is that 'BR is the sole judge as to whether it should continue to operate a service on a rail route and the DoT claims to be powerless to change it'. Who-ever made that claim in the DoT, must be unaware that government decides whether to subsidise. If they pull the plug, railway routes are closed. Unlike the conversion theorists, the road dominated DoT clearly recognises that there is a vital role for railways.

---

[42] See *Square Deal Denied* for a record of the problems imposed on bridges built long before the motor lorry, and the improper and unjustified pressure put on privately owned railways to strengthen their bridges to help competitors.

[43] The author travelled on the M6 & M1 on Christmas Day - it was like a desert. See photos of under-utilised roads.

The British Road Federation, which had around 100 companies and organisations as members, was formed in 1932 to 'promote intelligent, balanced and comprehensive transport planning throughout the country, and to press for an adequate network of national and local roads'. It ceased to exist in 1999/2000. It was by definition, in opposition to railways as a method of transport, and thereby had much in common with the conversion league. Each year, it produced a booklet entitled *Basic Road Statistics*, the purpose of which was 'to bring order to the confusion which arises from the use of contradictory or conflicting road statistics. It is hoped that these statistics will be adopted generally'. It was expected that the slant placed on this source of data would achieve their objectives. The booklet tended to become regarded as the 'tablets of stone' of road transport statistics. Regrettably, the source of this data can now be revealed to be less reliable and accurate than readers had assumed, (see pages 153).

The BRF 'Roadshow'

In 1984, the BRF held meetings around the UK to pursue a campaign - 'Room to move' - for improved roads. BR was invited to attend one in Manchester, on 20th March 1984, and the author of this book represented them. The speaker was a Director of the BRF. There were around two dozen present, who with few exceptions - were biased in favour of road transport. In addition to calling for more road construction, the speaker suggested converting under utilised or unused railways into roads. His views were in conflict with those of his predecessor at the Institution of Civil Engineers debate in 1955. On conversion, except for the author, none of the others present had any facts.

The author responded as follows:

- Only sixty out of 7,000 miles of track closed in the past twenty years had been converted into roads and before they set their sights on lines that *they* thought were under utilised, they should convert the 6,940 miles of closed routes begging to be used.
- An independent survey by Coopers & Lybrand Associates[1] showed that only one of ten lines recently considered for closure had any prospect of conversion. Even that line [Marylebone-Northolt], had less width than the standard 7.3 metres required by the Department of Transport for carriageways: being 6.7 metres or less, with 5.9 metres only at one location. Use would be limited to cars only, feeding into the already congested Baker Street. Widths on some other routes were down to 5.3 metres, also ruling out LGVs and large buses.[2]
- The glossy cover of their publicity booklet depicted a High Speed Train on a single line passing under a hump backed single arch bridge of low clearance. This clearly exposed the conversion problem.
- BR had to justify all of their investment by a rate of return expressed in pounds sterling, whilst roads investment is 'justified' by an aggregation of the *estimated* time that would be saved by users.

---

[1] British Rail internal publication *"Management Brief"*, 15.3.84. See also page 168.
[2] The Report circulated by the BRF after the meeting, misquoted these figures and then related them to a financial rate of return! (see page 93).

The speaker referred to the 'surplus £7,000m of road tax revenue'.[3] Chris Bannister, Lecturer in Town & Country Planning, University of Manchester, challenged this *surplus*, saying 'it disregarded the debit to the Health service and emergency services caused by road accidents'. Some said this was *academic nonsense*.

It is not *academic nonsense* when forecast reductions in accident costs are used to justify road improvements! The speaker also disregarded the costs of emergency services,[4] the effects of pollution, structural damage to buildings, pavements and verges and double glazing all of which fall on others. Contrary to opinion in the motor industry, road haulage pays much less than it should for road use. Recent research shows that 'LGVs only pay for around 59-69% of the costs they impose on society. Per tonne carried, rail produces around 80% less carbon dioxide than road'.[5]

In closing the Manchester meeting, Mr. H. Phillipson, [Director, British Aggregate Construction Materials Industries] said that the *'revelations on the 6,940 miles of [unconverted] closed railway and narrow widths were new to him, put a new perspective on the hypothesis of rail conversion and would doubtless open many eyes'*. This comment was not included in the BRF post-conference Report. There is no evidence that it opened *any* eyes, outside of that meeting.

In his internal report on the BRF Conference, the author recorded his views that the presentation was unimpressive compared to others experienced at conferences and public meetings. There were no slides or charts. It included, in the list of projected road schemes in the Manchester area, some which, it transpired from local authority representatives, who spoke later, had already been cancelled.

The BRF Report of the conference incorrectly stated that conversion of the Marylebone to Northolt railway line to a road would produce a rate of return of between 6.7% and 5.9%. The author wrote to the BRF, pointing out that figures of 6.7 and 5.9 quoted by him related to available *widths* in metres on the railway line mentioned, and were from a BR Management Brief, which made no reference to a rate of return. The standard MoT width was 7.3 metres. Furthermore, the BRF Report referred to '8,000 miles of railway closed *in* 1969', whereas the author, quoting from the Brief - and being well aware of the length of time taken to secure TUCC approval and Ministerial authority for closure of uneconomic lines - had spoken of 7,000 miles closed *by* 1969 (i.e. in the 20 years from 1948). On request, the BRF issued a brief, but incomplete, correction.

The BRF focuses undue attention on road related taxes: licences and fuel duty, which they believe should be spent on road improvements. During the 123 years when railways were privately owned, they were subject to corporate and other taxes, not a penny of which was ever returned to them to spend on their *highway*, which was built and maintained entirely at railway company expense. BRF moans regarding the 'raiding of the Road Fund' to aid the Exchequer in the years before nationalisation, are in respect of sums quite insignificant in comparison to what government skimmed from railways.[6] The

---

[3] This principle applied to tobacco would see those taxes applied solely to treating lung cancer, (see pages 94,95).

[4] A 1994 *Police Stop* video stated that road accidents cost £5.5bn p.a.

[5] *Goods without the Bads*, Transport 2000 Booklet

[6] In World War I, Government had free use of railways and was estimated to owe £400m for that use, (see *The Times*, 14.2.21), but paid £60m - less tax! In World War II it benefited to the tune of £1bn, (see page 6).

BRF in its annual publication *Basic Road Statistics* reprints - every year a section detailing amounts taken from the Fund[7] from 1915 to 1936, and totalling £42.1m

'Research by NERA and other consultants [working] for the government show that 40-ton 5-axle lorries are under taxed by £13,700 pa once pollution, health, road damage costs are included. Other consultants [OXERA] have suggested that congestion, accidents and interest on capital spent on roads need to be included, making the figure £30,700 pa'[8]

The idea that tax levied on road users should be spent on roads is from the Kindergarten School of Economics. Carried to a logical conclusion alcohol tax should be used to treat alcoholics, tobacco tax on lung disease, income tax for the sole benefit of taxpayers, etc. The quick witted will realise that nothing is left for NHS, police, fire services, unemployed, retired, defence or to pay government employees. Government never spent a penny of railway taxation to construct or maintain railways. These included one levied for 100 years only on *railway* passengers. In addition to corporate taxes, and sums skimmed from railways in two Wars, 'Passenger Duty'[9] - was imposed on railways from 1830 to 1929. It was originally imposed on stage coaches, but after their demise not transferred to other road transport. Not a penny of this tax, nor sums skimmed out of railways during Wars, was spent on railways. When government reluctantly ended this discriminatory tax, following pressure from rail passengers and a few MPs, the Chancellor insisted that railway companies spent the capitalised amount on works which were not otherwise financially justified with the declared objective of reducing unemployment. The Federation of British Industries[10] had the gall to propose to government that railway companies should spend this money in UK industry and none in railway factories!

No similar tax was levied on road passenger transport, despite them making substantial profits, e.g. the London General Omnibus Company - which later became part of the LPTB in 1933 - was making 10% profits and did not pay this tax.

During the two World Wars, government sequestrated railways and froze rail prices to hold down Government expenditure. After the First World War, railways' taxable profits were limited when government froze rail profits at 1913 levels - in perpetuity, and without adjustment for inflation, and set up a unique court of law to control railway freight charges thereafter, (see page 3). No comparable control was exercised over the profits or prices of any other industry or business.

During the Second World War, Government effectively skimmed over £1bn out of railways and imposed discounts[11] in addition to imposing taxation and Excess Profits Tax, whilst road transport profits were untouched, and even allowed to escalate.[12] Unlike all other businesses, railways were not refunded 20% of Excess Profits Tax after the 1939-45 War, nor a penny piece of the £1bn immorally sequestrated from profits. Nor when BR wished to modernise the assets which the public erroneously assumed were *bought* by the State, did Government donate a penny towards that task.

---

[7] The Fund was set up in 1909 to produce cash to convert roads from those suited for horse drawn traffic - funded by municipal Rates, to which railways were major contributors - to those suited for motor vehicles, which destroyed surfaces and caused massive dust clouds on property and people. Hitherto, motor vehicles paid nothing to use roads.

[8] Transport 2000 press release 7.3.01.

[9] *Square Deal Denied*, Page 18

[10] UK industry was struggling to compete with other countries.

[11] *Britain's Railways - The Reality*, Page 18.

[12] *Square Deal Denied*, Chapters 12 & 13.

In 1992, on BBC TV, the MoT said that unlike road transport, BR paid no taxes. Acts of Parliament did not require BR to make a profit, merely to break even, and not even that before 1962, when it was the BTC which had that directive. Government policies never allowed BR to earn profits from which to pay tax.

Interference by the Transport Tribunal - a court of law - and politicians held fares below industry-fuelled inflation for 40 years - peaking at 55 points below - thereby cutting potential profits by £11.6bn, excluding interest.[13] Politicians caused other losses. For 20 years, for political and social reasons, BR had to fund loss making services, whilst being prevented from charging sufficient on main routes to cross-subsidise - a situation which would have given road operators apoplexy. Ministers forced the payment of higher wages to rail staff, and blocked closure of uneconomic lines - all for electoral reasons.[14]

Studies have proved that road haulage pays less than its' fair share of road costs, (see pages 169-171,176,179) - ordinary motorists are subsidising hauliers. 'Non-payment of vehicle excise duty by illegal road transport operators is a significant problem', (Plowden & Buchan).

The road lobby ignores that the road users gain in several ways from the construction of new roads, motorways and road improvements. Journeys are quicker, accidents reduced and the facility to drive at more constant speeds reduces wear and tear. Fewer gear changes and less brake wear further cut costs. Journey time gains and accident reductions are used by the DoT when new road schemes are planned as a means of justification.[15]

Promoters of juggernauts - including the BRF - forgot that they had to leave motorways and enter towns where they cannot negotiate corners without crushing pavements and blocking traffic whilst deliveries are made. Repairs are not funded by the haulage industry. If rail operations caused damage to third party property, BR had to fund repairs.

To avoid delays to other traffic and damage to pavements, etc., would require costly compulsory acquisition of millions of perfectly good houses and commercial properties to create wider turning circles and more substantial road widths and depths. Damage repair costs are not paid by hauliers, but by ratepayers - another hidden subsidy.

Most hauliers buy imported lorries, some buy abroad. Some register lorries abroad, some fit double fuel tanks to enable them to use cheaper foreign fuel. Profits and taxes from those purchases goes abroad. The effect is that claims that hauliers pay more in tax than the UK spends on roads is even further undermined, increasing the hidden subsidy.

A Radio 4 programme 'PM' (17.1.96), included a statement by an AA spokesman, that *'Winston Churchill diverted money to railways'*. After prolonged correspondence,[16] the AA supplied the author with a copy of a BRF document, which was the source of this

---

[13] *Britain's Railways - The Reality*, Appendix A.

[14] *Britain's Railways - The Reality*.

[15] See *Juggernaut*, by J. Wardroper, Pages 36-43, which also reveals the limitations to objections at Public Inquiries.

[16] Initially, the BBC told the author that it was made by Lord Montagu, who told the author that he had not done so. The BBC then said it was probably the AA. The author was only able to obtain details of the source of this unfounded claim, after writing to the Director General of the AA, having failed to get the information from their spokesman. When the answer - that it was from the BRF - arrived, it was accompanied by a letter which ended 'I am sorry that you feel it has been necessary to raise this matter'. This is similar to replies to complaints from industry that 'you found it necessary to complain', which imply that a complaint was trivial. The author was concerned to establish the facts and for the statement to be publicly withdrawn. The BBC, when told the facts, did not broadcast a correction.

claim. It stated that Winston Churchill, in his 1926 Budget speech, 'wanted to protect railways as far as possible'. Hansard (vol. 194, col. 1710), reveals that he did not use the word 'protect' at all. He said that 'it was impossible to watch the development [expansion of road transport] without considering the reaction on railways'. The Budget did not allocate a *penny* to railways. This is confirmed by annual railway audited accounts, which had to be deposited with the MoT. Had any cash been conceded, railways would have been compelled, by law, to account for it. Government concern for the reaction on railways was not altruistic. They were concerned that loss of *profitable* traffic to road, may undermine the statutory concept of cross-subsidy to controlled low freight rates, which railways had to charge UK industry, to enable them to compete with more efficient foreign industry.

This erroneous BRF document inferred that pre-war railways were subsidised by road transport, when the boot was on the other foot.[17] Railways had to maintain and strengthen bridges for competitors' use and paid heavy municipal Rates to fund roads for decades, whilst road transport paid little or nothing. By 1926, they still did not produce enough to fund their own roads. Taxation of railways was always for use by the Exchequer, it was never re-deployed for railway benefit, their passengers or freight customers. Hitherto, the road fund had been applied to road costs, albeit small sums had been extracted, mainly to help the war. However, since government had subsidised the cost of buying motor vehicles before World War I, and after that war, sold surplus military vehicles - often in mint, unused condition, for a fraction of their value, this was not unreasonable. These were early examples of the favoured treatment government meted out to road transport. They were also free of restrictive legislation which tied and controlled railways. Later, when government was trying to cut unemployment, it offered interest bearing loans to railways to fund capital projects to that end, whilst providing substantial sums from the Exchequer for road building. Of these matters, the BRF made no mention!

This is not the only example of misinformation regarding pre-war railways. In 1946, an MP claimed that railways only remained solvent because of £27m given by government in 1929. This money was an *interest bearing loan*, repaid at the end of its term, (see page 11). It contrasts with £129m railway companies invested pre-war, plus £1bn in working expenses which included renewals of assets. Another MP claimed in 1951, that government bailed out railways after the First War, with £30m, (see page 11). This was a half payment of the sum paid to recompense railways for having screwed them in that War, having taken them over and had free conveyance of every person, horse, vehicle or item remotely connected with War. In contrast, road transport was paid *generously* for its wartime work. After both wars, railways were left to restore assets badly depreciated by unfunded government use, including thousands of wagons, coaches and locos, and miles of track transferred, in both Wars, without a by-your-leave of the owners to war zones abroad, where much fell into enemy hands when our Army retreated. The sum paid, after the First War was a fraction of that due, but was held down by duplicitous politicians, whilst nothing was paid after the Second War. No civilian road transport vehicle left these shores without full payment, and none were sequestrated by government for use in the UK, without generous payments, in either war. Despite these facts, the road lobby has the gall to claim it has funded the Exchequer, whilst railways have not.

---

[17] In 1938, the privately owned railways in their publication *Clear the Lines*, stated that Britain's railways were alone in Europe in not having been given any government subsidy. (See also *Square Deal Denied*, Page 102).

New disciples appeared to preach conversion. Unlike their predecessors, they made a serious error in trying to introduce a little detail on how it would operate.

Reading University Study

Prof. Hall was commissioned [29.8.74], to test claims which had aroused public interest[1] that converting railways into roads is feasible and would meet public transport needs of urban areas at reasonable cost. (Hansard 4.2.76, col. *631*). The terms of reference called for

- *Comparative average costs* of busways and surface railways;
- An assessment of conversion costs with specific attention to modifications to bridges & stations, track gauge & width, central barriers, bus terminal facilities [ticketing, *waiting room & other passenger facilities*], *access to the road network, metering, disruption costs during conversion*;
- An analysis of labour requirements - *subdivided by function* - for the efficient running of both modes;
- The analysis to *specify service frequency*, number of buses, a practical *procedure for dealing with accidents & breakdowns.*

The estimated cost was £8938. The DoE has a number of major reservations affecting the conclusions, (Hansard, 27.1.76, col. *147*). The reservations must have included disappointment that some elements of the terms of reference were not fulfilled, notably the italicised items above. As the specification related to urban routes, work on rural routes was outside the remit. Bus and lorry design was covered, but appeared to be outside the remit.

Prof. Peter Hall and Edward Smith had produced a proposal to replace railways by busways on six lines in East Anglia, including Liverpool Street station in London, which daily handled tens of thousands of commuters and thousands of Inter City passengers.

Following a leak, before the report was published in January 1976, Smith wrote to *The Times* (27.12.75) to 'confirm that his study *does* claim that buses will be safer than the trains they replace, as buses and coaches have a *passenger* fatality rate 38% lower than trains[2], that buses on converted railways will be safer than existing buses and the *passenger* fatality rate will *probably* be less than half that of the trains they replace'. He said that there would be fewer accidents to pedestrians and motorists by allowing existing traffic onto the converted system.[3] With excellent alignment and limited access, the new roads will be much safer than city streets or country roads. He referred to a letter to *The Times* from Mr. Kohr who was concerned that people now using trains would prefer cars to buses. On the Liverpool St-Harwich-Southend, this does not arise because there is not sufficient capacity in central London[4] for a significant percentage to use cars.[5] It is difficult to imagine travellers wanting to change to cars. With the subsidy BR receives, 'buses could operate a fare-free service at twice the frequency. If the subsidy was abolished when

---

[1] There is no indication where this interest was voiced. Most public comment in the media was anti, (see chapter 15)

[2] No source is quoted. The DfT told the author that 105 passengers were killed in PSV accidents in 1975. HMRI said 69 rail passengers were killed in 1975. Thus rail was 34% better, and would be lower, even related to the suspect DfT data on PSV travel, (see page 153). If the preceding year was his basis, rail fatalities were 26 and PSV were 64!

[3] If true, diverting buses with ex-rail passengers from rail formation to the A12 (see page 100) will increase accidents.

[4] Commuters do not all travel to central London.

[5] The reality is that a case can only be made for buses by making it difficult for cars to park or imposing toll or congestion charges, which means that, unlike BR, buses could not face car competition.

buses replace trains, fares could be cut by two-thirds.[6] At current prices, the cost of not converting the whole of BR is £1-2bn pa, plus at least 1,200 lives lost yearly'.[7]

11,000 miles of converted railway cannot provide alternative routes for traffic on 220,000 miles of road. Hence, *opinions* of what *may* happen on selected routes cannot be extrapolated. It was not proved that a claimed reduction in pedestrian deaths would not be more than offset by more deaths among thousands using 'level crossings'[8] bereft of barriers, and thousands walking between moving buses at Liverpool Street bus station.

If buses could operate fare-free services given a subsidy, why did they not do so when given a subsidy by BR, peaking at £1m pa in 1968[9] to take on passengers displaced from closed lines? Objectors to proposed rail closures often stated that comparable bus fares were higher than rail fares. MPs complained that bus fares *rose* after closures.[10]

The belief that buses would be safer, ignores that they would be travelling faster,[11] and hence accidents are likely to rise. Rail junctions are mainly on the flat, carrying more risk of accidents. Just as speed limits are ignored on existing roads with detriment to life and limb, so they would be on converted railways. Under the scheme, trains carrying 1000s of passengers from Norfolk and Suffolk would terminate at a station not designed for the purpose. The theory that all railways could be converted to roads, also founders on the fact that the original acquisition of land was ring-fenced to limit use to the operation of a railway. Other uses were legally excluded by original - still valid - Enabling Acts of Parliament. Owners, whose property was subject to compulsory purchase, after long hearings in Parliament, were given powers to demand the return of land, if it was not used for its intended purpose. Some may have to be offered to descendants of original owners, or current owners of previously severed properties, such as farmers. Some assets may already be under negotiation or review prior to sale without the knowledge of outsiders. The value of assets cannot be determined until they are put on the market.

The Hall/Smith scheme published January 1976

The lines embraced in the scheme were: two urban commuter lines [Tottenham Hale-North Woolwich, Romford-Upminster], three rural lines [Witham-Braintree, Colchester-Sudbury, Crouch Valley], and one main line [Liverpool St-Harwich/Walton/Clacton/Southend]. Allied aspects of the scheme are scattered throughout a 132 page book. It says that the line from Liverpool Street station is probably the busiest commuter line in the world, (Page 63). It wasn't - Waterloo had 65,000 commuters in 1976, and Liverpool Street 59,000.[12] Two of the six tracks from Liverpool Street would be converted to roads, whilst others on the same formation, would be retained for train services to Bishops Stortford and Cambridge,[13] (Page 69). The plan does not reveal that the station, was effectively two

---

[6] See analysis on page 139 which demonstrates that this would not be achieved.

[7] £1-2bn is a wide range for an estimate. It is not stated how 1,200 was derived. The DfT told the author they had no record prior to 1979, of pedestrian deaths involving a PSV. For 1979-81, the average was 251 pa. This is the *maximum* possible saving. Logic suggests there would be some at Liverpool St, and by continued *trespassing*

[8] 12 will remain on the main line route, (Pages 68,99,100,101,105,106), plus four newly created, (see page 143).

[9] See British Rail Annual Report & Accounts 1968, Page 31.

[10] See *The Railway Closure Controversy*, and Hansard vol. 590, col. 202.

[11] The average speed of buses on roads other than motorways and dual carriageways was 45 mph.

[12] See BRB Facts & Figures 1978.

[13] This route was used by 258 trains carrying 31,000 commuters to Enfield, Chingford, Hertford, plus main line passengers to Bishops Stortford, Cambridge & beyond, compared to 265 trains on the route in the Hall/Smith study.

buildings - divided by a brick wall - known as the western and eastern trainsheds, opened in 1875 and 1894. The plan was for the eastern trainshed to be a bus station, although they could have claimed part of the western trainshed, because some trains to be replaced by buses, ran from that part. That would have been difficult to use due to the dividing wall. Therefore, they opted for a cramped area, saying that west side commuters could have three extra platforms. The Treasury would not accept a debit for platforms for a service that hitherto did not use them. This contrasts with Manningtree, where they claimed a disproportionate share of the station facilities for road traffic, (see page 134).

Constructional work

Descriptions of structural alterations appear throughout the book for the six routes. Hundreds of altered locations are mentioned which, without drawings, are unclear. Of 256 km[14] total length of the six routes, only 1.7 km (0.6%) had drawings - none of which were suitable to give to a contractor to quote. The rest were mentioned in hundreds of short paragraphs. Difficult issues facing conversion are formation width, and the height and width of bridges and tunnels. Bridges should have been listed in a table, in line order, showing their displayed bridge number, dimensions, and whether under or over-bridges. That would ensure that none were missed, especially on farm or private land.

Five bridges are listed Romford-Upminster, one Witham-Braintree, four on the Crouch Valley line, a viaduct and a bridge Colchester-Sudbury, and *none* in the North Woolwich-Tottenham Hale section of the book, except a disused swing bridge. However, there are four railway bridges over this line: West Ham, Stratford, Clapton and Tottenham Hale. The Stratford bridge/tunnel is referred to in the main line section of the book as of 3.8m headroom, to be excavated by 0.8m. This underpass is vital for buses returning to Liverpool Street. Some lorries may require 5.1m. Either way, the formation would have to be excavated either side for a sensible gradient. Drainage pumps may be needed to clear underpass flooding. It seemed certain that there were road bridges, in view of its location. The London A-Z map, reveals 12 roads over and 3 roads under the line. OS maps show 17 bridges on the Crouch Valley line and 16 on Colchester-Sudbury. Potential problems with embankments and cuttings on these branches are not addressed.

The main line route shows 76 over- and 48 under-bridges.[15] Only 11 over-bridges are DfT height. Headroom is not recorded for 43. Some are shown, or inferred, as 'adequate', which is unhelpful.[16] To increase headroom or strengthen, some require rebuilding or re-decking and others to have the formation excavated.[17] The practicability of that could only be assessed by tests, which could not have been carried out without endangering trains, unless during a temporary blockage of a line. Some bridges including footbridges, are to be demolished, (Pages 48,54,99,103,108). Users will cross the new road on the level, contravening the aim to have no interface between pedestrians and vehicles to save lives, (see page 143). These locations will experience accidents, for which no debit is taken.

Smith measured bridge *widths* (*Autocar*, 8.5.76), 'by dodging between trains' - a danger-ous act. His letter did not explain how he measured *headroom*, which would have been

---

[14] Why they used metric rather than imperial distances, which were, then and now, the norm for UK railways and roads is not clear. It was a fetish of the conversion league, whose last chairman advocated its adoption (*The Times*, 5.1.78) claiming that most motorists travelled in Europe. In fact, they were a *minority*, as ONS statistics show

[15] Bridges are mentioned in about 100 brief paragraphs on 31 pages. Some bridges have been missed, (see page 100).

[16] As it is said (Page 15) that 4.2m is minimum & 4.6m desirable, it is not clear what height they are. (see page 108)

[17] Not merely *under* a bridge, but both sides to give a gradual gradient. Excavations may extend over a long distance.

even more dangerous, given the 25kv OLE suspended below bridges. BR staff would have had power off to take measurements. A railway over-bridge between Forest Gate and Manor Park has been overlooked. The London A-Z reveals road bridges not mentioned in the report, and hence, it cannot be known if they have adequate width and/or headroom: Primrose St., Worship St., North Folgate, Commercial St., Wheler St., Fleet St., Valance Rd., Globe Rd. and Morpeth St. Low bridge heights on this route led to it being initially limited to 6.25kv OLE, but later raised to 25kv, when DoT requirements were relaxed.

A link road would be built near Brentwood for vehicles to pass to the A12, and 26 miles of double track from Shenfield to Colchester abandoned. Conversion would have meant widening. It has 53 bridges and about 21 miles of embankment and cutting. Lloyd, who claimed that two tracks are ample for three or more lanes, must be turning in his grave. No increase in accidents nor travelling time lost has been included for this role reversal.

Three sections of the North Woolwich-Tottenham Hale line would be converted: North Woolwich-Silvertown, Custom House, Canning Town-Tottenham Hale. Conveniently, one abandoned section includes Silvertown tunnel. At the other end, 1.72 km of the railway to be converted would run alongside a line carrying services unaffected by conversion. It would be essential to build a 1.72 km robust wall between the rail route and the converted road to avoid a swerving road vehicle creating a 'Selby' accident.

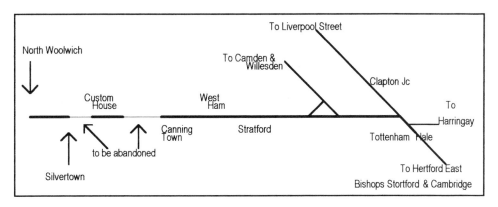

The report includes remarks, such as 'the cost of work *will* be less than the value of the steel and engineering bricks', (Page 76) - no £ sign appears. A report should show all facts and figures. Ballast is to be used as filling material in places, (Pages 75,76,101). It does not say that its quantity and quality has been assessed, nor are costs of collecting and moving it, mentioned. Asphalt will be laid on the bare earth formation under the ballast. It is scarcely credible that this would be solid enough for heavy road traffic, when rails, sleepers and ballast had spread train weight. Worse, at one location, it will be laid on the *cobbled* surface of a road to be developed as an underpass, (Page 77). Whereas minor track repairs are carried out between trains it could not be done with closely spaced road traffic.

Property is to be acquired due to inadequate width of the formation at 13 locations, (Pages 43,54,73,75,76,83,85,86,95,96,103). They involve 15 houses, gardens shortened, graves relocated, businesses relocated, two council car parks, tenanted property, part of industrial premises, a private carpark, a street closed, part of two vacant plots (which may have better sale prospects if not shortened), and a playing field 'moved' onto sidings (at no cost)[18]. How long it would take to replace well compacted, oil-contaminated siding formations with lush grass is left to the imagination. BR buildings are to be demolished, but it is imprudent to assume that 'none are of architectural merit', (Page 82), given the listing of that concrete monstrosity Birmingham New St PSB, (see also page 183). Ilford flyover is to be demolished (Page 84), and as this is going to be an essential part of the conversion of the first pair of tracks in the first week, it should have said how and when this would be done, as the lines to remain in use for that week are under the flyover. (see diagram, page 148).

Liverpool Street bus station

The greater part of Liverpool Street station which occupies 4 hectares [9.884 acres][19] will continue as a railway station. Their scale plan of the area to become a bus station,[20] with 30 bays holding two buses each is 50 metres wide by 155 metres long - about 7,750 square metres: 1.9 acres[21]. An adjoining area will be used to park an unspecified number of vehicles - whether it would meet all needs cannot be determined from the Report.

An arriving bus will pull into the first available bay, which may be part occupied. Buses will not be allocated to specific routes. A bus arriving from one place, will depart to any destination as required, when 100% full.[22] 380 vehicles will leave Liverpool Street in a selected peak of 58 minutes[23] - one every 9 seconds. Three minutes is specified as the loading time,[24] there is no mention of an unloading time, to enable terminal turnround time to be calculated. Incoming passengers would have to wait to unload until a bay became available. There may be long waits in the peak, for which no time loss is debited.

Manningtree

The route from Liverpool Street has Inter City trains to Ipswich and Norwich. Passengers will change at Manningtree to a train, at *the one platform to be retained*, (Page 100). Three of the four platforms/tracks at Manningtree would be converted to roads, for use by buses running towards Harwich, whilst one is 'retained for the Ipswich train'.[25]

Bus services

No timetables are intended. In addition to express buses, 50 stopping peak services will leave Liverpool St. in the peak.[26] Off-peak, most will stop as trains do now, but will be twice as frequent,[27] (Page 114). Not all destinations will have non-stop peak services, 23 will be served jointly, i.e. stopping, (Page 116). Except for a 58 minute 'peak', no rail timetable is shown, with which comparisons can be made. There is no Saturday nor Sunday timetable. In the peak, 108 express, and all stopping services will leave the converted

---

[18] The Conversion League had repeatedly claimed that no widening is necessary for conversion.

[19] In comparison, Victoria coach station occupies 3.3 acres.

[20] A belief that a bus service would be better if continued through central London (Page 114) instead of terminating at Liverpool Street *station*, shows unfamiliarity with the restricted width of Liverpool *Street* itself.

[21] 57% of the area of Victoria coach station.

[22] It is not explained who will decide which passengers to eject when a bus has 101% aboard. It will cause delays.

[23] Why this period was used is unclear. A 1958 CTCC study defined a $1^1/_2$ hour peak, as did the BTC 1968 Annual Report. 402 buses are required for his peak, (Page 116), but 80 make multiple trips = 482, not the 380 on Page 72.

[24] The author was told by the operator of 71-seat coaches that it takes 5 minutes to load through the one door. Each commuter train coach loads through two or more doors that equate to four PSV doors. Rail passengers load their luggage whilst a PSV driver does that, and could not take his place in the cab, until all luggage was stowed.

[25] This literally implies one train. The service to Ipswich and beyond is actually *twice* that going towards Harwich.

[26] Said to be less than in 'the narrower I495 bus lane in New Jersey', (Page 72). It is narrower by a mere 0.04m, if Smith's 3.3m lane were feasible, (see page 120). Speed is limited to 35 mph [56kph], not 72kph [45mph] quoted

[27] No running times are specified for stopping bus services in the peak or off-peak. However, the scheme forecasts that off-peak services will be quicker than trains, (Pages 118-119).

route at Brentwood to go via the A12, and thence other roads, to Ingatestone, Chelmsford, Hatfield Peverel, Witham, Kelvedon, Marks Tey, Colchester.[28] At Colchester, 16 express and all stopping services will revert to the converted system. No road capacity problem is foreseen, (see page 121). For the other five routes, no frequency or schedule is provided.

Bus Fleets

Bus design takes 7 pages, but width is not mentioned. 'Single-deck will be about 3.0m high, double-deck 3.9-4.4m high may not clear some bridges', (Page 8). Buses from Liverpool St will be 75-seat double-deck, (Page 116), and will run to any destination.[29] They will be 10m long, (Page 72).[30] A driver's last journey will be home, (Page 114).

The concept of buses pulling into the first available bay and departing to a random destination means that the prospect of them making the last journey to their home would be unlikely - even impossible - to ensure that it was completed within 8 hours.

To convert passengers to buses, a 65% average load is assumed, (Page 119). Peak buses are expected to be 100% loaded in *one direction*, the other will be very low. Off-peak is not predicted, but must be below 100% to avoid delays. A 65% average is improbable over the 20 hour time span of the BR timetable. It states that passengers will not go to the top deck for a journey less than 20 minutes, (Page 7). A total of 451 buses is envisaged for all routes. 10% is added (Page 119), for maintenance and breakdown of the main line fleet from Liverpool St, bringing the total to 494. There is no cover for buses on other routes.

Having calculated the buses required - from passenger data, which is not included in the report - three of the destinations from Liverpool St. are then reduced: Wickford, Witham, and Marks Tey, by 4, 3, and 1 respectively. The explanation, (Page 115), is that at these locations, which are the start of 'branches' this number can be used to go on to the end of the branch, rather than return to Liverpool St., thereby reducing the buses required for those branches, in their peaks, 'which are later'. Who will decide which of the drivers will go forward, and how they will get to their homes is not explained. Nor is there any reference to parking, fuelling, servicing, nor maintenance of buses based on the branches.

432 buses will be provided for the Liverpool St/Stratford/Colchester peaks, (Page 119). Even *if* this is adequate for an *average* day, the peak is not going to be the same every day. It is not enough to provide for an *average* peak, having claimed all will be seated. On some days, the average will be exceeded, and some will have to wait, where they would get into a 'full' train. In the table dealing with the 'main line' bus fleet, (Page 116), there is a reference to Prittlewell and Southend being served 'via A127[T]'. Ingatestone-Colchester inclusive, to be served via the A12, (Pages 90,97), are not similarly annotated.

Manpower

The number of drivers said to be required is shown for each of the six routes. A total of 676 drivers for all six routes is quoted. It is stated that the main line route requires '650 drivers and 750 other staff[31] including ticket sellers, bus manufacturing staff and the bus share of road maintenance', (Page 121). For bus drivers, the median cost has been taken.[32]

---

[28] All this new traffic will interface with pedestrians. More fatalities are probable, but this was not mentioned. Services calling at all destinations (Page 115), will be especially slow, as they pass over roads in and out of towns.

[29] Existing trains to Southend, Clacton & Manningtree have toilets. Toilets on buses will reduce seating below 75.

[30] Trathens appear to operate the biggest bus on motorways, it has 71 seats and is 13m long, 4.16m high, 2.8m wide.

[31] Such staff are not shown on other routes. 750 was derived (Page 24) by taking the median of *five* bus groups, covering 76 operators, with averages for 73 of them! To average averages is unreliable and statistically unacceptable.

[32] As part of London & the South East, costs will be the highest in the country - not the median, (see page 103).

Numbers of drivers working a 40 hour week on the main line route are assessed by multiplying the peak bus requirement by 1.5 which is said to be 'normal', (Page 119).[33]

Operating costs for main line buses (Page 120), includes £1.94m 'Other costs', a term whose definition (Page 23), excludes the 750 staff (Page 121). It is derived by taking the median value of nine unnamed bus companies, to produce £4500 pa. 'Costs for five PTEs are less relevant, but shown as a matter of interest'. They are far *more* relevant. Their median value is £4905. London & South East costs are, for cost of living and manpower availability reasons, the highest in the country. This means that they would be higher than the highest PTE which was £7820 pa. It is emphasised that 'electricity board staff are excluded from rail figures'. So *non-rail* staff should be, as none were included for oil distribution to bus depots. Fuel costs are estimated without disclosing the scheduled mileage!

Fare Collection

There will be ticket offices at 'Liverpool Street, Stratford and other busy points'. Other passengers must put the exact fare into a sealed box near the driver, who will not touch the cash. Prepurchased tickets can be put in the box. Books of season tickets can be bought from ticket offices *or the driver*. Tickets can be offered in bulk at a slight discount to shop keepers who otherwise would be pestered for change. (Page 114).

Maintenance of vehicles

The scheme envisages (Page 85), using the Ilford Multiple Unit Depot as a bus and lorry maintenance depot, and states that for all the routes studied only 496 buses and 350 lorries[34] are needed. The facilities are said to be adequate for maintaining and parking buses and lorries.[35] 'Parking for 300 buses and 150 18m lorries[36] will be enough'. Costs were estimated for surfacing and other work. There are no separate costs for maintenance and renewal of bus terminals. There are references to 'Other costs', which includes some provision for vehicle and building maintenance by bus companies, (Page 23), but that could not include bus station costs, which are invariably under separate ownership.

The study report mentions (Page 85), that BR had a plan to move diesel maintenance from Stratford to Ilford. The objective would obviously be for economy, and to release land for possible sale. There is no financial contra entry for this lost opportunity. The report lays great stress on opportunity cost gains, but fails to take the debit for this loss.

Finances

The study claims that [rail] 'fares could have been reduced 64% and revenue would still have covered operating costs', (Page 120), i.e. a £1 fare would become 36p, (but see page 139). The intention is that buses would have no subsidy, unless bus travel was free.

All six routes in the Study, include the same qualifying phrase: *assuming conversion costs have been offset by benefits to private traffic*. This implies that, despite a restriction on use of the new road by private cars from Brentwood to Liverpool Street, funding the conversion will fall on motorists - but not in cash. The backup plan to pay for construction in *real* money, seems to be the sale of land and property, (see pages 107,144), but that may take years to materialise. Contractors will want paying up front.

---

[33] There is no reference to the length of working day. The formula ignores Saturdays. *Bus & Coach Operators Handbook* by Dr. J. Hibbs does not mention such a formula, but advocates preparing duty rosters to cover timetables
[34] It is not shown that 350 lorries could move rail freight. Some traffic comes from as far afield as Avonmouth, Ince and Liverpool. 496 buses are shown on Page 85.
[35] There is no likelihood of having the same depot shared by one bus company and one or more haulage companies.
[36] These lorries would have to be built specially and would be confined to the route. The buses will be 10m length.

Intangible non-cash benefits claimed

A monetary value is attributed to benefits passengers and non-passengers will derive.

Formation opportunity costs

Defined as the value to private vehicles of a new road in annual terms.

Journey & waiting time savings for passengers

Time savings[37] claimed to arise from shorter waiting-cum-journey times for a bus[38] than a train, are converted to a *paper* value - £1.7m pa - to pay for conversion. 'Two minutes is allowed for [rail] passengers to walk from the ticket office to train or platform' - but none for bus passengers. If both were equal neither need appear. The time to book a ticket and walk to a platform 'was recorded for 64 peak and 62 off-peak departures from Liverpool Street station', (Page 115). Peak passengers were recorded over a 40 minute period[39], off-peak over an 18 minute period in late evening, (Pages 117-119). They bought tickets to 21 and 22, respectively of the 44 destinations on the main line route from Liverpool Street.[40] On the basis of a few passengers for some destinations, it is assumed that this broken one hour period is typical of the estimated 65m passenger journeys made each year. Figures are extrapolated to apply to all passengers, despite the fact that none are recorded for about 50% of destinations - *on this route* and *none* for branches or destinations beyond. A claim is made that 11 of the 62 off-peak passengers will save time, whilst not one is perceived to take longer. The scheme states that 'passenger time will be saved on services that are not grant aided[41], but this will be partly offset by time lost changing from bus to train at Manningtree', (Page 119)

'To avoid great expense, cross platform interchange between LT & BR at Stratford will cease, but walking time will only be one minute', (Page 82). Time savings would be cut.

Motorists and other private vehicles

There is no reference to a detailed survey of motorists or other road users to find their journey details and ascertain if they would benefit from being diverted by a new route, rather than assuming that thousands would benefit from using this new road, when it may really extend their journey time to do so.[42] Their assumed journey time savings are converted to a total of £19.25m - not in cash - and claimed as savings from conversion.[43] The diversions from existing roads to the new converted system are as follows:

• A new Canning Town-Stratford road *will* take 4m of the 4.2m vehicles pa now on the A1011, (Page 36). *Probably* 6m of 7m vehicles pa on the A112 and A1006 will divert to the new Stratford-Tottenham Hale road, (Page 37).

• The A124 has 9m vehicles pa, and an unclassified road 8.5m pa. Not more than 6m vehicles pa can be allowed on this new Romford-Upminster road, (Pages 41, 43).[44]

---

[37] The validity of time benefits used by the DoT were challenged by an expert, (see footnote, page 169).

[38] That passengers may wait less for an unscheduled bus, than an advertised train is implausible. It is unrealistic to specify a peak-hour bus departure interval (Page 116), when buses depart when they are full.

[39] Chelmsford shows rail 36 and bus 39 minutes, 'saving 3 minutes', (Page 117). It is minus 3, thus cutting 'savings'.

[40] 22 main line destinations were not in the lists, nor are 20 destinations on branch lines, nor 48 beyond Manningtree. Thus, a handful of passengers were timed, whilst none were recorded to 90 potential destinations.

[41] Those travelling to Ipswich, Yarmouth, Norwich, etc.

[42] An independent study stated that an existing road route was shorter than the new converted road - see page 123.

[43] Two routes in the study were re-examined by the Polytechnic of Central London (see page 123), who dispute the conclusions, particularly in respect of traffic diversion benefits. Motorists diverting to new roads are credited £0.60 per hour, whilst rail passengers diverted to existing roads during conversion are credited only £0.30, (Page 36),

[44] There is no explanation as to how 6m vehicles will be allowed onto the new road, and 11.5m kept off.

- The B1018 has 1.8m vehicles pa. It is *assumed* that almost all will divert to the new Witham-Braintree road, (Page 48)
- *It can be expected* that the private vehicle traffic will be about 25% of that on the B1018, *say* 0.5m vehicles pa, half diverted to the new Marks Tey-Sudbury road and half *newly generated*,[45] (Page 54).[46]
- 1m vehicles pa will *probably* be diverted to the new Crouch Valley road. *If* the running time is cut by 15 minutes, the saving will be worth £150,000 pa; if newly generated traffic averages 0.5m vehicles pa, the benefit will be £90,000 pa (Page 60).[47]
- Conversion *may* reduce traffic on the A11 through Stratford by a third. (Page 80).
- On the new Shoreditch-Brentwood road, to avoid delaying peak hour buses, not more than 2400 private vehicles per hour will be permitted (Page 110); access will be restricted by charging tolls,[48] (Page 111); the *probable* two way flow of private vehicles will be 50,000 daily - diversion of 50,000 vehicles will save 1,600 accidents, (Page 111); these vehicles will be replaced by 50,000 newly generated vehicles per day, (Page 112).
- The traffic on the A604 and B1352 is about 2.5m vehicles pa. *If* 2m pa divert to the new Colchester-Harwich road, the time saving is worth £0.2m, (Page 112).
- On the A133 and B1027, there are about 5m vehicles pa. *If* 4m of these divert to the new Colchester-Clacton/Walton-on-Naze road, saving 8 minutes per vehicle, the saving will be £0.32m pa. (Page 113).
- The new Brentwood-Southend road will take traffic off the A129, which has about 2.2m vehicles pa, and will supplement the A127. It can be *expected* to take 3m vehicles pa. *If* the average saving is 10 minutes, savings will be worth £0.3m pa. (Page 113)

Accidents

The study quotes 1973 rail fatalities[49] and claims £3.46m[50] will be saved by fewer accidents due to diversions onto the converted 'main line' from residential streets.[51] Comparisons between train and bus safety are related, in the study, to *passenger* mileage.

The Study claims (Page 18), that evidence shows that single carriageway converted railways, such as the Heads of the Valleys road[52] in Wales, are probably as safe as motorways

Freight Traffic

No estimate is made of lorries required for rail freight on the six routes. However, a figure of 350 lorries appears for the six routes, (Page 85) without demonstrating how it is derived. This is attributed to the unwillingness of BR and NFC to provide data[53] - perhaps due to a belief by BR and NFC of a preconception that railways should be converted. Rail freight information, scattered over many pages, is listed as:

- Short goods trains are occasionally seen Stratford-North Woolwich (Page 31).
- Braintree has on Mondays, a 350 Mg [sic] of fertiliser and a sporadic coal train (Page 46).

---

[45] Newly generated traffic is a trip that a user thought not worth making. (Page 2). The basis for estimating volume, distance and directional flow is not explained. It will add to city and town congestion, and must cause accidents.

[46] The relevance of the B1018 is unclear as it is many miles south of the Marks Tey-Sudbury line.

[47] Another study claims that existing traffic is on a shorter route than stated, so gains will be less (see page 123)

[48] Tolls may restrict usage, but a precise number cannot be pre-determined in this casual way. Tolls cause delays.

[49] These were higher than 1974 - whose figures were available before the Study report was published.

[50] A summation of accident benefits claimed on Pages 37,44,48,55,60,112.

[51] Buses cannot all divert from residential streets as that is their attraction - near to houses & shops.

[52] Users call it the Highway to Hell with 33 deaths in 6 years. (*Merthyr Express*, 25.3.93). It used short sections of a 20-mile closed railway, (see pages 143,166). Dalgleish praised its' safety record in *The Truth about Transport*.

[53] DoE is not criticised for not providing more important road traffic surveys, being the major source of benefit.

- Two trains of sand leave Southminster, and radio-active waste is brought twice weekly, by lorry from Bradwell to load on a special railway wagon for dumping at sea, (Page 57).
- A daily 2-way flow at Manor Park of around 70 freight and parcels trains with around 800 freight wagons and 100 parcel vans conveying 18,000 Mg per day. 18 of the 70 trains convey containers[54] to/from Parkeston Quay. Others carry farm produce to Harwich; sand from quarries at Marks Tey and Southminster; oil from Parkeston to Bow, Claydach and Channelsea; cars from Halewood[55] (Page 63).
- Mile End receives 0.55m Mg of sand from Southminster and Marks Tey, (Page 76). This will go direct to destination (Page 77), releasing land valued at £0.6m! [56]
- Milk arriving at Ilford (Page 85).
- Bananas to Fyffes depot at Goodmayes, (Page 86) - 'with the bananas taken by road, the land can be sold for £1.8m'.[57]
- Allied Beer has a private siding at Mistley. Traffic is light. The branch need not be resurfaced, the existing ballast would be adequate for lorries. (Page 101).[58]
- A 'coal depot at Hythe', (Page 104), which will have coal taken direct to the depot, by multi-bottomed lorry, or to the individual consumer from the colliery.[59]

From this information, an attempt was made to compare rail and road costs (Pages 25/26). This 'assumed a type 4 diesel loco and four sets of 20 wagons, *each containing £10,000* and a maximum payload of 40 Mg, with an average load of 60% [50% for minerals and 85% for containers[60]] and the loco running 60,000 km pa'. This *assumption* is compared to *Commercial Motor* cost tables, *but* with interest recalculated at 10%, licences excluded, fuel tax cut 50% to cover only road maintenance, 20% overheads, no profit,[61] a maximum payload of 22.4 Mg and 60% average load. 'On the basis of the unsatisfactory evidence available, it is concluded that there is no significant difference between the cost of trains and 32.5 Mg lorries.[62] On a road with excellent alinement (sic) and limited access, there is no reason to restrict weight to 32.5 Mg and length to 18m. In the USA, 33m long *multiple bottom dump trucks* of 57 Mg gross weight, made up of semi-trailers joined by dollies, are used on nominated roads. To leave those routes, each semi-trailer is taken away individually as a normal articulated tractor/trailer unit.[63] Ford UK said if *double bottom lorries* for two 9m containers were permitted, there would be a slight saving by road'. The Study postulates (Page 26) 100Mg lorries against existing train sizes.[64]

---

[54] Many containers were 8 foot 6 inches wide. Two passing each other in 9 foot lanes at 50 mph would be terrifying.

[55] The author recalls there was a daily flow of car parts from Dagenham to Halewood, which is not mentioned.

[56] There is no reference to consultation. Such depots exist to equalise varying demand to bulk supply.

[57] The company does not appear to have been consulted. Their policy was by rail from port to depots for distribution. It would not go direct to customers, but would still go to this depot - even if they agreed to road transit.

[58] This company and others are told that their traffic will be by road whether or not they like it.

[59] Coal direct by road would already take place, if it was economic. The lorries need a new road from the colliery!

[60] The source of these figures is not disclosed. They are not included in BR Annual Reports, as obtained pre-1963.

[61] No data is quoted to prove how much road renewal and maintenance arises from lorry wear & tear. TRL evidence proves that it eclipses cars, which bear an unfair share of costs. Why the specified items should be cut is not explained. How lorries which travel on both converted roads and existing roads will get this discount is not explained.

[62] A series of assumptions leads to a positive conclusion! It is assumed that customers will not object. They may move to a location where there is freedom of choice - creating local redundancy and destroying the assumptions.

[63] This requires a parking area and extra tractors and drivers at *every* access point! They are not costed.

[64] There is more prospect of bigger unstaffed trains. Comparison of futuristic road transport with existing trains is typical of conversion league/campaign practice. Future prospects must be compared with future prospects.

'Lorries appear on streets as they must even when the line haul is by train', (Page 17).[65]

Cash gains claimed

Property sales

A sample entry reads: As there is a shortage of jobs and housing in this area, it will be *assumed* half of the land will get planning permission for industrial development and half for residential use, (Page 38). 35 items on 26 pages, claim sales of £5.7m[66] including one of £1.8m, (Page 86)[67] to use for warehousing, factories or houses, without proving that there are potential buyers. The value placed on land for industrial use does not guarantee a single sale. It is doubtful that entrepreneurs are held back due to a lack of land for sale. Gains for selling land are mixed among constructional or other proposals, creating difficulty in analysis. They are also mixed with claims for the value of land turned into roads whilst financial benefit is also claimed for the value of time saved by diverted motorists. This sounds like double counting. A claim for £17m (Page 113), appears to be related to using the land for transport purposes, with no indication that cash will change hands.

Around Stratford, 34 hectares (Page 38), it is said, could be sold to fund conversion, but will be used as roads. It may have sidings required for stabling residual passenger coaches or freight traffic, which relate to unaffected routes. Lack of detail prevents confirmation.

Tenants will be moved to Mile End goods & coal depot, (Page 75). £20,000 opportunity cost is claimed for relocating tenants. (Page 76). There is no depot plan to show there is space nor prove it is suitable, nor confirmation that tenants were willing to move. Distances to their - and other displaced firms' - clients may be increased, affecting costs.

Assumptions are made regarding ownership of houses adjoining railways, including station and gate houses. Over the years, as their original purpose ceased, with abolition of station masters and modernisation of crossings, thousands were sold to sitting tenants or private buyers.[68] Estate agents trying to value houses, must surely have been told where to go, if they attempted to enter houses of railway employees and others, who may not intend to be evicted. Without interior inspection no meaningful valuation is possible.

Scrap sales

Sales of scrap railway materials are claimed, and applied to help to pay for conversion, rather than be paid to BR, which would seem to be the legitimate owner. It claims net scrap sales of steel, cast iron and OLE. The *net* value claimed is £0.39m, including £0.2m from OLE, (Pages 36,73,90,94,96,97,104,107,110). No costs are disclosed for recovery of materials. Which expert estimated the costs of dismantling OLE is not disclosed.

Cheap construction

It is claimed that the formation, having been compacted by train loads over many decades, needed only a layer of tarmac to provide a perfect running surface. (Page 16). However, in four of the six studies covered in the scheme, (Pages 43, 48, 53, 59), the lines were single on a double or near-double formation. The excess had been unused by trains and cannot be regarded as compacted. Without drawings of formation and ballast widths

---

[65] This popular belief is undermined by the facts. Fords traffic from Dagenham to Halewood and back, Fyffes from Avonmouth to Goodmayes, coal from collieries, sand from quarries and containers between port & Stratford do not touch the roads. 85% of BR freight was direct between private sidings, (see page 110).

[66] This would be reduced by the need to retain land to build two depots to replace Ilford, which is to become a bus depot. Ilford maintained multiple units for services which would continue under the scheme, (see page 138).

[67] Fyffes depot at Goodmayes (see reference on page 144).

[68] For example, the author discovered that the crossing house at Pork Lane had been sold in 1960.

for all routes, it cannot be said how much is compacted. It is stated that traffic can run on a bitumen bound base the day after it is laid, a wearing surface added later, (Page 16)

Given the perennial claims that railway formations are wide enough and bridges present no problem, it is interesting to note the changes that this scheme requires:

- Some 40 bridges have to be rebuilt, re-decked, etc., to give clearances still lower than DfT standards, (Pages 43,59,72,75,76,77,78,80,82,83,84,87,88,89,98,99,100,101,102,106,107).[69]
- Eight other bridges are to be removed due to insufficient clearances and to avoid the need to rebuild, (Pages 48,54,99,101,103,108,110) - but will users agree?
- Formations must be excavated to give headroom clearance at 13 other bridges, (Pages 78,80,82,83,84,85,86,89,95,96,105,107), and at Liverpool Street station (Page 72).
- Four bridges with less headroom than 4.6m[70] are not to be altered. (Pages 60,107,108,109). One is 4.2m, but another of 4.2m (Page 107), is to have excavation.[71]
- No revised height is specified for 22 bridges which are to be altered.
- The formation is insufficiently wide at several locations, and involves some acquisition and demolition of private property, (Pages 73,75,83,85,86,87,95,96,98,103,106,107).
- Some private businesses will be 'relocated' to create adequate space (Pages 76,85,86).
- New flyunders/underpasses will be built (Pages 77,90). There is no changeover programme
- At Stratford, which has cross-platform interchange with LT trains, north- and south-bound trains will use one island platform, by moving the former line, 3.3m. As lines are in single bore tunnels at each end of the station, (see photo), curvature may be a problem

There is no reference to the cost of drains, which road engineers say (see page 26), would be substantial. Instead, the formation will be *trimmed* to provide drainage, (Page 16).

Smith compared his plan (Page 94) with BR's successful and practical scheme, which raised £150m & £2m rental pa in cash. BR re-developed Broad St station site, diverting trains to Liverpool St, where offices and shops were also built over east side tracks.

Changeover tactics (Pages 90-91).

In the first week, two of the four tracks will be lifted from Liverpool St. to Brentwood. During the peak, two trains will couple into one [of 18 cars] at Liverpool St. and divide at Brentwood. Platforms are not long enough for 18. At some stations, temporary scaffolding will be erected to lengthen platforms. Where that is not possible, signs at Liverpool St. will show which carriages to board. *During the second weekend*, trains will use platforms 1-10, while the east half of Liverpool Street is converted (Pages 90,91), to a bus station & park. During the first seven days, after removing track and OLE[72], trimming the formation, a 150mm bitumen-bound base will be laid. After nine days, in time for the morning peak, the base will be complete for one carriageway to open for road traffic, used only by buses in the peak, and lorries outside the peak. The other tracks will then be lifted, to convert the other carriageway, which will be ready in two months. Four months from the start, the road will open to private traffic. There is no reference to staging work at Chelmsford, Colchester and Manningtree. For all other routes, buses will travel over existing roads during changeover. No debit is shown for delays or accidents.

---

[69] This includes two bridges on minor routes. It excludes 18 bridges missed on North Woolwich-Tottenham and some on other routes, (see page 99-100). Rebuilding would delay users and may disrupt water, gas and phone services.

[70] The scheme dismisses the DoE standard of 5.1m and opts for one of 4.6m as a standard minimum, (Page 15).

[71] 4.2m headroom would give an inadequate 4mm clearance for Trathens' size buses, (see footnote, page 102).

[72] It would be foolhardy to permit contractors to pick up track next to lines being used by trains. Contractors would not be permitted to use machines whilst OLE was still energised on an adjoining track.

£7000, [£875 per day], is included as 'a passenger time cost' for an average 5 minutes delay to long distance *peak* passengers, (Page 91), but nothing for 28,500 east side commuters. Commuters qualify for £1.20 per hour time value if their journey is quicker, (Page 2). Conversely, a twice-daily delay would cost £5300 for 5 minutes. A more realistic 20 minutes each time would be the likely delay, raising it to £22,800. All off-peak passengers would also be delayed, and there would be knock-on delay to west side commuters. There is no provision for increased costs arising from train delays and extra staff.

Presentation of Study

On 22 March 1976, the study was presented to the Institution of Civil Engineers, which published it in 1977, (see page 115), as a Paper referring briefly to the Study's conclusions.

DoT road design standards were not used, as rail 'formation widths were not always wide enough for everything that might be desired.[73] A lane 3.5m [9.6 feet] was adopted'.[74] For double-deck buses, 4.2m headroom was a minimum and 4.6m desirable.[75] Costs were synthesized. The benefit to private vehicles[76] and value of surplus land was calculated, and a bus service developed.[77] It was concluded that the community would benefit from replacing trains with buses and lorries and converting the rail formation to a public road where existing roads were not adequate. In one urban case, the value of surplus land was an important saving. ROI was 30-60% in rural cases, 210% to infinity [no net investment required] in the urban.[78] Construction costs could rise 215% in a rural, 2678% in an urban area, before savings were lost. Costs used were £40,000 per km [1973 prices], for a two-lane highway,[79] consistent with Conversion League figures, claimed to be based on data supplied by local authorities[80]. Environmental and accident benefits[81] would arise by diverting private vehicles from existing roads. Buses would be safer than trains.[82]

The terminal would have buses at 7 seconds headway loading 27,000 onto 500 buses in the peak on a single grade. The headway at the Manhattan terminal was 4.5 seconds. Others said that had several grades.[83] Prof. Hall conceded that more money might be needed for pedestrian segregation at the terminal, but believed buses could equal or better rail performance, particularly where a breakdown was concerned.[84] The authors thought[85] 'that *commuters, who would all have a seat*, would prefer this to crowded rail conditions'.

---

[73] This idea was not accompanied by demands to cut road costs elsewhere by reducing lane widths.

[74] This is barely more than Mersey Tunnel which has a 30 mph limit.

[75] Trathens operate 71-seat PSVs 4.16 metres high. A margin of 0.04 is inadequate for minor road defects.

[76] This is a non-cash item. Such benefits are ignored by the road lobby when comparing tax with roads expenditure.

[77] Those in *Better Use of Rail Ways*, cannot be termed as a *bus service*. There is no schedule for any route.

[78] Most ROI was non-cash benefits. Before cash came in from asset sales, interest bearing loans would fund costs.

[79] In 1967, a DoT engineer quoted £0.5m per mile for such a road, that is £0.3m per km, (see page 167).

[80] Local authorities (see chapter 13), had no costs for short lengths of disused track that became part of a road. In some cases formations were unsuitable and costs were no less, even more, than building a new road. (see page 190)

[81] Neither of these have hitherto been taken into account to help to justify any railway investment scheme.

[82] As no precedent was quoted, nor evidence given of field tests, this was a subjective judgement.

[83] The oft quoted New York City Transit Authority night time bus performance for the second half of 2004 was 73.5%. There is no day time data, which would be worse. There were accidents (see pages 167,168,179)

[84] There was no elaboration of this claim. The reality is that it takes a long time to get assistance to a bus breakdown, whereas one train can push another clear, and there was a Railway Control system to monitor and resolve problems.

[85] In this key claim of the proposal, incredibly, no market research had been carried out. The reality is that on two of the three train services - Southend and Clacton - using the east side the majority of commuters were seated. Only Shenfield trains, with an average journey of about 15 minutes had significant standing space. By no stretch of imagination were 50% of commuters standing, as had been suggested elsewhere.

Under-utilised roads —Top: Potteries 'D' Road; Centre: Shavington by-pass; Lower: A541

Top & Centre: Under-utilised M6, Crewe to Sandbach; Lower: Deserted dual carriageway, Stoke

Bridge bashing. Longton, Staffs.—A mother and child were lucky to escape death or injury. Top: by Carl Tart; Centre left: Advance warning sign at 8 times the braking distance; Centre right: Donated by an anonymous Australian tourist; Lower: by Mark Watson.

Top: Leeds guideed busway. Inset: Guide wheel; Centre: Wide turning circle of an articulated bus; Lower: Pennsylvania Turnpike (Jamie Orr)

Bridges, showing limited clearances and uncompacted cess covered by ballast. Top: Kidsgrove, Staffs.; Centre: Congleton, Cheshire; Lower: Hope Valley line.

Top: Bridge with OLE mast outside; Centre: Liverpool St-Bethnal Green cutting (DM Hibbert Collection); Lower: East Anglian four track gantry, (DM Hibbert Collection)

Top: Hartshill Tunnel, Newcastle, Staffs (Basil Jeuda);
Bottom: Totley Tunnel, 3.5 miles

Top: Liverpool St., East Side, Roof Support Columns (Bishopsgate Institute); Lower: Stratford, LT train entering north tunnel—viewed from platform 5 which these trains would use in the Smith plan

The Hall/Smith scheme was subject to some criticism and led to *Better Use of Rail Ways - Comments & Rejoinders* - referred to here as *Rejoinders*. There were 41 entries, of which, 18 were critical, with 16 *rejoinders*. The sole acknowledgement is to Mr. & Mrs. P.F. Withrington[1] for hospitality.

Conspicuous by its absence, is the lack of support from hauliers or any bus company willing to take on the job on the specified basis: fleet size, manpower numbers, no timetable; nor any construction company willing to undertake conversion at the price. If the scheme was practicable and profitable, there should have been a surfeit of bidders. A trawl of the well-indexed Times found no bidding interest, (see chapter 15), but includes four letters on the study - all are critical. With one exception, they are not included in *Rejoinders*. Media articles related to conversion, not specifically referring to this study are in chapter 14. Major defects and flaws have been identified by the author - see Part III. The scale of criticism shows that the Study had posed more questions than answers.

The introduction to *Rejoinders* (Page ii), states 'critics fail to substantiate their claim that replacement bus services on a converted railway cannot offer a level of service equal to that of the former railway'. The authors of the scheme failed to substantiate that it *can*.

'Many converted railways carry heavy lorries with a cost saving to the lorry operator', (Page iv). No facts are included to show savings have been made. The belief that an average length 1.8 mile conversion can noticeably cut lorry costs is untenable.

'Many objectors felt that the traffic flows assumed were excessive, but none produced any evidence', (Page iv). No evidence was produced by the authors to prove that theoretical flows were not excessive - other than to claim that *evenly spaced* traffic, unprecedented even on motorways, and free of surges and nose to tail - can do so.

No rejoinder to those largely supportive of the scheme

An article in the Guardian (29.4.74), claims railways carry less than 10% of traffic on roads.[2] It states that 'freight has to be brought to railheads by road', and that most freight trains operate with more empty capacity than long distance trucks - no source is quoted.

This was written before the Hall/Smith Report. Its inclusion is therefore mystifying, and outside their own criteria for inclusion. Most rail traffic never sees a road, passing from private siding to private siding. A diagram (see BRB 1976 Report), covering 1973-6, shows that traffic passing almost exclusively between private sidings - coal, coke, iron & steel, earths & stones, petroleum - accounts for 85-88% of all railfreight. BR statistics contain more detail than road transport statistics, which are now revealed as being unreliable, (see page 153). If railfreight transferred to road, it would incur *precisely* the same proportion of empty mileage. A critical article on same page of the Guardian is ignored, (see page 130).

An article in *Investors Chronicle* (12.12.75) referred to eminent geographer Peter Hall conducting research on lines, below bridges, in cuttings, prodding abutments and testing the compaction of formations. It accepted that sub soil would be of sufficient strength merely to require a layer of asphalt, claiming that local authorities have proved this can

---

[1] See chapter 11

[2] This is now open to question, as the basis used to calculate road traffic is crude and unreliable, (see page 153).

be done[3] and refers to the uninterrupted carriageway *straight* into city centres.[4] It adds that replacing trains by buses will save 75% of staff.[5] 'Sums in the study are said to be part fact, part judgement.[6] A saving is claimed by not having to build *any* roads in future'

The research was a revelation, given BR was criticised for refusing help, whereas these activities should not have been carried out without either trained protection staff provided by BR, arrest by BT Police for trespass, or accidental death due to being struck by a train.[7] Testing formations would have required qualified and suitably equipped engineers. Even they would need operating permission to make tests that may temporarily destabilise the track, and require suspension of services. Safe practices would have required prior publication of locations of site work in Engineering Notices. Suspending all road building cannot be achieved, when huge areas of the country had no railways to convert.

An article from *The Times* (17.12.75), suggests the study may embarrass government. It quotes highlight figures on savings & benefits, and refers to tolls for lorries and cars.

Hauliers avoid the M6 Toll road. The road dominated DoE paid for the study. The Treasury should have been drooling in anticipation. In fact, the DoE was unimpressed, (*Times* 23.12.75). Clearly, they must have discovered that the study had serious weaknesses.

An article in the *Economist* (27.12.75), refers to vain attempts by government to solve the rail problem. A radical solution is by Hall and Smith. The article repeats the claims made of national benefit, and reduced fares. It states that 'BR has a staff of 23 for every engine'

Had the *Economist* researched its back issues, it would have found that it recommended the solution - BR to have equal commercial freedom as road transport - (*Economist*, 10.5.52), long sought by railway managers. It was rejected by government which feared that it would leave rural areas denuded of transport, and could result in railways driving road transport out of business.[8] The manpower comparison overlooks thousands involved in maintaining infrastructure - whilst road counterparts are ignored. It ignores that multiple units, not engines were the dominant part of traction, (see BRB Accounts). It is noticeable, that *Rejoinders* did not include two other extracts from the *Economist*.

I would have liked to see a more perceptive review. It was expected that engineers would pick up the sloppy cost estimates. It is surprising that you accepted that conversion would be beneficial if costs rose 2000%. BR's annual turnover is £1bn. That means, we would get the transport service for less than nothing, (*Economist* 10.4.76).

During 1973-6, bus journeys have fallen 34%. In France, a doubling of the number of buses has led to hardly any increase in bus use. Could it be that people are not willing to put up with the motorised stage coach? Alternatives are proposed, but government's hands are tied by the opposition of *bus unions* to innovation, (*Economist* 17.4.76).

---

[3] The reality is different (see chapter 13).

[4] There are thousands of public and farm level crossings to restrict flows. Lines are *not* straight - see page 125. Moreover, streets adjoining many city stations - especially in London - are so narrow, congestion would arise.

[5] No independent source is quoted, and as no main line has ever been replaced by a road, it is not clear how there can proof. Comparison with closed lines is irrelevant. See also comparison of BR and NBC - page 181.

[6] Another independent study dismisses both - see page 123.

[7] In a letter to Autocar (8.5.76), Smith says he dodged between trains to measure width between abutments of every bridge from Liverpool St to Harwich. This was no mean feat for 8 bridges in Liverpool St-Bethnal Green cutting, (see photo & page 120). It was not said that Prof. Hall was likewise engaged. No measurements are listed for 51 bridges on other routes (see page 99). No data is given on formation compaction tests in the cess or banksides.

[8] See *Britain's Railways - The Reality*, Page 26.

An article from *The Times* (10.1.76), refers to an unrelated line, which BR claimed had no subsidy in 1966, but was subsidised in 1968. It urges the DoE to carry out a study on rail resources that could be more productively used by others.

Before the 1968 Act, no subsidy was given for uneconomic lines kept open by ministers. BR had to subsist with interest bearing loans.[9] A study should look at underused roads.

A quote from the *Evening Echo* (2.2.76) states that the thought of travelling by bus rather than train may horrify many, and of driving a bus may horrify rail staff. It notes that buses that took over from trains often ran into trouble, but assumes that this was due to using winding country lanes. It suggested minimising rises in rail fares. It said that this report did not come from an impractical man in an ivory tower, its main author is a civil engineer[10]. For some inexplicable reason, an extract from this article is printed separately, which mentions BR's unsurprising views. The article presumes that all replacement buses which ceased operation, did so because they were on country lanes.

The opportunity to glean readers' thoughts of conversion is denied by lack of knowledge of the paper's location. The assumption - initiated by Lloyd and pursued by Hall/Smith, that rail staff would turn to driving buses is improbable. It is more likely that they would seek jobs offering high wages in one of the factories forecast to spring up on railway land, not lower bus wages! Buses ceased to run where they had decent roads, and where they replaced steam trains on single lines, which, by definition, were not fast. On 'minimising fare increases', they would learn much from studying the reality of fare levels.[11]

An article in the *Observer* (8.2.76), stated: Many commuters will be giving undivided attention to planners who argue that rail lines should be converted to roads.[12] This study makes a prime facie case to turn part of the network into expressways.[13] Fares could be cut by almost two-thirds.[14] The conversion of rail tracks to roads would be a quick and relatively cheap process.[15] 'The main reaction has been to treat the proposals as an academic exercise. Criticisms have been superficial'.[16] It claims that the Report makes detailed engineering and operating costs.[17] The conversion to road would be a quick and cheap process.[18] Door-to-door service could be offered if buses ran onto ordinary roads.[19]

---

[9] See *Britain's Railways - The Reality*.

[10] A study needed experts in other fields: bus and lorry operating & scheduling, vehicle maintenance, stores control, accountancy & marketing. Their absence shows in the report. Other engineers disagreed, (see pages 25,26,166).

[11] By 1976, BR had lost over £11bn due to political and legal interference in fares. Rail fares trailed inflation for almost 40 consecutive years. See *Britain's Railways - The Reality*, Appendix A.

[12] There was little evidence of it. Where closures were proposed, opposition was as strong as ever. No one argued for conversion. Readers' letters columns bore no evidence of that, and those who wrote were opposed, (see chapter 15)

[13] *At face value*, there does *seem* to be a case. However, when one reads other opinions, and digs below the surface of the report - whose clarity leaves much to be desired - the risk areas and defects can clearly be seen.

[14] An analysis of the proposed costs and fares show that if fares were so cut, the bus company would have to be subsidised, even if one accepts the manpower and fleet costs, which are strongly disputed, (see page 139).

[15] This is rejected by non-BR engineers, (see pages 25-26). Other major flaws are exposed, (see pages 145-149).

[16] Many are not superficial. The author has studied the scheme and finds numerous serious defects, (see Part III).

[17] By no stretch of imagination can the costs be described as detailed.

[18] The conversion would most certainly not be quick, which becomes apparent when the flaws in the conversion process are dispassionately examined, (see Part III of this chapter). The estimated costs have been challenged by several independent parties, (see the criticisms summarised in this Part II).

[19] Door-to-door is a dream. There is *no* prospect that they could run via the narrow streets near Liverpool Street and other city stations, and onto congested London streets and get back to fit into an 9 second interval departure pattern.

An extract of an article in *Commercial Motor* (28.5.76), argues that as rail services have been steadily taken over by road transport, it is appropriate that the same thing should happen to the tracks on which those services are provided.

Bus travel had fallen steeply, that by train only marginally. Traffic per member of BR staff had doubled, rail passenger miles per coach were up 33% on 1948 by 1969.[20]

A letter to the ICE (6.4.76), refers to the Smith conversion costs as having been obtained by the League from county councils, 'when track and buildings were already demolished'. It quotes Southport and Radnor councils as proof that work can be done cheaply. It mentions cattle creeps under railways, and that farm severance had largely sorted itself out. It claims railway land is publicly owned, and selling to adjoining owners spoils the concept for long distance bridle paths, footpaths, lanes or trunk roads. Conversion League is the only body offering a solution to the BR deficit. There is no rejoinder.

The Southport scheme was less beneficial than claimed, (see pages 66,114,156). Radnor had a 'B' and a 'C' road scheme totalling 3 miles of the 56 mile closed single line. All track and equipment had been removed. Their costs are irrelevant to East Anglia. Radnor does not now exist, but other counties deny League cost claims. The Countryside Commission said severance has *not* been resolved, (see page 193). Rights under original Acts are valid. Offering land *back* to farmers is just. There are cattle creeps, but thousands of private level crossings are used to take cattle and equipment between fields. Farmers objected to conversion, (see page 124). The solution to the deficit spelled out long ago was to give BR freedom to decide its prices, determine which routes to keep and which traffic to handle - as mollycoddled competitors have been free to do for 85 years.[21] Conversion will lead to a long-overdue cut in drivers' hours, an increase in vehicle and oil imports, and an overburdened NHS and emergency services. Costs will spiral out of control. When someone wagers that this will not happen, and puts down cash to convert an operational main line will be the time to *hope* that they have a solution. This is an experiment from which there is no return. Conversionists will not offer their heads on a platter if it failed. Nor would they reimburse reversal costs or fund excess costs and ensuing national losses. Taxpayers will pick up the tab, and dreamers will find excuses for failure - *circumstances beyond our control* - the excuse reserved for the private sector.

The League's 1977 letter to the DoT claims that transfer of traffic from all purpose roads to converted railways *could* reduce accident rates by a factor of 4 to 20.

They say *could* rather than *will*. There is no point in being a hostage to fortune. They ignore the disparity between 220,000 miles of road and 11,000 miles of railway. Traffic would have to make *excessive diversions* to get onto the converted system to try to prove the point. They fail to bring into the equation, the conflict of 28,500 commuters cutting between buses departing every 9 seconds.[22] They ignore that buses will have to make two right turns against nose to tail cross traffic to return to Liverpool Street, and that traffic joining and leaving a converted system will make right turns - a well known cause of accidents. Not a single fatality has been conceded for these adverse factors.

---

[20] 1948 was BR's first year. See *Britain's Railways - The Reality,* Page 145

[21] See *Square Deal Denied & Britain's Railways - The Reality.*

[22] *Better Use of Rail Ways,* (Page 72) shows 380 buses will depart during the peak 58 minutes (Page 119).

Autocar reported (7.2.76) on the Hall/Smith proposal. They stated that every aspect of the conversion is looked at and studied - fares could be cut by 60% and bus operators would still earn good profits. It would give far more capacity for passengers. The result of the contract has embarrassed the DoE.

All aspects had *not* been looked into, (see Part III). There is no profit (see Table on page 139), much less a good profit, even before cost increases to reflect flaws discovered by this author and others. On their figures, the promised fare reduction creates a deficit, whilst correction of costs produces a deficit of £10m pa (see page 139). Reports in the media (in this chapter) and letters to the press (chapter 15) show others identified crucial weaknesses missed in the Autocar article. There is no doubt, that if the scheme would produce the gains postulated, the dominating Treasury would have had it implemented promptly. There is no prospect that they were unaware of it, given the claims made in parts of the media.

Not included in *Rejoinders* - largely supportive

An article in the *Surveyor* (6.2.76), carried an illustration of the proposed Liverpool Street bus station and some details of the Reading study, set out in a 126 page study[23] describing it as a 'limited access road', and stating:

- About half of the savings would be staff economies, as a bus service required 650 drivers and 750 other staff[24] including ticket sellers at two stations, staff making buses and maintaining roads, compared to 3,650 rail staff on the six lines.[25]
- The new road from Liverpool St to Brentwood would be motorway standard for most of its 26km length, and can be built to cater for ex-rail traffic for less than £3.5m.
- An extra £1.5m could cater for private vehicles as well, needing extra access points.[26]
- Rail fares would be cut by 60% and operators would still earn a profit.[27]
- At 30 bays, a bus would unload every 10 seconds.[28] Hall acknowledges that the safety at the proposed bus station would be unsatisfactory, and that a grade separation as at New York's Terminal would be appropriate.

    No cost was mentioned for creating a grade separation. It is incredible that a proposal would be submitted which depended on a major structural change which was not costed.

It mentions that the Conversion League 'wanted for years to carry out an appraisal of this sort'. What held them back, and why did they disregard three[29] by their founder! Contrary to their claim, their 1971 (dated 1970), dossier did not mention safety on any 'conversion' except at Southport, and *that* was not proven, (see page 66). The most telling comment by *Surveyor* was that Tyneside Metro opted for rail as it gave a better output per employee.

Rejoinders to those supportive of the scheme

An *extract* of a letter (9.1.76), from an unnamed senior BRB Officer is quoted. It expresses concern of problems of dealing with redundancy unless spread over some years.

---

[23] This is the book entitled *Better Use of Rail Ways* by Hall & Smith.

[24] A comparison of BR & NBC staff for 1976 - like for like - having deducted track maintenance & freight staff, was 0.5% less on BR for 41% more passenger revenue and at higher speeds! (*Britain's Railways - The Reality* Page 148)

[25] This is an unsubstantiated estimate.

[26] This appears to require land acquisition.

[27] A grossly erroneous belief, see page 139.

[28] Some show 7,8 or 9. Report (Page 69) indicates 9.5, but this may be too high, see page 136 & footnote page 113

[29] See chapters 3, 4 & 5.

The rejoinder suggests how staff can be transferred or retrained to perform road related occupations.

His field of expertise was not disclosed. Anonymity need not have been damaged by disclosing this. He may have been in the Clothing Supply Dept, with no experience of the problems likely to arise. Smith censures anonymous critics, (see page 122). He overlooks that retraining would occur *after* conversion, and only if staff *wished* to be trained in road transport. All staff required by highway and bus companies would have to be pre-trained.

Rejoinders not made to those not supportive of the scheme

The DoE which commissioned the Study by Hall and Smith 'had major reservations about some calculations in the study, and would not be publishing it'. (Times 23.12.75).

An article in *Planning* (6.2.76), described the conclusions of the Hall/Smith study as an 'academic nightmare' with no basis in fact. The ideas were completely fanciful.

The Hall-Smith report attracted a storm of criticism. The DoE which commissioned it has serious reservations but decline to say what they are[30]. BR describe the report as a sloppy study which fails to make its case. Where high capital cost and fixed systems cannot be justified, track[31] should be given to other modes, (Times, 5.3.76).

A verbatim copy of the ICE Report was included. The authors said 'that for longer journeys, trips to and from a station often mitigated the saving by train. It was a common criticism of railways, that passengers have to travel to or from stations by road transport', (see below). A claim was made that 'express coaches can act as feeders at both ends', and that standing commuters would prefer a seat. Resolving this appeared to be an objective.[32] The Conversion League praised[33] the report. What they said is not disclosed. Other comments made during the meeting were as follows:

- Opinions differed on the accident potential of a busway under different conditions. Some thought accidents would fall, pointing to average rates on motorways [0.15 accidents per million vehicle km] which they thought would apply to a segregated busway, (see below).
- Some stated that, in many cases, road standards were below those recommended by the DoE for new construction. Others thought that adhering to DoE standards was incorrect, as such an approach would lead to closure of 90% of existing roads.[34]
- Conversion costs were disputed. A county council which had converted 15km of disused line and was working on another 12km, quoted £206,000 per km. The main problem was *variation in the consolidation of the formation, drainage improvements required to create run-off from a road, and the removal of railway structures.* One private company had converted 3.5km into a 6.7m carriageway for £406,000 at 1969 prices. A GLC speaker referred to a study of a 5km section for an estimated £0.25m per km for a 6m

---

[30] They gave a reason in 1975, (see page 111).

[31] These would be uneconomic railways, kept open by the MoT.

[32] In the Journal of Transport Economics & Policy (Sept 1973), Smith said there was no assumption, peak passengers would be all seated. That would go down like a lead balloon. Standing rail passengers are a minority, (see page 116)

[33] As editors say 'when dog bites man, that is not news, but when man bites dog that is news'.

[34] This is a facile argument. If standards proposed are adequate, there was no justification for building motorways after 1976 to higher standards. There have been no calls to cut standards for new roads, nor to narrow existing roads.

carriageway and £0.35m per km for a 8m carriageway. It will be seen that these - by unbiased parties - were all significantly in excess of the figures used in the Study.

- A BR film showed bunched passenger arrivals at a main line station, whereas the study was based on random arrivals. BR referred to problems that must be expected at bus terminals: uneven loading, climatic conditions and breakdowns.[35] They disagreed with the conclusions and were dissatisfied with the standard and partiality of the study. They listed faults that were discussed by others. They objected to calculation of rail operating costs taking average values, whilst those for buses were incremental and marginal.
- A speaker said energy issues were important. Whilst, up to 76% conversion efficiency from basic fuels using electricity was provided, only 38% could be provided from diesel.

The belief that all passengers arrive at stations in road transport is erroneous. Many *walk*. Houses in walking distance of a station often have higher values than distant ones. Journeys by express coach involve changes, so there would be no improvement with conversion. If coaches were used as feeders, it would not affect the need to change twice, as every coach could not *possibly* perambulate round scores of streets collecting passengers for one destination. Increased journey times would signal an end to coach travel. If a coach collects passengers for other destinations, *they* would change twice. No matter how it is wrapped, they are going to change as often as rail passengers.

Commuters are under half of all passengers into Liverpool Street.[36] Not all commuters stand. Thus, to satisfy a minority, they will inconvenience the majority who have a seat which is far more comfortable than a cramped bus seat. Moreover, it is a known fact, that many stand near a door - of which there are more on trains than buses - to be first out. Even some with a seat, move to a door, before arrival. Over short distances, commuters often prefer to stand near a door. In the Cannon St accident in 1991, it was recorded that many were standing at the front when there were vacant seats at the rear.

Linking accident rates to the alleged benefits of segregated busways are misplaced. This was not to be a segregated busway - other traffic would share the system. Motorways are purpose built three-lane dual carriageway, with no right turns. These conditions would be absent on a converted railway, having right turns and cross roads. It was unclear how and by whom existing traffic would be directed onto the converted system. It would not occur if dependent on decisions by individual drivers, who would not know if it was congested.

Those not supportive or opposed to the scheme
In *The Times* (3.1.76). BR Chief Executive, David Bowick challenged the assertion that the fatality rate of buses was 38% below rail. He quoted 1973 figures showing bus fatalities were 2.5-4 times as many per passenger mile as trains, and that the ratio for serious injuries was 14-22 times as many. These are based on assumptions favourable to road: those killed and injured in rail sidings or maintenance depots are included, but persons similarly killed and injured in garages are excluded as being outside the public highway.

The rejoinder claimed that the figures quoted by BR were different from any reasonable interpretation of those published by the DoE, and added that 'the tone of the letter suggest Mr Bowick is worried about becoming redundant'.

---

[35] They overlooked short notice unavailability of the scheduled driver.

[36] In November 1975, total passengers were 156,700 daily see *Liverpool Street Station* by Robert Thorne.

Accident reductions claimed by the Study report and in the rejoinder are undermined by those supplied by the DfT (successor of the DoE) to the author, (see pages 97,98). The remark about redundancy is childish - a trait he criticises in others. Implementation of the Hall/Smith scheme would not have made the Chief Executive - left managing 99% of the system - redundant. In the unlikely event that the whole of BR was converted, Mr Bowick's legal entitlement to redundancy payments should have left him quite unworried.

A *Sunday Times* extract (1.2.76), stated the BR view was that benefits had been greatly exaggerated, no allowance made in respect of newly generated traffic which will use the roads, and no account taken of congestion costs of extra traffic off the busway.

The rejoinder was that it was *assumed* that parking restraint would be applied to stop new car traffic on the corridor. There was no response to the other criticisms.

The article mentioned - but this is not in *Rejoinders* - 'that passengers would have to dodge buses leaving one bay or another every nine seconds or so, struck one senior transport man, as horrifying to imagine'. It said that 'BR called the terminals layout ludicrously inadequate'. The article notes that Mr. Smith retorted that 'when a bus is about to leave it could turn on its headlights as a warning to passengers to halt. Alternatively, there could be a more ambitious layout with walkways *down* to each bay'. The article ended, but *Rejoinders* also ignored: 'things that run on tracks may still have a future'

A serious study should not *assume*. Half of the benefits claimed are for cars, whose lower loading would require an undue share of road space. The idea that drivers could stop passengers crossing by switching on headlights defies belief. Pedestrians *continually* cross roads between *moving* traffic. There is no prospect that they would be deterred by a vehicle starting from a stand and putting on its lights. A well prepared plan should have included walkways, rather than produce them like rabbits from a hat, when criticisms arose. An elevated walkway would need to be 5m above ground to clear double-deck PSVs, with long gently sloping ramps (to cater for prams, wheelchairs) down to platform level, and wide enough for a barrier to separate opposing flows. It would mean that excavation (see Page 72) would need to be about 3.5m, not 0.7m to be clear of the roof, and extend along the exit road. Platforms would have to be wider than if there were no ramps. A walkway would further extend walking time from ticket office to bus (see page 140).

Rejoinders includes an extract from Hansard (4.2.76), which records that the Minister has major reservations affecting the conclusions. There is no rejoinder. A statement by the Minister on the same day regarding coach safety and on measures being studied to improve safety, is overlooked. Without doubt, these would increase bus costs.

New Society (5.2.76), reported on the Study. It noted that the DoE, which had commissioned the study, had a number of unspecified reservations about the findings. *New Society* said that it must be something to do with the fastidious arithmetic and idiosyncratic methods of cost-benefit analysis. The plan for buses flying in and out of Liverpool Street at about six a minute could well lead to considerable loss of life, whilst the manpower needed to operate a bus service seems to have been badly underestimated. In considering how cars might use the busways, it [the Study] takes a cavalier view of the effect they would have at exit points. There is no rejoinder to some damning points.

Motor Transport (6.2.76): Before busmen rush for the crock of gold arising from the Reading report, they will have to ask if they can fulfil the task. The report assumes only *two* alternatives. A more realistic approach in 1970, found that the North Tyne Loop railway cost £6.9m pa, conversion to busway would be £6.3m, but light rapid transit cost £6.1m. Buses would be unable to avoid one another on single lanes without hard shoulders[37] as envisaged in the report. The manpower envisaged is lower than the 74 largest operators. The concept of metering is challenged. For the heaviest peak flows, buses are unable to offer the level of service, safety and efficiency that fixed track systems can.

A rejoinder focused on semantics: 'what is rapid transit'. It said Scottish Bus Group had less staff than planned. 'Metering is dealt with in the report'. To answer *road transport experts*' final point, it prays in aid a [USA 2$^{1}/_{2}$ mile] I.495 bus lane said to carry 25,000 seated passengers in a peak hour, at 43 mph which 'no rail track *can* match'

One expects curt dismissal of rail experts', but not *road transport experts*' views! LT 40mph, 2-minute headways are feasible on surface railways. Southend 12-car trains had 1032 seats, a potential 30,960 per hour. New York Transit Authority state that bus lane's peak [06.15-10.00], traffic is 62,000 commuters = 16,500 per hour, *including standees*. The bus lane is limited to 35mph![38] It has delays, (see pages 167,179). Metering is not adequately dealt with - a belief that metering will limit vehicles to a specified level, is untenable.

Country Life (12.2.76) criticised the Study, stating that it contained impressive figures, but some of the most significant were left out. Among those was a comparison of staff costs: the staff to commuter ratio being ten times better on rail than bus; and accidents: excluding pedestrian deaths, over 4,000 killed on roads compared to one on rail in 1974. It notes that the Study did not comment on skills required to control a 60 mph bus through a tunnel faced with one approaching at the same speed. Whilst that risk may be resolved by concrete flanges in the road, the friction on tyres may create problems, which could be overcome by steel flanges - an engineering concept that 'had a familiar ring'.

The *rejoinder* states only total staffing was considered and 'vehicles slow down in tunnels. Their accident comparisons may be due to their copy having 16 pages missing!'

Trains don't slow down. Road vehicles doing so would cut speeds crucial to conversion. Rail staff include track, bridge and signalling maintenance and electricity distribution. There are no comparable figures for roads and road transport fuel distribution. There is no holiday relief bus staff. Rail accidents include some caused by road transport or farmers at crossings which would continue and others referred to by Mr. Bowick (see page 116)

A letter in *Autocar* (28.2.76) asked what happens in fog, drawing attention to the BR automatic warning system, and suggests that buses would grind to a halt in fog.

The *Rejoinder* states: railway signals only warn a driver of other trains. He must watch out for obstructions. Motors have a shorter braking distance than trains. In practice, light fog leads to half of trains being cancelled. Road vehicles carry on, albeit at reduced speed.

Main lines had modern signals, that can react to obstructions by reverting signals to danger. Trains are *not cancelled* due to fog on such lines. Media reports prove that motor

---

[37] The road envisaged is 'dual carriageway with intermittent hard shoulders', (Rejoinders, Page 34). 'Hard shoulders will be provided where the formation is wide enough' (Study, Page 14). Elsewhere, breakdowns will block a lane!
[38] E-mail to the author. Outside that peak, the limit is 50 mph.

vehicles do *not* slow in fog.[39] The few who do, are passed by horn-blasting drivers, who swerve into pile-ups, when fog density changes without warning. Short braking distance is no help, when tailgating drivers see debris ahead, and have nowhere to swerve. Only someone trying to ignore the reality of higher railway safety could advance this claim.

Modern Railways (March 1976), in *Railways into Dodgems*,[40] identifies many weaknesses:
- Railways can only be converted by disregarding DoE desirable lane widths and shaving side clearances nearly 75% to 0.7m minimum, for free-steering vehicles at up to 70mph
- The study assumes the entire width of a double track railway has a standard solidity when it is obviously compacted to the highest degree in the area of the tracks only.
- The Study does not appear to contemplate expenditure on new drainage.
- The 40mph Runcorn busway is wider, has hard shoulders and has maintenance difficulties. This study has narrower lanes, no hard shoulder at places, and higher speeds
- BR would not run trains as close to bridge abutments as the study plans. There were 750 cases of bridge-bashing by road vehicles in 1972-4, 183 bridges had more than 4.2m headroom, the clearance that the study deems adequate. Bridges measured - for non obvious reasons in Glasgow for the East Anglian scheme - would have side clearance of 0.5 metres! This undermines claims that little bridge reconstruction would be necessary.
- Attention is drawn to the conflict between 450 passengers per minute crossing lanes occupied by buses on a ten second headway, and the ensuing chaos as passengers went from one bay to another seeking a bus with free seats - and, worse, paying on boarding!
- They scorn the idea that a pair of rail tracks can be macadamed in nine days, whilst trains carry on using adjoining tracks, and ridicule the proposal that trains should be doubled in length to 18 vehicles, for which platform extensions would be made. An interest is expressed in obtaining domestic quotes from engineers, who will move the Central line 3.3 metres sideways and demolish a wall for £5,000.
- They suggest that BR staffing has been exaggerated up to 300% whilst bus staffing has been minimised by assuming split shift working unlikely to secure Union approval.
- Their study ignores road lane closures, and appalling tailbacks from peak hour breakdowns. The expense of coping with vastly increased traffic in the City is ignored.
- Only the innocent would trust the assumed standard of bus timekeeping.

The rejoinder says 3.65m width is envisaged everywhere except a 520m length used by buses only, and accidents are caused by sub standard, not low bridges. Warning devices will prevent them, (see page 185). A breakdown 'will cause little delay; ask commuters about points failures'. Runcorn problems are dismissed: 'they *probably* arise from an unsuitable choice of road surface!' It claims that *this* conversion project is better than a motorway built from scratch, which 'involves slow and *costly property acquisition and earthworks*'. It did not answer compaction criticism, but irrelevantly referred to a letter which does not claim that full width is compacted, but speaks of bringing in material as fill. That letter says that in earlier conversions, all track and building had been removed, (see page 113).

In contrast, this conversion involves *property acquisition* that for unexplained reasons will be swift and cheap. If sub standard bridges are a criticism of railways which arrived

---

[39] '120 vehicles in M1 pile-up in fog', (*The Times*, 15.11.85).

[40] The word *Dodgems* is particularly germane, given the existence of roof supports, (see page 131).

long before double-deck buses and HGVs, it is par for the course. Accidents are caused by drivers, not bridges, whose locations have been fixed for 150 years. Warning devices do not prevent collisions, but if a driver reacts to a device, and retraces his route, traffic is delayed. No cash is allocated to install and maintain devices. Road operators went blindly ahead, buying higher and heavier vehicles, and looking to BR to pick up the tab for re-building bridges - a cost that should have fallen on those creating the problem - not on all road users, and certainly not on a competitor who was in the field first! Nor should government pay. The irony is that the Smith scheme will *increase* the number of sub standard bridges, (see page 99). It is incredible that a claim is made that *vehicle breakdowns will cause little delay*, given no provision in the Study for breakdown trucks or crews. Providing space for one disabled vehicle per bus bay (Page 13), will not ensure breakdowns only occur in that utopian location. The 520m section - in a cutting near Liverpool St (see photo) - envisages one 3.3m lane each way, between a two-lane bus station, and a two-lane road. In fact, there is insufficient width for two 3.3m lanes in the cutting, (see page 146 & photo). BR *operating* supervisors quickly learn to resolve points failures!

A report in *Traffic Engineer & Control* (March 1976) - another unbiased source - is critical of several aspects of the Study. It argues that, whilst the case for four lightly used lines is convincing, they are hardly typical. When it comes to the main line from Liverpool Street to Harwich and Clacton, which is one of the busiest anywhere, it is not possible to be otherwise than sceptical. The chaos that can be envisaged with Liverpool Street converted to a bus station with 30 bus lanes loading and unloading a vehicle every ten seconds is frightening. It is difficult to believe it is feasible to cope with buses on lanes of less than 3.5 metres and 380 buses in a peak hour. Insufficient consideration has been given to consumer choice - the cost of travel is not the sole criterion. The authors have been rash and unscientific in extrapolating the cost/benefit studies to the whole BR network, from 1.8% of the system. It is hardly surprising that the DoE has reservations.

The rejoinder states that it is surprising to speak of comfort when as many as half the passengers are standing[41]. Bus passengers between London and Glasgow have to book a week in advance. It quotes a report by Commercial Motor (20.5.77), of objection by BR to 'choice' to a licence for a new express coach service for cheap student travel.

Bus operators also oppose licence applications by operators seeking to cream the market. The main reason for low coach fares is an insistence on advance booking to achieve maximum loads. The practice will not change, no matter how many extra roads are created, nor railways converted. Hence, it is irrelevant to conversion. When BR tried, in the 1960s to introduce compulsory advance booking, linked to a guaranteed seat it was opposed by watchdogs who treasured the facility to get on any train without prior notice, and to complain if there was no seat, because BR had failed to invest in crystal balls.

An article in *Municipal Engineering* (12.3.76), an unbiased source with relevant expertise said: benefits are overstated, there are many assumptions and errors in bus operating costs, peak capacity of roads and valuation. The Report uses an arbitrary average rate for time saving for motorists. Opportunity costs are overstated by assumptions of other traffic

---

[41] The Study (Page 63) mentions only one such train! Smith stated (Journal of Transport Economics & Policy, Sept 1973): *there was no assumption peak bus passengers would be all seated,* That would go down like a lead balloon

using busways. Bus speeds on the narrow lanes appear high. 'Several million car trips pa' are mentioned but no indication given of origin, destination or distribution by time of day. On one line, 6m car trips pa are *assumed* to be diverted. Taking typical distributions, and a peak factor of 10%, this implies 1,000 cars per hour in a single carriageway two-way road. This would be close to, if not above, the capacity of such a road, and if attained would imply a much reduced speed. No discussion is devoted to junction capacity, a critical constraint on traffic flow, which would reduce bus speeds and time saved by cars. The Liverpool Street scheme is not operationally feasible nor supported by the economic evaluation produced. Signalling would be required to ensure smooth departures of buses on the 9-second headway. Incoming buses going to the first available stand to pick up would confuse passengers seeking to locate buses. The cost of the Liverpool Street scheme is estimated at £50,000 which the *New Scientist* states might cover a set of drawings, but little building work. The new roads would need retardation and acceleration lanes and signalling to ensure safe merging. This would require a 4-lane width on many sections, eliminating much of the benefit from sale of land. The extraordinary assumption that buses could use A12 without delay, is not backed by peak hour flows for this busy road.[42]

The *rejoinder* sees no problem with junction traffic: critics are confusing motorways with roads laid out for horse traffic. Rates of loading and unloading have been observed of 1.5 seconds to load and 1.0 seconds to unload. No problem is foreseen with conflicting departures, as buses will work to the UK rule - those in the out lane will have priority over those pulling out.[43] 'A passenger will find the stop that serves his destination and **wait** if his bus is not already there'. The lane capacity limit is challenged on grounds that the DoE recommend 2,000 vehicles per hour, with no frontage access, and negligible cross traffic. Stress is placed on the fare-box idea to speed journeys. It stated all tickets at the main stops will be pre-purchased as proposed in the Study, (Page 114).

By no stretch of imagination can the proposed road be compared to motorways, which have no right turns and no traffic entering from the right - as at Liverpool Street bus station. The study shows provision for right turning lanes - a notorious collision risk. Hard shoulders and central reservations are not provided throughout. Loading rates observed at Crewe bus station exceeded his observed figure. Trathens estimate 5 minutes to load 71 passengers - a rate of one every 4.2 seconds. The concept of fixed locations for each bus stop for particular destinations had not been spelled out previously. However, given 30 bus bays, and 36 destinations served directly from Liverpool Street, plus one stopping service, it should have been spelled out which seven bays would suffer the confusion of having queues for two different routes. The problem is worsened, if platforms have to be wider, when 25 bays would serve 37 destinations. There has been no previous reference to passengers having to *wait* at a stop, and no time adjustment for it. Where two destinations were served from one bay, the platform would have to be wider to permit passenger flow around the first bus stop. Some confusion would arise as to which destination, the first available bus should run. *Negligible cross traffic* is unhelpfully subjective. Frontage access would not cease - the depot at Ilford, freight installations, houses and shops will remain. Not all level crossing traffic would cease. The fare-box is an ill conceived idea, doomed to failure, (see pages 103,135). The Study does *not* state all tickets

---

[42] A lorry driver spoke of frequent lorry accidents and high speeds on the A12. (See *Juggernaut* by J Wardroper)
[43] Another rabbit from the hat not seen before. It will delay buses starting out of bays.

will be purchased at main stops, but that: 'individual tickets *can be* bought at ticket offices at Liverpool Street, Stratford and other busy points'. The verb is not *'must be'*. It adds that 'tickets can be bought from the driver' - there is no limit to the locations so involved. Putting the fare in the fare box, unchecked by the driver is a recipe for fraud. The rejoinder ignores the crucial point on the origin and destination of road traffic.

A report[44] by the *Surveyor*, (26.3.76), stated sale of surplus property[45] could take place, whether or not conversion occurs. BR engineers pointed out that the railways have no drains[46] and the run-off from a road laid on top would be disastrous, whilst embankments, which were solid in the centre, but not the edges, would require excavation, backfilling and retaining walls. Smith and Hall had said that underslung girders on one bridge could be brought up flush with longitudinal ones to create more headroom, but overlooked that gas mains were concealed under the bridge. Conversion costs envisaged were well below those experienced by local authorities and others. A recent GLC study on one of the lines in the Hall/Smith Report showed £260,000 per km as the cost for a 6m carriageway, and £350,000 per km for an 8m one, both to single- decker clearance, unlike the double-decker provision in their Report. English China Clays built 3.2 miles of 22 ft road on an old railway track for £406,000. Critics said that 300m acceleration/ deceleration lanes were needed, and that much of the Liverpool St-Brentwood section would have to have an extra lane. The gap was also vast between idea and reality for building a 30 platform bus station at Liverpool Street for £50,000. The article includes examples of conversion costs of closed lines, which were substantially higher than those in the Study, even where they were only for single-deck bus clearance. Taking all objections to the arithmetic, there was a strong impression that conversion costs were grossly underestimated. On inter city routes, people prefer the train to their cars. If inter city conversion went ahead, there would be a substantial switch to cars, and city centre roads would not cope with it.

The *Surveyor* would seem to qualify as unbiased, with relevant expertise. The *rejoinder* includes a sarcastic response that anonymous critics who demand acceleration lanes 300m long, when 90m is adequate, must be told to land their Concorde elsewhere.[47] He explains an error regarding a bridge as being due to a failure of BR to help. On the subject of construction costs, the rejoinder refers to a letter (Pages 51-52), which says that figures quoted at the ICE meeting were obtained by the Railway Conversion League from local authorities. It mentioned that work had been done cheaply, where *the profit margin was not a factor.*

Approaches by the author to every local authority listed in the League's 1970 booklet (see chapter 13), elicited that they had *no* conversion costs for the small sections (an average of 1.8 miles per scheme). It would not have made sense for them to calculate costs for such minor parts of a road scheme, especially when many sections had to be widened, (see chapter 13). Where work was done by private companies - and that would be inescapable on the Liverpool Street scheme, profit would certainly be a factor. Whilst censuring

---

[44] An earlier report on 6.2.76 is not mentioned in *Comments & Rejoinders*, (but see page 114).

[45] BRB Accounts for 1976 refer to property sold for £200m and several major developments in hand, including 1.2m square feet of offices, shops and other amenities at Liverpool Street.

[46] This - and other problems - was revealed 20 years earlier at an ICE debate, (see chapter 4).

[47] In another rejoinder, (Page 27), he criticises the writer for 'childish name calling'.

anonymity among critics, he has, himself, quoted anonymous BR officers who seem to support him, (Study Report Pages 58,78 - pages 115,125 herein). The study report quotes other information, including, for example, bus company costs, without naming the companies. To blame BR for overlooking the gas mains is unacceptable: (a) the DoE were paying *him* for the study, not BR; (b) elsewhere he reports checking every bridge en route, (see page 125)

In March 1977, the Transport Studies Group of the Polytechnic of Central London published a re-examination of the Reading Report. It took two of the six case studies embraced in the Report, namely, the Crouch Valley and Colchester-Sudbury lines. It was packed with data and statistics from named sources to support its conclusions:
• The analysis of revenues and costs for a bus service do not describe flows and service.
• Bus costs need to take account of empty bus return running in peaks.
• Time savings by diversion to the new Crouch Valley road would be less than forecast as the road used by existing motorists is shorter than that specified in the Study. Savings cannot be assessed without detailed traffic flow data, which did not appear to exist
• It is assumed that all current rail travellers will go by bus, despite evidence that 73% of south east workers own cars. Substantial diversion to car is more likely than to bus.[48]
• The accident rate on rural roads with low-volume traffic is of a low order and therefore the estimate of saving is far too large.
• Railfreight included radio-active waste, and the daily equivalent of 100 lorry loads of aggregate, which would slow down other traffic.
• On one of the two routes examined, replacement buses could not earn enough to cover costs. In the other, costs would only just be covered. (In fact, they would not be, see page 139).
• Rates of return were low and the case for either conversion was weak - between negative and 2.9%, compared to up to 60% claimed and 10% regarded as normal.
• Private user benefits - which account for a large proportion of the total benefits of conversion - were overestimated by as much as six times.
• Bus operating costs would be significantly higher than in the Study.
• Terminal costs were unlikely to be saved where a terminal is shared by a continuing part of the railway system.
• Their Study had quoted £5/m² for surfacing the railway formation. Actual conversions and plans reveal a figure of £41/m².
• Bus operating costs are under estimated. Manning levels suggested are unrealistic.
The rejoinder refers only to an extract of the Polytechnic Report, that ignores the first eight of the 13 crucial points. It dismisses the basis they used for costs as hypothetical. It claims that money spent on verges (Page 5), is unnecessary. It claims that manpower numbers are accurate as they are similar to an average gleaned from a bus company, and based on drivers not working longer than 4 hours without a break, an 8-hour day, and a 40-hour week. On terminal economies, it claims that only 6% of stations on the continuing railway will be shared. The Polytechnic had highlighted boarding times and the effect of mixed traffic on bus schedules and time savings - the rejoinder refers them to sections of the study report. Replying to alternative land values, e.g. for agricultural purposes - the sarcastic rejoinder states: 'turnips do not grow well in ballast'.

---

[48] An RAC 2004 Motoring Report states that most motorists see rail as the best alternative to the car. The converse must be equally true. If they were barred from converted routes, they would use existing roads & increase congestion

Hall/Smith costs are hypothetical. Cost levels elsewhere are not valid, any more than a house price can be taken as a UK standard. The only costs which are not hypothetical are written quotes by contractors, who would demand precise drawings, not a series of brief paragraphs. The concept of using manpower data of companies, which almost certainly do not carry 28,500 commuters plus others, is valueless. The only way is to prepare a timetable and driver rosters. That expertise could have been co-opted. The report does not mention limited working hours and breaks for drivers. The basis for 6% of stations is not explained but presumably arises by counting Liverpool Street and Manningtree - one continuing to deal with 258 trains daily, and the other with 90, as of equal value as stations dealing with a dozen or so. The sarcastic remark about turnips is an own goal. Firstly, farmers who bought hundreds of miles of disused track, used it for internal farm tracks, erection of buildings, storage, slurry pits, etc., (see page 195). Secondly, the rejoinder overlooks that good grass doesn't grow on ballast either, but that didn't prevent them proposing that a playing field be annexed and relocated on railway sidings, (Page 103) Removing existing verges would allow cheap widening of many roads, cutting congestion.

Autocar reported again (24.4.76) on the proposal for an 11.5ft carriageway in each direction with 2 ft wide central reservation. The benefits were obvious, more so if it opened out to four lanes in the suburbs as the railway gets wider.[49] If cars are diverted into suburban tube carparks, benefits would not be eroded by congestion.[50] Allowing an 8ft bus, 18 inches clearance, at speed past hefty bridge abutments in cross winds caused many people pause for thought. *How one tackles bridge abutments and cutting walls being so close to the sides of buses needs more than the airy dismissal of the Report.* The DoE said such widths were unacceptable. As many roads are below 12ft, they are over cautious. At the ICE meeting, BR criticised costs of converting bridges, cuttings and embankments, and clearances for double-deck buses to pass bridge abutments at high speed. Runcorn busway[51] is 11 ft wide with buses at 40mph. The value of land which would be released was questioned as were wildly inaccurate estimates for a bus terminal at Liverpool Street.[52] A problem experienced by councils trying to convert *closed* lines into roads, was that railways tended to use bridges over roads, where councils wanted traffic lights.[53] Farmers were happy to use unmanned crossings where trains were infrequent, but less happy about a constantly used road crossing their fields. Norfolk Council has shown the principle is workable, but *at much higher costs than the Hall-Smith* estimates.[54] They said the rail subsidy was 'an attempt to transfer traffic from road to rail',[55] and suggested converting *under-utilised* lines.[56] It asked if 'unions will allow

[49] The further away from terminus, a railway gets narrower because traffic is less.

[50] There would be a cost of creating parking. Most drive to the suburbs and park in residential streets to use the tube.

[51] It was designed with *a town built round it*. Parking was made inconvenient. It is the lowest car owning area in the country, so is no guide. The carriageway is 22 ft wide, with 4 ft clearance on both sides. Speeds are limited to 30 mph at some places, (see pages 119,159).

[52] The opinion on Liverpool Street costs was supported by an independent source - see page 122.

[53] This was not the attitude they took over the introduction of light controlled level crossings.

[54] These are in rural areas, with fewer bridges.

[55] It wasn't. It was to avoid transfer *from* lightly used, uneconomic rural lines. 'The DoT does not want to transfer freight from road to rail' (*Juggernaut* Page 106). No business provides uneconomic services without subsidy. When lines closed, bus fares rose and buses had to be subsidised by BR until 1968, then by local authorities or government.

[56] Not all lines, not even all *under-utilised* lines. Subject to MoT approval, they would close.

computer controlled unmanned trains, and goods handling will be modernised'.[57] Two undated photos of unidentified bridges, show road traffic - one on the *right hand side* - and no trains on the railway. A third is of a car-carrying train and concludes there is plenty of headroom for high vehicles. A fourth shows a disused line near Bourne End, serving as a refuse tip, which, it was claimed would form a natural bypass for a village. The article concluded: The study is 'now apparently discredited on a large number of technical and cost grounds'.

Smith responded (Autocar 8.5.76), that the most important cost - **paving** was from a study published in the Highway Engineer, and that it would be worth converting a railway even if it were used only by buses and lorries replacing trains.[58] He said that he had measured every bridge between Liverpool Street and Harwich by dodging trains.[59] He criticised BR for not substantiating criticisms with maps, plans and diagrams. An anonymous BR officer (see also page 115), told him BR would not allow open discussion. He undermined his scheme by stating that where clearance is restricted, drivers would reduce speed. It would cut road capacity! He again criticises *extravagant DoE requirements* for road widths. He disputed that his 1973 based figures were low compared to Norfolk County Council costs, saying that they took place in 1976/7, and asked if no one had heard of inflation.

Dalgleish wrote (to *Autocar*), that conversion costs were not from the League. Those costs may be arguable, but bus costs and benefits to other traffic are unchallenged.[60]

Responding to the Article

• Photos of track and road use may have been taken when lines were closed for renewal or Christmas Day, and reflect the situation for $^1/_{250}$ of a second in 365 days. Locations will be found where a bridge is closed for road repairs whilst trains run below.

• To get the same headroom, HGVs and PSVs would have to reduce wheel diameters to that which enable wagons to pass within railways' restricted loading gauge.

• The local authority did not agree that the Bourne End line could be a bypass, because part was turned into a footpath, whilst the rest is disused. A map supplied by the County Council shows the route of this disused line as being a virtual semi-circle round Flackwell Heath hill, contradicting claims that railways were straight.

Responding to the Rejoinder

• Drawings are thin in his book. Of the 256km in the scheme, the length of infrastructure set out in drawings in the book, aggregates to just over one kilometre. No engineering project of this magnitude would have been submitted without comprehensive drawings.

• Bridge measurements should have been tabulated in chronological order allowing DoE, BR and others to check the accuracy of measurements and ensure that no bridge was overlooked, especially one on farming or other private land. Measurements made in haste are wisely subject to caution - remember the adage: 'measure twice, cut once'.

---

[57] Goods *handling* was modernised in the 50s. One may forgive a *car magazine* for being unaware of freightliner & non-stop 1000 ton trains. Union views on private sector made computers were irrelevant. Managers knew they were unreliable in less safety-critical areas and that a 100% reliable computer to safely control trains was some way off

[58] The scheme depends on conversion costs being covered by private traffic (see pages 104,139). Moreover, at the fares claimed, bus services would not be profitable even if others did fund the conversion and most of its maintenance.

[59] BR reporting procedures would bring reports from drivers, signal box or station staff to Control 'of someone criss-crossing the line'. In the prevailing situation of bomb threats, which frequently included railways, police should have been called, and the army alerted. The incident indicates a serious security weakness in that area compared to those where the author worked. In the light of current internal security fears, the area should be thoroughly checked now.

[60] This book tabulates facts which challenge and demolish that scheme and other conversion proposals.

- Doubtless, many others were aware of inflation, but they would also be aware that construction and operating costs were higher in London & the South East!
- He ignored that one company quoted costs at the ICE meeting at ten times the cost he had used - and they were at *1969* prices! The issue of cost was addressed in a re-examination of two of the Hall/Smith case studies, by the Transport Study Group of the Polytechnic of Central London. They concluded that inflation over two years *cannot* account for the discrepancy. They said that £300,000 per km for a 7.3m width was a reasonable estimate compared to the Smith cost (£40,000). He ignores the inflation on an estimate of £29,000 *per mile* 20 years earlier for a long, largely rural, route (see page 50), which, by 1975 would equate to over £82,000 per mile, or £132,000 per km!
- Paving costs would not cover costs of building the bus station, slip road construction, excavations, altering bridges, flyovers etc., which would seem to be far more significant
- He does not answer criticisms on 'the value of the land and the wildly inaccurate estimates for a huge bus terminal at Liverpool Street' and ignored farmers' concerns.

A letter from independent experts - the Technical & Engineering Committee of the Confederation of British Road Passenger Transport (27.4.76), to Hall & Smith, with a copy to the DoE - contained 14 criticisms. *Rejoinders* includes a brief extract of that letter that is limited to the last three of the 14 criticisms shown below. The rest were unanswered

- The study implied that specially designed vehicles may be required but no mention was made of the high capital cost that this would involve.
- There was considerable evidence of a lack of experience and inadequate detailed knowledge of the subject.
- There were factual errors and a notable omission was any reference to reliability.
- The British legal limit for the front axle is 9,150 kg not 6.1Mg as shown in the report.
- To state that the transverse rear engine is usual in Britain, and universal in the US is misleading. This is only true of double-deckers in Britain, and in the US there is a significant number of buses with longitudinally mounted engines. No mention is made of these latter engines which is the most usual for rear-engined single-deckers in Britain and is in sizeable numbers in most European countries.
- Independent front suspension is not standard in America, nor in Europe. A reference to independent rear suspension does not mention that it is impractical with twin rear tyres.
- Hydraulic retarders are only used for a much more powerful engine than would be used for bus work.
- It is stated that an integral body is lighter and less expensive but many integral buses are heavier and more costly than their counterparts with separate chassis and bodywork.
- The 8m double-decker mentioned, is obsolete. The worldwide standard is 11-12 metres
- It referred to a misunderstanding of conventional leaf springs and their linkage.
- It referred to the 'possibility' of placing a horizontal engine under the driver, when it already exists in Paris.
- The conclusion that a nose heavy vehicle was preferable takes no account of the virtually universal use of twin rear tyres on buses and coaches. These give correct tyre loading and hence the desired stability on vehicles.
- The claim that for equal length, the double-decker has twice the seating capacity ignores the space for the staircase, occupying 4-5 seats space.

- Articulated buses are manoeuvrable, but it is important to note their effect on street congestion and garage space.

The *rejoinder* by a *civil engineer* tells the auspicious *Technical Committee* that their views on engine placement confuse stability in sidewinds with stability in corners! It disputes their view on comparative double- and single-decker seating. It argues that one articulated bus will take up less road space[61] than three rigid buses they would replace.

There is no consideration in the rejoinder nor the original report to the implications of an articulated bus using the Liverpool Street bus bays, nor turning into the out lane, with its limited space. Most importantly, they have overlooked that having some articulated - presumably intended for destinations where bridge heights are limited - and some double deck vehicles, means that buses cannot pull into the first available bay - a cornerstone of their plan, but must only pull into a bay which requires that type of bus. This could leave an articulated bus blocking an inbound lane, whilst waiting for another articulated to depart - as there would be insufficient length for both clear of the inbound lanes.

Rejoinders has an undated extract from a Working Party Report of the Conservation Society. It was to be published April-May 1976, (*The Times*, 31.3.76). The Extract mentions:
- North Tyneside scheme road conversion costs were prepared in 1970. With inflation, these would have risen to £0.4m per km. That scheme was based on limited station facilities and ramps every 5km in comparison with 2km in Hall/Smith.
- Long bus deceleration lanes were a major omission in the original Smith paper.[62]
- Costs envisaged for 14 proposed ramps are suspiciously low; they include major works, roundabouts, tunnels. and a new length of road adjacent to a major suburban location
- If costs for the major works at Liverpool Street, Shoreditch and near Brentwood are eliminated, it leaves £29,000 per km for the rest for busway only, which is unrealistic.
- The proposed average 80 kph bus speed would mean a top speed of 110 kph. Double-deck buses were limited to 80 kph, after one overturned on the M1.
- The only bus which would meet criteria for a front engine and one man operation was a disaster, only 70 were sold. Two caught fire and burnt out while running. The only bus scheduled at high speed led to one overturning with fatalities and serious injuries. It is permitted on motorways only in the summer at 50 mph. The operation looks unsafe.
- The estimated main line fleet seems underestimated even on the authors' own principles. Instead of 475, 530 would be needed. If running speeds average 75% of that envisaged, it would need to increase by a third; 15% spares are usually held by operators, not 10%.
- Busmen do not like split turns.
- Much of the benefit comes from additional car traffic created. The maximum level of traffic assumed is 2,400 vehicles per hour, which equates to 1.5 seconds gap between each. TV advertising warns that 'only a fool breaks the 2 second rule'.
- There are access points every 2km, a bus 'station' every 2.5km. [These are hazards].

---

[61] See photo taken in London. When one negotiated a corner, vehicles in the opposite direction were stopped. The ensuing delays clearly reduce road capacity. When two met at a corner, traffic was stopped in both directions.

[62] It appears that the 1976 Book, found after prolonged national inquiries by the author, was followed by an amended Report which preceded the 1978 *Comments & Rejoinders*. He has been unable to find this edition. To produce three editions of one Report when all aspects should have been covered in one, is a clear indication of the weakness of the argument. Undertaking a task such as this is like sitting an exam - you get one shot, and that's it - right or wrong.

- One bus failure can start a snowballing effect. there could be little certainty of reliability. This means either more spare buses or journey time losses for passengers.
- If 60 kph is taken as feasible, the benefit of £1.67m becomes a disbenefit of £2.3m.
- There are no figures to back up the claim that freight trains run only generally at night[63] and lorries in the daytime.
- Environmental conclusions are biased.[64] They claim that OLE is a visual intrusion, but do not refer to lighting and huge road signs that would be essential, particularly for private car traffic.
- Oddly, they throw in construction costs as a single annual cost rather than use the conventional approach of measuring construction costs, then assessing the resulting annual running/social costs of the changed system.
- Opportunity costs describes the next best alternative use that could be produced costing the same amount of money. In section 16 of the paper they mix economic evaluation of social costs from financial cost accounting. Doubling the existing cost of BR services with a theoretical cost is hardly good analytical practice. It ignores a vital point of economics - if consumers prefer X to Y, they will pay more for X than Y.
- Using conventional accounting and as the system is incapable of carrying the private car volume envisaged, nor of achieving more than a quarter of the property sales in this area, net capital costs will rise to £90m, and annual savings/benefits will fall to between -£0.03m and £4.4m depending on whether speeds of 50 or 60 kph are achievable.
- The scheme, assuming it works with high level of efficiency and complete safety, could yield at most, 5% - half of the DoE test discount rate. The economic case is weak
- The scheme assumes property prices will be high enough to make a significant profit. This is unrealistic. BR's record for disposal of property is reasonable, with income of £20m pa. Property in East London is not easy to sell, partly because the GLC seeks to stop further migration from London. The area is run down, and to expect sales of any size shows a lack of realism.
- Only rail can meet urban need. Urban areas have been built up because railways existed
- Why were the effects on lifestyle and land use not analysed more closely.

Rejoinders were made to only 16 of the criticisms and several 'rejoinders', were at best partial responses, to these 21 damning and well structured criticisms:-

- ♦ The bus bay figure includes deceleration lanes but was not explicitly stated.[65]
- ♦ Small island roundabouts have proved a satisfactory alternative to expensive junctions[66]
- ♦ The critics do not understand the difference between cruising speed and average speed.
- ♦ The cause of the bus overturning was that a lorry jack-knifed in front. Jack-knifing can be prevented by fitting an accessory to the brakes.[67]
- ♦ Comments on the vehicles needed are based on a misunderstanding of cruising speed.
- ♦ A bus built of reliable components can operate with 10% reserve, it will have more seats

---

[63] The branch lines covered in the study which have freight are not open at night!

[64] Rail freight is much less intrusive environmentally and is much safer than road freight, (Plowden & Buchan)

[65] To have clarified such an oversight after an exam would still result in failure. It is not acceptable to produce points like rabbits from a hat. He envisaged some bus bays sharing deceleration lanes (Study Page 13), a recipe for accidents

[66] Except where used by LGVs and articulated buses! The Study mentions two small roundabouts, one large & two undefined, (Pages 92,104,107,110). The largest is 178 metres in diameter & has an underpass, (see Page 92).

[67] There is no mention in the book of restricting use of the converted system to lorries so fitted, nor of the cost, which most hauliers have not been prepared to pay, and the DoT has not enforced, (see *Juggernaut,* Page 71).

- Most of the fleet will be available for maintenance during the day.[68]
- The possibility of both carriageways being simultaneously blocked by a 'crossover' accident is precluded by the central barrier assumed in the study ![69]
- A breakdown will only cause a problem on the 520m bus-only 6.6m single carriageway just outside Liverpool Street. A tow-truck stationed there could reach it in a minute.[70]
- Claims made by the Working Party that passenger time is overstated, are wrong because the comment on running speed is wrong.[71]
- The rejoinder to a criticism on lack of evidence that 'freight trains commonly run all night', whilst 'lorries run all day', is that the full sentence includes numbers of trains at Manor Park, and the lorry aspect is conditioned by when not affected by congestion. It is also stated that lorries run in the day because employers have to pay extra at night.[72]
- Lighting is dismissed as unnecessary - 'a legacy of an age when public spending on roads was less constrained', (Page 37).[73]
- No new flyover is needed on any of the routes studied.[74]
- The Report says buses on the Liverpool St line will offer a seat for every passenger.[75]
- Every property value was arrived at by asking an estate agent or valuer.[76]

A *Rejoinder* is made (Page 30) that if enough lines were converted to require several thousand buses, a purpose built 100 seat, 110 kph double deck bus would be viable[77]. Figures are not produced to validate this claim. A production line for such a small one-off order, with no indication of when replacement would arise, is improbable, (see page 31). A rejoinder is made (Page 37), that road users are so sensitive to the community that they unfailingly obey an unenforceable ban on using horns at night, despite slamming car doors and shouting in the early hours. It is untenable. Drivers ignore red traffic lights, make prohibited right and 'U' turns, go the wrong way on one-way roads, use bus lanes irregularly, tailgate, make risky changes of lane, overtake on the left, fail to give way at major junctions and roundabouts, and do not keep vehicles in good condition. Many of these dangerous offences occur within sight of CCTV, which are unlikely to detect misused horns[78]

---

[68] This, like a gearbox change in 5 hours will be at Ilford, needing drivers to take buses there. Those on services may not have time, (see pages 137-8). What matters is not that most are available, but whether those due maintenance are.

[69] Thirty years later, we have yet to see a central barrier with such attributes!

[70] The book does not mention a truck. Two 3.3m lanes are not possible, (see page 146). If they were, it would *not* get to a bus so quickly. *After* advice is received, a driver found & instructed (no supervisors are envisaged) it would take 5-10 minutes. The road will be blocked as it gets ahead of an outbound bus. Many buses will be stopped. The station would be heaving, a peak in chaos. If the breakdown was inbound, it would take longer, causing more delay. A bus towed to Ilford at 20mph will delay buses. There is no debit for *one* incident per year against passenger time savings

[71] The author has identified other serious flaws in the claims of time saved, (see pages 140-141). They claim an average of 5 minutes for all passengers, (Page 115) despite having no data for 90 destinations, and 0.2% for others

[72] The report itself refers to freight from branch lines which are closed at night. Hauliers have never been inhibited by congestion. The belief that lorries run during the day, has no bearing on self employed drivers, and is not borne out by endless heavy vehicles on the M6, whose noise can be heard day and night at a range of one mile, unlike nearer trains.

[73] If Treasury officials had been standing knee deep in gold, they would not have allocated an unnecessary penny. Lighting was installed to reduce accidents. Non-provision invalidates comparisons between safety on converted roads and motorways. If superfluous, all lights should be switched off to cut global warming, and later removed

[74] A substantial dual carriageway structure is envisaged at Brook Street, between Harold Wood and Brentwood, (Page 92). It is described as a flyunder, but is a flyover in which four lanes pass over four lanes.

[75] That idealistic objective is undermined by Smith in the Journal of Transport Economics & Policy (Sept 1973).

[76] That does not guarantee buyers will be found, nor that in this rundown area, the price would not fall like a stone. Sellers always start by pitching the price high. The caution advanced by the critics is well judged. (see page 107).

[77] This *Rejoinder* does not appear to be prompted by a criticism on the subject. It implies an uncosted new type.

[78] Rail horns are used *solely* for safety reasons. Failure to use horns properly causes avoidable road accidents.

Transport Policy, an MoT consultation paper (April 1976) stated that the study costs were under-estimated, savings claimed doubtful and new traffic questionable.

The *Rejoinder* claimed that costs were realistic, it dismissed bridges built to *idealistic* DfT standards, and claimed that a 2-track railway will convert to a road with a width of 6.8-7.3m. It claims that MoT criticism is based on generalities.

This book shows that costs are unrealistic, not all bridges were measured, and a 2-track section will not convert to such a width (e.g., see page 146), and the changeover is impractical

Neutral report included in Rejoinders - neither for nor against
Nobody cares for freight (*Commercial Motor* 13.2.76) bemoaned public dislike of lorries, that may have encouraged a belief of an intention to exclude lorries. There is no rejoinder.

Not supportive - not included in Rejoinders
A *Guardian* article (29.4.74), adjoining one included in *Rejoinders*, stating that road transport appears incapable of developing beyond a point where 50 passengers or 30 tons can be handled by one driver, whilst one train driver can cope with 500 passengers or 2,000 tons. 'Trains have a 4-to-1 energy advantage over road, ton for ton'.

Professor Hall expects 'an *experiment* to be carried out on *a lesser used line,*' (*The Times,* 2.2.76). The inference is a lack of conviction about routes carrying heavy traffic.

A letter in *New Society* (5.2.76) doubts assumptions on time savings. It refers to an article by Peter Hall, [*New Society,* 29.1.76], and says that, although 10-times as much saving for bus passengers was claimed on a new road, compared to car users, it did not tempt people out of cars. This casts doubt on the validity of savings calculated by multiplying thousands of tiny daily reductions in travel time to make thousands of hours a year. It says that Hall might reflect on the light this throws on the willingness to switch to buses on converted railways. An article in the same edition of *New Society* is in *Rejoinders*. (Page 71).

Criticism in *New Scientist* (5.2.76) is missed, although it was quoted in *Municipal Engineering* (12.3.76), an extract of which is in *Rejoinders*. Having said that £50,000 would pay only for drawings of Liverpool Street bus station, it points out that the much-quoted bus lane in New Jersey leads to a multi-storey multi-million dollar terminal, compared to a single level terminal proposed by Smith, with 27,500 peak hour passengers crossing the bus flow. By looking at annual traffic, the [Smith] report fails to take account of peak road saturation and substantially underestimates loading time for one-man buses. Other costs have been substantially underestimated. On one route which requires four drivers in the peak, it assumes the need for only five drivers. It doesn't allow for drivers who go sick or have holidays. The report failed to consider adequately what happens at junctions.

The introduction to *Rejoinders*, says as criticism was expected, it was decided to collect all *criticisms* and give a *measured* rejoinder. Measured rejoinders should eshew sarcasm, but some did not. Some criticisms are reduced to extracts, some are left out. Had *supportive* views been left out, there would have been room for full reprints of criticisms. Readers are left in the dark as to what else was in an article, when an extract is used.

Serious flaws in the scheme were identified in reports, articles and letters set out in the preceding part of this chapter and chapter 15. However, there are other serious defects.

Crucial flaws & defects

First to the generality of the proposal. It lacks proper plans and drawings for the whole length, without which it would have been shredded by any Board. There is not one cross section nor side elevation drawing. The four top elevation drawings lack detail, and relate to 0.6% of the route. Locations where constructional problems need to be addressed are described in a few words instead of standard before and after drawings, backed by contractors' written estimates. Photos of Liverpool St. station interior were essential. The study frequently uses *assume, if* and *probably*, but concludes with definite consequences! The limited consideration of the down side risks ignores the worst scenarios.

Issues which stand out to a transport manager, and are crucial to proving *practicability* before considering financial aspects, are the design of the Liverpool Street bus station, ticket issues, accidents, use of the route for other traffic, no reference to fuelling/coolant or top-up/water supply for windscreen washers, no timetable and Post Office mails.

A diagrammatic representation of the passenger and vehicle flow at the proposed Liverpool Street bus station exposes serious problems:

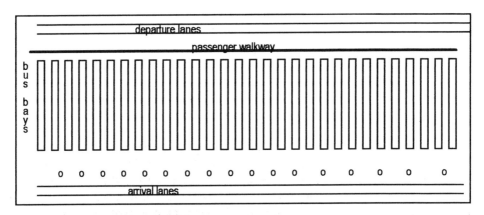

The 155m long bus station will have 30 bays: 3m per bus lane (Page 13) and 2m width per 'platform' for passengers to load and unload, which may be inadequate. If they were wider, there would be fewer bays. Barriers would be needed to minimise accidents. A passenger walkway would be about 3m wide to cope with bi-directional flows. The plan lacks a crucial passenger/vehicle flow chart, from which the dangers to passengers would be apparent. As buses depart from their bays, they will cross the walkway. The plan should have been put to the H&SE - in like manner to new rail plans that are put to the HMRI by BR for approval. The drawing (Page 71), has three rows - each of 17 - unexplained dots (shown in the diagram above as small circles). Investigation reveals that they were roof support columns. One row is next to the inbound lanes - the others (not shown above) are expected to be on the platforms. Buses - including articulated - will turn between them.

They will need to be in the outer lane to do so.[1] Other rows are on the bus platforms. If they are widened, problems will arise. A row of unexplained boxes in the drawing are the bases of arches of a brick wall separating west and east trainsheds.

An arriving bus will pull into the first available bay, and will, sometimes, be behind one that has broken down or whose driver has gone for a break, or to 'inspect the plumbing'. There is no reference to what will happen if a bus arrives at the closed end of the bus station, because all sixty spaces are occupied. It would be dangerous and impractical for it to reverse, hence it would have to wait a space at the end bay. Should it wait more than a few seconds, others will be waiting behind. Such problems will occur after the peak. No mention is made of relief drivers to cover breaks, nor for holidays or sickness. Without supervisors who are not mentioned, there will be chaos. The scheme envisages that drivers will run at random to any destination except on the last run, which will be home.[2] The prospect that the aggregate working time will precisely correspond to the legal hours limit with such random sequential journey times is virtually nil. As is the prospect that maintenance can fit into the time when the bulk of the fleet is at Liverpool Street - as is envisaged. As there are no rosters, as buses flow in after the peak, drivers will go into the first space available or congest the bus station, as there is no one to direct which are to park and which are due maintenance at Ilford, of which a driver will have no knowledge.

In a 'peak' of 58 minutes,[3] 380 buses will depart - one every 9 seconds. A loading time of 3 minutes is specified.[4] No unloading time is mentioned, hence turnround time cannot be calculated. If all had tickets, the driver would have to check validity at the rate of one every two seconds. They failed to mention that drivers will have to inspect seasons, nor to specify how they will deal with tickets out-of-date or short of destination. The scope for buses varying from an 9 second slot by a few seconds either way, is a recipe for chaos. It is said that buses will depart when 100% full. There is zero prospect that *all* will achieve this in precisely 3 minutes, even in the peak. At the tail end of a peak, the bus to each destination will wait longer to fill to 100%, than during the height of the peak. No reference is made to this. Nor is it stated whether off-peak buses will wait until they have full loads. There will be some tailgating and some longer gaps. Buses departing every 9 seconds from one or other of the 30 bays is impractical. To claim that this task could be performed - day after day, in all conditions - from 19 bays, (see Page 69), is incredible.

A bus departing every 9 seconds means one arriving at the same frequency. If it takes five minutes to unload, and five to load, during that time, 86 buses will arrive - exceeding the dual capacity of 30 bays. If turnround time averaged half that, 43 buses would arrive, and as they waited for a vacant bay, a queue would develop. Things would be worse off-peak. To avoid chaos, each bus would need to unload and load in a few seconds. When a sealed fare box, (see pages 103,135) - which would need to be secured to the floor - has to be changed, turnround time would increase. The concept is a recipe for disaster

---

[1] See photograph. The narrow gaps between columns are also illustrated in *Liverpool Street Station* by Robert Thorne & *Railway Stations of Britain* by Geoffrey Body.

[2] The reason is not explained. His home may not be on the route. Is the vehicle to be parked in the street?

[3] Why such a strange period has been selected is not explained. A CTCC study of peak travel in 1958 covered a $1\frac{1}{2}$ hour period; BTC 1968 Annual Report references to heavy peak flows are over a $1\frac{1}{2}$ hour period.

[4] An operator of 71-seat PSVs told the author that it takes 5 minutes to load through the one door. A train coach has two or more doors, which on many trains are as wide as two PSV doors each. Rail passengers load their luggage, but a PSV driver does that and could not take his place in the cab, until the luggage of the last passenger was stowed.

The passenger walkway (see diagram, page 131), will have 28,500 departing passengers[5] moving on it in, in one direction, in the peak 58 minutes - an average of 490 per minute[6] past a given point. In that minute, they are going to have 6-7 buses *trying* to depart across the walkway, taking say 14 seconds out of their minute. Commuters hurrying for a bus further along will risk life and limb to push through. Some will divert off the walkway onto road lanes to get round the crush. Those encumbered by small children, luggage, or in wheelchairs are going to be in particular danger. Departing passengers would have to cross the flow of incoming passengers going in the opposite direction. The flow would be increased by passengers who, intending to board a particular bus, found it fully loaded and went to another bay. Passengers will be unable to get to buses quickly, and the time savings envisaged (see page 104), will not merely evaporate, but become negative.

Departing and arriving passengers will each have to be restricted to one half of a 3m wide walkway, which will need designated directional flow separation to avoid total chaos. If the walkway is made wider, there is less turning area for arriving buses, and more opportunity for conflicting movements between departing passengers trying to cut through to a bay, between other departing passengers heading for a different bay, arriving passengers and moving buses. The Study makes no provision for the costs of a CCTV system, which would be essential and require staff to operate and maintain it.

Delays would occur in boarding due to passengers fumbling for the correct fare, which they are hardly likely to be carrying in their hands as they hurry to find where their bus is located. How those who board in excess of capacity are to be ejected is not mentioned.

As they depart from a bay, each driver would have to manoeuvre through the passenger flow into one of the two departing lanes, sometimes in the path of another bus. Drivers will have great difficulty forcing a way through. The aggregate time taken for departing buses, to cross the walkway at, say two seconds each - it could be longer - is 16 minutes of delay to passenger flow in the 58 minute peak period. The first minor accident will bring the station to a halt. Working hours will be completely unpredictable. Drivers may insist on taking overdue breaks at the outstation, disrupting the flow.

In contrast, Victoria coach station has 21 bays, holding between two and four vehicles to accommodate 53 coaches, plus 6 parking - that is about the same number of bay spaces as the proposed bus station at Liverpool Street, which will have about half of the area of Victoria. Their departures in the busiest hour are about 50. The separate Arrivals area has 10 coaches unloading at any one time. They don't like more because of the vehicle/pedestrian interface problem. They allow 15 minutes to unload and move clear. Thus, in a site about 50% of Victoria's area, the Liverpool Street bus station will hold up to 60 buses in 30 bays, and achieve a departure every 9 seconds, compared to Victoria's one per minute. Victoria's frequency is conditioned by bay occupation and internal movement rather than egress onto roads. Victoria allows departure coaches to be in their bays or on site for 30 minutes. It is clear that the planned occupancy and flows envisaged on the Liverpool Street site are wildly optimistic and dangerous into the bargain.

---

[5] i.e. 75 passengers on each of 380 buses, each fully loaded as claimed. If each person's stride occupies one metre, and has a half a metre space ahead for a smooth flow, and two persons occupy 1.5m of width, 490 will occupy a length of 342m, which is double the length of the walkway. The number of incoming passengers is unknown.

[6] BR filmed arrivals which showed the flow was uneven, which makes matters worse, and undermines the claimed time savings. Clearly, some days would be above average, requiring more buses and more staff.

Clearly, the whole Liverpool Street operation with its hoped for flexibility of buses running on any route, would require one company to have the licence or contract. Established bus operators would jib at the prospect of driving a bus, every 9 seconds, through a two way flow of milling passengers. It is doubtful that any insurance company would give accident cover, but if they did, premiums would probably be penal. Cynical brokers would not depend on assurances by academics that there would be few accidents. Noticeably, there is no reference to insurance. BR, of course, made insurance provision.

Another staffing element that has been ignored is assistance for disabled passengers. The effect on loading times of wheelchairs, prams, and luggage is overlooked. Victoria coach station provides assistance. In the 1970s, there was no blanket restriction on cycles on trains, although it was not practical on peak commuter trains. However, long distance trains in the peak and off-peak carried cycles, as did off-peak shorter distance trains. Obviously, no cycles will be conveyed by bus.

Manningtree

The route from Liverpool Street carries Inter City passengers to Ipswich and Norwich. They will go by bus to Manningtree, and change to a train, at the one platform to be re-tained, (Page 100). Three of the four platforms/tracks at Manningtree would be converted to roads, whilst one is 'retained for the Ipswich train'. This gives an impression of one plat-form, literally, one train. However, the service via Manningtree to Ipswich and beyond is *more than twice* that going towards Harwich. The single track station would have 92 daily trains to and from Ipswich and Norwich. The scheme takes three-quarters of the station for less than one-third of the traffic. A salutary indication of the wasteful use of roads compared to railways. This disproportionate alteration to rail facilities at Manning-tree does not merit a penny for alterations to the residual railway infrastructure: carriage cleaning & fuelling (hitherto done at Colchester), signalling, or track. No provision is made for the costs of staff required at Manningtree to look after passengers, and see to departing trains. Nor is mention made of transfer of mails and parcels which are carried in passenger trains.

Other changing points

Many travelling from Liverpool Street will change to another bus at Stratford, Romford, Witham, Wickford and Colchester. Some form of supervision would be essential to minimise chaos, and arguments in case passengers arriving at these locations from both directions, try to board buses in numbers which exceed their capacity. There needs to be supervision to deal with problems of drivers absent from work, and the handling of cash, (see below). The plan makes no provision for toilets or shelters at these or other locations.

Destinations for which no provision is made

No provision is made for passengers (Page 116), to Alresford, Hythe or Weeley, on the Clacton line, or for Mistley, Wrabness and Dovercourt on the Harwich line, hence, they will have no direct service, other than the service stopping at all 'stations'.

Fare Collection

The idea conceived to attempt to reduce delays and keep costs down by not having ticket offices at all 64 stations involved, would fail. 'Books of tickets of (sic) season tickets can be bought from ticket offices or the driver'. The belief that shopkeepers could be per-suaded to 'obtain tickets in bulk at a slight discount' clearly indicates that the authors have no knowledge of the trade terms required by retailers. The belief that they would stock tickets as an alternative to 'being pestered for change' shows that the authors are out of touch with reality. Retailers would *not* supply change, just as they ceased to oblige non-customers long ago with change for payphones. A notice would make that clear, as in the past, and those ignoring it, would be told quite brusquely where to go! Those who tried to get change for a note, by making a small purchase, and requesting the change to be in a number of specified coins would quickly get their come-uppance. Busy retailers working on tight margins have no time to waste on such unproductive activity. If they agreed to sell tickets, they would demand a normal trade discount of at least 33-50%,[7] and credit for a month. They may decline to stock a full range of tickets, including season tickets, to all stations. Re-booking at shops at junction points would extend journey times. The commuter used to buying a ticket with seconds to spare, would have to join a queue of those buying groceries, papers, confectionery, etc. Problems of security, accountancy, etc., would be significant. An annual season ticket would be valuable and bigger target for thieves than a few cigarettes. Their insurance would rise. It is a complete non-runner. Retailers' terms would make bus operation totally uneconomic, even with a subsidy, even if it were not torpedoed by other impracticalities, including shops closing at 6pm. The idea of 'ticket offices at Liverpool Street, Stratford and *other busy points*' would have to be replaced by one at every station, some open around the clock. Their failure to name all locations is incomprehensible. One cannot determine whether the staffing levels are adequate without that information. Passengers requiring season tickets would expect the prevailing discounts against the much trumpeted low bus fares. They would not pay weeks or months in advance merely to travel on cramped buses at fares which did not offer similar discounts to BR. Commuters would not tolerate withdrawal of seasons, which enable them to avoid delays at both ends - and government dare not oppose them.

Another idea to reduce terminal time is for passengers without tickets to 'put the exact change into a sealed fare box, drivers would not touch the money'. The driver would be unable to account for *his* ticket sales - he could give them to friends, or sell them in a pub. There would be no check on how far passengers were entitled to travel. They state that tickets may be dropped in the box. Ticket validity would not be checked. The opportunity for fraud is immense. No one with practical transport experience would propose the idea. Passengers changing at Stratford, Romford, Witham, Colchester and Wickford will pay into another fare box. Who, at each location, would replace boxes, check and account for their contents is not mentioned. Boxes would need to be replaced before becoming full. They would have to be removed or emptied before buses went to Ilford for maintenance, and at close of work, *after* drivers made the last journey home. Standard security practices require two persons to handle loose cash, and record the number of foreign coins. How boxes would get to a main location from branch routes is ignored. It would not be possible to pay by credit card or cheque - an acute disadvantage at locations without ticket offices.

The boxes would need to be of a size which allowed a huge number of coins to be inserted, or turnround times would be extended. The weight of the boxes could prove daunting. The contents would have to be checked and bagged, before being sent by security vehicle to a bank, which charges for checking coins. The scope for fraud is incalculable. The revenue is forecast at £4.5m pa, (see Table on page 139). Of this, about 25% of

---

[7] No comparison can be made with Travel Agents who sell products allied to transport.

London fares would be in seasons (the national percentage is 20%). That leaves £3.4m. If half was in pre-paid tickets, that leaves £1.7m pa in cash - by inference (Page 114) - most in coins. Given the scope for fraud, the amount would be less. The operator would be ruined.

Bus services

Traffic for Ingatestone, Hatfield Peverel, Witham, (for Braintree), Kelvedon and Marks Tey (for Sudbury), travelling on the A12 and local roads (see page 149), will be slower than rail, but are shown to have faster journey times, (Page 115). Their interface with pedestrians risks more fatalities. Stopping services (Page 115) serving these points will be especially slow. Clearly, stopping services cannot wait until 100% full, or otherwise there is a risk of a long wait and/or having no room to pick up. They must have a specified departure schedule, or otherwise the decision will be left to the random wishes of staff. There should be an allowance in time saving calculations for a counter loss by commuters using stopping services which would take longer to fill, and have longer gaps between.

Bus Fleet size

The fleet cannot be derived by relating a theoretical running time, which makes no provision for problems and using it to calculate a theoretical fleet. The risk of time loss by buses transferring from outbound to inbound lane at out stations, with the consequences of making two right hand turns across unyielding traffic[8], does not register a mention.

The 'main line' will have 75-seat double-deck buses. It is stated that passengers will not go to the top deck for a journey under 20 minutes (Page 7). Despite that, the scheme uses double-deck buses, 100% loaded in the evening peak from Liverpool St to 11 destinations whose journey is 20 minutes or less, (Page 116). These involve 99 buses making 160 peak journeys. If they do not use top decks, that requires 99 extra buses. 17 buses starting from Stratford have journeys under 20 minutes. There will be similar problems with the 50 all-station buses, (Page 115), which will involve journeys under 20 minutes. These buses will need to be single-deck, increasing the size of the fleet and manpower. If articulated single deck buses were used, to provide 75 seats, they would cause further problems, when trying to pass between roof supports to enter a bay at Liverpool St. If all were occupied by a bus, the tail would obstruct arrival lanes. Should they get into an occupied bay and have to reverse out due to a breakdown of a preceding bus, it would be chaotic. An articulated bus would cause delay to other buses and passengers, on departure, by taking longer to exit a bay. They would have problems at mini roundabouts. If single deck or articulated buses were used, the random use of buses to any destination would be impractical. Moreover, the belief that commuters will squeeze into a bus, whose knee room is less than a train, and worse than some of the worst airlines, for a 1-1½ hour journey is unrealistic.

No one would undertake to operate a service at the fares claimed and reliability promised, on the basis of these fleet estimates. The Report does not show total peak passengers. The proposed 380 peak hour buses (Page 72) equates to 28,500 passengers. In 48 trains (Pages 66-8), that *averages* 590 per train which had between 504 and 1032 seats, 'average' 768, suggesting avoidable standing or too few buses. The authors added a percentage of spare vehicles to cover maintenance and breakdown for the main line flow from Liverpool St - which may be unacceptable to operators. None were provided for

---

[8] At two places, right turns will cross flows of 25,000 vehicles: one every 3 seconds. Peak hours will be worse. One turnround point has only 16,000 vehicles crossing! As no return route is planned at Maryland, buses will make 'U' turns, causing delays. The return trip time (see Page 116) does not allow transfer elsewhere to inbound lanes.

other routes. No breakdown vehicles were provided. For buses to run at random to any destination requires *every* bridge en route to be of the minimum height necessary for double deck buses. As will be seen (page 108), nearly half of all bridges need alteration: re-decking, re-building, replacement[9] or excavation of formation to create the *limited* headroom envisaged. Excavation assumes no mains services exist, and that bridges had deeper foundations than necessary, which is doubtful, given that the original railway company was not prosperous. No data is shown for 18 bridges on the North Woolwich-Tottenham line, and others on the main line which may need attention, (see pages 99,100).

Manpower

Manpower is under estimated. A route with a current service from 05.50 to 23.00 is said to need 4 buses/drivers in the peak, and 'because only one bus is required outside the peak, only 5 drivers are required'. Another with 7 buses in the peak, hence 7 peak drivers - would have a total of eight drivers - to cover a 16 hour time span! It is doubtful that employees would tolerate the implications, and in the absence of a timetable and rosters, it may contravene legal driving hours. A total of 676 drivers for all six routes is quoted. No mention is made of relief staff for holidays, sickness, etc., which BR figures include.

The 'main line route' requires '650 drivers and 750 other staff[10] including ticket sellers, bus manufacturing and the bus share of road maintenance', (Page 121). No cost is shown for the 750 - which should be split into the three categories mentioned. How the manpower required to manufacture buses, (Page 9), was calculated is not revealed. There is no reference to supervisors, admin staff, cleaning staff for buses/stations/depots or breakdown crews. Liverpool Street bus station would need supervisors on each shift at several places, and in the adjoining bus park. A control centre with CCTV would be vital. Supervision at turnround points would be vital, otherwise, in the absence of a timetable, not all drivers would return promptly. Operating costs for the main line service (Page 120), include £1.94m 'Other costs', a term whose definition (Page 23) excludes the 750 staff and those overlooked, (see above). Electricity board staff are excluded from BR figures - so they should be! - as none are included for staff distributing oil to bus depots. BR staff 'distributing' electricity should also be excluded for the same reason.

In contrast to the assessment of manpower required for the six routes, NBC (1976 Accounts) had 3.4 staff for every bus and they excluded bus manufacturing and road maintenance. By NBC standards - and they were almost certainly not affected by heavy commuter peak operation - at least 1,530 would have been required in relation to the proposed fleet, the size of which has not been proven to be adequate in the absence of a timetable. The method used to assess fleet and manpower will *never* catch on in transport circles. Stagecoach had 3000 vehicles and 11,000 staff; i.e. 3.66 staff to each bus.[11]

The average cost of a bus driver for a 40-hour week including employers' contribution to NHS, pensions, etc., for one-man operation (OMO) is £2200 pa, (Page 22). In the mid 1970s, the average for LT OMO drivers was £5400 pa. There would be no applicants for £2200 jobs when they could get £5400 from LT. This would increase costs, (see page 139).

In the chart overleaf, a bar represents 125 drivers required for the hours shown. It provides, in round numbers for 500 during peaks, and half that outside peaks for a service

---

[9] Bridge reconstruction will cause serious delays to existing road and rail traffic. No time loss debit is shown.

[10] No similar provision is made for such manpower on the other five routes.

[11] 1976 Buses Yearbook, by S.J. Brown.

half as frequent. In mid-shift, drivers require a legal break. To move, park or operate their buses may require more drivers. Without a timetable, it is not possible to calculate manpower precisely. Based on the Hall/Smith approach, over 1,000 would be required, (see below), Mondays to Fridays, rather than the 650 postulated. A further 99 are required (see page 136), an increase of about 450. This excludes Saturdays, holidays, sickness, etc. Drivers scheduled to an 8-hour shift will not drive for 8 hours. When a driver picks up a bus from the park, time is occupied in checks on a vehicle's readiness for work. Shifts starting and ending at 01.00 will be very unpopular, but to cover existing service times would be unavoidable. These manpower levels may be reduced if split shifts are accepted, but a *penalty payment* is often made for the period between peaks. On this long route, they are unlikely to have time to go home. Whether there would be sufficient spare time in the off-peak to cover ferrying to/from Ilford can only be established by duty rosters.

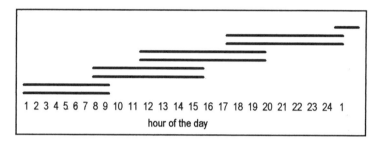

The Study ignores Saturdays. To determine manpower for Saturday services, given a 40 hour week (Page 22), a form of Rest Day roster is required, which gives all drivers one day off in six, which will not always be Saturday. For every five drivers required on other days, one extra is required for Saturdays. This principle will apply to the other 750 staff mentioned (Page 121). Relief staff for out-based depots - which have low service levels - will tend to be a higher percentage than at a main depot.

Maintenance

The scheme plans to use Ilford Multiple Unit Depot for bus and lorry maintenance, (Page 85). How costs were assessed for the area and buildings, was not explained. For safety reasons, no visitors are permitted in sidings or buildings unless accompanied by a manager or supervisor responsible for a visitor's safety. Staff in such locations were notorious for challenging strangers - even in uniform - and rightly so. Crucial tasks are overlooked. In addition to maintaining east side multiple units, Ilford maintained those which operated services from the west side of Liverpool Street, which under the plan would continue. It also carried out heavy maintenance on multiple units from the LT&S line. With Ilford closed, and the rail link to the LT&S severed, two depots would have to be built for them. Conversion of Ilford depot would have to be done over the second weekend!

There are no costs for maintenance and renewal of bus terminals. There are references to 'Other Costs', which mentions some provision for vehicle and building maintenance by other bus companies, (Page 23), but that would not usually be for bus stations, which are invariably under separate ownership. The approach used to arrive at these figures is not likely to catch on in the transport industry. They will continue to set out the manpower and forecast value of materials required. Any operator providing the services would determine the fleet and manpower required to operate and maintain it, on the basis of a timetable, and the cost of a depot on written estimates.

Whereas gaps between trains enable rail staff to carry out minor adjustment to the formation, it would be impossible on roads. Lane closures will be necessary.

Finances

The study claims if buses were subsidised, no fares would be charged, or that rail fares could be cut 64% and would still cover bus operating costs, (Page 120). *Covering costs would not be enough for the private sector.* The financial details set out in the six sections of the report are not brought together, in their sections, nor as a whole in the Report. They are summarised below. It is claimed that the bus company can stand on its own feet - and it must do so, even if the fleet and staff are inadequate and need to be supplemented.

	rail revenue[12]	bus revenue[13]	bus costs[14]	'profit'
	(£000)	(£000)	(£000)	(£000)
Tottenham-Woolwich	46	16.6	39.1	-22.5
Romford-Upminster	30	10.8	22.9	-12.1
Witham-Braintree	43	15.5	39.1	-23.6
Colchester-Sudbury	26	9.4	23.8	-14.4
Crouch Valley	79	28.4	66.9	-38.5
Liverpool St-Harwich	12315	4433.4	4400.0	33.4
Totals	12539	4514.1	4591.8	-77.7

On their fleet basis, with *7 day revenue* and *5 day costs* there is a loss.[15] At their wages: drivers for weekends, holidays, sickness add £0.6m; 450 extra drivers (page 138) add £1m; key staff (page 137) add £0.5m; 750 staff (page 103) not all seem to be costed, add £0.5m; total £2.6m. London area wages (page 137) would increase £2.6m to £6.4m (£2.6/2200 x 5400); and their 650 drivers would cost £2.1m more. Fares commission would cost about £1.5m, (page 135). There would be £10m pa deficit. There would be costs for breakdowns, accidents and ensuing revenue loss. Fuel costs are not properly calculated, (see page 103).

Every one of the six routes in the Study include the same qualifying phrase: *assuming conversion costs have been offset by benefits to private traffic.* This implies that motorists will fund conversion. However, their *burden* will not be in coin of the realm - essential to pay for construction - but by the theoretical value placed on time saved by motorists (see page 104), who, it is *assumed*, will transfer from existing roads to the new road system. If this does not happen, the whole fabric collapses. The motorists' share would be paid in cash by government. The only other cash for conversion, would be from land sales. But surplus land was being sold off as buyers became available, or was developed jointly by BR Property Board and outside bodies. As a rule, if the whole of a property portfolio is dumped on the market at the one time, the price falls. The reality is that the gain from most surplus land was accruable equally to BR, and therefore, must be left out of the equation - a point made by independent parties, (see pages 122,128). BR, in contrast to the

---

[12] *Better Use of Railways*, Pages 31,41,46,51,57 & 63. These are 7-day revenue figures.

[13] Rail revenue less 64%.

[14] *Better Use of Railways*, Pages 38,44,49,55,61,119-120. *As a minimum*, their figures must be increased for Saturdays: 20%, holiday/sickness relief: 12%, Sundays: 10%, & for other staff, (see page 137).

[15] Including a derisory 0.8% main route 'profit' Operators said buses replacing trains would be unviable (page 51)

bus operator has to fund its own infrastructure, and when it failed to do so - mainly due to political interference in fares and charges, and in closure of uneconomic lines, was required for 21 years to take on interest bearing loans.[16] This was the cause of deficits. Government belatedly accepted that services required for social reasons should - as applies when bus operators are required to provide uneconomic services - be funded by government. If BR had been allowed to 'fund' its infrastructure on the basis envisaged in this scheme for bus operators - including monetary credit for time saved by commuters when electrified services were introduced - it would have had no problem in operating with fares up to 55 points below inflation, as it was compelled to do by politicians.[17]

Intangible financial benefits claimed

It is claimed that substantial benefits will derive to passengers and non-passengers to which a monetary value is attributed. Without them, the scheme would not have attracted support of any journalist, nor even of the anti-rail lobby. They are non-cash items, and cannot, therefore, pay contractors. That leaves the government holding the baby.

Journey & waiting time savings for passengers

Shorter waiting-cum-journey times are claimed in respect of buses, converted to money, and prayed in aid to fund conversion. The time taken to book a ticket and walk to a platform 'was recorded for 64 peak (0.2%)[18] and 62 off-peak departures from Liverpool Street' (Page 115). Peak passengers were recorded over a 40 minute period, and bought tickets to *only* 21 of 44 destinations on the main line route. The 18-minute off-peak survey covered *only* 22 of the 44 destinations. Any time saving for off-peak passengers is challengeable, as off-peak, 'most buses will stop as trains do now, but will generally be twice as frequent' (Page 114). No departure times are listed for trains, nor for buses *departing when full*. How can a realistic difference be assessed? Nevertheless, a claim is made that 18 of the 62 passengers will have a shorter wait-cum-journey time, whilst none would be longer. These records - which exclude 90 stations served directly or indirectly from Liverpool St (see footnote page 104) - are extrapolated to cover journeys to all stations!

It is stated that 'two minutes is allowed for [rail] passengers to walk from ticket office to train or platform'. No time is mentioned for bus passengers. Most commuters - probably 95% - have seasons or returns and would not go to the ticket office, but take the shortest route from street to platform, whose number is engraved on their hearts. They know the time to reach the station, to the *minute*, and aim to get *just within the barrier* and into the *nearest* carriage. Any unable to find a seat, may walk through, as a train is moving - this cannot count in time comparisons. Some may go further along a platform - but only to use waiting time, for which Smith has taken credit. The few observed buying tickets in the peak, will allow extra time to be on the safe side. They are not representative. In contrast to walking to this *nearest* point, most bus passengers would walk further. As the first bus bay will be just inside the location of existing ticket barriers, it follows, that those joining buses at bays 2 through 30, will walk further. Given an equal distribution of departures over the 30 bays, that means that 96% *must* walk further. A 150m walk would take 1.75 minutes for an average person if not impeded by others. Each bus lane crossed is likely to cause 10 seconds delay as a bus departs. The time to the last bay would be 7 minutes.

---

[16] See *Britain's Railways - The Reality*, Chapter 15.

[17] See *Britain's Railways - The Reality*, Appendix A

[18] There is no evidence to show that the other 99.8% would not have a faster overall journey by rail.

Walking time to buses will average 3.5 minutes, plus 2 from the ticket office - worse than the 5 minutes claimed for 64 rail passengers. The total time claimed for the 64 equates to 7 seconds for 28,000 passengers! Anyone missing a bus will wait up to 10 minutes

The scheme states that 'passenger time will be saved on services that are not grant aided,[19] but this will be partly offset by time lost changing from bus to train at Manningtree', (Page 119). It is *completely impossible* to make such a claim in the absence of a plan of the bus/rail station layout, the times of arrivals of buses and departure of trains - neither of which are specified. Arrivals at Manningtree of buses routed via the A12 (see diagram, page 149), will be unpredictable. It is certain that these journeys would be longer, and the authors would have gained credibility by admitting the inevitable.

26% of passengers (see Page 116), will travel over the A12 from Brentwood.[20] Four of the destinations reached by this road claim a peak time saving, none are longer. It is *inevitable* that there will be traffic delays. In the off-peak, no time saving to *any* destination can be assessed from the period studied, as not enough passengers were observed to fill *one* bus. With no bus departure times, how can time savings be claimed? How will a driver know when to depart? Buses twice as often as trains means nothing to a driver. Even in the peak, 75 passengers may not board a particular bus within the allotted terminal time.

No mention is made of increased costs nor revenue loss to main-line passengers during changeover. There is no reference to a survey to ascertain if passengers were waiting for someone who finishes work at a different time, intended to buy a paper, magazine, take refreshment, join a train which a friend or partner will join en route, or needed to fit in with domestic plans to be met at destination by a partner whose own work dictates the time at which a lift home can be provided. No gains would arise for them. In the absence of such a survey, the £1.67m *paper* savings claimed therefrom, that would be severely cut (see above), and then further cut by an inevitable switch to car - cannot be counted as a benefit. The reality is that when lines have closed in the past, far more switched to car than bus, and in many cases, the bus service - despite being subsidised by BR - was eventually withdrawn. If not all rail passengers transfer to bus - a scenario which is not considered, yet is the reality - there will be long gaps between buses, and hence longer waiting times. The massive sum attributed to the passenger time savings will evaporate.

'To avoid great expense, cross platform interchange between LT & BR at Stratford will cease, but walking time will only be one minute', (Page 82). This is not referred to in the time gains as the one minute loss for thousands of passengers daily that it would be.

'A shorter subway will halve walking time from bus station to platform', (Page 82). It will not benefit those who walk from home, nor those on buses unless bus times are altered.

Motorists and other private vehicles

There is no reference to a survey of journey details, to see if any would benefit from diversion to a new route, rather than assuming that they would, when it may extend their journey time.[21] Some drivers on an existing route may be stopping to pick someone up, or make a purchase before continuing. The mind boggling £19.25m value attributed to time saved by private vehicles, which is prayed in aid of conversion, is speculative, and cannot be accepted as justification for converting the route *on a trial basis*.

---

[19] Those travelling to Ipswich, Yarmouth, Norwich, etc.

[20] This excludes passengers on the Yarmouth train (Page 63) & other expresses who would travel over the A12.

[21] An independent study established that an existing road route was shorter than the new converted road, see page 123

Gains for diversions of road traffic from existing roads, some of which it is claimed will be replaced by newly generated traffic [22] (see page 105), are converted into monetary value and claimed as the source of funding for the constructional costs of conversion, (see page 139). Noticeably, they are phrased in conditional terms:

- *Probably* 6m of the 7m vehicles pa on the A112 and A1005 will divert to the new road between Stratford and Tottenham Hale, (Page 37).
- The A124 and an unclassified road have 17.5m vehicles, not more than 6m vehicles pa can be allowed on this new Romford-Upminster road, (Pages 41,43). This *assumes* more than that number will wish to divert - but it is not supported by traffic surveys. How the balance would be blocked is not explained.
- It is *assumed* that almost all 1.8m vehicles pa on B1018 will divert to the new Witham-Braintree road, (Page 48).
- *It can be expected, say* 0.5m pa vehicles will divert to the new Marks Tey-Sudbury road and a similar volume *newly generated*, (Page 54).
- 1m vehicles pa will *probably* be diverted onto the new Crouch Valley road, 'and *if* the newly generated traffic averages 0.5m vehicles pa ...' (Page 60).
- On the new Shoreditch-Brentwood road, not more than 2400 private vehicles per hour will be permitted, restricted by tolls, (Pages 110-111); the *probable* two way flow [of private vehicles] *will* be 50,000 per day, (Page 111); these 50,000 vehicles will divert and be replaced by 50,000 newly generated vehicles per day, (Page 112). All are given a money value. *Tolls will not restrict traffic to a pre-determined volume.*
- *If* 2m pa of the 2.5m vehicles on the A604 and B1352 divert to the new Colchester-Harwich road, the time saving is worth £0.2m, (Page 112).
- *If* 4m of 5m vehicles on the A133 and B1027 divert to the new Colchester-Clacton/ Walton road, saving 8 minutes per vehicle, the saving will be £0.32m pa. (Page 113).
- The new Brentwood-Southend road can be *expected* to take 3m vehicles pa from the A129 & A127. *If* the average saving is 10 minutes, it will be worth £0.3m pa, (Page 113).

There is no traffic data to show what proportion may be to/from locations on existing roads or turning off at a junction on an existing road, and would not gain from diversion. These *if, assumed, probably* or *expected* diversions are converted to a *firm* time saved, then to money. Two routes in the study were examined by the Polytechnic of Central London (see page 123), who dispute the conclusions, particularly in respect of traffic diversion benefits. In one case, they state that the new route would be longer.

Accidents

The Hall/Smith study claims £3.46m, will be saved by fewer accidents due to diversions from residential streets, including £3m onto the converted 'main line'. Comparisons between train and bus safety are related, in the study, to passenger data which, for buses, is unreliable, (see page 153). The number of non-passengers killed by a train or bus is not influenced by the number of passengers in either. The only accurate data supplied by the industry to the DfT relates to stage services (i.e. local services in towns and villages), and this traffic will have to continue operating in residential streets or else run empty. Passenger mileage on express, contract and excursion services are estimated. Local

---

[22] Newly generated traffic is a trip not hitherto thought worth making, (Page 2). The basis for assessing the volume & journey length is not explained. Journey purpose is unkown. If a fall in traffic cuts deaths, this *must* increase them.

services accounted for 72% of vehicle mileage in 1973. For what it is worth, local passenger mileage in 1973 was 77.2% of total estimated passenger miles/km.

If traffic is diverted from 11,000 of the existing 220,000 miles of road to 11,000 miles converted system, the remainder will travel faster, and cause more deaths. Moreover, the *newly generated traffic* will fill up the roads. As pedestrians and cyclists will still share existing roads even, if with less traffic, it does not ensure even one fewer death. Well documented causes of accidents are traffic speed, tailgating, mechanical failure, tiredness and misjudgement - all of which are equally likely on a converted system.

Flat junctions mean right turns across traffic, and whether provided with lanes or not, will lead to collisions. They require a break in a central reservation. The Study mentions 14 such places on the main line route, (Pages 75,86,87,99,100,101,102,104,105,106,108). It does not mention Ilford, where lorries and buses will be maintained, serviced and parked, and to which, other transport will arrive from unspecified directions with parts and fuel. Mile End depot will involve right hand turns. A similar problem will arise at 'level crossings', as buses would be more frequent than trains (longer delays to cross traffic, including farm traffic, would induce pedestrians and drivers to take risks). Men maintaining roads are more likely to be killed than on railways, given the greater number of road vehicles and their facility to swerve into workers, whereas trains cannot swerve. Liverpool St bus station with its dangerous conflicting interface of passengers and vehicles, is certain to lead to fatalities. Four new level crossings (Pages 54,103,108,110), will be hazards, but no allowance is made for more accidents, although the converse is expected to cut accidents. If central reservations on motorways cannot prevent head-on collisions, it is obvious that a lack of them, and narrower lanes on a converted system will cause more accidents.

Claims are made of the safety of the Heads of the Valleys road - of which 4 miles, in sections, was partly built on a closed 20-mile line. No before and after data was produced to substantiate these claims. It has a bad record now, (see page 105).

The study makes comparisons with 1973 rail fatalities, which were higher than 1974 - whose figures were available before the study report was submitted.

Freight Traffic

No assessment is made of lorries to convey rail freight.[23] This is attributed to BR and NFC being unwilling to provide data - perhaps due to a belief that conversion was behind the request. Some data can be assembled from the Annual Reports of BR and NFC, DoT and Select Committees. BR produced three relevant Reports[24] a decade earlier, which could have been adjusted for inflation, and other known changes. None are mentioned.

It is stated that there is no rail freight on two routes: Romford-Upminster (Page 41), Marks Tey-Sudbury (Page 51). The rail freight traffic on the other four routes is listed as:

- A daily 2-way flow at Manor Park of around 70 freight & parcels trains with around 800 freight wagons and 100 parcel vans daily. 18 trains take containers to/from Parkeston Quay. Others take farm produce to Harwich; sand from quarries at Marks Tey and Southminster; oil from Parkeston Quay to Bow, Claydach and Channelsea; cars from Halewood[25] (Page 63),

- Short goods trains are occasionally seen on Tottenham-North Woolwich (Page 31),

---

[23] However, a figure of 350 suddenly appears on Page 85.

[24] The Reshaping Report, Trunk Route Development and Road & Rail Costs

[25] The author recalls there was a daily flow of two trains of car parts from Dagenham to Halewood.

- Braintree has on Mondays, a train of fertiliser and a sporadic coal train (Page 46),
- Two trains from Southminster carrying sand. Twice weekly, radio-active waste is brought by lorry from Bradwell to load on a wagon for dumping at sea, (Page 57).

From this vague data, an attempt was made to compare rail and road costs (Pages 25/26). This 'assumed a type 4 diesel loco and four sets of 20 modern wagons, *each containing £10,000* and a maximum payload of 40 Mg, with an average load of 60% - 50% for minerals and 85% for containers[26] - and the loco running 60,000 km pa'.[27] This *assumption* is compared to *Commercial Motor* Tables of Costs [1973], *but* with interest recalculated at 10%, licences excluded, fuel tax cut 50% to cover only road maintenance, 20% overheads, but no profit,[28] a maximum payload of 22.4 Mg and average load of 60%. 'On the evidence available, it is concluded there is no significant difference between the cost of freight trains and 32.5 Mg lorries.[29] On a road with excellent alinement (sic) and limited access, there is no reason to restrict weight to 32.5 Mg and length to 18m. In the USA, 33m long *multiple bottom dump trucks* of 57 Mg gross weight are used on nominated roads. They are made up of semi-trailers joined by dollies. To leave nominated routes, each semi-trailer is taken away individually as a normal articulated tractor/trailer unit.[30] Ford UK said if *double bottom lorries* for two 9m containers were permitted, there would be a *slight* saving by road'. The SMMT and RHA have no knowledge of these vehicles, which, if suitable for converted railways, ought to be in use now on motorways. There is no reference to customers being asked if more frequent entry to premises was acceptable. Most coal merchants will not accept coal tipped to ground as it degrades the quality - they take it direct from wagon to sack. One cannot assume, because transfer to road seems academically better, it will be accepted in the commercial world.

Cash gains claimed

Property sales

One entry reads: 'As there is a shortage of jobs and housing in this area, it will be *assumed* half of the land will be given planning permission for industrial development and half for residential use' and claims £615,000 for it, (Page 38). That assumption cannot be made. A shortage of jobs does not equate with business buyers. Some 36 items on 27 pages, are claimed to give sales of over £6m - including one of £1.8m (Page 86)[31] - for land to be used for warehousing, factories, houses, etc., without proving that there would be buyers. Thousands of acres of brownfield sites lie unsold. Former stations and houses have proved unsaleable. Claimed gains for selling land are scattered through the book among constructional or other proposals. They are mixed with claims for the value of land turned into roads, whilst financial benefit is also claimed for the value of time saved by diverted motorists. A claim for £17m (Page 113), appears to be related to using the land for transport purposes, with no indication that cash will change hands. There is no proof that there is market interest in the land that would become available, and if there is that it

---

[26] The source of these figures is not disclosed. They are not included in BRB Annual Reports.

[27] No source is shown. BRB 1975 Report shows the loco fleet averaged 103,000 km pa, there is no split for freight.

[28] No data is quoted to prove how much road renewal and maintenance is caused by lorries. There is much evidence to prove that the wear and tear they cause eclipses many times over, that of cars, which bear an unfair share of costs. Why licences, interest rates & other costs should be cut, is unclear. Lorries will travel beyond the new route

[29] A series of assumptions leads to a positive conclusion!

[30] This means having parking, plus extra tractors and drivers at each access/exit! These are not costed.

[31] Fyffes depot at Goodmayes (see reference on page 106).

would not be counter balanced by tenants leaving existing premises empty and derelict. Sites would be needed for rolling stock maintenance displaced from Ilford, (see page 138).

Of 36 properties to be sold, 26 would retain a frontage on the new road. If that was denied, they may prove unsaleable, being condemned as fire hazards, and tantamount to slums. If they did retain front access, they will have a frontage onto the converted system, despite protestations that this will not apply, in order to claim fewer deaths.

'Tenants will move to Mile End goods depot. Other tenants can be moved to the depot. Tenants under Malcolm Road bridge can be moved to Mile End depot'. (Page 75). '£20,000 opportunity cost is claimed for relocating tenants'. (Page 76). There is no depot plan to show there is space, nor prove it suitable, nor confirmation tenants have agreed to move.

There has been no deduction of Estate Agents' and Solicitors' fees for selling. Valuations by Estate Agents are gross before deducting their fees and those of solicitors.

If the grasping Treasury believed that the amounts stated could be gained, by replacing some or all rail by road transport, it would have left no stone unturned to cash in.

Scrap sales

The scheme claims sales of rail assets to pay for conversion. BR may wish to re-deploy their own assets. The book claims profits from scrap steel and cast iron worth £17,000 (Page 36); and from dismantling OLE of £0.28m (Pages 73,90.94,96,104,107,110). Assumptions that contractors would be allowed to remove OLE, would not be fulfilled. There is a need when removing redundant OLE to re-plan the lengths and route of the remaining overhead wires - one does not simply chop a piece out. An electricity sub station is to be demolished at Mile End, (Page 78). There is another at Chadwell Heath. Both are on the nearside from which the first two tracks are to be removed. If these were removed as part of the initial conversion, there would be no power to run trains during the week in which conversion of two tracks was proceeding. If they weren't removed, given post-privatisation experience, it is likely that contractors would cut power cables in the process of ripping out tracks, taking down OLE, etc., and bring trains to a stand.

Cheap construction

It is claimed that the formation, compacted by trains over decades, needed only a tarmac layer to provide a perfect road, (Page 16). On four routes (Pages 43,48,53,59), the lines were single on a double or near-double formation. The unused excess would not be compacted, nor would the cess or verges on any line. All lines have a 'cess' each side: an uncom-pacted walkway about 1m wide, (see photograph). Heavy road vehicles would be on uncompacted land! A proposal that traffic can run on a bitumen bound base the day after it is laid, and a *wearing surface* added *later* (Page 16), is a recipe for chaos, and analogous to Lloyd's plan to widen tunnels later if they were found to slow traffic down, (see page 23)

'Mr. Lever believes Wimpey Asphalt would be able to follow *this timetable*,' (Page 91). There is *no* timetable to reveal the time allocated to asphalting or other tasks. The book is silent on whether they would do so within an [undisclosed] contract cost.

An advisory booklet issued by UKRAS, stated: 'on clay or alluvial soils, deterioration will set in rapidly under heavy traffic, especially in cuttings. To check the sub formation, it will be necessary *to undertake soil mechanics investigations. This geophysical research is specialist work.* Underline bridges should be subject to stress analysis by calculation and strain gauge measurements. In cuttings, soils usually contain undrained water. There will be continuous upwards movement of clay or silt through the ballast. The exposed soil must be covered over to a depth of twelve inches or more with fine stone dust or graded sand well compacted. Fresh clean stone ballast can then be added. Under heavy traffic, soils of this character break down at the approximate rate of one inch pa'.

There is no specific reference to the cost of installing drains, which according to road engineers (see page 26), would be costly. 'Trimming' the formation to provide drainage (Page 16), is inadequate. Plans provided to the author by county highway departments, in response to queries regarding the extent of conversion (see chapter 13), include new drainage, and some bridges whose foundation or structure had to be rebuilt.

The scheme plans a 6.6m road (see page 120) and 4 tracks in the 21.5m wide Liverpool St -Bethnal Green cutting (see photo). A 4 track line (see page 198) with space to re-locate the east side OLE masts (see photo), leaves only 5m for a road and a pavement for passengers to unload in the event of fire, accident or breakdown, and a wall between rail and road.

The outbound LT line at Stratford is to move 3.3m (Page 82), from LT platform 6 to 5, now used by BR trains to give cross platform interchange to LT trains on platform 3. The six line paragraph is ambiguous without a present and proposed layout drawing, which would show that it was not simple. A diagram (Page 81) shows no platform numbers, nor that LT lines are in single bore tunnels at both ends. Ensuing track curvature would be tight. No space would be created for a road lane between the tunnels, due to the deep cuttings leading to the tunnels. Platforms to be demolished are on uncompacted ground.

It is planned to abandon 20km of *two-track* line from Brentwood to Chelmsford (Page 94), and 22km Chelmsford to Colchester, (Page 97). Ex-rail - and other traffic - using the new road from London, would divert onto the A12, (see diagram, page 149). These sections include some 60 bridges and viaducts, about 21 miles of cuttings and embankments, plus walls and fences, which would require ongoing maintenance, for which no cash is allocated. These sections had five level crossings, which may, with the bridges, etc., have influenced its abandonment. The cost - along with three unwanted platforms at Liverpool Street - would fall on BR. Capacity for extra traffic on the A12 is disputed, (see page 121).

Construction costs, including slip roads, roundabouts[32], flyover, demolition and relocation of occupied property, conversion of Liverpool Street to a bus station, conversion of Ilford depot, the purchase of 494 buses & 350 lorries would have to be incurred, before any income was earned. There is no reference to DCF or NPV - commonly used in such projects. A project of this size should also be subject to a Critical Path Analysis,[33] but there is no evidence of one. It would quickly expose the crucial problem areas in sequentially planning construction, demolition and materials delivery.

Houses are to be demolished, parts of industrial premises compulsorily acquired, private and public carparks reduced in size, and businesses relocated. This, of course, contravenes the concept of conversion: to use formations as they stand, without widening, which was proclaimed by the Conversion League, (see page 79).

Changeover tactics (Pages 90-91).

The changeover plan - to convert Liverpool Street-Brentwood in nine days, (see page 108) - is impractical. An idea to double train length whilst two tracks are converted is doomed, (see page 147). The plan to lengthen 10 stations is not so simple, (see page 147). Neither is the

---

[32] Seven are mentioned, (Pages 92,97,99,104,107,110). Traffic will be delayed during and after construction.

[33] Sometimes called Network Analysis. This vital project technique had been used on BR at least two decades before, for example, the shipbuilding industry debated it, (see *Britain's Railways - The Reality*, Page 91).

plan for trains to share platforms 1-10, *during the second weekend*, whilst the east half of Liverpool Street is converted to a bus terminal and bus park. Alterations to bridges, Ilford flyover, OLE and crossovers represent crucial and potentially insurmountable difficulties.

Lifting two tracks, will cut off Liverpool Street platforms 15-18, halving the commuter trains, as there is no link between them and the tracks to remain! Services would have to be reduced. Many commuters would be unable to board overcrowded trains, and would be delayed. No cost debit is provided for their delay.

The belief that one can simply lengthen any platform is ill-founded. No drawing nor sentence, is included to prove that any location has the space in the right place for an extension, which may well necessitate alterations to signalling, crossovers and other infrastructure, and new earthworks. Coupling is impractical.[34] The moment one was drawn forward - over several crossovers and junctions - to back on another, other trains would be unable to leave or arrive. Safety procedures require a driver to change ends, so that in setting back, he was in what would then be the leading cab. This involves applying the brakes, shutting off power, climbing down from his cab, walking the length of the train, climbing into the rear cab, and starting up again. In doing this, he would walk along the ballast, which is not an ideal walking surface. Reversing towards a platform containing a train full of commuters carries risks and would, almost certainly be vetoed by HMRI, should BR managers and staff lose interest in safety. Only someone, without knowledge of safe railway working methods and train operations, could make such a suggestion. This would inevitably cause delay to other trains. Likewise, the arrival of an 18 car train, which needs to split, would stop most of the station. Due to the longer running times created by coupling and dividing at both ends of the route, additional rolling stock would almost certainly need to be acquired - from whence would be a problem for the dreamers. The service would have to be heavily cut during changeover.

There is little prospect that trains usually using platforms 11-18 could be loaded in the west side commuter platforms, which are in constant use in the peak - in any case, four platforms have no access to the tracks that will remain in use for one week. Only one of the main line platforms could, at a pinch, accommodate one of the trains which would be usually in platforms 11-18. The operation of coupling up and dividing at both ends of the line, would require a review of track layout and signalling to see what costly changes were necessary. Additional staff would be required at both ends to perform coupling and uncoupling. If the task could be left to traincrew, the time taken by them to do so would be longer. No one would be allowed to couple or uncouple, without another person who could stand alongside the middle of the elongated train, within sight of the driver, and signal when it was safe to move. There is no reference to ensuing costs.

Temporary platform extensions would have to be inspected by HMRI before use. If half of each elongated train was restricted to passengers for particular destinations, trains will be have to overrun stations so that passengers in the rear half can leave. Experience from earlier years, when trains had to 'draw-forward' was that it was a time consuming practice. Having part of a train off the platform was frowned on by HMRI. Extra trains would be needed from manufacturers, to meet peak needs, due to the longer terminal time

---

[34] There were three types of commuter trains, operating to Shenfield, Southend and Clacton respectively. They were incompatible for coupling together, having different motors, maximum train speeds, couplings and unit/train size. One type had controlled doors. Double length trains would be up to 24 cars in length. It would delay all other trains.

at Liverpool Street and the other end. Running time would be longer. It is possible, that 18 cars cannot be operated in multiple. As there would have been no expectation to have trains of such length, it may have been pointlessly costly to build in such a facility.

The plan to lift two 'nearside' [east side] tracks (Page 91), using two for trains to Brentwood, overlooks that a flyover to be demolished at Ilford, carries tracks from east to west side. A single line (see diagram), connects to west side tracks beyond the flyover, for which speed would be 20mph at both ends. It cannot be used in the opposite direction without new connections, signalling and OLE. A single line would not cope even with a reduced peak service. Trains would terminate at Manor Park, 6 miles from Liverpool Street.

This problem apart, a full width road could not be laid on the lifted 2-track section as OLE masts supporting hundreds of 4-track gantries stand in the cess, (see photo), which, along with any verges, is an essential part of the width needed for a road. Their removal would be essential before slip roads could be completed. Any 2-track gantries over tracks to remain for a week, and located in the middle of the formation, would limit road width.

From Liverpool St. to Brentwood, 20 crossovers link east to west side tracks. Removal of their OLE would cause costly delays, and could not be done during the changeover week. It is not a matter of cutting wires, which would electrocute the cowboy who did it, and stop trains on west side tracks in a tangle of wire, due to cross runs of wire.

Four-track gantries (see photo), could not be removed while trains still used the two tracks to Brentwood. They would have to be replaced by new 2-track gantries, requiring changes to the control systems of OLE and electricity distribution. The OLE would have to be re-designed involving preparation of drawings. Labour would be required to implement the changes. Speed restrictions would be imposed on all trains whilst alterations took place, causing more delays and creating a passenger time debit. No allowance has been made for these potentially heavy costs. A simplified diagram shows the flyover and tracks relevant to the removal plan. It does not show all 20 crossovers which will have an OLE changeover problem. Had the Study included all track diagrams and OLE structures, these crucial defects in the changeover plan would have been seen.

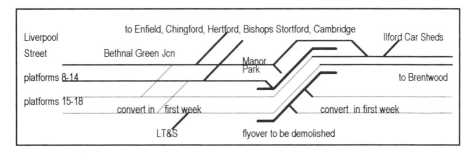

The changeover plan does not mention that from Liverpool Street to Brentwood, 12 bridges are to be rebuilt or redecked, and formations excavated at 9 others. Before redecking, etc, OLE attached to bridges would have to be replaced by gantries for a week. Excavation under bridges - which really means excavation over a much longer length than the bridge itself - would destabilise ballast on the formation of the two tracks in use. This work cannot begin until trains cease, and must be completed during the second weekend. Nor does it mention major works on the rail formation at Brentwood, Chelmsford and Colchester, (Pages 90,95,97-98), which cannot begin until trains cease.

'During the second weekend, trains will use platforms 1-10, whilst the east half of Liverpool St. station is converted' to a bus terminal and bus park. That involves excavation to create headroom, and doing so between columns (see page 131). It may not be possible to limit trains to 10 platforms instead of 18. A timetable would have to be compiled to see what was feasible. Assumptions by non-railway operators should not be made.

If changeover was not demolished by problems itemised herein, and the 'first carriageway opened', it would have no west side exits, until all tracks are lifted. Until both carriageways opened two months later (Page 91), there would be no east side exits. Buses would unload in a construction site and turn at Brentwood. More buses would be needed.

Rail route is to be abandoned, (see diagram). Traffic will leave the system at Brentwood and go to the A12[35] via a new link road, (Pages 92-93), which will cause delay during construction of a huge roundabout/underpass complex. No time loss is debited for this task, which may take a year. Building a link can be partly done in advance, but the flyover at the railway end can only be done during the second weekend. At Brentwood, the road to Shenfield and Southend will be slewed, (see diagram), onto new 'uncompacted' ground. At Chelmsford traffic will rejoin the formation for a short distance from existing roads, and exit to existing roads to go to Colchester. At both places, major construction is required to connect existing roads to the rail formation. Neither can be done until the second weekend, as trains will run until then. Between Brentwood and Colchester are Ingatestone, Hatfield Peverel, Witham, Kelvedon and Marks Tey, to be served off the A12, via local roads. Abandonment abolishes five level crossings which would be inconvenient flat junctions, and avoids other problems, (see page 146). These diversions onto existing roads *must* increase accidents and slow traffic, but no financial debit is admitted for either.

Until the Brentwood-Southend line is converted, 137 buses, in each direction, will use existing roads in the peak, plus other off-peak. This task is to take two months, (Page 91).

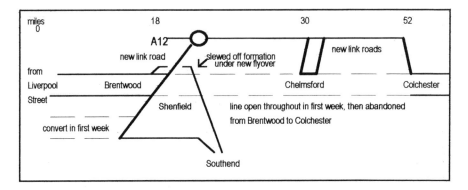

Previous conversionists avoided being specific on changeover. By wandering into this marsh, the impracticability of conversion of main lines - regardless of how much money is thrown at it - is exposed. Users of rail and road, who would be delayed by a changeover should be grateful that this attempt to spell out changeover has been fruitlessly made.

---

[35] The capacity for this traffic is disputed, (see page 121). Up to 65% of the distance will be on existing roads!

Conclusion

Doubtless, media comment on the highlights - *fares down by 64% and still profitable, £billions of gain to the country* - were made without realising that most was not in coin of the realm, nor that many crucial elements had been overlooked. It has been shown (see page 139), that with a 64% fall in fares, a bus company could *not* operate without a subsidy.

The outlay, before a penny is earned, would be £22.3m [construction £11.5m[36], acquisitions £0.2m[37], new buses & lorries £10m[38], staff training £0.6m[39]]. To this is added wages for staff recruited in weeks preceding conversion. Against this, over an uncertain period, an inflow of £6.1m cash [property sales £5.7m, scrap £0.4m[40]] is claimed. A £16m bank loan will be needed. Loan interest of about £2m pa, and a bus subsidy of £10m pa (see page 139), will leech £12m pa away - four times the BR subsidy. Paper gains from private motorists will not produce a penny to fund capital investment or cover revenue losses.

The practicality of handling traffic, fleets, manpower costs - including weekend services - should have been *precisely* determined by relevant experts. A detailed survey of existing road journeys should have been included to ascertain if there were any benefits from diversion. Data on formation widths relates to about 18% of the total length of route. Detailed drawings showing compacted and uncompacted formation widths throughout, and a table of before-and-after bridge heights and widths were essential.

This review and other comments (see Part II, page 199, chapter 15) shows that the proposal is wholly impractical, and the benefit claimed invalid. The Study postulates *its* worst scenario of costs and benefits, which this chapter shows is well short of the worst scenario. Attempts to validate claims by references to sensitivity tests of selected elements in the scheme, take little account of the most crucial issues. They assume:

- that all passengers would transfer to bus, and none to car, despite past evidence,
- that a bus service of such magnitude on a shared road could operate without a timetable,
- a financial benefit for passenger time based on extrapolation of unrepresentative data,
- that the fare box concept outlined would be practical and financially sound,
- that retailers would sell tickets for a *slight* discount,
- entrepreneurs, held back by lack of a site in East London - would spring up to buy land,
- that the staff would be available and would work for wages well below south-east levels,
- no extra cost for strengthening uncompacted areas outside those occupied by tracks.
- 30m cars *may* transfer from existing roads to converted roads, and fund the conversion,
- that all users of new roads will drive and maintain vehicles responsibly,
- that barriers will prevent cross carriageway accidents, when this has yet to be achieved - and that barriers will not cause vehicles to rebound back across their own carriageway,
- there would be no - or significantly fewer - accidents on these converted roads,[41]
- that delays will not be caused by breakdowns and collisions with bridges both above and below the converted system, contrary to current experience, (see page 185).

---

[36] *Better Use of Rail Ways*, Pages 36,43,48,54,60,94,96,104,106,110.

[37] Plus six acquisitions which are are not priced, (*Better Use of Rail Ways*, Pages 73,75,76,85,86). It cannot be assumed that acquisitions will be unopposed, with costly legal consequences and delays.

[38] £5.8m for buses and £4.2m for lorries is shown *Better Use of Rail Ways*, Page 121.

[39] *Rejoinders* Page 16.

[40] See page 107.

[41] e.g. the Study forecasts (*Better Use of Rail Ways*, Page 48) that diversion will eliminate all accidents and fatalities. This is unreal, when traffic diverted to higher standard motorways still experiences accidents and fatalities.

The Railway Conversion League, (aka Railway Conversion Campaign), pursued conversion until 1994, when Angus Dalgleish, its last chairman died.[1] Its demise suggests that it had become a virtual one man band, as was rumoured. The *Directory of British Associations* listed it under its original title until 1996. Unlike thousands of others listed, the League had ceased to mention the size of membership - a fair indication that it was *very* small. Its membership was last listed in 1988 as 26, having fallen from 75 in 1972.

The Internet Age

Transwatch uses the Internet to try to revive the lost cause: 'Re-igniting Conversion'. Director, Mr. P. Withrington, calls on people to submit information on conversions. The website 'attempts to provide a list of all locations in the UK where disused railway lines have been re-used as roads, giving details, *where known*, of map references for the road and original railway, and the date the conversion took place'.

In this list, the routes of the railways concerned are not clear, and are less easy to identify than those in the 1970 list, (see pages 64,187-192), which was by no means perfect. Although, with that, one could often compare a railway atlas with a current OS map.

Transwatch list (5.3.05), 204 conversions - few of which specify identifiable *railway* locations. Some can be identified as sections of the same line or road and should be treated as one. Their total length is 254.8 miles, an unimpressive average 1.2 miles. 'Rules' are specified for inclusion of conversions in the web site:

- The road must join the formation of the railway line, run along for some distance and then leave it again.
- Only publicly accessible roads are included. Farm tracks, private drives are excluded
- Industrial or housing estates are generally excluded because it is too difficult to follow the route and the routes are generally too short to be worth recording.

What is meant by 'some distance', rather than, say, ten miles, is unclear. It is a highly subjective definition. *Rules* are not rigorously observed.

The list contains many *ultra* short sections proving nothing about the practicality of wholesale conversion. Nine are less than $^1/_4$ mile, 75 are $^1/_2$ mile or less, and 131 are under one mile, only one of the 204 listed is in double figures - and then only just: 10.2 miles.[2]

Despite the Rules, some industrial roads *are* included, together with roads which cross a disused line at a tangent (e.g. M25 over the former Westerham single line branch).

The list includes entries which read: 'it is unclear if the road has been widened onto the railway or just very close'; 'A466 widened onto the railway for 0.6 mile'; 'road took route over river, but unclear if railway bridge re-used'; 'line closed in 1930s, not clear if bypass actually built on railway'; 'conversion not confirmed'; '*looks like* realignment'; 'A148 round Hillingdon - this make[3] [sic] not be a conversion, A148 may just be running close to railway'; '*industrial estate road* - less than $^1/_2$ mile'.

---

[1] Transwatch website. The *Directory of British Associations* list it in 2004, but with no chairman, and no members.
[2] A local group aged over 55, regard a 4 mile walk as a minimum distance for relative beginners! Walks by the group up to 10 miles take place almost weekly. It is hardly worth getting a car out of a garage to travel less than a mile.
[3] Presumably should be 'may'.

'Cambrian Moat Lane Jcn to Tallyllyn line' appears three times between other entries. Stoke-on-Trent people would be surprised to learn that the Potteries Loop Line [Stoke-Etruria-Hanley-Kidsgrove] extended to Shrewsbury; and more surprised that the single line Jamage colliery branch was wide enough 'to create the A500/A34/A527 junction'. Large scale maps for the area around that junction show that the roundabout is 140 yards wide, excluding slip roads, as it crosses at right angles across the former branch line. 'The A66 *widened* onto the trackbed' cannot conceivably rank as a *conversion*.

Thirteen entries relate to conversions to motorways! It includes 'conversions' listed in earlier reports, e.g. the 12 foot wide Barton line *widened* into a 102 feet motorway[4] (see page 65) - and the single line Westerham branch 'converted' into the M25, (see page 189).

Only one complete disused route has ever been replaced by a road[5] confirming the inaccuracy of the long-standing claim that railways were straight between towns, wide enough and therefore ideal for conversion. More significantly, after 10,000 miles of railway have closed, it can only be claimed that 2% has been converted, even applying a very loose meaning to the word *conversion*!

A conversion *date* is only quoted for a minority. 70 entries record that 'conversion' took place 'before 1984', and 90 'after 1984'. The nature of this landmark year is unclear. It is unhelpful in obtaining information from local authorities. The list is largely silent on the crucial issue of the extent of widening required to provide the essential width for a road. Only 20 of the 204 entries name the person who provided the data, precluding amplification.

Roads built on *closed* lines are irrelevant to the conversionist objective - converting all railways. Using a closed line as the foundation for a new road is not conversion in the sense that it would apply to an operating railway. Such schemes involved no concurrent displacement of existing rail traffic, with its consequential costs of tens of thousands of new road vehicles to new designs, nor the provision of transfer stations whilst conversion took place. The anti-rail lobby is willing to see roads on converted railways without verges and ignores the problem of uncompacted cess, verges and open ditches within the boundary fence. However, should they ever be converted, it is likely that delays and accidents will *justify* compulsory purchase to provide extra width and verges.

Practicality & costs

Transwatch said that government should remove all impediments to converting railways to roads, but doesn't list them. First refusal of closed lines has been to local authorities, who, BR stated (Conversion Report 2.3.84) 'have had pre-emptive rights since 1966'. What, then, are the impediments? Clearly, inadequate widths led to local authorities converting more closed lines to footpaths than roads. Sustrans has just announced that there are, in the UK, 10,000 miles of cycle and footpaths, including lengths of closed lines that are significantly longer than the pathetically short lengths of *conversions* to roads

Transwatch compares the *contract* cost of upgrading the West Coast main line from 110 to 140 mph - involving track and signalling renewals, station rebuilding etc., - with a *non-contractual* Treasury *paper figure* for building a 70 mph motorway - a chalk and cheese comparison. It is a fact that the cost of building the M1 substantially exceeded forecasts, (see page 169), whereas BR schemes were within budget. The rail cost includes:

---

[4] For comparative dimensions of motorways and railways - see page 199.

[5] Spalding-Boston - some 10 miles long. The scale of widening is not now known.

- Electrification costs which are not comparable with concrete as they are part of fuel distribution, and comparable with fuel distributed to filling stations, bus and lorry depots
- Diversion costs of rail traffic during engineering work which has no parallel in building motorways in green fields - but would arise in a conversion of an operational line.
- Track and bridges are built for 22.5 ton axle weights - *in the ballasted area*. Motorways cater for 11.5 tonnes[6]. If they were built solely for cars, the required axle weight would be about 0.5 tonne, illustrating the excessive extra cost of roads suitable for HGVs.

Traffic

Transwatch refers to making '*reasonable assumptions* about the capacity of rail and road alternatives'. Conversion schemes seem to be based on *unreasonable assumptions*: on transfer to bus, traffic diversions to new roads, track width, etc. Assumptions should not be made. Researched facts should be used. The fact is that road transport requires 22 times as much road mileage - much of it wider than railways - to carry ten times as much traffic - even on the unreliable basis by which road tonne-miles/km are estimated, (see below). If nine foot widths without verges on converted railways - are adequate, no widening of the M6 is necessary, lanes can be reduced to nine foot and verges concreted to provide five lanes. Congestion would be solved, cheaply, at a stroke.

How many would divert from the M6 to a converted west coast main line with its delay-inducing flat junctions and traffic lights? None. All would wait for someone else to do so. There are few railway routes close to motorway junctions to take diverted traffic. Hence, in the event of conversion, existing roads will continue to experience congestion arising from diversions from blocked motorways.

Like its predecessors, Transwatch compares the the *whole* railway system with only motorways and trunk roads. The DfT say there are *no* reliable statistics of freight *volume* on motorways either in terms of tonnes or tonne-km. The only data available is *distance* run on motorways by goods vehicles over 3.5 tonnes gross weight.[7] They travel an *estimated* 11.5bn vehicle miles on motorways [2003] - 40% of *estimated* total vehicle mileage [28.5bn] for all roads. DfT has a *figure* for tonnes carried by all vehicles on all roads, which is 1.6bn. The basis used exaggerates road freight tonne-miles/km. The DfT explained that if a vehicle starts with, say, 10 tonnes at A, unloads half at B after a mile, then picks up 2 tonnes, the tonnes conveyed are counted as 12 for the full journey! If the full length of the journey is, say 50 miles, 600 tonne-miles would be counted instead of 353! From this inaccurate base, an *estimate* of traffic on motorways is made by taking 40% of 1.6bn tonnes = 657m tonnes. Applying 40% to the *estimated* 152bn *tonne-km* on all roads, produces 60.8bn tonne-km on motorways. No statistician should accept it

DfT statistics for road passenger transport are equally suspect, being based on vehicle mileages and various assumptions. Little definitive data is submitted by operators. There is no data on loads - and hence passenger miles/kms - for long distance, contract or excursion coaches. There is some for local services, but it is not precise outside London.

Clearly, road traffic *figures* are not as accurate as rail. Hence, their use to calculate road utilisation and compare it with rail, cannot be justified. Some accuracy needs to be imparted into recording road traffic figures, which are also used to justify road building.

---

[6] The railway axle weight was established when the UK used imperial tons which are slightly heavier than the metric tonnes now used. One ton = 1.016 tonnes. The road axle weight was quoted by the Highways Agency.

[7] The gross weight of a vehicle if fully loaded by weight. Vehicles well above this minimum do not compete with rail.

A claim that BR misled the public by comparing a train load of passengers with the low known occupancy of cars is incredible, not least because it prays in aid a national rail average train loading depressed by the low load of rural train services, which BR was prevented from closing by politicians. Those routes, when they are closed are mostly not converted to roads, nor do they lead to good PSV loads. Operators required subsidies to replace rail - initially paid by BR - and even then, many bus services had a short life.

Transwatch claims that 'fewer than 1 in 50 motorised journeys are by rail'.[8] It does not state what percentage of journeys is on those roads, whose mileage it excludes in comparisons. It overlooks that 73% of car journeys are under 5 miles. Many must be in areas with no nearby railway, therefore conversion could have no effect. An RAC 2004 report shows that the most frequent purpose of car journeys is shopping - accounting for 25% of annual mileage - which does not compete with rail. The Report quotes the average car journey as 8.7 miles! If diverted, it would travel further. Over 75% of bus mileage is on local roads, and if diverted from roads which have houses, shops etc. on them, they would run empty. These facts seriously undermine claims on diversionary gains.

It is stated that 'commuters with prepaid tickets may board at the rate of one per 1.5 per second [sic], and alight at one per second, totalling two minutes for a 50-seat bus'. It does not say how long those who haven't prepaid would take. Runcorn bus passengers, 'most of whom have the fare ready, load at the amazingly fast rate of one every two seconds'.[9] *Municipal Engineering* (12.3.76) quotes 'fastest loading times of 3 seconds per passenger, and says that from Liverpool Street, with different fares, 7-10 seconds is likely'.

Bus terminals
Transwatch states that: '*Probably* a bus would use terminal space 3-4 times as efficiently as the train.' It goes on to say that 'with similar calculations, it can be shown that, in terms of both capacity and use, road transport out-performs rail by a factor of 3-5 across the network'. A claim must not begin with *probably* and conclude with *certainty*.

'If these [buses] are spread over three levels, there would be some 30 bays on each'. There is no assessment of the cost of a terminal, nor the ground that would be occupied with ramps, nor of the length of time required to pass between street and upper levels.

According to Transwatch: 'terminal capacity is a separate issue and more difficult to demonstrate simply'. It is crucial and only difficult in the absence of a timetable based on a full analysis of the precise journeys which passengers make. Conversion proposals have tended to ignore the practicalities of operation, which any transport operator - road or rail - would regard as the first essential step. Lloyd sought to dispense with timetables for the very reason that they would prove the impracticability of his dream, (see page 22).

Despite that, Transwatch claims that 'the 50,000 passengers who alight at Waterloo could all find seats in 1,000 50-seat coaches – sufficient for one lane of a *motor road* **managed** in a way that avoids congestion'. That will be the day, when any road is managed so as to avoid congestion. That will also be the day when *all* buses depart with a full load. Not a penny has ever been allocated by conversion theorists to a management system. An assumption that all passengers would present themselves in orderly groups of 50 all conveniently going to one and the same place within the space of a minute before departure is untenable. It assumes that buses would run at the same speed as trains -

---

[8] The meaning of this definition is unclear.

[9] From a report on the Runcorn Busway supplied to the author by Halton Borough Council, 22.7.05

which obviously, they would not. It makes no allowance for those with luggage, cycles, or prams, passengers in wheelchairs or other disabled, and those with dogs, which would prolong idealistic loading times. They say that their claim is consistent with American research and the *approach* to the New York bus terminal.[10]

Transwatch states that Victoria Coach station 'is said to be able to handle 10,000 passengers per hour' = *50m* pa on a 16 hour day/6 day week. Data supplied by the coach station shows it has *10m* pa. One must *not* compare what one system *may* be *able* to handle with what another is *actually* handling. Liverpool St east side is *actually* handling 28,500 in a peak hour in an area half the size of Victoria coach station, (see pages 101,133).[11]

Accidents

It states: 'In comparison [with rail delays] disruption when there is a major motorway accident seldom lasts more than a few hours'.[12] That ignores the ensuing chaos on other roads, and the total delay of thousands of vehicles, which is *never* evaluated, and for which, unlike rail, there is no compensation paid by the culprits. It is selective in focusing on motorways. The scale and consequences of road blockages is under-estimated. There is not a day, when radio reports of accidents - with staggering delays - do not reach double figures. The zillions of minutes delay to tens of thousands of vehicles daily are convertible into money, just as reducing delays are taken as financial justification to improve roads.

Following a road traffic accident on a converted railway, thousands of vehicles would divert to village and residential streets, creating congestion and accidents there.

The attempt to address casualty figures follows the same path as vain attempts to prove that roads are better utilised than railways. In this, every person who had been injured or killed anywhere on the whole railway system is counted, (see Bowick page 116), whilst pedestrians, cyclists and motor-cyclists on roads are excluded as they are 'seldom met with on railways'. By the same token, as cars, buses, lorries are seldom seen on railways, casualties caused by them could be excluded and, hey presto - there are really no deaths on roads at all. The classes they seek to exclude use level crossings, where accidents are more often caused by the failings of road users than by trains.[13] Such deaths appear in railway statistics, but should be debited to roads - a level crossing is part of a road, and analogous to a cross-roads, except that level crossings are safer. Likewise, when road vehicles crash through barriers or fall onto the line (e.g. Selby - which was not a unique event), ensuing deaths appear in rail not road statistics. Had that line been converted to a road, and the same vehicle had crashed at Selby, the fatalities would have been far higher. Trespassers are, by definition pedestrians, as they are not in vehicles. These *pedestrians* - 'seldom met on railways' - are taking a short cut across the railway, but are included in rail deaths. Pedestrians are likewise killed taking a short cut across a road instead of using a controlled crossing. Pedestrians used roads long before motors, and trains crossed roads long before motors. A proper comparison requires all fatalities to be counted in both modes. In this context, converted railways will not be pedestrian free. 'Trespassers' will continue to take short cuts and those using level crossings, will continue to use the same

---

[10] The research has been challenged, as has the relevance of the New York terminal, which is on several levels (see page 109). Moreover, bus lanes in New York have problems, (see pages 167,168,179).

[11] Buses then have to reverse out of bays. At Crewe bus station, buses take about 20 seconds to reverse from bays.

[12] The reason for the relative brevity of a closure is that, unlike rail, less effort is expended to establish the cause.

[13] According to the strictly independent HMRI.

route, but without the protection of barriers. Deaths will soar as they try to cross between closely spaced 60 mph vehicles.

Hall-Smith study

Transwatch states that rail lobby criticisms of the Hall-Smith study are risible and vitriolic. It does not divulge where these offending criticisms may be found for others to consider the validity of such emotive adjectives. The only record of BR comments found by this author were at the ICE discussion (see page 109), and the media (see pages 110-130). Neither the official record of the ICE discussion nor the media contain words which can be so described. Local authorities - often critical of BR, and never considered to be a rail lobby - dismissed the Study's figures. A Transport Study Group unconnected with railways, comprehensively dismissed it, (see page 123). The DoE,[14] which commissioned and paid for the Study, dissociated itself from the findings, as it 'had major reservations about some of the calculations in the study' (Times, 23.12.75). It is impractical, based on unwarranted assumptions, and has many flaws and defects, (see chapter 10, parts II & III).

These many defects are *not* answered by the book [*Rejoinders*] as claimed by Transwatch, which states that it 'exposes rail lobby comments'. That book refers to criticisms and comments from 41 sources, (see chapter 10, part II).[15] Critics include the DoE, *Hansard*, technical journals, Professors Cooper and Spaven of the Polytechnic of Central London.[16] None of these are part of a rail lobby. Only BR and its Chief Executive are paid-up members. *Modern Railways*, which criticised the study, was openly critical of BR on many issues. Only since privatisation has it tended to concede that BR was not as bad as it was painted. Any rail lobby is seriously outnumbered by road transport operators, who have been silent on this Study in particular, and conversion in general. Revelations from the detailed examination of the Smith study report, (see previous chapter), indicate that current faith in the study, is misplaced. When conversion was first debated at the ICE, in 1955, it was rubbished by road engineers and road transport operators! (See chapter 4).

It is claimed by Transwatch that the cost of conversion could be cheaper than the Smith estimates, praying in aid a 7.3-metre carriageway built on a closed railway at Southport through flat country, said to cost £140,000 per km at 1991 prices.[17] It is overlooked that they got land-fill material free, and that the Engineer who built it, said that sub soil was favourable.[18] Figures quoted by contractors at the 1971 ICE meeting were up to £406,000 per km for a 6.7m road, (see page 115), ten times the study figure. This damning fact from non-BR speakers is ignored. The argument about what conversion would cost for any given location can only be established by contractors' written *quotations* for that location.

Transwatch criticise BR for refusing to help the Hall-Smith Study. Their book acknowledges help received from BR! Any research costs would inflate BR *losses*, giving more cause for criticism. Clearly, BR would not be asked to help with a bus timetable. Bus operators would have been happy to do that, but there is no evidence that they were asked. Aside from staff numbers and costs, which would incur costs to determine re-

---

[14] The DoE was a conglomerate, embracing that most notorious of *road* lobbies - the DoT!

[15] The chapter includes an assessment of the validity of the Rejoinders and notes that several criticisms are ignored.

[16] The author has tracked down most of these parties - see chapter 10, part II, which contains an assessment of the Rejoinders by Smith, and notes that some valid criticisms have not been addressed.

[17] A. C. Dalgleish, *The Truth about Transport* (1st edition published by Centre for Policy Studies, March 1982; 2nd edition, December 1993, published by the now disbanded Railway Conversion Campaign). See chapter 8.

[18] Dalgleish dismissed costs advanced by critics on grounds that the sub soil was unfavourable! (see page 79).

allocation where duties embrace services not included in the Study, the only help that BR could provide would seem to be the dimensions of bridges, tunnels and land occupied. Much of this is available on maps in the House of Lords Record Office and Public Record Office. Data on formation suitability as *roads*, required on-site test borings, soil analysis, etc., a costly exercise which would have interfered with train services, and delayed passengers. Money - well in excess of the fee paid for the Study - would need to change hands. BR had no expertise in building permanent roads on a railway formation, so they would be unable to help in that direction. It is significant that the DoE - then, BR's political masters - which commissioned the Study, did not direct BR to give more help.

Fuel consumption

Transwatch tries to prove that road transport is more fuel efficient than rail, making an *unchallenged* statement that given rail rights of way, coaches and lorries could discharge a national rail function using 20-25% less fuel. *The statement is hereby challenged*

It takes the average lorry load as 15 tonnes[19] [30 tonne load, returning empty]. Included for rail is an unwarranted presumption of 20 miles road transit. This inflates rail fuel consumption as *85% does not travel on roads,* (see page 110). No data exists on the distance of road delivery for the rest.[20] Speed - crucial in consumption - is ignored. Freight trains are up to 75mph, lorries 60mph. The lorry fuel basis is '*If the lorry runs at 7 mpg, it requires 5.7 gallons*'.[21] No source for 7mpg is shown. It is statistically unacceptable to take an *average* of *all* rail freight services to create an *estimated* train load, to compare with *one hypothetical* lorry carrying a maximum load. That should be compared to a train load of 500 *tons*, [1000+ out, empty back]. DfT data gives tonne kms for all road transport over 3.5t gvw in 1998 as 159bn, and vehicle km for goods vehicles excluding light vans as 32bn. This puts the average load of a heavier lorry at 5 tonnes, and even this is overstated due to the unreliability of road statistics, (see page 153). Thus, fuel consumption per tonne-mile for one lorry is underestimated by a factor of three. This worsens road consumption from the claimed 120 to 40 tonne-miles per gallon, compared to 181 tonne-miles per gallon for railfreight, excluding the erroneous 20 miles road transit. Allowing for some road transit on 15% of traffic still leaves rail consumption far better. Plowden & Buchan say that diesel consumption per tonne km by road haulage, is five times greater than rail.

Transwatch claims that system-wide rail returns the equivalent of 115 passenger mpg - less efficient than an express coach returning 10 miles per gallon with 20 people on. It is statistically unacceptable to take an estimated national average of all railway passenger services - for urban and rural routes - and compare it with *one hypothetical* PSV carrying 20 passengers. The DfT say that no reliable data exists for average PSV loads (see page 153). PSVs seen locally by the author are frequently carrying one or two passengers!

The *average* train load is compared with *one* diesel-powered car with an *above average* two people, to claim that rail energy use is no better than a car. The speed disparity, crucial in fuel comparison, is ignored. The average car load is 1.6. With two people, it must average 60mpg, wth 1.6 people, 75mpg. The comparison is untenable. One could equally compare one well-loaded train with the average of all passenger transport.

---

[19] A large percentage of mileage is driven with loads well below the vehicle capacity, (Plowden & Buchan)

[20] The author worked at goods depots, at which delivery distance for the most of this traffic was under 3 miles.

[21] Using a *global* approach as Transwatch did, an average lorry achieves 5.9 mpg. This covers all vehicles from light vans to HGVs. A lorry carrying 32t would use more. Source: National Fuel Use statistics & DfT vehicle miles.

Transwatch states: 'Rail data depends primarily on information provided by Network Rail for 2002/3. Diesel consumption by passenger rail is the same as freight, following the *approximate* division of diesel provided by Network Rail'. Data 'includes Network South East: 108 mpg, Regional: 123 mpg, InterCity: 123 mpg, system wide average: 115 mpg'. Where did Network Rail obtain *2002-3* data for these three groups which ceased to exist in *1994*, and were fragmented into 25 businesses? Pre-privatisation, audited BR Annual Reports did not include it. Network Rail had no role in the supply of diesel for trains. Transwatch say[22] that as their source was 'no longer at Network Rail, and her successor claims to have no such data[23] - it probably means there is no person in the nation that has today's electricity and diesel consumptions used by national rail'. Each rail operator has its own data. *No person has such data for HGVs or PSVs.* It is unclear why a precise national rail mpg is sought to compare with imprecise road traffic data.

No deduction is shown of fuel used for engineering purposes - whose comparison would be with highway authorities: track maintenance and renewal, building new road bridges, repairing bridges bashed by lorries; test running new rolling stock on behalf of suppliers, and operating charter trains whose passenger numbers or freight tonnages are not recorded. Fuel used by trains diverted due to bridge-bashing should also be excluded.

Bad weather

Transwatch dragged in the 'wrong sort of snow'.[24] This phrase originated with jour-nalists, not BR. In February 1991, snow was getting into train motors. BR's spokesman said that snow was unusually dry and powdery. The Evening Standard (11.2.91) reported verbatim. Others - who have probably never tackled wind blown snow to satisfy their *own* customers, much less evacuees from competitors - coined this sarcastic phrase. Unlike many countries in Europe, the UK has some years with virtually no snow, and in others, winter comes and goes several times.

Transwatch proclaimed that road transport carries on in most conditions.[25] 'On Monday after a weekend of flooding in November 2000, the entire rail network came to a virtual standstill. On Tuesday, the Today programme interviewed a road haulier, who said that his organisation had reached virtually all its customers.[26] No doubt there was disruption but *probably* 95% of road journeys were unaffected[27] compared with a completely paralysed rail system'. Unlike *The Times* reports, which are available from 1785, and can be read to ascertain the full context, obtaining a transcript of that radio interview has proved impossible, as it has been, in the author's experience, even only a few weeks later.

The date was not mentioned, nor was it provided on request. Research of principal newspaper reports for the whole month, revealed serious flooding in the early part of the month. 'Nothing like it had been experienced since records began 273 years ago', (*Financial Times*, 11.11.00). *Roads* were closed, but there were no reports of the *entire rail*

---

[22] In a letter to the author dated 2.8.05.

[23] The original source may have given off-the-cuff estimates in order to close off the inquiry.

[24] Snow gridlocked several motorways. Airports had problems. Rail was not mentioned (*New Statesman* 10.2.03)

[25] That is not the author's experience. His book *The Railway Closure Controversy* contains many documented objections to closures, because road users and industry admit to depending on rail in bad weather.

[26] It does not indicate if the haulier said when this occurred. Common experience is that road transport cannot predict the day of delivery, much less, the time, even in good weather - 'within 24 hours' is commonplace. To say that they had 'reached their customers', without saying when, is, therefore, nothing of which to boast.

[27] This seems to be an assumption. No haulier could know that for the whole industry. There is no industry-wide data

network coming to a stand - a failing which would *not* be overlooked by the media, always hypercritical of railways:

- Hundreds of roads remained closed in Wales and southern England. The AA predicted some areas would not have time to recover before the predicted return of bad weather late tonight or tomorrow. Train services recovered very well from Monday's storm, with the vast majority of services running without major delay. (*Independent*, 1.11.00).
- Few will forget the extreme conditions experienced this week. Railways did remarkably well. Ferries were unable to dock at channel ports, (*Guardian*, 1.11.00).
- A renewed threat of petrol shortages, with supplies low at some filling stations.[28] Panic buying is threatened. Overflowing rivers added to rail disruption, (*Financial Times*, 3.11.00).
- Travellers faced continued misery on road and rail services. *Some* train services in the West Country, South Wales and North East were delayed or cancelled. Flooding closed several main roads in Yorkshire and the Midlands, (*Daily Telegraph*, 3.11.00).
- Trains were running London to York, and Newcastle to Edinburgh, but not York to Newcastle. On Thursday, passengers were put on buses at York for Newcastle. One returned because of flooding, and passengers were put up in hotels, (*Independent*, 4.11.00).
- Motoring organisations discouraged journeys unless absolutely necessary. This is one of the worst weekends for travel in years and it will be days before things improve, said the AA. Ferry crossings from Wales to Ireland and Dover-Calais were disrupted yesterday due to high winds. Eurostar was experiencing only minor delays, (*Financial Times*, 7.11.00).
- A tree fell on a car killing two passengers and critically injuring the driver. It narrowly missed a coach travelling in the opposite direction, (*Independent*, 7.11.00).
- Floods returned, cutting off homes and closing roads and railways. 301 flood warnings were in place. A man stranded when his car was swept off the road near Sturminster Newton was winched to safety by a helicopter. (*Daily Telegraph*, 7.11.00).
- Many towns inaccessible by rail yesterday as floods continued, thousands evacuated[29] (*Daily Telegraph* 9.11.00). In contrast, *The Times* and *Guardian* - on the same day - reported instead on main roads blocked by floods, 200 houses flooded and villages swamped.

The classic rail-bashing was a photo of cars in a flood, headlined: 'Rail travellers face delays after flood damage', (*Daily Telegraph*, 23.12.91). There were only two railway locations mentioned - compared to a dozen roads listed.

Some other typical examples of bad weather transport problems include:

- Freezing fog & ice disrupts flights & makes 1000s miles roads dangerous. (*Times* 1.12.75).
- In dense fog, I arrived Euston, early. Others using the motorway were dead (*Times* 15.1.85)
- 50-car pile-up on the M2 in blizzard, other roads were blocked by snow. (*Times* 9.2.86).
- 67-vehicle pile-up in fog closed 7 miles on the M4, (*The Times* 12.12.89).
- Roads closed, villages flooded, bridges closed. (*Times* 10.1.92).
- Last weekend anybody attempting to drive to the south coast needed blankets, food and a torch. Driving north is a nightmare, (*Times* 24.10.04).
- Homes and businesses flooded as 80 mph winds and heavy rain lashed the south coast. *Two* trains were halted at Dawlish by high waves Train drivers said it was the worst they could remember. Brittany Ferries cancelled a ferry, (*Times* 28.10.04).

---

[28] Which are all supplied by road.

[29] Which would not be a consequence of flooded railways! Invariably, houses get flooded because roads are flooded.

- The M11 suffered gridlock on 30 January 2003. Drivers were snowed in up to 17 hours; 12,000 people were affected and left without heat, water or food, (*C4* programme, 6.7.05).

Road disasters occur in good weather. An M6 crash killed 13 in bright sunshine, causing a 35 mile jam. Six serious motorway crashes are listed, including a 120-vehicle pile-up, and several coach collisions. (*Times* 22.10.85).

A search of the 'quality' media found no remarks by BR that seemed vitriolic or risible, (see page 156). What is risible is an inference that road transport virtually always delivers on time. Many people will have experienced them failing to call at a specified time in *good* - much less - bad weather. The norm is to be told to expect them morning or afternoon. Often, even the day is not predicted! In contrast, railways are criticised for failing to keep to a schedule timed to the nearest minute! In wintry conditions, a modest gradient finds road vehicles skidding because gritting has not taken place. If a delivery arrives at a house at which there is *apparently* no one in, no delay will occur in putting a card through the door telling the occupier where a package can be collected. It is not unknown for a card to be put through the door of the wrong house. When road haulage publishes a timetable specifying delivery time to the *nearest quarter of an hour* will be time for them to boast about keeping to schedule. Several new and extensive road delays are reported by the BBC *every* hour. The gross time delay is never calculated. Until they do, any 'comparison' with rail delays is impossible. Road transport would need to invest in a large number of staff to keep and disseminate delay information currently, and retrospectively, before they can indulge in self praise about standards. By failing to offer a proper schedule and answer for it, hauliers keep costs artificially down. The much vaunted 'just-in-time' delivery by road is a myth. There would never be an empty shelf, or a missing product if they could fulfil *that* promise. That a haulier may make such a sweeping claim of reliability is no surprise. Only the anti-rail lobby would accept it at face value. The evidence of history, is that when bad weather strikes, motorists, anxious to avoid getting stranded, and avoid having cars ruined by salt, whenever possible, head for the nearest railway station, passing several bus stops en route!

Railfuture

Transwatch tries to dismiss the views of a body called Railfuture, published in *The Case for Rail* on grounds that they are inaccurate, but, in so doing, advances invalid claims:
- Railfuture make an unreasonable comparison of the length of the rail network with the entire road network. That network is nearly 400,000 km long but most consists of minor rural roads and urban back streets. Transwatch claims that the reasonable comparison would be with motorways and trunk roads, which have a length of 15,500 km and a lane length in the range of 52-60,000 km. In comparison, the national rail network is some 16,000 km long and offers a track length of 32,000 km.

   This comparison - not Railfuture's - is invalid and unreasonable. No traffic begins or ends on motorways and little on trunk roads. If traffic originating on non-trunk roads was ignored along with non-trunk road mileage, comparative road traffic volume would be derisory. In fact, every part tonne and every person travelling on local roads for a short distance is counted.

- On the tricky ground of safety, on which, even the biased media, tend to give railways the edge, Transwatch, having excluded non-trunk roads in comparisons (see above), slips back to praying in aid of passenger mileage, *all* car mileage: 'currently there are 18 times as many passenger miles by road as by rail'. Subjective judgements are made as to how safe converted roads would be, if free of pedestrians, motor cyclists and cyclists.[30]

> *Trespassers are pedestrians taking a short cut across - sometimes, along - the railway. All three classes use level crossings, hence they cannot be discounted for rail, whilst being counted for roads. As 73% of car journeys are less than 5 miles* (see page 71)*, most will never be on a motorway or converted system. They refer to suicides and trespassers as if neither will feature in a converted system,* (see page 62)*. Where those intent on suicide will go is not explained - maybe a motorway. Trespassers taking short cuts would not diminish.*

- It dismisses Railfuture comparisons of passengers by rail and roads by claiming that motorway and trunk road lanes handle nearly 4 times as many passenger-km as rail.

> *The DfT say there are no accurate passenger/km for roads, nor motorways,* (see page 153)*. Hence this comparison is invalid. Again they compare all rail mileage with 15% of roads.*

- It also dismisses Railfuture comparisons of freight by rail and roads, by claiming that motorway and trunk road lanes handle 3 times as many tonnes-km as rail.

> *The DfT state that there are no freight tonne figures for such roads. There are figures for vehicle miles, but in the absence of data as to the contents - and many vehicles are known to be travelling empty or part loaded[31] - there is no weight data available except for the whole road network. Even that data appears to be over estimated,* (see page 153)*.*

- Averaged over the network as a whole, the average flow by rail is equivalent to 300 buses[32] plus lorries per day per track – a flow that would be quite lost on a motor road capable of carrying 5-10,000 vehicles per day per lane.

> *This is a chalk and cheese argument. Rail traffic is averaged over its whole network - main lines and rural lines - and peaks flattened - and then compared with a theoretical capacity of a hypothetical road which would not be the standard of a converted railway!*

- Railfuture claims on speed differential are dismissed on the grounds that the express coach would match the train for journey time, given the rights of way.

> *This is a remarkable claim, given that passenger train speeds are 100-125 mph and rising, whilst coaches are limited for safety reasons to 60 mph, and not rising, on purpose designed motorways. It is inconceivable that they would be safe at over 60 mph on a converted system at headways as is proposed. Delays and accidents arising from. flat junctions, traffic lights and farm crossings would extend journey times even more.*

- Transwatch says that 50% rail journeys are less than 25 miles, 90% less than 80 miles.

> *It ignores that 50% of road passenger mileage is by local PSVs, whose passengers average 3 miles per journey! The rest is by contract coach - school runs, excursions - and express. Their journey length is unknown, but the DfT has estimated a 30 mile average. It fails to draw attention to the length of car journeys - which represent most passenger travel - 73% of which are less than 5 miles. The RAC 2004 Report says the average car trip is 8.7 miles.*

- They claim that the environmental consequence of preserving railway rights of way is that the immensely wide routes serving the heart of London are substantially disused while lorries and other traffic clog unsuitable city streets.

> *Given conversion, more lorries would enter cities to make extra delay inducing calls, and existing and new PSVs would do likewise. All rail freight travelling to private sidings -*

---

[30] Three groups which Transwatch say are 'not normally found on railways'.

[31] Lorries travelling with wheels elevated are either part loaded or empty. Many open lorries can be seen to be empty. 'Heavier lorries partly loaded use more fuel than lighter vehicles.' (*Juggernaut*, Page 16).

[32] The Smith scheme requires 475 for 90 miles of converted railway! (Page 119).

85% of all traffic - would travel through industrial and residential streets to reach destinations. There is no evidence - and neither can there be, without a detailed traffic survey of vehicle journeys - that a single vehicle will benefit by diverting. Many lorries are making deliveries on existing roads. Buses which did not run along residential streets would have no passengers. The proximity of buses to houses is their attraction.

'Lorries account for 6% of energy consumption in the UK, but responsible for 31% of emissions of black smoke, 17% of nitrogen oxides, and other pollutants', (Plowden & Buchan)

- Transwatch disputes a statement by Railfuture that 'it is certainly not true that most rail passengers are well heeled'. Transwatch notes RAC's 2004 report on motoring states that 50% of fare revenue comes from households within the top 20% band of income.

  Inquiries of the RAC regarding its Report on Motoring revealed that there were two in 2004. They said that neither refers to rail fares. Such a claim is not borne out by the volume of passengers on cheap tickets, Student, Family and Senior Citizen railcards, etc

- Transwatch criticises a claim by Railfuture that a twin track railway has six times the capacity of a 6-lane motorway, by praying in aid a single express bus lane serving New York Bus terminal.[33] That lane is said to carry 700 45-seat coaches in the peak providing 31,500 seats – said to be four times the peak hour passengers alighting per track at London Victoria.

  The comparison is invalidated by the reality that many displaced UK rail passengers do not switch to PSVs, but to cars. The criticised claim was in respect of what is happening on UK motorways now. The passenger capacity of a bus-only lane is irrelevant. If one lane of a converted system is reserved for PSVs, many will travel with part loads, leaving no room for cars, thereby congesting existing roads. The value of the New York situation is undermined by evidence that bus punctuality is not good and that collisions occur, (see footnote - page 109).

Transwatch believe that in the national interest, Railfuture claims should be investigated by a body such as the Advertising Standards Authority. It should consider also the validity of all road traffic figures quoted by the DfT, BRF and others, and their use in justifying road building.

Propaganda

Transwatch concludes that *The Case for Rail* is consistent with the rail lobby's propaganda, and that the propaganda has created a myth that bears no relationship to reality. They claim that the railway function could be carried out by express coaches and lorries, given the rights of way, at one quarter the cost of the train, halving the death rate, using 20-25% less fuel[34] and offering all London's crushed rail commuters seats at a fraction of current fares.[35] National road traffic figures are unreliable (see page 153) as a basis for fuel consumption and single vehicle performance is irrelevant. It says that no unchallengeable case against this claim has been presented. An unchallengeable answer is made herein.

Propaganda is an emotive term used to describe information disseminated by the opposition; propaganda disseminated by the home side is called information!

Reality

Transwatch claims 'if railway rights of way were available to express coaches, fares would be reduced by a factor of at least five or at least that is often the current

---

[33] The New York bus service has deteriorated, and accidents cause delays, (see pages 109,167,168,179).

[34] These claims are untenable. No acceptable proof can be tabled on the effect on fatalities.

[35] The main author of the East Anglian study - praised by Transwatch - states a seat is not guaranteed, (see page 115). The claimed fare reductions are unattainable without a subsidy, (see page 139).

differential'. It is a recorded fact that when PSVs replaced trains after closures they were subsidised by BR, and that objectors to closures had stated that they would have to pay higher bus than rail fares. Complaints were made in Parliament that bus fares increased after closure, and objectors to closures often proved bus fares were higher.[36] *The claim that fares on the East Anglian study would fall by 64% has been disproved,* (see page 139).

In trying to claim that express buses would achieve speeds to match those of Inter City expresses, Transwatch overlooks the need for buses to leave the converted system and go onto existing roads to get to bus stations. The alternative would require buses to use locations away from town centres, requiring feeder services, the cost of which, together with bus shelters needs to be embraced.

Conclusions dependent on assumptions, DfT road traffic figures and opinions on accident reductions are not a sound basis for costly conversion. As is pointed out on the Internet (see page 206), if road transport is so beneficial, why has conversion not taken place in the major economies of Europe? It is not due to BR being backward. In 1980, a Leeds University study found that BR compared favourably with European railways.

The reality is that if railways were converted for one route as suggested in the Hall-Smith study, and were found to fail, reinstatement would be very costly. This is an issue that those concerned have not addressed. By definition an experiment is something that can be reversed if it proves impractical or too costly. Reversal may not be feasible. If an experiment proves the theorists are wrong, who picks up the tab?

If PSVs of modern design, using motorways for almost their entire journey, cannot attract *all* existing rail traffic, despite some of the latter being at higher fares, how can anyone realistically believe that they could do so on roads with one lane and flat junctions at thousands of cross roads? It is claimed that PSVs could be equipped with every comparable facility found on trains. That would reduce seating, increase costs and fares.

It is incomprehensible that anyone can ignore the evidence that railway formations are generally unsuitable for conversion to roads. The repeated failure to calculate the vehicles required, after Lloyd's embarrassing re-calculations is proof that these are dangerous waters. How dangerous is revealed by the calculations in the East Anglian case. Only by ignoring history can it be claimed that buses would do the job, when the reality is that passengers displaced by rail closures mostly switch to cars. When one converts rail passengers into average car loads, which have not materially changed for decades, the headway for cars carrying the same number of passengers as a train is ten times that of a train, (see page 199). The downside scenario which must be considered, is that of a main line service carrying one Inter City train every five minutes being replaced by 3,600 cars per hour *in one lane*, or one every second. At 60 mph their headway would be less than half the prescribed safe headway, even if they flowed along like computer controlled robots instead of in unregimented surges. When account is taken of cross traffic at flat junctions and farm crossings - whether light controlled or not - other vehicles entering the road, whilst others wait to turn right to exit, accidents would not halve, but would soar out of control. Why conversionists believe that displaced passengers would turn to buses instead of cars is no mystery. Towns would be gridlocked if they turned to cars. The conversion theorists, who

---

[36] See *The Railway Closure Controversy*, Pages 37,75,95,109,134,170.

would not lose a penny in an *experiment*, were blind to the reality. It should be easy to find someone to blame for failure

Motorists will have seen HGVs swerve out of lane, and back in, which would be dangerous on the converted narrow roads which conversionists will accept - *initially*. Given the admission of HGV drivers in the Selby TV re-enactment, that they drive when very tired[37] the reason for swerving is obvious - as are the consequences which are ignored. Selby led to the installation of costly protective barriers for bridge abutments on motorways. Work is proceeding elsewhere. As with earlier hindsight expenditure, such as *hard* shoulders, roadside signalling, lighting, warning signs, central barriers,[38] etc., these are costs that are overlooked in superficial comparisons. The discovery that motorways - especially slow and middle lanes used by HGVs - are wearing out in half the design life, (see page 182), is a hidden cost for road haulage which is also ignored in paper comparisons.

Irrelevancies

A quote dragged in by conversionists, is that of Stewart Joy, (see page 87), an Economist moved to BR, for three years, by his employer, the DoT, as an extra mouth to feed. Transwatch mentions that in a book, he accused the BTC of tricking government[39] into subsidising railways, and of being fools or knaves, and infers that as there were no libel actions, the allegation must have been true. Leaving aside its irrelevance to conversion, the assumption overlooks the obvious. It is improbable that there was a mad rush to buy his book by railway managers, and hence the alleged libel would remain unknown. As he named no one, no one had grounds for action. He had an academic background. His obituary[40] states his railway experience was that of a supernumerary clerk with Victoria Railways [Australia]. This author was a line manager when Joy was with BR, but was unaware of his existence until 1992, when Joy's book - published 1973, eleven years after the BTC ceased to exist - was chanced upon in a library, whilst killing time, awaiting the arrival of files from a storeroom. It reveals Joy's lack of comprehension of railways. He ignored the ruinous effect on BR finances caused by the Transport Tribunal's inequitable control of fares and freight rates - admitted by its President - which were held well below inflation, and the effect on BR of industrial decline. He claimed that the BTC rushed to buy 0.5m decrepit colliery-owned wagons, which they were *required to do by the 1947 Act*, and at a specified price of £43m. Government had been trying to force railways to buy them and replace them with a modern fleet, to help cut unemployment, for 20 years[41] but railway managers would have none of it. There was no protest from wagon owners! He displayed a lack of knowledge on the external control of closures, commercial freedom, common carrier obligation, rolling stock, finance and productivity. His claims on these subjects, were rebutted - with fact and figure - in *Blueprints for Bankruptcy* published 1993 (updated 1995), and *Britain's Railways - The Reality*, published 2003.

---

[37] More evidence of tired drivers is revealed in *Juggernaut* by John Wardroper.

[38] Which had to be replaced as the original barriers are found to be insufficient protection against juggernauts.

[39] The idea that railway managers - long denigrated as of low business ability - had the skills to trick the highly educated and knowledgeable men who stalked the corridors of power - was aired in 1920, when railways were accused of tricking an earlier generation of senior civil servants into signing a wartime document without understanding it. It was ridiculed then by the media, and must be now. If anyone should have sued for libel, it should have been some of these highly placed civil servants!

[40] *Rail*, September 1998.

[41] See *Square Deal Denied*, (Page 87) and PRO: MT47/128.

Conversion assumes that the railway should be given free for road building purposes, and that surplus land and assets should be sold to finance conversion. No mention is made of the £1.3 bn debt to be paid to former owners - with annual repayments of £3.2m and annual interest of £45m. BR had been paying these sums, and as they were deprived of income due to political interference and incompetence, had to take on interest bearing loans. By 1962, this had cost BR £680m.[1] The previous owners were not finally repaid until 1988. The conversionists overlooked others with a claim. After paying off creditors, repaying loans, continuing to fund statutory fencing and other costs, the residue should next be applied to paying staff in lieu of notice and outstanding holidays, redundancy pay and pensions.[2] Railway owned houses would, following prevailing UK practice, be offered to sitting tenants, at prices which, following normal practice, would be below market value. Whether *anything* would be left to fund conversion, as is believed, is open to doubt, but it would be much less than postulated.

The basis of conversion is a house of cards depicting claimed benefits: less congestion, less fuel, fewer deaths, faster and more reliable road transport. These unsubstantiated claims were handed down from generation to generation, until they became believed - but only by the devout conversionists. They, in one of their wilder allegations, linked those who opposed conversion, to the propaganda of Dr. Goebels, whom they quote as saying 'that constant repetition of propaganda would make people believe it'. The irony is that, that is *precisely* what a handful of conversion supporters have been endeavouring to do for 50 years. Remove any card and the edifice collapses. Among the most unreliable of their many claims is that of reduction in road deaths, particularly among pedestrians. What they ignore is the probability that there will be a pro rata increase in fatalities among other users, even in the unlikely event that pedestrian deaths fall on existing roads

The unsuitability of railway infrastructure for use as roads

The MoT said that, *except in a few instances, it is prohibitive to convert redundant railways into roads*,[3] When Lloyd made his presentation to the ICE, annual BTC Reports showed that over a third of route mileage was single, and a further 54% was double track:

N°. of tracks	Route miles
Single line	6,773
Double line	10,302
Triple line	448
Four or more lines	1,503
Total	**19,026**
Track miles	35,704
Average	1.88

[1] See *Britain's Railways - The Reality*, Page 176.
[2] It should not be overlooked that BR had, effectively been buying itself from previous owners, which, together with external directions to hold fares below inflation, pegged salaries and wages well below industrial trends. Negotiations on pay always produced a reminder by management that free and reduced rate travel, secure pensions, and post-retirement travel concessions were part of the deal, and 'justified' lower pay levels.
[3] Hansard, 16.2.55, vol. 437, col. 47.

The DoT publication *Railway Construction & Operation* which sets out railway construction standards shows that track widths were too narrow for use as roads. Moreover, some rail routes were below prescribed widths for historical reasons.

Conversionists overlooked that some railway formations were shared with LT, e.g. Queens Park-Watford; and London-Upminster which had LT tracks alongside BR tracks. They overlooked that the concept of 60 mph vehicles at 100 yard spacing would be rudely broken by swing bridges over navigable waterways. There were several locations where one railway line crossed another 'on the flat', and thousands of level crossings of minor and major roads (including then, the A5 near Lutterworth). Rail junctions would cause delays, as traffic turned right. Examples of these inconvenient locations will be found in scores of books on railways, which tabulate details of junctions, crossings, viaducts, bridges, tunnels and swing bridges - on single and double lines - illustrated by photos.

Norfolk County Council stated[4] that: 'Land required for roads that have overlaid these former railway routes considerably exceeds the original land take for railway construction, so that, apart from minimising disruption to communities along the line of route, there is little advantage in following these alignments and costs incurred may have actually been higher than those of following totally new alignments. In most cases, to allow road construction to take place, the vertical profile of the former railways has been altered significantly with embankments lowered and cuttings infilled to allow for the greater width needed to construct a new road'. This destroys the claim that railway routes were of adequate width, or could be converted into roads at a fraction of the cost of new roads. Other authorities made the same point, (see chapter 13). Widening and infilling cuttings to raise a roadbed to a level providing adequate width were not uncommon.

A report on the conversion of a short length of closed railway to be part of the [40 mile] Heads of the Valley road, in Wales stated that 'consulting engineers recommended a short section be incorporated in the new road, but not the rest. Other parts of the line were found on investigation to be unsuitable for engineering reasons'. (Times 27.5.58).

In 1967, the Institution of Civil Engineers published *Developments in Railway Traffic Engineering*. Two key findings were:

- A 4-track railway occupies half the width of a dual 3-lane motorway. 12 acres per mile are required for such a railway, as against 24 acres for a motorway. Because of this, an average motorway will incur greater construction costs than a comparable railway: 3-lane motorway £0.7m per mile; 4-track railway, including land: £0.5m per mile. (Page 1).
- Ballast is normally nine inches deep. Only where a railway cutting acts as ditch to the countryside are drains usually necessary. A road with concentrated run-off at each side requires drainage costing £70,000 per mile. BR has 64,000 bridges, of which 25,000 are over-bridges. Of 39,000 under-bridges, approximately 18,000 are wrought iron or steel construction, the rest are brick, masonry or concrete. Metal bridges incur an average annual expenditure of repairs, renewals and maintenance amounting to £10m, (Page 2)

American experience

Conversion supporters repeatedly quote the 'conversion of an American railroad into the Pennsylvania Turnpike'. Lloyd wrote to *The Times* (4.7.81): 'In doubting whether

---

[4] Letter to the author 3.2.05

conversion is a business proposition, Mr. Posner (*The Times* 18.6.81) is ignorant of the success of the Pennsylvania Turnpike, which bought an old railroad, turned it into a motorway and from profits, paid bondholders years ahead of their obligation. It should then have passed to the State, but they preferred to leave it with the Turnpike Commission'.[5] He envisaged a 'modest 2-track railway converted to an unluxurious road at, say, £0.1m per mile, carrying a typical rural trunk road flow of 6,850 vehicles'.[6] It is *irrelevant* to his objective - converting all railways, displacing rail traffic and diversion during changeover. The South Pennsylvania Railroad was not a *closed* railway, as it never opened! Begun in the 1880s to compete with the Pennsylvania Railroad [aka the Pensy], before it saw a train, it was sold unfinished to the Pensy, and abandoned. In 1934/5, the idea of using the abandoned trackbed to build a road was advanced by State officers in response to the federal New Deal job creation plan, which would improve transport in the war that was on the horizon. They persuaded government to *give* $29m in Grants, and fund a $41m loan [bonds] to cover the forecast $70m cost. It opened in October 1940. It was totally unlike Lloyd's concept[7] The design features were:

- A 200 ft right of way.
- Four 12-ft wide concrete traffic lanes.
- Maximum curvature of 6°; banked corners and separate grade crossings.
- Limited access with 1,200 foot long entrance and exit lanes.[8]
- 10 ft median grass strip (central reservation) & 10 ft wide berms (verges).
- Ten service plazas along the right of way.
- No cross streets, traffic signals, driveways or railroad crossings.
- Eleven interchanges[9] (along the 160 mile route).
- Speed limit 35 mph in tunnels (through which flammable loads are banned).

Although it had one of the lowest fatality rates, safety improvements had to be made to meet rising accidents. This led to a 300 foot wide right of way with a 60 foot median. $100m (£49m) was spent on bypasses in the 1960s to eliminate three of the tunnels.

Lloyd would have been wise to study the figures. The reality is that the 160 mile Turnpike cost $437,500 per mile in the late 1930s. At $4.89 = £1 (the 1938 rate) that equalled £89,470 per mile. By 1981, inflation would have lifted that to £1.5m per mile! His road would be half the width of the Turnpike, for one-fifteenth the price! Banning flammable loads through UK tunnels would put BR's huge oil traffic on existing roads.

Another favourite of conversionists is the capacity of New York's Lincoln Tunnel. *The New York Times* reveals delays occur. Two buses going in opposite directions, collided head-on, injuring 12, when one swerved to avoid a car-lorry collision, and then skidded

---

[5] The original 3³/₄% bonds were redeemed, not from profits, but by new 2¹/₂% bonds to save $0.5m interest pa. The bondholders were the federal government as part of the New Deal. The Commission was created by the State, it was not a private company, and remained a State body.

[6] The source of the £100,000 is not mentioned nor justified. 6,850 cars per day would carry about 10,000 people. 28,500 are carried in an hour in one direction on one line from Liverpool Street, (see page 133).

[7] Only 34 miles of the 160 mile Turnpike were part of an unused railway formation. Six of the tunnels built for a single track railway had to be enlarged. (R. Calvert, *Railway Magazine*, January 1965).

[8] The East Anglian scheme envisaged equivalent acceleration and deceleration lanes of 90 feet! (see page 122).

[9] These were huge, see photograph. A typical one spread over land ten times the width of that occupied by the *dual carriageway* road! For source see http://users.zoominternet.net/~jamico/Turnpike_Page.htm.

on a wet road, (14.9.00). Two buses and two other vehicles were involved in collisions, injuring 57, and blocked the Tunnel in the peak for over 2 hours. They were travelling at 20 mph! (24.2.01). Gridlock was caused for two hours in the peak by an oversized lorry, despite a signed height restriction, (9.4.05). A two hour blockage on the Liverpool Street route would hold up 800 buses!

UK conversion studies

The League could have commissioned consultants but failed to do so. In contrast, BR commissioned such a study. They found that the only roads possible - without excessive and costly reconstruction of many bridges, tunnels and other structures - were below the standards laid down by the DoT for new through roads. The *Report on the potential for the conversion of some railway routes in London into roads*, was published in March 1984, by Coopers & Lybrand together with G. Brian Parker, an independent highway planning consultant. Ten radial or orbital rail route sections - all less heavily used than the main trunk routes - were looked into for the prospects of converting some of London's railways. It shows that only one of routes examined could be, considered a prima facie case for conversion. In all cases it proved uneconomic to meet the design standards laid down by DoT highway engineers because of the very large capital sums that would be needed to reconstruct bridges, enlarge tunnels and widen the rights of way. In three cases the double-track formation would not even accommodate *any* width of two-way road. Some 200 kilometres of rail route were examined, including orbital and radial routes, but ignoring the most heavily used lines. The ten schemes were picked in the hope that some could be linked together to provide a new Inner London road 'box' running round from Lewisham in the south-east to Peckham, Clapham, Kensington, Willesden, Islington and Hackney. The two radial routes were from Fenchurch Street. and Marylebone-Northolt, which the conversion league claimed was ideal for road traffic. On all routes where roads might be physically possible no adequate financial case was made apart from Marylebone-Northolt, which presented, prima facie, a case for further study.

The Report states that: 'the narrowest point of that route is the tunnel under Marlborough Hill, which is on a curve of 380 metres radius, with a clear width of 7.75 metres only up to a height of 2.5 metres. The route passes over a viaduct 800 metres long. Another tunnel is 7.3 metres wide, and there are bridges with width limitations. It would be difficult to provide any road links at the Marylebone end due to much of the first 4 km being in tunnel. A road resulting from conversion would be only 6.7 metres wide as against the standard 7.3 metres, with one section only 5.9 metres wide. The line would need to be widened in three locations, but the stretch of only 5.9 metres could not be widened. User would be limited to cars only, feeding into the congested highway network north of Baker Street. Single deck buses would only be possible if subject to light controlled alternate working at the narrowest part, if the MoT approved such a restriction. The capital cost of £16m excludes the cost of a bus terminal at Marylebone, or any land'.

The other radial route examined - Fenchurch Street to Shoeburyness - would convert into a single lane road only. Even if it was good enough to take buses, the Steering Committee said that it would be less economic to carry commuters by buses than continue train services, even assuming conversion could take place overnight. BR said: 'imagine buses being steered between massive steel structures with six inches to spare at each side;[10] hardly a recipe for safe transport'. BR considered the study was worthwhile as it throws an objective, independent light on a controversy which has raged for 25 years.

Comparative costs of rail and road transport

Roads are built on the basis of social benefit, an ingenuous formula based on the time road users *may* save by using new roads.[11] BR had to justify investment in money terms - either lower working costs or higher revenue.

In 1964, the BRB prepared a Report,[12] as part of its evidence to the Geddes Committee, which had been set up to consider the comparative costs of road and rail transport. The Report stated that it was essential in any proper study of the relative roles of rail and road freight transport to establish the hitherto unresolved problem of system costs: the cost of providing and maintaining the highway, its ancillary services, structures and equipment,[13] signalling, policing, etc. In contrast there was an abundance of data on rail costs.

Operating costs were compared for a 10 ton wagon, 12.5 ton container, a 10 ton lorry and a 16 ton lorry[14] all involved in carrying general merchandise. The system costs were on the basis of a new railway being constructed, including land purchase. Road costs are based on new construction published in a paper[15] in 1963, which exclude the cost of major bridges and land purchase. Nothing was included for land purchase at present, but land purchase was based on 80% of the distance being through rural areas and 20% urban - the same formula as for the railway assessment, and the same values per acre assumed.

Annual road maintenance costs, snow clearing etc. were based on MoT data for the year to March 1963. Expenditure on road policing and lighting were taken from National Income & Expenditure, 1963. Total costs were then divided into those costs which are occasioned solely by the need to provide roads able to stand up to heavy traffic.

The additional construction costs attributable to heavy vehicles have been assessed as the difference between published construction costs of trunk routes catering for all traffic and costs of routes if they had been built for light traffic only. Construction costs had been inflated by the higher cost of moving earth to reduce gradients to facilitate reasonable speeds by heavy lorries. Before the M1 was started the cost per mile was expected to be £250,000 per mile, in the event it was £400,000, whilst today [1964], excluding major bridges and land acquisition, it is estimated to cost £750,000 per mile. In contrast to this latter figure, a motorway built for light vehicles only would be £200,000 per mile.

The study revealed that the cost of a 4-track railway was less than a 2-lane dual carriageway, and very much less than a motorway. The relative traffic volumes which could be carried by either system were taken from MoT data, to which was applied running costs and an allocation of track/highway costs, from which it was demonstrated that rail freight transport costs per ton mile were around 50% of the cheapest road alternative. The BR Report demonstrated that the road freight operator pays no more than

---

[10] At the 60 mph speed planned by Brigadier Lloyd and never really moderated by his successors.

[11] An advisor appointed by the MoT in 1979 said that the DoT method of estimating time savings were far fetched, unduly simplistic and grossly over-estimate the tangible benefits of road improvements, (see *Juggernaut*, Page 40).

[12] *A study of the true costs of rail & road freight transport over trunk routes.*

[13] Over the succeeding years since the first motorway was built - at ostensibly low costs, we have seen progressively more and more add-ons: hard shoulders, more service stations, lighting, huge numbers of illuminated signs, etc.

[14] These were the prevailing standard sizes of rail and road transport. Both have increased.

[15] *Roads in England & Wales.*

a third to a half of trunk road costs. The Report showed the sources for all data, in contrast to the unsubstantiated figures used in the conversion campaign, which invariably shows no independent sources or, at most, edited extracts of quotes, (see pages 73,75-77).

If haulage drivers' hours were cut to rail levels, they would need 50% more drivers, who would want higher wages to compensate for lost overtime. Together with NHS costs, it would increase road hauliers' costs. A change will be enforced by the EEC directive.

Responses to the BRB Report

The BR study of true costs presented to the Geddes committee shows that hauliers were only paying one-third to one-half of their actual track costs. The argument is fairly convincing. It is in the national interest to reveal that the haulier has been doing things on the cheap. (*The Times* Editorial, 24.6.64).

Douglas Jay, MP wrote there is substantial truth in BR contention that lorries are under-taxed. Figures supplied by the Treasury show that Duty paid by lorries is hardly higher than in 1933, and in some cases lower. To have kept pace with inflation, lorry tax should be almost three times as high as it is (*The Times*, 26.6.64).

Motorway slow lanes wear out much faster than others, confirming USA studies that heavy vehicles are responsible for a disproportionate share of road costs. They reveal that 1,000 12-ton axle loads create the same wear as 160m car axle loads. (*The Times*, 26.6.64).

'The MoT claims that out of each £700,000 spent on new motorways, only £124,000 was attributable to heavy lorries. The manner in which MoT evidence to the committee was published suggests a strong desire to avoid embarrassing comparisons. Whereas with railway evidence the press were given ample explanatory material, time to study it, and a press conference chaired by Dr. Beeching, MoT evidence consisted of a mass of qualified statistics slipped out quietly late yesterday with no comment. The DoT said that it had not attempted to make a comparative study of road and rail costs, which - they claimed - they were hardly qualified to do! BR said that the MoT figures show that HGVs do not pay full track cost. The major difference is the amount allocated of capital costs', (*The Times*, 19.8.64)

The RHA admitted that hauliers in heaviest class may not be paying enough tax to cover their full track costs, but claimed that BR assessment was too high. MoT claims that lorries over 8 tons incurred track costs of 5.2p per vehicle mile. (*The Times*, 8.10.64).

It is astounding that the MoT conceded that lorries did not pay their full share of road costs - but were unsure what the share should be! How had they justified spending on motorways without establishing the effect on capital and maintenance costs of heavier vehicles? How had they approved heavier axle loads without a sound basis for assessing what hauliers should pay? It was not rocket science. They had ignored USA research. It is notable, how often the road lobby has tried to use USA experience to justify building motorways and to advocate conversion - but on this crucial aspect affecting taxpayers and dispossessed property owners - they, and the MoT - are silent, (see also page 130). The grudging admission by the RHA that some heavy vehicle taxes do not *quite* cover costs should be seen as confessing to a lesser charge, in the hope of getting off lightly.

Other Reports relating to competition

The Highway Economics Unit, of the DoT, stated in *Developments in Railway Traffic Engineering*, (Page 62), *published 1967* that a 4-lane all purpose road would cost about £0.5m per mile. Costs in recent cases ranged from £0.25m to £1.25m.

Brian Fletcher, manager of Staffordshire County Council Engineering Consultancy Group stated: We think we are doing well if a motorway lasts for seventeen years.[16] In contrast, railway track and bridges last for many decades.

'It costs £7m pa to police abnormal loads on motorways and dual carriageways. We are seeking to reduce the burden on police forces and encourage transfer to private escorts which would of course transfer *part of* the costs to hauliers involved in abnormal loads.'[17]

A major Report on road pricing produced in 1964 by the government, was put aside quickly under political pressure.[18] Another Report by consultants for the DoT in 1973, which advocates transfer of some freight from road to rail for economic reasons, has been kept under wraps, (see page 210).

A report *The Transport of Freight* [Cmnd 3470], published November 1967 stated [Para 6]: 'the legal limits on the working hours of professional drivers have played an important part in protecting public safety since they were introduced in 1930. The present limits have remained unchanged for 33 years'. Appendix 1, Table 1 shows that road hauls are mostly short, 70% of tonnage being carried less than 25 miles, and only 7% above 100 miles. Of rail traffic, 45% travelled less than 25 miles and 20% was more than 100 miles. Appendix 2 stated: the Transport Bill will reduce the maximum permissible length of a driver's working day from 14 to 11 hours, and this will include an allowance of no more than 9 hours at the wheel compared with 11 out of the present 14. The minimum daily rest period is to go up from 10 to 11 hours; a new limit of *60* hours total work in any week will apply and a new requirement for at least one 24 hour rest period each week.

In 1967, the MoT Paper *Public Transport and Traffic* [Cmnd 3481], examined PSV drivers' hours: 'Legal limits on hours of PSV drivers have been unaltered since the 1930s.[19] The maximum length of the working day will be reduced from fourteen to eleven, except stage services which may spread eleven hours work over $12\frac{1}{2}$ hours; with not more than nine hours at the wheel. The rest period before work will be increased from ten to eleven. On one day per week, it may be $9\frac{1}{2}$ instead of the present 8 hours. There will not be more than *60* hours per week. Many bus and coach drivers are working hours substantially in excess of these limits' (Pages, 23-24).

The ensuing Act was less severe, reducing hours at the wheel to 10, and a $12\frac{1}{2}$ hour day for an HGV or PSV driver. All railway staff had had an 8 hour day, with a 12 hour rest period since 1919, when it was imposed by government against employers' wishes. If lorry and bus hours were the same as rail and operators had comparable safety conditions imposed, road transport costs would have risen, making rail competitive. It is no surprise that BR lost so much traffic,[20] when competitors were:
- allowed longer working hours by law, and exceeding those permitted hours,
- overloading their vehicles and exceeding statutory speed limits,
- keeping costs low by a failure to use comparable safety devices & inadequate maintenance.[21]

In 1976-77, a Select Committee stated: 'One argument about competition is that government is not taking an impartial attitude towards EC Regulations in respect of road

---

[16] Sentinel 23 May 1997.

[17] HoL Hansard, 7.11.00, vol. 618, col. 1361. Transfer to private escorts has occurred, but delays continue.

[18] *Ways of the World*, by MG Lay, Page 330.

[19] Prior to that there was no legal limit whatsoever to the hours of drivers of road passenger and goods transport.

[20] Unlike BR, hauliers had pricing freedom, and were empowered to refuse unprofitable traffic.

[21] All these failings are exposed in *Juggernaut* by John Wardroper. It should be read by all motorists and voters.

and rail freight. It is phasing out rail subsidies - paid for socially necessary but uneconomic lines - and not implementing regulations on drivers hours and tachographs. The Secretary of State saw neither as affecting competition'! (Report Pages 72,73).

Limit the Lorry, a Report by Transport 2000, stated that HGVs cover only 50-70% of their full costs, and cause 100,000 times as much damage to roads as a car.

Road & rail capacity

In 1961, *The cost of roads* by PEP included an extract on research by Dr. Smeed of the Road Research Laboratory, who calculated that 'the total area [in square feet] required to move one person one mile in the peak, was fourteen for a car, four to ten for a bus [depending on the width of road] and one for rail'. This represents a resounding case for the economic and environmental benefits of rail passenger transport over road. (Page 123).

In 1963, Sir Robert Hall's Group reviewed the likely future demand for inland transport. Members of the Group came from within and outside government departments. *Transport Needs of Great Britain in the next twenty years* stated that BR studies showed that about 95% of *all* traffic is carried on only half the railway system, 99% of *freight* was on 70% of route mileage, (Para 13).

Assistant General Manager G. Wilson of BR/Scottish Region, in an address to the University of Glasgow[22] said that the design capacity of various categories of road, as stated in Road Research Laboratory reports were:

	passenger car units	heavy vehicles
2-lane single carriageway	6,000	2,000
3-lane single carriageway	11,000	3,700
2-lane dual carriageway	25,000	8,500
3-lane motorway	37,500	12,500

The Reports show that a 3-lane motorway capacity in 24 hours is 150,000 tons, assuming that heavy vehicles have a capacity of 12 tons, all fully loaded. The normal width of a 3-lane motorway is 130 feet, so that one mile of motorway will occupy 75,000 square yards of land. The capacity ton-mileage per square yard of land is 150/75 = 2.0 ton-miles per day. A four track railway is stated to have a capacity of 200m gross ton-miles pa, i.e. each track can carry 10 trains per hour, each of 600 gross tons, say 350 capacity tons. Four tracks in 24 hours have a capacity tonnage of 350,000. Such a line occupies a width of 80 feet; one mile will take up 50,000 square yards of land. Capacity ton-mileage is therefore, 335/50 = 6.7 ton-miles per day.

Comparative figures of other widths of rail and roadway are:-

	types of rail/roadway	capacity ton-miles per square yard of land
rail	two track	5.7
	four track	6.7
road	2-lane single carriageway	0.9
	3-lane single carriageway	1.3
	2-lane dual carriageway	1.9
	3-lane motorway	2.0

---

[22] BR Management Quarterly - N° 11, February 1967.

Turning to passenger transport, Mr. Wilson quoted an article in the Financial Times (17.10.66) which included the following figures relating to urban passenger systems:

	Capacity (seats per hour on one lane/track)	Equivalent (seats per hour per foot width)
cars on urban motorway	1800	150
buses with exclusive use of single lane	3600	300
suburban railway	25000	2240

J.P. Weston of the Highway Economics Unit, MoT, stated in *Developments in Railway Traffic Engineering,* (Page 62): 'We have a problem in the roads sector of under utilisation'

Dalgleish in 1982, urged transfer of all long distance traffic to a segregated route, (see chapter 8). He claimed to show the spare capacity of railways converted to motor roads. The diagram in his book, is of dual carriageway throughout, with bridges and no junctions, which would rule out conversion. He claimed the system 'could carry 219bn passenger-km + 50bn tonne-km. All purpose roads would then need only to carry 178 bn passenger-km + 41bn tonne km, instead of 443bn and 105bn respectively'. BR was then carrying 30.6bn passenger-km and 17.4bn freight tonne-km on a network $\frac{1}{20}$ the size of the road network. That means a transfer from existing roads of 188bn and 33bn respectively. Traffic on roads is crudely estimated (see page 153). The idea that 220,000 miles of road could transfer about 40% of its traffic to an 11,000 mile network is patently absurd. It is noticeable that no one offered to back these ideas with their own money.

Utilisation of rail and road

In 1989, a conversion campaign regurgitated the discredited Lloyd theory, in the media,[23] claiming that railways were grossly underused. The author's unpublished response demonstrated that road utilisation was worse than rail, having 22 times as much road mileage amd disproportionately more acreage, for ten times as much traffic.[24] There were under-utilised lines in *rural areas*, that were kept open by political decision, and for which there had been no subsidy for the first twenty years of nationalisation. British Rail had to fund them from interest bearing loans, which together with fares held below the RPI, had caused the crippling deficit.[25] Thousands of miles of railway had closed since the 1960s - most of it was available for conversion but remained unused. After standing derelict for years - in the ownership of local authorities - much was brought into public use as footpaths. The letter reminded readers that track widths were inadequate even for single carriageway roads, whilst limited bridge heights would restrict use to cars and small commercial vehicles. Due to the poor utilisation achieved on roads, converted railways would not accommodate road transport carrying existing rail traffic, leaving no

---

[23] In an advertisement in *The Daily Telegraph*, 26 July 1989. (See page 88)

[24] Based on the common practice of adding freight tonne miles/km to passenger miles/km to produce total traffic, and comparing the totals for rail and road transport to the total route mileage of road & rail. (See CSO Annual Abstract of Statistics for traffic data and route length). Also based on the relative shares of traffic by road and rail, then being claimed by the road lobby, but now discredited, (see page 153).

[25] See *The Railway Closure Controversy*. No bus operator, nor other business would have provided a product below cost by government directive without subsidy. See also *Britain's Railways - The Reality*, Page 176.

space for traffic to be transferred from existing roads. In addition to converting railways, it would be necessary to build an equal length of new roads merely to cope with traffic displaced from rail, due to the poor utilisation achieved on roads.

There is a lack of efficient management of the existing road system, with poor signing, and inadequate arrangements for limiting congestion after an accident. Diversions for accidents or major road works around 'three sides of a square' is typical, when good organisation would limit extra mileage. Congestion could be cut with imagination and manpower. Such measures should be considered before new roads are created.

After forty years of motorways, no system has been developed which effectively diverts traffic held up by an accident onto alternative routes until a very long three-lane queue has formed. Radio warnings usually come *after* one has passed the last exit, and arrives behind a three hour queue. Additional routes such as railways converted into roads would therefore be wasted. Neither has a system been introduced to separate traffic travelling at different speeds so as to maximise road utilisation and therefore tackle the self-created congestion problem. Heavy freight confined to night travel and particularly outside city commuter periods would reduce congestion. The reality is that those concerned with road traffic have a one track mind - create more road capacity to wastefully use.

A principal cause of poor utilisation of roads is speed variation: 30-100 mph on motorways, 10-75 mph on other roads. It is bad management in commuter peaks, to permit horses, 10 mph tractors and lorries so heavily loaded that they cannot exceed 20-30 mph on a 60 mph road. Delays are also caused by very wide loads that make their majestic progress at horse drawn speeds. Some wide loads are encountered on minor roads causing delays and potential danger for other road users. The implications of meeting a wide load on converted railways with their projected nine foot lanes was completely ignored by every conversion plan, since loads wider than nine foot are legal, (see page 185).

The road lobby ignores the fact that juggernauts have to leave motorways to deliver in towns and villages, where they negotiate road junctions by halting traffic movement in all four directions. Some commercial premises have such restricted access that vehicles shunt to and fro for up to five minutes to effect entry. Delays can only be reduced by gutting premises and reconstructing local roads, with its attendant compulsory purchase of property. More delays are caused by hauliers using roads to unload car transporters and by other deliveries to firms with inadequate access to premises. Selfish conduct, bad lane discipline, and failures to observe the Highway Code exacerbate the problem.

Despite the appalling under utilisation of roads, users create worse problems. Ultra brief media reports inform of mind-boggling hold-ups due to lorries turning over,[26] jack-knifing[27], shedding their loads and losing tyres, and many other vehicles travelling too fast and too close. Ensuing delays are never translated into time or money loss. No compensation is paid by offenders - if it were, road delays would plummet. Converting railways serving small towns and villages into roads would not change this situation. The tracks, being double or single, would not offer the huge turning areas required for LGVs to leave the converted system and turn on to the local road.

---

[26] *Juggernaut* by John Wardroper reveals that large articulated vehicles are inherently unstable, due to a high centre of gravity, and, for that reason, are limited to lower speeds in Europe.

[27] The means to prevent jack-knifing was developed in the 1960s, (*Times*, 29.9.66), but most hauliers resist the cost.

Another factor in poor road utilisation was revealed in a Study[28] which stated that, at any one time, 30% of lorries run empty. It also stated that government research into the food industry revealed that only 50% of the *cubic capacity* of *loaded* vehicles[29] is used.

Road safety standards

The conversion campaign ignored the tendency of government to direct much higher and more costly standards of safety must be implemented by BR, than were demanded from other transport, including permitting excessive hours of working on road transport.

In 1964, 'the MoT was surprised at the number of lorries found in a dangerous condition in road checks. I pointed out (*The Times*, 10.12.57), that the DoT *Summary of Road Accidents*, was misleading. It claimed that less than 3% were caused by mechanical defect. Later, the MoT said it was 20%. The MoT intended to introduce an annual test of HGVs, but it was *not practical at present*. If a vehicle is stopped for a check, it gets a free examination. If it is seriously defective, it is ordered off the road. The only deterrent is a fine, but the average is £3.' (AL Goodhart, *The Times* 24.8.64). HGV testing began in 1968, PSVs in 1981. Testing of other commercial vehicles and cars over ten years old began in 1959.

In May 1992, government imposed a six month time limit on BR to resolve an alleged safety problem with carriage doors.[30] No similar time-scale was imposed on improving safety of HGVs or PSVs which caused road pile-ups.

Media reports (24.12.94), on a proposed restriction of PSVs to 65 mph to comply with an EC directive, stated: 'It will be similar to existing restrictions on lorries, which are fitted with limiters'. Many would be surprised to learn that juggernauts were so restricted. If PSVs are likewise 'restricted' it will be a case of 'Plus ca change, plus c'est la même chose'. Ministers *consulted* [the industry] on this safety measure. With BR, whose safety standards were far higher, Ministers issued *instructions*, regardless of practicability, cost or effect on competition, with tight time scales.

A TV programme which reconstructed the Selby accident caused by a motor vehicle falling on the track, included HGV drivers admitting that they drove when tired. A BBC1 programme (21.11.05) revealed 20% accidents are caused by lorry drivers falling asleep.

A new Framework for Freight Transport, (Plowden & Buchan), lists many serious problems:
- The existing road transport safety rules are not being enforced.
- Tachographs can be tampered with easily and cannot be detected in roadside checks.
- The impression that lorries have a better safety record than cars is incorrect. Fatality rates for lorries are 2.4 times those of cars. 25% of lorries fail the annual maintenance test at the first attempt, even though it takes place at a pre-arranged time!
- Lorries are frequently overloaded. Spot roadside checks found 17.6% overloaded on M1, 12.6% on M6; up to 24.5% on 'A' roads. A random survey at Carlisle in 1988 found 21.5% lorries overloaded. Immediate prohibitions issued 1985-93 in up to 8.9% cases and delayed prohibition in up to 12.9% cases.
- The Metropolitan licensing authority said driving hour regulations were widely abused.

---

[28] *Goods without the Bads* by Transport 2000
[29] Loads of cereals & food products to supermarkets & retailers would not give full loads by weight, and they would return empty.
[30] Which the H&SE found was mainly due to irresponsible conduct by passengers. (See BRB 1990/1 Report, Page 7)

- One haulier had 18 vehicles and 14 trailers, but no maintenance staff and no records. One facing prosecution was allowed extra vehicles. A third was allowed a large increase in vehicles despite four prohibitions and three defect notices on five vehicles.
- Illegal 'cowboy' operations are believed to be significant. The licensing authority for the Metropolitan area said that 5-10% operators are illegal. The problem has been recognised since the 1950s, and was mentioned in official inquiries in 1965 and 1978.
- In 1979, a DoT report said licensing authorities were too lenient and often gave an operator another chance, even those with a bearing on safety. One operator worked for 22 years without a licence, was prosecuted eight times and fined a total of £300.

In *Juggernaut*, John Wardroper catalogues his research into unsafe practices in the road transport industry. It should be mandatory reading for all road users. Examples of *some* of his findings in respect of unsafe practices in HGV operation include:
- Defective vehicles found in road side and *pre-planned* depot checks of HGVs, (Page 68).
- 94% articulated vehicles had a tendency to jack-knife, (Page 71).[31]
- In 1966, the RRL said that spray thrown up by lorries contributed to one in 77 motorway accidents. Tests showed that mudguards would cut spray by more than one half. (Page 73). Private companies produced a means to cut spray, improving the visibility of following vehicles from an existing 30% to 70%. Hauliers were disinterested.[32]
- Articulated vehicles with high loads easily overturn, even at slow speeds, (Page 70). Legal speeds for these vehicles are higher in the UK than Europe or America. A survey in 1971 revealed that 71% of articulated vehicles were exceeding the legal limits, (Page 75).
- Under-run guards - to prevent a vehicle running under the back - were still being debated in 1979, (Page 74).[33]
- Instead of having vehicle suspension which is less damaging to roads, (Page 99), suspension is designed down to the minimum, (Page 118)
- Drivers sleep in the cab or drive home illegally, (Page 51).
- In 1968, the haulage industry became subject to *quality* licensing instead of *quantity* licensing which still continues in Europe and the USA. Examples of the quality of road operations include: a haulier who ran a haulage business from home, kept and 'serviced' lorries in a council carpark; another 'serviced' 6 artics in a railway arch 20 ft by 9 ft; another 'serviced' 36 lorries and 50 trailers in 5 railway arches, (Page 53).
- In 1973, the EC required that tachographs be fitted to all vehicles by 1977. UK delayed action until 1981, (Page 54). Their purpose, which was welcomed by drivers and owners in Europe, was to monitor drivers' hours to prevent accidents caused by tiredness, and to prevent overspeeding which could cause overturning and other accidents. Drivers admit to falling asleep at the wheel and working excessive hours. (Pages 64,65).
- Between a third and a quarter of vehicles checked were overloaded, 1 in 16 were so dangerous, they were prohibited from going further, (Page 61)
- Undermanned inspectors ordered 8,000 very unsafe lorries off the road in a year (Page 49)

---

[31] A means of preventing it was invented and successfully tested 10 years earlier, (*The Times*, 19.3.65 & 20.5.68).

[32] From 1986, MoT tests included checks that spray suppression is fitted, but they do not measure the spray.

[33] Guards had been called for by an MP in 1914 and recommended in 1919. The subject was raised in Parliament in 1946 and kicked into touch. (See *Square Deal Denied*, Page 60). It is unsurprising, that with unequal pressure on railways to spend vast sums on safety, that the economy minded road haulage industry could poach so much traffic.

In its 1993 Report, *Taming the Truck*, Transport 2000 stated: 'Since the introduction of the 38 tonne limit for lorries, the mileage of the heaviest lorries has increased by 82%, much with part loads. It has meant a less efficient industry, more pollution, road damage and accidents'. The Report drew attention to the risk of damage to gas mains by HGVs. It stated that it is more common for HGVs to break the speed limit than to comply with it, that 7% of HGVs last year had very serious faults resulting in immediate prohibition notices, that between 7% and 24% of lorries were overloaded, that licences are often granted to operators who admit to operating without a licence, often for long periods and with long records of maintenance faults. The RHA recommended impounding lorries of illegal operators. Instead, it seems that derisory fines are imposed.

Accidents

Brigadier Lloyd - the father of conversion - did not claim that it would cut deaths of pedestrians and cyclists. His disciples initiated this claim to bolster their flagging and discredited campaign, seeing its emotional appeal, coupled with the monetary value placed on deaths. In 1977, the chairman of the League claimed that 3,000 lives could be saved by segregating them from motor vehicles by conversion. Five years later, in *The Truth about Transport*, he had reduced his claim by one sixth. He did not explain, nor justify the basis for either figure. In 1977, 2,313 pedestrians and 301 cyclists were killed. Five years later, 1869 and 294 respectively were killed. His claim of 3,000 was 45% of all 1977 road fatalities. The total in 1982 was 5934. Both claims were completely unrealistic. Converting 11,000 miles of railway could not conceivably eliminate all such deaths on 220,000 miles of road. Clearly, deaths in other forms of transport are a greater problem. Providing pavements on all roads would make a bigger impression on pedestrian deaths.

Claims that lives will be saved by conversion are pure speculation. There has not been one properly assessed case to prove it. Research by PACTS[34] reveals that 90% of pedestrians killed or seriously injured occur in built-up areas.[35] Traffic in built up areas will not diminish as a result of conversion, it would increase as more lorries, PSVs and cars fed into urban areas. If a transfer of traffic to converted roads did take place, it would lead to vehicles travelling faster on existing roads, and, what would otherwise be injured pedestrians on those roads, would be killed. Nowhere, does they concede that there may a counter increase, proving that they have not considered any downside aspects.

The road lobby dons its blinkers when speed limits and enforcement are mentioned. The reality - which independent research has *repeatedly* shown - is that speed kills. Naturally, the road lobby must try to deny the undeniable, because speed reductions make road transport more costly. PACTS says that excessive speed is the single most important contributory factor in fatal car crashes. Tony Grayling of the Institute for Public Policy Research says that a cut in the limit to 20 mph. would reduce casualties by 60%. (New Statesman 5.2.01). The Association of British Drivers (representing a *minority* of drivers), is particularly dismissive of the benefits of speed enforcement. It can only believe that all drivers and their vehicles are perfect, and that no vehicle will *ever* suffer sudden mechanical breakdown. An RAC 2004 Report states that 5% drive without insurance -

---

[34] Parliamentary Advisory Council for Transport Safety comprises politicians, academics, retired public or private sector leaders and consultants.
[35] Source: Road Casualties, Great Britain 2003.

and hence no MoT - and 20% of cars are not serviced. Risks to safety posed by such vehicles ahead or alongside arrogant speed merchants is ignored by the road lobby.

In claiming that vehicles on a converted system with 9 foot lanes would travel at 60 mph - by inference - without a single accident, they ignore that on three lane motorways, when lanes are temporarily narrowed to similar widths, speed limits are dropped to as little as 40mph, despite which, vehicle collisions have caused death and injury and road workers have been killed. They ignore that vehicles crash through central barriers and cause many deaths, but blindly assert that converted roads of minimum width without barriers would be virtually accident free at 60mph. Nothing would eradicate as causes of collision: tiredness, inattention, misjudgement, road-rage and tailgating.

Media reports of road accidents often give barest details, never establish how many are delayed nor the scale of damage. In the 1990s, deaths in minibus crashes appeared frequently, often with little coverage. Other examples include a lorry overturned in a con-traflow on the M6 (15.9.91) blocking it for nine hours; 18 miles of the southbound M5 closed (23.11.93) between Bridgwater and Weston Super Mare by a spate of accidents. *A tragic accident* blocking the M40 killing thirteen (18.11.93), merited 581 col. cms., including photographs, equating to 44 col. cms. per fatality. The RAC reported jams aggregating to *230 miles*, (12.8.94) delaying an undisclosed number of holidaymakers. A minibus crash killing 13, merited 77 col. cms, (17.12.98). About the same time, an articulated lorry crossed the central reservation on the M5 killing four, was covered in 4 col. cms. An army tank transporter crashed through the central barrier on the M1, killing five, injuring many more and causing huge delays. (12.6.03). They were en route from Southampton to Catterick and could have been on rail. In 2000, a new loading dock for tanks was built by the army at a station near Catterick, at a cost of £0.75m. The Cannon Street *rail disaster* in which one fatality was reported, got 578 col. cms. (January 1991).

John Wardroper writes in *Juggernaut*, of 678 accidents in the West Midlands in 1976, involving HGVs, in which other road users were killed: 391 were in cars, 112 on motor-cycles, 46 in small goods vehicles, 8 in lorries, 47 on cycles, and 159 were pedestrians. (Page 66). The two groups on which the emotive conversion case is based totalled 30%. The other 70% would be on converted routes and deaths would, inevitably, increase. If some traffic is diverted from existing roads to converted routes, the traffic remaining on existing routes will be able to travel faster and kill more pedestrians. That is the reality.

The BRB Annual Report for 1976 drew attention to significant disparities between rail and road transport. It stated that casualties per passenger mile or per ton mile were -

Car: fatalities are eight times as many as rail; serious accidents are 70 times as many as rail;
Bus/coach: fatalities are 3-5 times as many as rail; serious injuries 20-30 times as many as rail;
HGV: fatalities are 12-17 times as many as rail; serious injuries are 35-50 times as many as rail

The road lobby argues that road casualties are greater due to the mix of pedestrians and vehicles. This is easily resolved - at the expense of those who began to use roads *after* pedestrians, viz. motor transport. Roads could be fenced along their entire length as railways were statutorily compelled to do, with controlled gaps at selected places.

Bus services

Lloyd - and others - forecast that road transport operating on a converted network would cut fares for those who hitherto used railways. The reality is that when railways have closed in the past, leaving no competition for buses, fares have risen.[36] There is little doubt that in the absence of railways, pressure would be put on road operators to cut hours and increase wage rates to compensate. The consumer will foot the bill.

Conversion proposals ignore costly terminal facilities for passengers and those waiting to meet them. Facilities, the like of which are rarely found on the road scene, will have to be provided. Toilets, waiting accommodation, catering, inquiry offices, etc., will be required. In 1984, the author discovered how the road passenger industry was living off the backs of BR to keep costs down. A Liverpool coach driver had the gall to complain in a letter to the Liverpool Echo about Lime Street station men's toilets - then under reconstruction during station modernisation - into which the driver took it upon himself to conduct *female* coach passengers. BR replied: 'This is how they cut costs'. Unlike railways, they were not monitored by a hyper-critical government watchdog, CTCC, which pressured BR to provide platform shelters, whilst saying: the provision of bus shelters, *because of cost and usage factors*, was one for councils to decide, (1965 Report). In fact, street bus stops without shelters were often used by more passengers than nearby rural stations. It is significant that bus shelters, lay-bys and raised kerbs for improved access are funded by local authorities - a hidden subsidy. Any unbiased person would have had the grace to take these costs into the equation when criticising BR costs and subsidies.

The assumption that bus transport would be more effective given its own dedicated routes is false. The conversion campaign has often prayed in aid the New York City busway system. It 'once had the best surface transit system in world. Today, the system has declined to point where New Yorkers skip taking the bus because it is often no faster than walking. It is certainly slower than taking a cab or driving your own car. Buses don't work because they are high capacity vehicles stuck in traffic behind low capacity vehicles. The city has tried bus lanes, but they fail consistently without heavy enforcement'.[37]

National Express does not publish statistics on punctuality or reliability.[38] It contends that unexpected problems: roadworks and adverse traffic signals, which it encounters on roads would invalidate such statistics. Timetables state that whilst published departure times are precise, arrival times, at intermediate and final destinations are approximate. Consequently, maintenance of connections between services cannot be guaranteed. They state that they will make every effort to provide a full range of facilities, but reserve the right to operate any or all services without advertised facilities. That would blow a big hole in the fond belief that a 100% standard would be provided by bus companies on converted railways. These conditions may well apply generally with other bus companies.[39]

The company's representative claimed that publishing punctuality data is appropriate for rail, which they see as being 100% in control of their highway, but not for road

---

[36] See *The Railway Closure Controversy*, Pages 16,95,170.

[37] Source: Internet - New York Transit Authority/Transportation Alternatives.

[38] The author, when working for BR, requested sight of their performance data and timetable planning basis to compare with BR's much criticised standards. He did not disclose that he was with BR, which he expected would produce a rejection. Instead, he said that he was working on a thesis. They declined. He has no doubt, that any other bus company would have declined.

[39] It was rich for the Chairman of FirstBus - owner of the unreliable PMT buses in North Staffs to say - when First Bus entered the rail business - that trains must be more reliable! Unlike BR, PMT published no reliability data

transport.[40] It believes customers are satisfied with current performance. He did not seem to realise that snow falls equally on road and rail; nor of the ability of road vehicles to use diversionary routes, whilst rail has less opportunity to do likewise. Bus operators do not realise the effect on train running of very bad weather, albeit railways keep running whilst road transport skids to a halt. Lloyd's dream of 'prompt sanding and snow clearance' remains just that, even 40 years later - a *pipe* dream. The media still catalogues serious failures in various parts of the UK *every* year

Conditions of Service [National Express, Winter 1996/7] are more restrictive than rail:
- Passengers must arrive at the boarding point at least five minutes[41] prior to scheduled departure. They must allow at least one hour before the departure time of other connecting services or before important appointments.[42]
- The company does not accept responsibility for delays caused by circumstances outside its control.[43] These include: accidents causing delays in the service; exceptionally severe weather conditions; fire and/or damage at a coach station; compliance with requests of the police; deaths or accidents on the road; vandalism or terrorism.[44]
- The company does not undertake that services will start or arrive at the time specified in timetables nor that they will connect with services shown as connecting services.
- No refunds will be made after the time/date of departure of service on which a passenger is booked without evidence [e.g. medical certificate] of inability to travel. No refunds will be given for lost or stolen tickets.[45]
- The company is not liable for loss, as a result of any delay to services or by the same not operating in accordance with their published timings.
- The company reserve the right to alter timetables, suspend, cancel or withdraw services without notice, whether before or after a ticket has been booked and a seat reserved.
- No smoking is permitted on buses.[46]

This is the reality of what passengers, who transfer to bus, will face with conversion. There will be no capacity for passengers who have not pre-planned and pre-booked their

---

[40] In reply to the author's request for information.

[41] BR was expected to allow passengers to buy a ticket and board a train if arriving seconds before departure or board without a ticket, having arrived at the station at the last second. This unforecast passenger expected there would always be a seat available. BR was viciously criticised by rail watchdogs if a passenger with this tight margin missed a train, or faced a penalty charge for travelling without a ticket. Replacement bus services will incur longer waits.

[42] In 1985, the author conducted an analysis of complaints against BR. One of these was from a passenger whose train arrived late in Birmingham from Liverpool. He was scheduled to give a talk in Birmingham, which was due to commence nine minutes after the train was due in Birmingham.

[43] British Railways, in contrast, was not allowed to plead *circumstances beyond its control*.

[44] BR was not allowed to exclude from its performance data, trains delayed by these causes. The chaos caused by heavy handed police interference in train services after, for example, a suicide, had to be experienced to be believed.

[45] In contrast to rail. BR was savaged for not accepting the word of passengers on trains without tickets, or with damaged or defaced tickets. (See *Blueprints for Bankruptcy*, Pages 177-8). The basis of some refund claims - often supported by watchdogs - were on the most incredible grounds, (See *Blueprints for Bankruptcy*, Pages 122-3).

[46] BR attempts to end smoking in buffet cars - which ought to have been supported on hygiene grounds led to BR being taken to court. Attempts by the author in 1984 to persuade Merseyside PTE to agree to a smoking ban in the underground services were rejected, despite the safety implications.

journey, which is a flexibility offered by train. The idea of buses departing from tens of thousands of towns and villages, when they are 100% full and to run without a timetable, is unrealistic. Clearly, many buses will have to pick up en route, at an unpredictable time. Experience of past railway closures proves that a large proportion will transfer to car. It is a scenario that the conversion campaign tries to dismiss.

Bus companies have insufficient resources to prevent delays from bad weather - but that always passes unremarked. Spare PSVs and drivers are too costly to provide. Passengers divert to rail, at short notice, and BR was expected to conjure extra rolling stock from thin air. This often occurred when roads were blocked by snow.

An opinion has been expressed that replacement of trains by buses will cut manpower. Norman Fowler stated in his political biography that 'everyone knew that the [railway] business was overstaffed'. There was no comparison with industry, other than to point out: 'BR had 230,000 staff in 1976 whilst the NBC had 20,000 buses and 68,000 staff.' No conclusion can be drawn from that. BR staff operated twelve times as many passenger *and freight* vehicles as NBC! Moreover, the effective size of the NBC fleet is reduced as vehicles were cannibalised to keep others in service, (see NBC Annual Accounts). Fleet size related to manpower is meaningless in productivity terms. For an effective comparison, statistics must be put into context. By law, PSV drivers were permitted to work 11 hours daily - it was 14 until 1968. The law imposed no limit on other bus company staff. In contrast, government forced railways to adopt the eight hour day for *all* staff in 1919, without concern for cost. The sole reason for bus drivers being allowed to work such long hours - which a Government White Paper (Cmnd 3481) stated were being 'substantially exceeded' - was cost. That increases 68,000 staff to an equivalent of, at least, 93,500.

Total BR staff included shipping, hovercraft, workshops, hotels and property; excluding these, leaves 182,695. (BRB 1976 Report). Unlike BR, NBC do not maintain *their* highway, whereas BR maintained theirs *and* thousands of bridges over which NBC buses travel. BR Annual Reports provided far more data than NBC, but did not separate staff employed on BR's 'highway'. When infrastructure maintenance transferred to Railtrack, BR Reports show a 17% fall. Applying 17% to 1976 manpower reduces 182,695 to 151,600. One must then deduct staff devoted to freight, which is not one of hundreds of statistics demanded by the MoT - even when they covered an expensive 300 pages! The freight element can be estimated from traction hours on non-passenger duties. Non-passenger traction hours were 38.6% of the total. (BRB 1976 Report). Deducting 38.6% from 151,600 leaves 93,080 rail passenger staff - 0.45% below the *realistic* NBC figure of 93,500. With this *relevant* manpower, BR earned 41% *more* passenger revenue than NBC!

The real cost of road haulage
The haulage industry is really subsidised by other road users and government inertia. A major post war study[47] of the effect of heavy axle loads on road wear was undertaken some sixteen years after the War by the USA Army. They drove on a road in different vehicles for two years. Wear caused to the structure of the roads related to the fourth power of the axle weight - if axle weight is twice as much, it will do sixteen times as

---

[47] See Transport Research Laboratory Report LR 1132 [1984]

much damage. Car traffic had little effect. Most road construction costs arise from the weight of lorries. A USA official study of highway wear, 15 years ago, revealed that the damage caused by a 6-ton axle load was 10,000 times as much as a car, and a 12-ton axle load was 160,000 times more.[48] Research shows that 'HGVs only pay 59-67% of costs they impose on society'.[49]

Transport 2000 state that per tonne carried, rail produces 80% less carbon dioxide than road. HGVs produce 40% of all diesel particulates which can cause or worsen bronchitis or asthma, and half of sulphur dioxide emissions.[50] An increase in road transport will worsen the nation's health.

Lorries are 7% of vehicles on roads, but responsible for 20% of all deaths. EU figures show that rail is 27 times safer than road. In 80% accidents, the HGV driver is not a casualty.[51]

A letter in the Daily Telegraph (7.6.94), demonstrated that former Ministers are not the only ones to believe in the myth of 'Just in time' deliveries. If it existed, there would be *no* empty spaces on shelves, no instructions to return in three weeks for something needed now and no goods arriving in twelve weeks instead of the promised two. Personal experience is that shops *routinely* tell customers they are out of stock of something the needed today. Many garage staff tell customers who require repairs on a car, that a part is not available today. However, the task of feeding industry - which would have faced hauliers, had they taken over supply of raw materials to industry in 1955 - has virtually vanished with the decimation of UK industry in the face of efficient foreign competition.

Many examples of the overt and covert subsidy to road haulage may be found in *Juggernaut*. They include:
- A USA study showed that the extra cost of building a motorway for heavy lorries was 28-35% more than envisaged for light vehicles, (Page 134), and they have a lower axle load than the UK. Their study envisaged narrower lanes and shoulders, if a road was built solely for cars, unlike a study by the DoT, which envisaged no such change.
- DoT data in 1975/6 showed that a 32t lorry underpaid for its share of maintenance of roads by 83%. In 9 years, DoT data showed that heavy lorries were subsidised by other users and the taxpayer by £1.2bn compared to £192m for rail freight, (Pages 136-8).[52]
- Incredibly, in calculating shares of road maintenance cost, the DoT begin by deducting £139m as attributable to pedestrians! This is made up of 50% of all road cleaning, 50% of all lighting (although most is on motorways), and 35% of some other costs, (Page 132)
- County Surveyors said that overloading accounts for a 50% increase in damage to roads, in some cases for 100%, (Page 61).
- Motorways are breaking up halfway through their 20 year design life. The cause is heavier axles, not more traffic. The ROI on the M1, M5 and M6 is negative. (Page 126).
- An RRL study showed that road damage is double what road builders had been told to plan for, (Page 128).

---

[48] R Calvert. *The Times*, 18.6.76.

[49] Transport 2000: *Goods without the Bads*.

[50] *Limit the Lorry*, and *Goods with the Bads*.

[51] Transport 2000 *Limit the Lorry*, and *Goods with the Bads*. *Juggernaut* (Page 67) by J. Wardroper says HGV drivers are not casualties in 95% accidents.

[52] The rail freight subsidy was ended in 1977. The HGV subsidy continues.

It has been overlooked by the conversion and road lobbies that BR costs included maintenance and renewal of bridges - a cost which is really attributable to highways, and hence the road transport which passes over them. In the event of conversion, bridge costs, hidden in railway *losses*, would fall directly onto the roads budget, where they should have been since 1930, as the Minister of Transport had agreed.[53]

It has been claimed that heavier goods vehicles reduce the cost of goods to the consumer. No account has been taken of the *increased* costs borne by motorists who are delayed behind heavy vehicles on *A*, *B* and other roads, or accident damage and road repairs caused by HGVs. Most road mileage is on routes that are not paralleled by railways. If 11,000 miles of existing railway were converted to roads, it would not benefit one jot, millions of delayed journeys on 210,000 miles of roads remote from a railway.

Converting railways into roads will have no real impact on the trillions of minutes delay caused to other traffic by double parking of HGVs to load and unload, or shunt to and fro to gain access to the back door of retail and business premises. The road haulage industry and the DoT ignored the problem of huge vehicles needing to enter towns, villages and farms to collect or deliver, when they authorised bigger HGVs.

Fall-out from Conversion

An assumption - that replacement road services would slash travel costs - was rudely dashed by experience. 'No sooner had a rail service closed, than bus fares rose to heights which made it difficult for constituents to go about their business at reasonable prices,' (Hansard, vol. 590, col. 202). Bus fares and haulage rates were held down by the level of rail fares and freight charges. If all railways closed, road charges would be free to rise, allowing shorter drivers' hours and higher wages. Pressures for improved safety would lead to higher vehicle building costs. Road construction and maintenance costs will rise with more lanes, traffic signals, traffic police etc.

Converting railways into roads would produce an unending and inescapable burden, far in excess of the subsidy paid to BR. An inability of the Exchequer to swallow the increasing burden of road costs would focus economies on other public expenditure. The burden on the State would rise due to more fatalities and injuries. In a letter to the Daily Telegraph in 1991, the author pointed out that rail accidents from 1952 - which the Telegraph had used as a base line[54] to criticise BR - had killed an average of eight p.a. compared to an average of nearly 5,000 p.a. on roads. The number injured by accidents in both modes is equally disparate. The cost of this excessive number of road casualties is a hidden cost of road transport. If there was about ten times as much traffic on roads as railways in 1991 - as was claimed[55] - conversion would have increased fatalities of those hitherto using rail by one-tenth of total road fatalities - about 500 p.a. If conversion did increase fatalities, would those who proposed conversion be charged with manslaughter?

BR was burdened with the cost of preserving historic structures, a task not faced by competitors. In 1985, 1256 were listed, it is now over 2,000, including 128 viaducts,

---

[53] *"Square Deal Denied"*, Page 64

[54] *Daily Telegraph*, 9.1.91. This was the year of BR's worst accident, the death toll of which could largely be laid at the door of government that had prevented BR from using their own money to provide new signalling and steel coaches. (See *Britain's Railways - The Reality*).

[55] This figure is now revealed to be unreliable, (see page 153).

including Bishopsgate, which Hall/Smith plan to alter by creating a slip road from it. This may not be permitted. Who would pick up the tab for preserving these structures is never mentioned in any conversion. The East Anglian scheme has six listed structures.

The BRB Annual Report for 1976 drew attention to the disparity in the use of energy between rail and road transport. In terms of energy consumption per passenger, compared to a passenger in a suburban train, it stated that a car commuter used eight times as much, and a bus commuter used two thirds as much.[56] In terms of energy consumption per tonne of freight, an HGV load used three times as much as a load on a freight train.

The same Report drew attention to noise pollution caused by road transport on people as compared to rail. The number dissatisfied with noise from all roads was 11m, from trunk roads was 4.8m, and from rail was 0.1m.[57] Even allowing for a lower volume of traffic on rail, there is a serious disparity. John Wardroper revealed[58] that a survey by consultants for the DoT showed that people say the noise *when a train is passing*[59] is less than lorries. Those living by a line are less disturbed by noise than those on roads. The problem was capable of alleviation - at a cost, which hauliers will not pay, and government will not enforce: Rolls Royce designed a quieter 320 hp engine in 1981. In 1979, the estimated cost of building a 3-mile motorway with walls and banks to muffle noise was £55m.

Staff required to run an infrastructure corporation - managers, supervisors and maintenance staff - was not mentioned by Lloyd nor his successors. Conversion proposals ignore admin staff, managers and supervisors needed by operators. Freight operators would also need staff to calculate haulage charges and issue invoices. All operators would need staff for vehicle servicing and maintenance. Hauliers would require even more staff - clerical and maintenance - if government took effective enforcement action on standards. Staff are needed to cover holidays and sickness, and for staff working the five day week which originated in the private sector. These manpower needs would further increase, due to the inevitable fall in working hours which would follow conversion. Union power would see to that! Fares and freight charges would soar to pay those costs.

The presumption that rail passengers would transfer to bus after line closures, is not backed by experience. Passengers turned to cars. DoT statistics reveal that rail travel declined slightly, car usage soared, and bus travel declined steeply.[60] The reality is that road congestion would become worse as more travellers switched to cars after railway conversion. Conversion means many thousands of additional road vehicles - especially cars - entering towns and creating new congestion on routes not designed to take them.

Conversion without lifting *all* overbridges to the DoT standard would increase the scale of bridge bashing from the current 2,000 cases pa, which cost £10m pa. There would be many blockages of converted railways as juggernauts came into contact with low bridges and tunnels,[61] including some raised to the 4.6m envisaged by Hall/Smith. A study last

---

[56] In comparison with rail, each passenger on a BA domestic services used four times as much as BR InterCity.

[57] In respect of air noise, it was 3.4m people.

[58] *Juggernaut*, Pages 82-83,90,95.

[59] Without any evidence, based on subjective opinion, those who advocate conversion have claimed that rail noise only appears to be less, because there is less freight on rail than road. This survey focuses on when a train is passing.

[60] Transport Statistics Bulletin, published by the DETR in 1999, shows that, comparing 1954 and 1970, rail travel declined by 7%, bus by 35%, whilst car rose by 312%. By 1995, compared to 1970, rail travel was unchanged, bus had declined a further 27%, whilst car travel had doubled.

[61] See photos of Longton (Staffs) bridge which is 14 ft 6 ins (about 4.5m) high, and has advance warnings. Goods and fuel were discharged onto the road and pavements, putting lives of pedestrians and other road users at risk.

year for the DfT defined low bridges as those with a clearance of less than 5.03 metres - well above the 4.6m height considered adequate in the Hall/Smith study.

A DfT 2004 report shows that a principal cause of lorries striking low bridges - despite low clearance signs, with a 3 inch safety margin - is that drivers did not know the height of their vehicles. The most common cause of double-deck PSVs striking bridges is that drivers *forgot* that they were driving double-deckers. These problems will continue at under-bridges and cause delay to traffic above on a converted system. It will occur on a converted system if all railway over-bridges are not lifted to the required DfT height. Signs, 'warning devices', nor assurances by conversionists will not prevent it. The DfT report says that sensors are expensive and not 100% reliable. They are useless unless a driver reacts. The consequence will be injuries, fatalities and serious delays to traffic

A claim by local authorities (*The Times* 14.6.87), that it is BR's job to replace low bridges by higher bridges to meet safety standards, is out of touch with reality. No other company would spend a penny to provide greater facility for competitors who have imprudently increased the size of vehicles to poach traffic, without ensuring the infrastructure was able to take them. Local authorities should practice what they preach, by widening every junction where lorries mount pavements, creating separate lanes for cyclists and providing fenced off, well lit pavements along both sides of *every* road to improve safety.

Defending drivers, the RHA blamed government for not introducing rules to display vehicle height in cabs, when self interest of operators should have brought action. Moreover, the DfT report shows that many drivers did not know their vehicle height even when it was so displayed. A bus operator claimed the problem was 'a failure of signs' in a case where a driver had ignored a no-right turn sign and low bridge signs. The bus height was displayed in his cab, and it was 2 feet higher than that on the sign for the bridge!

Where a converted railway crosses an existing road, it would need to have costly protective 'Selby' barriers fitted. The already narrow traffic lanes arising from conversion would be further reduced as a consequence.

DfT statistics show that the average speeds on dual carriageways and motorways are PSVs: 58mph, cars: 69mph, and HGVs: 52mph. On single carriageway roads, they are PSVs: 45mph, cars: 44mph and HGVs: 42-46mph [dependent on axle configuration]. The ever optimistic conversion theorists forecast all travelling at a constant 60mph on converted railways with *nine foot lanes*. PSVs and HGVs would be faster on these economy sized roads than on dual carriageways! It defies belief. They overlook that the width of a lorry is commonly 8ft 5ins. DfT regulations specify that an overhanging load, up to 9ft 6ins [2.9m] wide requires no special arrangements, and could be met anywhere. Loads wider than that have to be notified to the police. Given the higher speeds and the risk of meeting loads exceeding the nine foot lane width, delays and an increase in accidents would be inevitable. Conversion to economy sized roads, *will* cause more deaths as motorists, who are behind HGVs and unable to safely overtake, take risks to do so.

Increases in the cost of oil imports is an inflationary factor which pushes everything up. More demand will increase fuel prices, hence, importing more oil to feed road transport replacing trains will create a cost to the economy that is being ignored. More imported lorries would have a similar effect. On the other hand electric power can be produced without burning oil, and will not adversely affect the balance of payments.

It was necessary for BR to dispose of unused land as quickly as possible, both to raise capital, and terminate statutory maintenance costs for bridges, fencing, drainage, etc. Other industry would do likewise. Where there was no longstanding legal obligation to return it to the original owners, land had first to be offered to central government, and if they had no need, to local authorities, who may need it for road building or other development. If they rejected it, it could be offered for sale to others, usually to adjoining landowners - farmers, estates or domestic householders.

Despite the publicity surrounding a claim in 1992, by Bart's Hospital for the return of land no longer required for railway purpose, the conversionists continue to ignore this restrictive aspect and to claim that the land on which the railways were built belonged to the nation. They never understood the legal restraints, nor political directives and control, on disposal of land no longer required for operating a railway. Land was frequently acquired by the original railway companies under compulsory purchase after they had secured a private Act of Parliament against stiff opposition. Many deprived owners were able to insert into the Act, a clause requiring land to be returned to them if it should cease to be used for the purpose for which it had been acquired. In some cases, it specified that the land - and it later transpired that this could include buildings erected by the railway company thereon - had to be returned to the erstwhile owner at the same price as the railway company had paid for the land, and in some cases, were to revert without payment[1]. Land acquired for railway building, almost invariably, cut through farms and other estates. Companies were required to provide bridge or private level crossing access between the separated areas. Thousands of these level crossings remain to this day.

The MoT was asked about the possibility of redundant railways being converted into roads. He replied that, except in a few instances, it is prohibitive, (Hansard 16.2.55, vol. 537, col. 57). In answer to another question, MPs were told that the Merthyr-Abergavenny branch had closed and part was brought into use as a road, others were spread from Wales to East Anglia and County Durham, (Hansard vol. 590, col. 210). In April 1960, the MoT said that six sections of disused line had been converted to road - some 23 miles in total, mostly single line. The six sections ranged from 0.25 miles to 9.0 miles, (Hansard vol. 620, col. 173). By that time, some 1,400 route miles of railway had been closed.

Claims by the Conversion League

The League's 1970 booklet (see chapter 7), catalogued sections of railway line already 'converted' into roads. Tragically - for their cause - there were only 29 sections[2] from 109 yards up to maximum of six miles and with an average of $1^1/_2$ miles. Widening outside the railway boundary was clearly mandatory, especially when it included examples of a single line widened up to 190 feet to create dual carriageways.[3] The list was in a minute font, requiring good eyesight and dogged determination to elicit the facts. They did not explain, why, despite this evidence of a handful of clearly minor cases, and 'conversions' requiring significantly wider areas, they still believed in conversion.

---

[1] The Appleton Report for the Countryside Commission quotes an example, (see page 193).
[2] Which was really only 25 schemes, totalling 43.7 miles (see following pages and page 65).
[3] Most of the 'conversions' in their list were widened beyond the width of the rail route - see page 65.

In their book, following the chairman's introduction, they squeezed in a NOTE referring to the term 'motor road being frequently used in the Report'. It claimed that a Motor Road - a term unknown to the DoT or any of the Counties which were supposed to have them - has the following characteristics: 'No frontage, no standing vehicles, negligible cross traffic'. Of the 29 listed conversions, there were none; of the 112 maybe schemes (see below), there were eleven, of which five became roads totalling 5.9 miles. Nowhere, do they set out any data to demonstrate that they have surveyed cross traffic at level crossings or new road crossings to prove that there is 'negligible cross traffic'.

So desperate was the League, after preaching their dreary and uninspiring sermon to the clouds for fifteen years, that they tried to expand their pitiful catalogue of claims of conversion, with nine pages of 'maybe' conversions. These pages list 112 different sections of mostly single line, in 45 different local authority areas[4] and totalling 211.5 miles. This equates to a monumental average of 1.88 miles per scheme, which is hardly breathtaking. These rejoice under the heading 'Railway conversion schemes under construction and proposals for future schemes'. Once again, they scrape the barrel with proposals for 'converting' 500 yards here and 500 yards there, and even down to 207 yards (190m). Of these 112 items, 35 had no length shown. It is safe to conclude that they were ultra short lengths, as no opportunity would have been missed to list any item which was of any significant length, whereas including them would have exposed the League to further ridicule. Eighteen were so unspecific as to location that it was impossible to even identify the precise location of the railway line expected to be converted.

Regrettably for their cause, the total mileage from this list, actually converted fell well short of their hopes. Inquiries of the local authorities concerned, revealed that many routes were not used at all. A large number were converted to cycle tracks and footpaths, some were crossed at right angles,[5] one in a very deep cutting was filled - at unspecified cost - to gain the required width of road required and most of the rest required substantial widening, involving land acquisition and property demolition. Some closed railway lines have re-opened as tourist attractions - rather than as part of the transport infrastructure, and some were sold off to other parties to use for non-transport purposes.

Specific comments by local authorities on the relevance and value of conversion of closed railway lines set out in the 1970 'maybe' list are as follows:

- Aberdeen: The one mile section was used for road works, no data was available on the extent of widening.
- Argyll: Referred the inquiry to the Scottish Executive, who were unable to assist. No distance had been specified in the 1970 booklet.
- Ayrshire: No section of the 2.25 mile railway has been converted to road due to the cost implications. It is now a footpath/bridleway.
- Berkshire: The 1.5 mile disused line was not used for a road. It was sold to adjacent landowners and developed for residential or industrial units.
- Brecon: Five separate schemes were listed, but no mileage was shown for any of them. The locations were inadequately identified for them to be traced by the local authority.

---

[4] There were 45 in the League's 1970 list. Lincolnshire was split in two parts in that list, but is here as one.
[5] By no stretch of imagination can a closed railway line, which has been crossed at a virtual right angle be regarded as a conversion. That word implicitly means that a road has been built along the length of a closed railway. There were two such examples in Kent and East Sussex.

Without more detail as to the precise locations, the local authority demanded an up front payment of £450 for further research, but that did not guarantee any productive outcome.

- Buckinghamshire: Neither of the two schemes which were forecast to cover 2.5 miles were progressed as roads, one is a walkway, the other is merely a disused railway.
- Caernarvonshire: Part used as a road, part as a footpath, some route was resold, some became footpaths or cycle ways, and there were various other non-road applications. The League claimed that 23.95 miles was to be converted to roads, the length converted was about 2.2 miles. The council said that little data is available on the extent of widening, but a single carriageway would be wider than the trackbed of a single track railway. A glossy report on the A487 improvement states for much of its length, the new road runs *alongside* the Caernarfon-Afon Wen railway, now the Lon Eifion cycleway.
- Cambridgeshire: A bypass was built on the closed single line listed, but additional land had to be acquired on both sides for verges and drains. Only four miles of the forecast 7.5 miles of railway was used. The new A141 has a carriageway 8.3m wide plus verges 2.3m each side = 42 feet. A new bridge had to be built with deep piling because the depth and stability of the foundations of the existing railway bridge were unknown. Drawings supplied show that the new width required for roads including drainage was about 3.3 times as wide as the former rail formation.
- Carmarthenshire: The 0.85 mile road is twice the width of the old line.
- Cornwall: Only one scheme was listed, with no mileage: conversion of a mineral line between Devoran and Penpol to a County Road. Why they specified *County Road* as if this was something special - like their much loved Motor Road - is unclear. No other scheme mentioned a *County Road*. Roads are either the responsibility of the DoT or a County. This railway originally ran from Perranwell station to Penpol via Devoran to serve local tin mines. The section from Perranwell to Devoran has become a Trailway for pedestrians, cyclists, horses, and is about 3m wide - much less than half the width required for the most basic road. The section on to Penpol has been subsumed under residential development. At no point can it be said that the railway became a road, nor that it was any wider than the width recorded above.
- Cumberland: No mileage was shown for the one scheme listed. It is believed by the Highways Agency that some sections of the old railway may have been used, but they were unable to identify them, nor to indicate their length or width.
- Denbighshire: No mileage was shown. One scheme was not pursued and the railway became part of an industrial estate; a second forecast road was not constructed; the third forecast road was not constructed, and part was used by the Llangollen preserved railway and part became a carpark.
- Dorset: A total 8.8 miles of closed railway was forecast to be used. The actual total used was 0.7 miles. Two sections of closed railway were used for short lengths of road; two road schemes were not progressed; in another case a road was built, but the railway line was not used; one section became a cycle way; one is now an operational railway
- Durham: Three schemes were progressed totalling approximately 0.9 miles, instead of the 3.5 miles forecast. A fourth scheme was not progressed.[6] The local authority stated

---

[6] In contrast, the County had converted 40 miles to cycleways, footpaths, bridlepaths - 40 times as much as to roads. It drew attention to the high costs of repairing and maintaining fences, culverts, bridges & viaducts, (*Times*, 31.5.83)

that 'any costs for sections of converted railway will have been subjective'. All involved property demolition, roundabouts requiring substantial widening - plans show that one was eight times the railway width - and earthworks to match road to railway levels. All four were designated to be Motor Roads in the Report.

- Glamorgan: Due to re-organisation, the locations fall into other areas.

  Now in Caerphilly CBC: One scheme, claimed to be 0.85 miles. The location was insufficiently clear for them to relate it to a road scheme.

  Now in Rhondda Cynon CBC: Only two of the three schemes were progressed, but additional land had to be acquired beyond the railway boundary in both cases. A total of 5.1 miles became part of roads, instead of the 10.2 miles forecast by the League.

  Now in the City & County of Swansea: A five mile conversion was forecast. Only 0.3 miles was progressed.

  Now in Neath & Port Talbot CBC: Two of the three schemes were progressed, but the lengths were less than forecast by the League - a total of 2.4 miles instead of 2.6 miles. One has been abandoned.

  Now in Bridgend CBC: One of the two schemes was progressed, one is footpath, with part subsumed into an industrial estate.

  Unidentified locations in a number of unknown local authority areas: The 1970 list included a claim, that in Glamorgan, 'further sections of railway are to be used for trunk road construction'. Obviously, it is impossible to ascertain whether there was any such development in this attempt to clutch at straws.

- Hampshire: Four schemes were listed, with no mileage shown. Each one related to part of a line. The council stated that some disused lines were known to have been converted to public rights of way, but further research would not be carried out without payment of an unspecified sum. There was no guarantee the information sought was still available[7].

- Hertfordshire: The League listed three schemes with a total mileage of 2.2 miles One route was converted to a cycle track, footpath and horse trekking route, the others were abandoned.

- Huntingdon & Peterborough: No mileages were shown for the two schemes listed. No reply was received to repeated letter and phone calls asking if conversion occurred.

- Kent: No mileages were shown for the three schemes listed. A new road [the M25] does not - as claimed by the League - 'make use of the old Westerham Railway', but crosses it at a tangent. It is not along the length of the line, as the wording was clearly intended to imply. The one benefit arising from closure was that the M25 did not require to bridge over the line. The Canterbury-Whitstable line is now a footpath - the Council said: 'it was never planned to be a road' although the League claimed that 'a road had been planned for some time'. The former Tenterden-Headcorn branch line is being developed as a cycleway.

- Lancashire: Three sections of line were listed totalling 4.25 miles. The County Council could not trace the first location listed: Toruer. It is untraceable in maps of the UK. Two of the three schemes, including the untraceable location were designated to be Motor Roads. Although the Council was helpful, they were also unable to trace any record of the other two schemes.

---

[7] Evidently, *Freedom of Information* comes at a price, which the ordinary man in the street may not be able to afford.

- Leicestershire: Three schemes were listed totalling 5.9 miles - all to be motor roads. Not one of these schemes was progressed. One of these lines is still in use as a railway. Part of one closed line became a footpath. The County converted 24 miles of railway to paths
- Lincolnshire: No mileage was shown for the one scheme. No reply was received to a repeat letter and phone calls asking what happened to the railway.
- London (Merton Borough): A section of railway line a mile in length became part a road. It was designated to be a motor road. It involved acquisition of extra land to create the width for a dual carriageway.
- Merioneth: The forecast 1.2 mile length of railway was converted, but mostly to single carriageway, not to dual carriageway as claimed.
- Monmouthshire: One 0.37 mile length of line was replaced by a 7.3m carriageway road with 3m verges, about 3-4 times the width of the single track railway. The other line (now in Caerphilly CBC) was only 0.25 miles and the road was also wider than the land . occupied by the railway and required lowering by one metre to match the road level.
- Norfolk: Of eight items listed, only two had roads built on top of a closed railway. These totalled 13.5 miles instead of the 20 miles forecast. One bypass built does not use a closed railway line. One line may re-open as a preserved railway. 'Land required for roads that have overlaid these former railway routes considerably exceeds the original land take for railway construction, so that, apart from minimising disruption to communities along the line of route, there is little advantage in following these former alignments and the costs incurred may have actually been higher than those of following totally new alignments. In most cases, to allow road construction to take place, the vertical profile of the former railways has been altered significantly with embankments lowered and cuttings infilled to allow for the greater width needed to construct the new road'. *This would not be compacted by trains.*
- Northamptonshire: The League gave no information regarding the proposed length of railway to be used in the one scheme mentioned. A short section of line was used for a bypass. It required a new bridge over a river and a new roundabout - costs ignored by the League. Inclusion of its length would invalidate comparison with the League's aspirations, because it would compare their zero miles with a specified distance.
- Nottinghamshire: The League had claimed a 2 mile length was to be converted. The council was unable to provide any useful information.
- Oxfordshire: A 1.1 mile line was bought in 1972. The bypass was not constructed. The 'railway width was 15-28m, a road required 30-60m'.
- Renfrew: None of the 6.3 miles lines listed have been converted to roads.
- Selkirk: One 1.75 mile scheme was listed. The council said that 'majority of the line was used'. No drawings could be traced. A further inquiry produced the response that it was assumed that land alongside the railway would have been acquired, but records are no longer available
- Shropshire: No mileages were shown for the three lines in the League's list. One scheme was not progressed. Of the others, short lengths (100 yards or less) were used in constructing the A53 and A518 bypasses. Road width was a minimum of 15.6 yards overall between fences. Formations were poor quality material and needed replacement.
- Staffordshire: Six schemes were tabulated by the League totalling 26.5 miles. Two were to become 'all-weather roads', (which seems to imply under surface heating to keep

roads clear of snow and ice, and some means of clearing fog).[8] A 6.5 mile line was converted to a cycleway; another to a 2.5 mile footpath; a third to a 5.5 mile footpath; a fourth 8.5 mile line is now a preserved railway; and a fifth became a footpath. The whole of the 26.5 miles of railway forecast to be converted to roads in the county was, thus, not used for roads. Altogether 42 miles have become footpaths or cycleways.

- Suffolk [East]: Two locations shown by the League, viz. 'Belton, near Great Yarmouth', with a total length of 0.4 miles, have apparently always been within the county boundaries of Norfolk. This careless error caused difficulty in trying to track down what had happened to the proposed conversion. Maps provided by Yarmouth library reveal that only about $^1/_4$ mile of road sits on the formation of the closed railway, some remains unused, whilst some is covered by houses.

- Suffolk [West]: In respect of the two locations listed, for which no mileages were shown, one bypass was built, but the disused railway was not used. In the other case, part of closed single line railway was used, but its length cannot now be determined, but the 'width would have been 21 metres', considerably in excess of that of a single line.

- Sussex [East]: The League list two: 1.3 km and 2.3 km respectively. The 2.3 km section [of the 22.4 km Lewes-East Grinstead line] was not converted, and is still disused. The longest section is a 15km preserved steam railway - the Bluebell line - due to be extended by 3km. The southern part of the line was crossed by the Phoenix Causeway at right angles and cannot, by any stretch of imagination, be called a conversion.

- Sussex [West]: An 0.8 mile length of single track railway was used as part of a road. The League's 1970 book stated that considerable acquisition of land would be needed for this 100 ft wide road! The council confirmed that *considerable* area of land was acquired to obtain the necessary width. This is not a *conversion*.

- Warwickshire: Of the three schemes listed representing 5.5 miles, only one scheme was progressed and that was 0.9 miles in length.

- West Lothian: One scheme was listed, but no mileage was shown. No reply was received to repeated letters asking if the conversion took place.

- Westmoreland: A 4 mile section of closed railway was used to lay an improved road. Some widening was required. This was designated by the League to be a Motor Road.

- Wiltshire: Neither of the two forecast conversion totalling nine miles took place. Part was sold to adjoining landowners; the other became part of a long distance cycle track and footpath, some 7-8 miles long!

- Workington Borough (renamed Allerdale): There were three schemes totalling 3.25 miles; 2.5 miles was used partly as a service road to shops, and partly for carparking. A 0.3 mile road to a swimming pool and sports centre was built on a closed railway line. Another section of road was built over 0.18 mile of closed railway. The rest became a cycle way, or was landscaped.

- Yorkshire East Riding: Five sections of closed railway route were listed as planned for conversion to roads. Of these, four totalling 34.5 miles have been used as recreational routes for horse riders, cyclists and walkers. The fifth route for which no mileage was quoted by the League has been built over by a mix of housing, works and a car park.

---

[8] The concept was greeted with derision at Alston, which was at the end of a branch line from Haltwistle and was closed in 1976. (See *The Railway Closure Controversy*). Such roads are still conspicuous by their absence. (See also page 50 for misplaced belief in *all-weather roads*).

Consideration is being given to the need to revert one of the recreational routes to commercial rail use.

- Yorkshire West Riding: One location is now in Bradford MDC. The schemes for converting Shipley-Bradford, for which no mileages were shown, were never implemented. The other location is now in Leeds MDC. They were unable to provide any information.

Several conversions involved property demolition to provide adequate widths and to create large roundabouts to connect into existing roads (one example in County Durham was eight times the railway width), major earthworks to match road and railway levels. Several others required wide areas for earthworks to reconcile road and rail levels.

The response from the local authorities covering the maybe lists was mostly very helpful, varying from answering the questions posed, to providing detailed scale maps. Only three local authorities did not reply. Two others replied, but only to seek payment for providing the answers. Four councils were unable to provide information, due to the length of time that has elapsed, or due to local authority re-organisation. The vagueness of the League's data as to the location of a disused line was not helpful in some cases. In total, the data from local authorities reveals that only 48.1 miles of closed railway have been replaced by roads, instead of the 211.5 miles which the League forecast in its 'maybe' list. Add this to the 43.7 miles listed in the 1970 Report as already converted (see page 65), and it produces an underwhelming total of 91.8 miles compared to the 9,000 miles of railway route closed by 1980. Moreover, most of the closed lines converted had to be widened to create the width necessary for a road.

Conversionists failed to notice that the main competitor for BR passenger services was the car - not the bus. BR managers kept telling ministers and MPs that this was the reality, but they still seemed to think it was the declining bus industry. They also held the illusion that one railway company could compete with other train companies serving - not the same towns - but towns many miles apart on opposite sides of the country!

The fact that 15 years after their 1970 publication, only a further 0.8% of closed railway routes - which had ranged from about 20 to 180 miles in length - had been 'converted' to very short sections of new roads, serves to show that railway lines are *not* suitable for conversion. Their 1970 publication includes four photographs to 'prove' the adequacy of rail widths for road conversion. Two were of closed lines in the most isolated rural areas imaginable, the combined length of which appears to be about $1^1/_2$ miles, representing about 0.02% of lines closed at that date. One was taken at a considerable distance, making it impossible to judge the original width of the closed line, and hence how much of the adjoining land had been included in the new road. The other showed - at a considerable distance a car - of indeterminate size - parked unrealistically close to the pier of an overbridge, so as to exaggerate the space available for other vehicles. It would have been foolhardy to drive at 60 mph so close to a concrete pier. The car was so far away, it could well have been a child's pedal car. The two other photographs - of lines still in use, which they claim could be converted into wide roads - have a total length of one mile - about 0.009% of operational railway. One photograph shows a train conveying cars in an endeavour to demonstrate the adequacy of railway width. The cars were minis!

Against these few locations, many more will be found, often in deep cuttings, on high embankments or viaducts or through tunnels, which alone demonstrate beyond dispute, that railway widths are inadequate for multi-purpose roads. Confirmation of this can be found from perusing the many books written about railways which contain photographs of daunting infrastructure. These include books devoted solely to tunnels, of which there at least, two, and others covering viaducts, bridges, etc.

In contrast some 404 miles [290 of standard gauge], of closed railway has now been re-opened as preserved railways. These are not serving a standard transport purpose, but are tourist attractions. That the formations of those closed railways should have been devoted to this purpose rather than become roads, proves the unsuitability of railway lines - by virtue of route or width - for conversion to roads. Inquiries of local authorities reveals that even more are to be re-opened as leisure railways.

Brigadier Lloyd claimed that the full length of British Railways could be converted - not a few yards here and there. Therefore, it is incredible that his successors can crow about 'conversion' not realising that the use of a very short length here or there - of lines previously closed due to lack of traffic - proves conclusively that railway routes do not go in the direction in which roads are needed. A few yards or quarter of a mile of a long branch line (see chapter 7), proves the reverse of that intended! The extent of widening also shows the impracticability of conversion. A recent list on the Internet contains examples of 'road actually built alongside railway', 'not sure if road built on railway'. Also, despite a new 'Rule' that a road must be built on the same line as a railway, they retain examples - such as the M25 and the Phoenix Causeway that were built across a railway at a tangent. Rail routes widened by a factor of 9-10 are included in *conversion* claims.

The unambiguous evidence that the pipe-dream of conversion had been demolished by experts, and by the reality of a mere handful of minor length schemes was, doubtless, the cause for the Conversion League's successor, the Railway Conversion Campaign, to disappear with the death of its last chairman in 1994.

Countryside Commission Report on Disused Railways
In its 1970 booklet, the League quoted one paragraph occupying 3.5 col. cms from an 82 page Report prepared by Dr. J.H. Appleton, comprising 3,100 col. cms. Most of the Report, whilst looking at alternative uses for disused railway lines, is *not* devoted to its use as roads. The inference which readers are invited to draw from the League's highly selective quote is that railway land can be put to best use as roads.

The Appleton Report mentioned the statutory and contractual obligations for disposal of surplus land, well known to BR management, but which the League studiously ignored. The report reveals that 'even the passage of a century, has resulted in little adjustment of farm or even field boundaries to fit the new circumstances. Restoration of unity is sufficient incentive to farmers to purchase disused railway land'. (Para 5.29). Farmers could also put sections of closed line to other non-growing purposes.

A few examples were quoted in which short sections of disused railway were converted linearly into roads - albeit, invariably widened - the Report states that 'there is a much larger number of cases in which very short sections of railway have been acquired in connection with road development *transverse to the route*'.[9] The saving was merely that a bridge or level crossing was not needed. No document published by the League ever admitted this fact. The Appleton Report included eight pages devoted to the use of disused railways for agricultural related purposes - the volume of which eclipsed all other uses put together.

The Report lists all alternative uses, which included agricultural use, recreational use [parks, footpaths, cycleways, bridle paths, caravan parks], building and development, preserved railways, nature reserves, industrial archaeology sites, pipeline and electric cable routes, motor rally and scrambling routes, refuse disposal. The Report said the latter use was widespread.

A list of disused railways converted to recreational use was included in the Report. Eighteen cases were listed. The length was shown in eight cases, and these totalled 74.25 miles, or 69% more than the total claimed by the League to have been converted to roads by the same date. The mileage of the remaining ten conversions to recreational use was not shown. The Report points out that many railway lines are *not* ideally located to be converted to bypasses - as the League loves to claim. The Report saw a high potential of disused railways as recreation routes. The scope for using disused railways as bridleways or cycleways is also mentioned. Although it was not mentioned, these would reduce the incidence of horses and cycles - even joggers - on roads, and thereby help to reduce traffic delays and accidents.

The Report did not include a summary of the uses to which all disused railways had been put. The reason was, doubtless, the tight time limit imposed by the Countryside Commission for the production of the Report. A consequence of this, is that the Report included erroneous claims by the Conversion League: 'that the railways were owned by the nation', (see page 60), and that 'hundreds of sections of railway had been converted to roads', when in reality their own 1970 Paper only itemised 25 (see page 65). It also included statements by the League as to the cost paid for closed railways for road building and conversion costs. It would have been more appropriate to have asked local authorities. However, Dr. Appleton was faced with a time limit. The Report notes that the cost of 'most of the conversions [to roads] worked out considerably higher' than figures quoted by the League, indicating that some data was gathered from other sources. The Ramblers Association also saw closed railways as having a national use - other than roads.

The Report states that 'much of the criticism levelled at BR has been grossly unfair. Many tributes have been paid to BR for acting within difficult limitations with sympathetic understanding'. It reveals that by 1968, of 2,126 miles of railway closed, 1,037 miles had been sold. This means that, of the closed lines put to other use, only 4% was used in the construction of a public road. The Report does not analyse how the remaining 96% was distributed among the other uses.

Had the League read beyond the first page of the Report, and not closed its mind to alternative uses of closed lines, they would have noted - among other considerations of

---

[9] A closed railway crossed at a transverse tangent is not a conversion.

the redeployment of closed lines - a call for a recognition of the benefit to the economy of converting disused railways to agricultural use, which is 'in the public interest'.

In December 1970, the Commission produced a further Report, as recommended in the Appleton Report, to update the uses of disused railways. This listed 74 sections of railway comprising over 460 miles[10] of railway converted to footpaths, cycleways and bridle paths, seven locations converted to caravan parks and picnic areas, and 22 closed lines that had been re-opened as [preserved] steam railways, with a total length of 103 miles[11]. The average footpath scheme was six miles, and the average railway re-opening was nearly five miles - both much longer than routes converted to roads, and none were as short as the ultra short sections garnered together in the railway conversion report.

The length of main line railways is 10,400 miles. Hence, since Brigadier Lloyd initiated his campaign, 9,600 miles of railway route - almost half - has been closed. Had there been *any* merit or advantage in his theory, the whole of these closed routes would have been converted to roads. Instead, the reality is that 'conversion' to roads is the exception rather than the rule. To claim - as Transwatch does (see page 151) - that 250 miles[12] has been converted by 2005, demonstrates that there is no case. In contrast, by 1989, over 1360 miles of closed lines had been catalogued[13] as being converted to non-vehicular use: footpaths, cycleways and bridlepaths. No widening was required and their average length was 2.47 miles compared to road 'conversions' average of 1.2 miles, (see page 151).

If BR's 20,000 route miles, in 1955, had been closed and converted at the rate claimed[14] to date, the country would have gained only 500 miles of new road. In contrast, at the same rate 800 miles would have become Preserved Railways - used for leisure purposes, whilst some railway would have re-opened for real transport purposes. However, the bulk would have become footpaths and cycle ways or reverted to agricultural use. Congestion would have strangled the country's transport, and, hence, its industry and business activity. Brigadier Lloyd's envisaged basis of vehicles travelling at 60 mph, 100 yards apart, over the 24 hours and over the four seasons would have been seriously undermined. Based on his calculations,[15] the available headway for former rail traffic in new road vehicles, on this length of new roadway would - night and day - be 2.5 yards [2.3 metres], the safe headway for 2 mph - with no space for traffic to transfer from existing roads!

The fact that local authorities - having been invited to buy disused railways, after central government had first refusal - used them to create footpaths, cycleways, etc., is clear evidence that either they are unusable as roads due to width restrictions or are on the wrong alignment. Why else would they miss the opportunity to relieve road congestion? Sustrans has created 10,000 miles of route for pedestrians and cyclists, the greater part of which are on ex-railway routes.

---

[10] The Report quotes the mileage for some schemes totalling 276 miles. The mileage was not quoted for a third of the schemes, but could be ascertained from details of the locations.

[11] The total length has further increased over subsequent years, (see page 193).

[12] Not all of which qualifies as conversion within the meaning of the word.

[13] *Railway Rights-of-Way* (Branch Line Society) by Rhys ab Elis.

[14] As that list includes discrepancies (see pages 151-152), and the identification of rail locations is less than helpful, the author has been unable to investigate the validity of all claims. Lines crossed at tangents, or widened ought not to count, nor should any below, say, five miles in length.

[15] He said rail traffic could be carried in road transport with headways of 100 yards, (see pages 21,23).

Comments and criticisms appeared in the media in response to the Hall/Smith Study, (see chapter 10, part II). Other comments were made on earlier proposals, (see chapters 7,8).

An article *(Times, 23.2.76)* stated: in Nottingham, *deliberate* delays are imposed on cars in peak periods to force users onto buses. PSVs can be made more attractive by equipping them with bars, kitchens, toilets and other features. He overlooks that re-design would increase costs of building, operating, maintaining and cleaning PSVs, whilst reduced seating would cut income. The fact that it is necessary to restrict cars to force users onto buses, undermines comparisons with trains. He mentions East Anglian lines in advocating conversion on the grounds - which others dispute - that road traffic produces a profit (see page 139), and railways are under-utilised compared to roads, (See pages 73,88,198,199).

A further article *(Times, 11.6.81)* criticised rail performance, extolled the concept of railway conversion, and referred to Prof. Hall's report.[1] It stated: 'BR has been helped to resist change by the MoT [as almost all nationalised work simulation and waste centres are by their departments]. It [BR] has exploited its bureaucratic wiles to this end'.

BR audited Annual Reports, which were debated in Parliament, and were not challenged as inaccurate, record the adoption of work study, method study and other management techniques beginning some 50 years ago, long before most of UK's backward industry[2]. Developments included the first labour saving machine in 1948 - BR's first year of existence, followed, *every* year, by many more, until hundreds were operated. BR developed new signalling systems, later adopted in other countries, which reduced manpower drastically and improved the speed and safety of trains. *Every* year, managers and engineers throughout the system implemented thousands of their own schemes to improve asset life and utilisation, and reduce manpower. Most changes were implemented without publicity and with little or no industrial dispute, unlike timid attempts in industry.[3]

It claimed that electrification only increased speeds marginally. When it began on the West Coast in the 1950s, the margin was 11% over new diesels built by UK industry. The claim that railways can be converted to roads 'without digging up a field or demolishing a house' is not borne out by actual 'conversions' nor the Hall/Smith study, (see chapters 10,13)

It said that BR had cost the public billions of pounds. This ignores the requirement for BR to subsidise inefficient industry by legally controlled below-inflation freight charges so that 'work simulation' - to borrow the phrase - could continue in those industries, until they eventually threw in the towel. It overlooks that fares trailed inflation for 40 years as a consequence of the decisions of a unique court of law and ministerial interference, so that the government and the public really owed BR £11.6bn plus interest[4] at the time of privatisation. It disregarded that, for decades, politicians blocked closure of uneconomic lines - many struggling even in the heyday of railways - which managers wanted to close, but government decided to retain, but not to fund. Objectors to closures mainly argued on

---

[1] It will be seen from Chapter 10, Part III that the scheme would not work, nor produce the claimed benefits.
[2] See *Britain's Railways - The Reality*, Chapter 9.
[3] See *Britain's Railways - The Reality*, Chapters 13, 14 & Page 145.
[4] See *Britain's Railways - The Reality*, Appendix A.

their value in winter and wartime[5]. Some industries - which, unlike BR, pre 1969 - *were* subsidised, had the gall to suggest that railways in these remote areas should be able to cut their costs and operate without a subsidy.[6] BR was not compared with industry.[7] An analysis of the ratio of rail manpower to workload reveals remarkable improvements from the earliest days, not matched in UK industry. True, the scope for comparing UK industry with BR is limited, because they - unlike BR - have prudently not been required to expose complaints and other damning statistics to public view. The grouping of types of industry by the ONS limits comparisons. Inadvertently, the writer drew attention to industrial apathy by stating that there was no export market for electrical equipment, since other countries would manufacture their own. The converse scenario has not prevented other countries from exporting cars and all other goods to the UK!

The article refers to the use of non-trunk roads by road traffic, which, it implies ought to be on railways-converted-to-roads. However, 11,000 miles of converted railway could never replace the use of 200,000 miles of non-trunk roads, as they do not cover the same geographical area. Moreover, as the utilisation of rail capacity is higher than the road network, (see pages 88,173), a converted railway could not cope with rail traffic in road vehicles, much less provide relief to under utilised, and inefficiently managed roads.

It stated: 'In a few cases, bridges may cause difficulties, but almost none are insuperable.' By definition, that means some are insuperable. The faith in the reliability of the pneumatic tyre is not shared by all. Many have had to block half of a road to change a tyre, have been delayed whilst someone else does so, some have had their vehicle struck by burst lorry tyres, or have seen tyre debris on the side of roads - much of it, clearly, from large vehicles. This contrasts with railways, where broken wheels will *not* be seen. According to an official source[8], 'if higher speeds are maintained there is a greater risk of mechanical failure, e.g., a burst tyre, which has a more serious effect on handling at high speed'. The skid resistance of a wet road decreases as vehicle speeds rise. Hence, if speeds advocated by conversion theorists are implemented, accidents will increase.

Conversion was advocated in the *Sunday Telegraph* (3.12.00). It spoke of railways as *straight lines*. Records show that many routes went round hills to avoid tunnelling and due to early loco power limitations. Some were forced to circumvent private estates. The editor was referred to *Blueprints for Bankruptcy*[9] which summarised the first conversion proposal and views of experts - road engineers[10] and operators - who stated, inter alia:
  • lines were not straight,
  • major clearance problems would restrict their use to light vehicles,
  • bridges, tunnels, viaducts and drainage would pose serious problems, which could only be resolved at formidable cost.
The experts included one from the BRF. The book refers to a letter from the author in 1989 to the *Daily Telegraph*, (See pages 88,173), in response to an advert advocating

---

[5] See *The Railway Closure Controversy*.
[6] See *The Railway Closure Controversy*.
[7] The author claims to be the first to make meaningful, non-subjective comparisons between BR and other industry in *Blueprints for Bankruptcy* and later in *Britain's Railways - The Reality*.
[8] PACTS - Parliamentary Advisory Council for Transport Safety.
[9] In a letter from the author. *The Daily Telegraph* had purchased the book in 1995.
[10] At a meeting of the Institution of Civil Engineers, see chapter 4.

conversion. Statistics in that letter exposed the weaknesses in the idea. Like the 1989 letter, that to the *Sunday Telegraph* was acknowledged, but not published, nor was it embraced in an article.

A second article (17.12.00) reports on copies of booklets - supplied by the widow of Angus Dalgleish - with photos of road traffic using converted railways, (see pages 90,91), stating 'as, so often, our readers know much more than the editor!' (See above!).

A third article (24.12.00), highlighted longer gaps between trains compared to road vehicles. It quoted a former minister who, whilst flying to Northern Ireland, had observed a stretch of the M6 close to the main London to North West railway that 'was jammed solid[11] while the rail line which was slightly wider than the M6, had almost no traffic on it'. The actual location was not specified. Inquiries of Air Traffic Control as to the flight path revealed that the location was probably Crewe. There, four routes: from South Wales/Shrewsbury, Derby/Stoke, North Wales and Manchester - join the London-Scotland main line. The width occupied by platforms and tracks is about 190 yards, some in a cutting. To the south of Crewe lies Basford Hall sidings, which covers a wider area, about a half mile in length. The next comparable location is 150 miles further south! These areas are of no value in creating motorway width for the 158 miles London-Crewe, and might well be on the far side of the moon for its potential value as road lanes.

The rail junction at Crewe, has *four* diverging routes. The M1/M6 junction has twelve parallel road lanes plus hard shoulders - for only *one* diverging route, which together occupy a land area around 1200 yards by 1200 yards! The mind boggles at the number of parallel lanes and flyovers necessary to provide for around twenty different traffic flows travelling through a converted system at Crewe, at Lloyd's 60 mph - much less the current 70 mph legal speeds. It would be completely impossible without costly grade separation, and substantial acquisition of adjoining land. To convey existing rail passengers through the Crewe area by bus or car and rail freight by lorry would require so many vehicles on so many conflicting routes that the term 'road congestion' would take on a new meaning. Road traffic would, often be stationary through this area.

According to the Highways Agency, the width required for a motorway, with three lanes each side, is 35.6 metres. The DoT requires an overall width of 16.5 metres for a four-track railway and 8.08 metres for a two-track route.[12] The London-Glasgow west coast main line has two tracks for over half of its length. The railway is wider at stations, but these must be compared to nine motorway service areas south of Crewe that occupy far more land, and to the huge clover leaf junctions on motorways. Junctions on the M1/M6 and M6/M5, M1/M25 etc., are in a league on their own. The requirements for motorways and railways are depicted in a diagram (see next page). The outer box represents the land width and bridge height required for a three-lane motorway; the larger hatched box that required for a four-track railway; the smaller hatched box for a double-track railway. The space between would take a further three-track railway. It will be seen that the width required for a three lane motorway is wide enough for three main lines!

---

[11] Hold-ups are mostly due to the higher incidence of accidents. They would be reduced by better driving, improved vehicle design and better maintenance, (see *Juggernaut* by John Wardroper). Photos taken by the author reveal seriously under-utilised roads in Cheshire, Staffordshire and North Wales, including the M6. (see photo pages).

[12] Department of Transport *Railway Construction & Operation Requirements.*

The headway comparison, made in the article, between rail and road, overlooks relevant facts. Cars have an average load of 1.6 persons.[13] A passenger train carries as much as 300 cars, at almost twice their speed. As the safe headroom between vehicles is one metre for every one mph[14] the aggregate headroom for 300 cars, at 70 mph, on one track/lane, would be 21,000 metres, ten times the *long gap* maintained, for safety reasons, ahead of a 125mph passenger train.[15] If cars travelled 50% faster, their headroom would need to equate to 15 times the *long gap* between trains.

The average load of a lorry being 5 tons,[16] a freight train can convey as much as 200 lorries, and travels 25% faster. At 60 mph, with a braking distance of one metre for every one mph, lorries require an aggregate 12,000 metres headroom, seven times that of a 75 mph freightliner.[17] At 75 mph, 200 vehicles would need 15,000 metres aggregate headroom - ten times as much as a freightliner. The following illustrates headroom disparities:

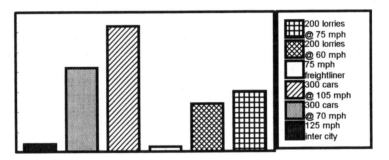

If, the railways - hitherto owned by the State - are under used, whilst the State owned roads are over used, it is evidence of gross mismanagement by the owners! In reality road utilisation is poor. Much congestion on roads is caused by bad driving and the ensuing accidents. We are as far away as ever from the utopian standards of driving which Brigadier Lloyd saw as crucial to conversion.

An RAC Report (Motoring Facts, 2004, Page 31), shows that drivers who exceed speed limits frequently, are three times as likely to have accidents, as those who exceed it infrequently.

What conversionists fail to appreciate, is that if railways are closed, the daily hours of road drivers will fall like a stone and their wages will rise to compensate, like money was going out of fashion. The consumer: public, industry, state, et al, will pick up the tab.

---

[13] Annual Abstract of Statistics, 1998, Tables 14.2 & 14.4
[14] Highway Code & LGV School Instructors.
[15] Railway Signalling Standards.
[16] Annual Abstract of Statistics, 1998, Tables 14.1 & 14.4
[17] Railway Signalling Standards.

The Conversion League failed to convince road transport operators and road engineers of the practicability of their dream, (see chapter 4). They failed to convince Transport Ministers, who were mostly road-minded, in particular Ernest Marples, partner in a road construction business. They failed to convince MPs, who noticeably did not take up the cause. Their white knight - Sir David Robertson, MP - deserted the cause, (see pages 52,53,55). Finally, they failed to convince the public. They tried to give an impression of support, by some selective editing of media reports, (see pages 75-76).

The public clearly saw through the generalisation and irrelevancy. Views on the subject in the Letter pages of *The Times* are a good indicator, because of easy accessibility through its comprehensive index. In addition, a computer programme - Infotrac - available in Cheshire libraries, brings up a list of relevant letters. A search from 1954 onwards, revealed that, excluding letters from the League chairman, the ratio of letters *against* conversion, compared to those in favour was 15:1. This was during the era when criticisms of BR were the bread and butter of the Letters pages of newspapers, and it was rare to see *one* voicing support for BR.[1]

Significantly, no letters of support appeared in this search from anyone connected with road transport, proving that such roads would be of no benefit to them. A director of SMMT wrote that 'in 1981-2 taxes paid by *all* road users were £8.3bn including £1.6bn VAT on new vehicles[2], whilst road building and maintenance by local and national government amounted to £1.7bn', *(The Times, 30.6.81)*. This is a chalk and cheese argument. Besides its irrelevance to conversion, (see pages 93-94), the *real* question is what is the tax paid by road haulage, and what is the amount of extra costs of road construction and repair caused by their heavier axle weights? The road haulage industry is hiding behind the subsidy which they get from taxation of motorists, for whom road costs would be much lower, if public roads catered only for cars, and HGVs had to use segregated roads

Operators have not *objected* to conversion. The reason is clear. They know a converted system would be useless for them because of the restrictive loading gauge and flat junctions. Their hope of benefit from conversion, is that motorists would use a converted system, and free up motorways and dual carriageways for them. Motorists would not use the system. They urge transfer of freight to rail. If railways were converted, they would look for freight to transfer from trunk roads, unaware of physical constraints. Every user of trunk roads would hope that someone else will take to 50-60mph roads with flat junctions, thousands of traffic lights, no roundabouts and little scope for overtaking.

Letters to *The Times*, from *the public* in favour of converting the whole rail network - as advocated by the League, for use by existing road traffic as well as traffic conveying ex-rail traffic - were:
• Peter Masefield[3] quotes LT data showing the hourly capacity of a bus lane is two per minute, but it is only relevant to a normal street, interrupted by intersections. A lane on

---

[1] The author has written over 90 letters on railways and road transport to the national media, mostly to the *Daily* and *Sunday Telegraph*, all based on researched fact and figure. Not one was published.

[2] BR is not exempt from VAT on new vehicles or any other of its £1.2bn of external purchases. It cannot quote prices exclusive of VAT to customers, as hauliers, car dealers and other industry do, as if it were an add-on optional extra.

[3] See his letter - page 203.

a motorway [which a converted railway would be] with no buses stopping in the lane has higher capacity. Statistics are available from New York where one lane in the Lincoln tunnel carries a peak hour flow of 600 buses plus 100s of cars. (N Seymer 19.1.76).

- Mr. Posner[4] challenged Professor Day to debate conversion and posed the test whether money could be raised in the City for conversion. There have been examples of conversion.[5] As far as I know, no group would be allowed to operate a toll road.[6] (N Seymer, 30.6.81).

- Specially trained drivers on a converted network would not be required for safe higher speeds. Electromagnetic cables in the road could guide vehicles, as I proposed in 1957. Drivers would only be required at both ends of the journey.[7] (RH Tizard, 14.12.82).

Some 45 letters in *The Times* opposed the concept:

♦ *As an engineer*, I can see a very large number of problems in conversion. Most railways use the DoT formation width of 30 feet - down to 26 over and through bridges, (see photos). A moment's thought will convince one that the wholesale reconstruction and widening of cuttings, embankments, bridges, tunnels, and viaducts could not be met from our capital resources. (J Aitken, 6.7.54).

♦ A Saturday at Woking, Ealing or Willesden would destroy this dream [conversion]. A visit to congested rail networks in South Wales and the Midlands would make him wonder why he had entertained this illusion. What happens to his system in fog? (N Williams, 8.7.54).

♦ Branch lines may be capable of conversion, but it would be a national folly to scrap main lines and substitute a form of transport relying on imported fuel and rubber. (D Day 8.7.54).

♦ A train carries 600 or so passengers with luggage and a crew of only three[8], compared to a bus with a crew of two. This is the reason we have trunk line railways, which are bulk carriers. (A Mordaunt 9.7.54).

♦ Several years ago, a not very serious suggestion was made in Parliament to tear up the GC [Marylebone-Nottingham railway line] and make way for a road. (J Pertwee, 9.7.54).

♦ It must have been obvious to most readers - unlike those advocating conversion - that the width of land for a road is not the distance between the fences, but the formation which, for a two-track railway, is 23 feet. The cost of widening embankments and cuttings to provide additional width involving heavy earthworks and massive retaining walls would be out of the question. Some years ago, conversion was considered at Canterbury and dismissed, after a very brief examination showed it would be quite impossible to provide any greater width than the existing 23 feet. Any large scale proposal would only provide a comparatively narrow roadway. (C Gribble, 9.7.54).

---

[4] See his letter - page 204.

[5] Posner was referring to the real cost of total conversion, not short pieces.

[6] The DoT may have welcomed a proposal. Toll roads include the Mersey tunnel, Dartford bridge, M6 Expressway and Severn Bridge. There is a conventional alternative - funding by Treasury Stock. Given their conviction of the success of conversion, Treasury Stock at par, and a very low interest rate should have quickly sold out to the lobby. Putting money where the mouth is, sorts out the realists. His negative assumption is symptomatic of the apathy of UK businesses, which caused it to lose a centuries old lead in exports, (see *Britain's Railways - The Reality*, Chapter 14).

[7] It would need close control to have drivers ready for vehicles at the end of a converted road, and would cause some delay, unless they were going to snooze in cabs en route.

[8] This was in the steam era. It has reduced to two, and even to one man operation, (see page 205).

- The York-London service is three hours for 188 miles and is usually very punctual, often early; good catering, comfortable trains ride well. What has the League to compare with this? (J Latter, 19.3.71). *There was no response.*
- No country of our size can function without a modern railway service. (R Bonwit, 27.3.72).
- There is inadequate width, lines are not necessarily correctly sited in relation to the road system, and would require construction of additional access and junctions. Because only 20% of freight goes by rail, does not mean there could not be more. The Conversion League should re-name itself the 'Railway Re-construction League'. (G Jenkins, 12.4.72).
- If similar investment as is needed for conversion were put into railways it would go as far, if not farther to solving the problem of inadequate roads. Railways have to observe strict safety procedures. If one person is killed on railways, it is of national importance, whilst 20 killed on roads in one day are not mentioned. Any attempt to impose similar standards on motor transport would be crippling. (P Sain-Ley-Berry, 12.4.72).
- The eulogy of road transport depends on being *given* the necessary routes. Why should taxpayers *give* operators routes the railways maintain, control and police? BR is only compensated for running uneconomic services[9]. (W Whitehead, 13.4.72).
- Those who are not train drivers can travel by rail, but non-car drivers seldom go by road; road speeds cannot increase whereas trains can achieve vastly superior speeds; road travel results in great loss of life. (R Colyer, 14.4.72).
- Disturbed by devastating cuts in what is the safest and least polluting form of transport. Do the plans involve an increased allocation to the NHS to deal with increased casualties on roads which would result? Another objection is to the spurious argument that rail transport does not pay. Road transport is heavily subsidised by the public. (Dr J McFie, 11.10.72).
- The recommendation for railway cuts is based on narrow accounting considerations, without relevance to social and environmental needs. (A Holford-Walker, 11.10.72).
- If it is correct to claim [*The Times*, October 17], that rail is outdated as a means of carrying freight, how is it explained that West Germany, the most prosperous nation in Europe, sends 40% by rail, 23% by road and the rest by water. It is claimed that road transport is flexible. How flexible will it be when they are limited [by their size] to the present route system of the railways. (Dr L Taitz, 21.10.72).
- Has no one the courage to suggest that the rail network should be increased? There would be no risk of industrial action by the medical profession if casualties were reduced by a transfer of traffic from road to rail, (Dr J McFie, 7.3.73).
- An £0.45m conversion of railway to road in Cornwall was shortsighted. (D Lock 14.4.73).
- The US Dept of Transportation study of the problem [bus v. train] fails to compare like with like. Unlike buses, trains are separated by a signalling system which is proof against weather and sudden illness of the driver. American trains - but not buses - are forced to carry three redundant staff, in addition to the crew. Rail can be automated in response to chronic staff shortages. No technical innovation seems likely to eliminate the need for a driver on every bus[10]. The bus weight per passenger is less than a train, because of reduced space and comfort. (R Hope 28.1.74)

---

[9] These are retained by political decision. They were not funded by the taxpayer before 1969.

[10] First Group is recruiting drivers from Europe and the Balkans. Bus unions complain that wages are inadequate to attract staff. This distorts comparisons. Higher wages are paid to BR drivers, but these are less than industrial wages.

♦ People have been immobilised by rail closures and the withdrawal of replacement buses. A recent study shows if accident costs are taken into account, many subsidised lines are profitable. (R. Colyer, 30.8.74)

♦ I have news for those who see no role for railways in a small island surrounded by all-weather ports - Japan has opened a new line and is extending it, as passengers carried soar. BR is to introduce 125 mph running next October. Professor Hall's unpublished report[11] is alleged to demonstrate that buses can provide a faster service than trains on a converted double track railway where overbridges and tunnels are 25 foot wide. This conveys the spectacle of buses, running in poor visibility without signalling, some three feet from similar vehicles moving in the opposite direction, at a relative velocity of 250 mph - for how else could a bus service be faster than rail? (R Hope, 17.12.75).

♦ A *confidential study by the DoE*[12] suggests that £1,000m could be saved [*The Times* December 17] by changing from railways to busways. It assumes the majority of those using trains would switch to bus. With every railway closure the vast majority change to cars; transport costs will rise, not fall. (L Kohr, 23.12.75).

♦ The League claims [*The Times*, December 19], there is no role for railways in a small island surrounded by all-weather ports. The Isle of Man, Channel Isles and Malta closed theirs long ago. I hope he is not putting Britain and Japan in that context. The League had unparalleled opportunity to prove its convictions. BR has released 8,540 miles of track bed over 28 years but only few hundred miles[13] are converted. We could have led the world - but where to? (M Page, 23.12.75).

♦ Critics of the Study into conversion of railways into express busways must await publication, but it is ironic that the announcement appeared the day after [*The Times*] report *Fog and ice affect flights and roads*, with a 17 mile queue in fog on the M4; and A12 closed for hours after 30 vehicles collided. (S Hawtrey, 23.12.75).

♦ Not impressed when the government proposes to wield another axe on the railways, which we shall need when exhaustion of oil supplies results in the extinction of the internal combustion engine. (D Green, 23.12.75).

♦ The Transport Studies Group, Polytechnic of Central London had evaluated conversion based on studies in recent Report. It concluded that the case for conversion was weak, and costings assumed were highly suspect, especially in respect of road construction where there is an under evaluation by a factor of eight. (J Cooper, 25.4.77)

♦ In response to the Hall/Smith study, whatever the theoretical comparison between BR and a hypothetical new busway, for routes of any substantial density and distance a railway is inherently cheaper and faster. Practical statistics are published by an operator of both: London Transport, which shows virtually the same passenger miles by bus and train. For one exclusive track or bus-lane, the practical capacity is 120 buses per hour carrying up to 8400 passengers compared to 20,000 per hour by rail. A 7-coach train having about 65m passenger place miles pa requires 43 operating and maintenance staff. The same annual output is achieved by 24 buses requiring 134 staff. On energy consumption, BR electric InterCity trains achieve 295 capacity ton-miles per million BTUs compared with about 260 for an inter-city road coach. (Sir P Masefield, 5.1.76).

---

[11] See page 97.

[12] It was not *by* the DoE. It was the Hall/Smith report funded by the DoE, who told the authors they could publish.

[13] By 1975, it was only a few *dozen* miles.

♦ The lunacy of DoE transport plans is illustrated by Hall's crazy scheme to pave over miles of excellent track, and transport commuters in buses we don't possess, (J. Daly, 21.1.76)

♦ A USA study of highway wear, 15 years ago, revealed that damage caused by a 6-ton axle load was 10,000 times as much as a car, a 12-ton axle load was 160,000 times more. (R Calvert, 18.6.76).

♦ The [alleged] positive tax contributions by road users are turned negative if true environment and other costs are taken into account. A recent true, rather than *perceived* costing has given a debit approaching £1 bn pa, plus the cost of accidents. Far from rail freight being subsidised, it meets track and signalling costs that would be avoided if there was no rail freight business, together with administrative charges. Most freight is on InterCity routes which are not subsidised. (D Henry 25.4.77).

♦ The eccentric fantasies of the League are still given credence. Most of their claims and statistics were long ago shown to be bogus. It was never clear how Prof. Hall supposed that two coaches could pass on a 15 foot carriageway at speed. They will still be uttering platitudes about alternative fuels when the last oil well runs dry. (J Nearstead, 13.6.81).

♦ To suggest replacing rail by juggernauts and coaches is to fly in the face of all logic and experience. By the time railways are converted, oil will be prohibitively expensive. This is the conclusive argument for rail electrification to proceed. (S Steward, 13.6.81).

♦ Criticises anti-rail views of A. Sherman. Their factual basis is exposed. (M Oakley, 13.6.81)

♦ Sherman's concrete solution for railways is insubstantial in many respects, but becomes flimsy when applied to cities like London. Twice as many people come into central London by train than by car. Before investing capital in another panacea, it is time we learnt to make better use of what we have got. (H Sherlock, 13.6.81).

♦ Some champions of conversion have done more harm by making excessive claims. It is unlikely that objective study would justify converting the whole network. (A Day, 17.6.81)

♦ The plan for electrification was examined as a business proposition [not a cost benefit analysis, as applies with roads], but a hard headed examination of the commercial ROI of 11%. I have always regarded concreting over as a humorous introduction to an academic lecture not a serious suggestion. If any experienced businessman can produce a serious business proposition, I will debate it with him [Prof. Day, *The Times* 17.6.81] before a jury of our peers. My test would be whether its supporters can raise enough in the City to buy a bag of readymix, let alone a few million tons of concrete. (M Posner, 18.6.81)

♦ A comparison of changes in Europe 1955-80 shows our railway route cut by 41%. The average is 10%, and 12 of the 25 countries in Europe have extended route miles. Who is right - Britain or Europe? Our poor industrial[14] and economic performance hardly justifies the sublime insular conceit that rest of Europe is wrong. (E. Nicholson, 30.6.81).

♦ It is never in question that it is *technically* possible to convert railways into roads. It is cripplingly expensive. Trackbeds have been converted with a loss to the nation of the potential to rebuild the [rail] network. What converters fail to show is why it is desirable to emasculate the only large scale transportation this country possesses, which could be made invulnerable to interruption of oil supplies. (J Nearstead, 4.7.81)

---

[14] This is a crucial point. If major UK industry: shipbuilding, cars, engineering, etc., had been expanding instead of contracting, UK railways would have been highly profitable. See *Britain's Railways - The Reality*, Chapter 14 for some interesting revelations.

♦ Letters from the vociferous lobby which wishes to convert railways into roads are silent in one highly relevant point - safety. Every year, thousands are killed on our roads. It is reasonable to predict an increase in road mileage will lead to an increase in casualties. This is inevitable with a system that relies on people using millions of vehicles, many in a dubious state of roadworthiness. Perhaps the lobby can suggest an effective way of reducing road deaths before they deprive us of our one safe system. (A Everson, 4.7.81).

♦ The study of conversion, [*The Times*, March 24], leaves much unsaid, casting doubt on its conclusions. The DoT recently turned down electrification to Cambridge as the ROI is only 18%. What ROI is expected from conversion? A double track railway is 20 ft wide - the same as a suburban back street. Unless a modest road is accepted, the cost of building a road will not be reduced because a railway once ran there, on an alignment that would never have been chosen for a road. (W Barter 31.3.82).

♦ Guided transport systems allow uninterrupted services in poor visibility, very high safety standards, high levels of energy efficiency from a variety of fuel sources, and free of pollution. BR anticipates running one man operated trains, carrying up to 1,000 passengers[15]. If the roads system proposed by Mr. Ibbotson, (see next page), is restricted to existing rail users with people and goods in buses and lorries instead of trains, the same level of infrastructure costs will have to be covered by the same customers. If, on the other hand, the road is open to all and sundry, the discipline necessary to secure high standards of operation will be lost. No mention is made by him of the cost of converting or the need for extensive access works, to safely allow buses and lorries to join in a closely spaced procession of vehicles moving at 80 mph. A fraction of the investment required would thoroughly modernise railways. In the movement of bulk loads of freight and passengers, railways provide excellent value. (W Bradshaw, 4.12.82).

♦ That London's commuter trains could be replaced by buses running in a disciplined manner on converted routes has mainly academic support[16]. It falls down at practical hurdles: system control, junction working, terminal layout and safety. (D McKenna, 4.12.82)

♦ How unfortunate for [the League] that on day you publish their letter - which flies in the face of all intelligent and technical reasoning, you carried a report of the first of this winter's motorway pile-ups in fog. When will they grasp that uncontrolled movement of road vehicles is *bound* to lead to accidents in fog, heavy rain or snow. If drivers are unable to behave sensibly on roads built specially for them, how can any rational person believe they will do better on roads made out of railways. (R Faulkner, 13.12.82).

♦ Why are we arguing conversion of highly developed railways into undisciplined roads without considering a device that combines both: RoadRailer? It has interchangeable rear road & rail wheels, and used in USA. It was tried in the UK, but displaced when the container [revolution] began. US tests prove it is four times as fuel-economical as trailers. It would rid trunk roads of many juggernauts. (G Freeman Allen, 5.1.83).

♦ 55% of UK railways have closed. We are not alone. This action was taken by Cyprus, Guyana, Haiti, Libya, Mauritius, Sierra Leone, Surinam, Trinidad and Venezuela. Five of these forward looking nations have eliminated railways altogether. There are signs of backsliding by Libya and Venezuela which are toying with the idea of building new lines - in the former case with the aid of British consulting engineers. (R Hope, 12.1.83).

---

[15] The first such service began in March 1983 between St.Pancras and Bedford.

[16] This is an important point. Conversion has never been supported by practical people in the road transport industry.

◆ In the fifties, we had a thriving motor industry. Costly state intervention is the reason it still supplies 30% of demand. The attempt to boost private transport has been disastrous - BR's record is a comparative success. As you observe [editorial, 21.1.76], why do other nations not concur with those, who wish to scrap railways. Perhaps the answer lies in the influence of irresponsible interest groups such as the road lobby. (Prof C Harvie, 1.2.83)

Three were neither for nor against League policy, but favoured conversion of lines not required for rail use, or a network limited to high speed vehicles, excluding existing road traffic. The League opposed such concepts. If the system was not open to all, the claim that it would ease congestion falls, and the main reason for conversion disappears:
1. Government should fund a 20 mile trial conversion with separate routes for fast [200 mph] and slow traffic and road freight 'trains' like those in Australia. (C. Nockolds, 3.7.54)
2. The solution to congestion is to convert *some* lines. No new land would be required[17] and construction limited to surfacing. A 2-track line is 23 foot wide sufficient for a 4-lane road! Where widening is expensive at tunnels and bridges,[18] roads could narrow to two lanes. It may be possible to use parallel routes as one way roads.[19] (Prof. Bondi, 7.7.56)
3. Railways should be converted to roads, reserved for 80mph public transport. The system would not be open to all traffic.[20] Buses would call at locations not served by rail and go into centres of population from which, stations are remote.[21] At the terminal, buses could turn round, or go on into central areas[22]. (L Ibbotson interviewed, 29.11.82).
   The League disagreed (The Times, 7.12.82) *with high speed only traffic, but envisages low speeds on converted railways which would increase capacity.*[23]

On the Internet[24], it is asked if conversion is a good idea, why hasn't anyone else done it? No major developed country has done so. Most, with similar distances and population density [France, Germany, Italy, Japan], are investing *more* to improve rail. The UK has closed 10,000 miles, but less than 5% has turned into road. The USA has many busy and expanding commuter rail networks round major cities, and enormous amounts of long-distance bulk rail freight. Most closed railroads in the USA have simply been abandoned. Even where small countries such as Mauritius abandoned rail, trains have been replaced by buses and trucks on existing roads, and tracks left to be recolonised by nature, or, turned into leisure footpaths. Many new interchanges with the existing road network would need to be created, requiring a large amount of additional land. If buses provide such capacity advantages, the best way to take advantage would be to encourage their use on existing roads in preference to cars. Our transport problems require large-scale investment in rail and road. Creating false 'either-or' options is mischievous and counter-productive. So if railways did not exist, we would probably end up inventing them.

---

[17] This belief was not borne out by experience. See chapter 13. The Hall/Smith scheme requires acquisitions.
[18] In reality, all tunnels and viaducts and virtually all bridges.
[19] He had made this suggestion at the ICE meeting in 1955. It is an impracticable proposal, (see page 27).
[20] He need have no fear, motorists would not wish to share a single carriageway with lorries and buses at that speed!
[21] He did not explain how buses calling at additional points and going into town centres could run at faster schedules than trains permitted to run 20 mph faster!
[22] They would add to congestion. He did not state that lorries would not be allowed on commuter routes during peaks
[23] This is nonsense, any transport operator knows that higher speeds improve vehicle and manpower productivity and produce the best utilisation of track capacity. Utilisation is worsened by variations of vehicle speed.
[24] www.speedlimit.dreamwater.org/railconv.html.

Chapter 16

The idiosyncratic proposal to solve road delays advanced by the theorists, namely that 11,000 miles of railway be converted into roads to solve delays occurring on 220,000 miles of road is - to coin their word - risible. The theory is founded on eight assumptions:
- 'Single carriageway' motorways with nine foot wide lanes are adequate.
- Accidents on these new lower standard roads will be lower than those experienced on existing roads - including 3-lane motorways.
- Passengers displaced from trains will transfer to buses not cars, despite evidence to the contrary following closure of 10,000 miles of railway.
- Buses, even if impeded by cars will travel at 60 mph in all conditions and circumstances
- There will be limitless capacity on city roads for the inflow of thousands of extra buses and for those who insist on using cars, whether on these new roads or existing roads.
- Ample parking will be available for motorists at the end of a converted rail route. None will cross a city - adding to congestion - to get to a new carpark nearer to a workplace.
- Oil[1] will never run out, nor the country be held to ransom by supplier countries, and forced to pay ever increasing prices.
- Other European countries are pursuing the wrong course.

Weaknesses in these assumptions are air-brushed out. The average speed of buses on 2/3-lane motorways, which have no flat junctions, is 58 mph. Their speed on existing single carriageway roads with flat junctions is 45 mph. The belief that there would be no frontage access is misplaced. Selfish motorists and selfish professional drivers, will rarely give way to vehicles emerging from premises still on converted routes, nor at junctions.

The only nine foot lane roads identified by the conversionists are those in tunnels such as the Mersey Tunnel, where the speed limit is 30 mph.

The belief that accidents will fall, is based on pure speculation. No case study has been properly evaluated - before and after - as is essential. Claims in respect of improved safety on the Southport road conversion (see page 66), are expressed in woolly terms which would be thrown out by any Board of Directors.

Passenger mileage by bus has fallen steeply, whilst that by rail fell slightly, and that by car has soared.

Oil is of finite quantity, depends on nature and has taken millennia to create. Reports of over-estimated reserves are a warning. New oilfield discoveries tend to be more costly. Renewable energy sources generally have little effect on global warming, are unsuited to road transport, but ideal for railways: nuclear, wind or water powered electricity.

The conversionists count only the length of motorways and trunk roads in their comparisons with railway mileage, despite little traffic originating on either. They ignore that most fatalities occur on those roads, whose existence they endeavour to air brush out of any comparison with railways, but from which traffic originates. They keep losing the plot and using figures which are chalk and cheese comparisons.

If full scale conversion of railways into roads went ahead, government would have to enforce transhipment as a means of avoiding heavy costs to repair town damage.

---

[1] It is overlooked by the road lobby that oil imports have a bearing on the balance of payments - as do imports of foreign built road transport of all kinds. The effect of reducing this should be brought into any rail/road equation.

The new railway companies have been paid far more subsidy than BR ever dreamed of - to achieve less. It will lead to more closures, and open the door for pipe-dreamers to hope to 'convert' a few more miles to roads, although it will probably create more footpaths.

Effective management of roads & road transport

Misuse of bus lanes by motorists and commercial vehicles is endemic. Other lanes are wastefully used by vehicles hogging middle or outer lanes. As accidents happen on motorways, so they will happen - in spades - on a converted, mainly single carriageway system, and there will be little prospect of squeezing round an accident.

The first step in tackling delays is to *manage* the existing road system, as there is no system of management worthy of the name. More off-road cycle tracks and bridleways would reduce delays. Many local authorities are alive to this and have taken action by converting many closed railways to such purposes.[2] More remains to be done. Some under-utilised roads should be converted. No road should be without pavements on both sides. This will keep pedestrians and hikers off the road. These policies cost money, the burden of which must fall on road transport. Attention needs to be given to the use of roads, especially during peak commuter hours by farm tractors, that use roads without paying for them. They should be barred in peak hours. This would pressure them to create off-road inter field routes, or seek to re-arrange land ownership so that they own fields linked other than by public roads. Purchase of closed sections of railway will continue to help in this direction. Horse riders should be prohibited on roads in peak hours.

The second step is to adopt as standard, the lane width which conversion theorists say is adequate[3] for speeds of 50 mph: shorten deceleration lanes to 90m, tarmac up to the boundary fence, dispense with hard shoulders or reduce them to the one metre width mentioned in the Hall/Smith study and elsewhere. Three-lane motorways would then become five lanes. Accompanied by an enforced speed limit of the 50 mph deemed adequate by Hall/Smith, it will ensure that smooth flows are not interrupted by those maddening delays which are probably caused by vastly differing vehicle speeds. Congestion and accidents will decline, further reducing delays. In any future building, the recommended headroom of bridges can be cut to 4.6m from 5.1m with huge savings.

The third step is to reduce the permitted working hours of road transport drivers and impose effective controls to ensure that they are observed. This would be accompanied by a fourth measure imposing tougher maintenance standards on all road vehicles, especially lorries and PSVs, and to eliminate the cowboy element. An annual MoT test for such vehicles is inadequate. A high mileage vehicle should be tested more frequently than low mileage cars. Garage standards have been recently reported to be unsatisfactory with 25% of vehicle faults remaining unresolved. Firm corrective action is needed by the DfT.

The fifth step should be effective action on illegal hauliers, and unlicensed cars esti-mated by the RAC to be 5%, (see Report on Motoring 2004). These hauliers and motorists are thereby opted out of MoT tests, and more likely to cause accidents, which cause delays.

---

[2] They have discovered there are unforeseen costs to be borne - the like of which is outwith the comprehension of the conversion campaigners. Maintenance of fences, ditches, culverts, bridges, viaducts, embankments, sea walls - the latter, rarely found on roads - is a heavy, unending burden. Farmers are vociferous in their demands for fence repairs and control of weeds. Vandalism is a serious problem.

[3] An RAC 2004 Report on Motoring recommends tackling congestion including variable speed limits on motorways and narrow lanes to improve the use of existing road space.

The next step would be to take penal action with tailgating drivers, who are likely to cause accidents and certainly cause delays to cars seeking to overtake.

Finally, there must be an end to the use of lay-bys as overnight parking for lorries, which is commonplace. They should be parked in safe secure compounds. This should be obvious in normal crime ridden times, and especially in current terror ridden times. 'LGVs have to be based at authorised centres. There is reason to believe that non-compliance may be a serious problem. Licensing authorities dealt with fifteen operators regularly parked away from authorised centres'. (Plowden & Buchan)

Smith wrote in the Journal of Transport Economics & Policy (September 1973): 'any railway physically suitable should be considered for conversion to a road'. Any *objective* approach would consider the converse. Later, he wrote: 'I am not advocating that all railways should be converted', (*The Times* 30.1.74). The DoE grant to Hall/Smith would have had more value had it been applied to a study of the Better Use of Road-ways, because the network is not managed so as to make best use of them. Such a study is long overdue.

Guided busways

One idea is to convert railways into guided busways. Inquiries about them of MPs, technical press and libraries were unfruitful. Research led to a reference in Parliament, (Hansard 2.2.93, col. 231) which mentioned the 'Oban guided busway'. Inquiries of the helpful librarian at Oban revealed there was no guided busway there, but he found on the Internet, that the O-Bahn guided busway system originated in Essen, Germany. There are guided busways in Bradford, Crawley, Edinburgh, Leeds[4] and Ipswich, but not in Aberdeen where an MP forecast them. Buses are fitted with side guidance wheels. UK routes total 10.4km, most, in short sections - the longest is 1.5km in Edinburgh. They are costly. The Edinburgh scheme cost public authorities £10m. The Crawley scheme was about 50% over budget.

Problems arise from replacing railways with guided busways: at level crossings - public, farm, private and footpaths - and junctions. They are only usable by specially designed buses. Blocking devices may prevent access of standard buses, cars, or goods vehicles. A breakdown or collision blocks a lane until a rescue or emergency vehicle arrives. If a railway was converted to a two-lane guided busway, a bus could not pass a broken down vehicle. Changing a wheel could prove difficult. Resurfacing such roads requires buses to divert to ordinary roads. A driver told the author that as they are deemed light railways, in the event of an accident, British Transport Police attend from the nearest major station

Guidance over short distances are of limited value. When buses leave the system, they revert to the frail hand of drivers working long hours, and often are delayed at round-abouts by traffic from the right. Replacement of trains on rural routes is being encouraged by the SRA and some local authorities to try to limit out-of-control subsidies.[5] It is unlikely that bus operators will pay all infrastructure costs of railways converted to busways, just as they do not pay for bus shelters, bus lanes, red routes, raised pavements and lay-bys. Guided busways may prove to be a nine day wonder. It is also worth noting

---

[4] The author travelled on Leeds guided buses (see photo). They rattled and were a noisy uncomfortable ride at 30-40 mph. Vehicles like these would replace trains in the Hall/Smith scheme. Transfer to car would be inevitable.

[5] Which eclipse those given to BR, which were to support rural or secondary operations, but have been granted for main line services, which under BR received no subsidy, (see *Britain's Railways - The Reality*, Page 183).

that they do not subscribe to the Hall/Smith concept of operating without timetables. Nor do they fit the profile envisaged by the Conversion League/Campaign, which wanted converted railways to be used by all forms of road transport. Repairs to surfaces were required twice in the first year of busway operation in Edinburgh, which was on the route of a former railway. 'Ever since it opened, it has been one disaster after another. It was closed twice for repairs, following complaints of bumpy rides, once for a week, and once for ten days.' (Evening News, 15.11.05). It had cost £10m to build, plus £4m for special buses.

Under original Enabling Acts, which gave compulsory purchase powers, current owners of land crossed by railways may still have legal powers to seek restoration of land, when it ceases to be used for its original purpose. Those owning land bordering railways would be well advised to research land and Parliamentary records and lodge objections and claims.

Alternative strategies

Super juggernauts, 33m long, which may tailgate another, are not an answer. They are on trial on a disused airfield. That would confirm suitability for the Sahara desert, not the M6 or M1. Lay-bys, funded by the haulier, would be needed near motorway junctions to drop-off or pick-up a trailer as envisaged in the East Anglian scheme, (see chapter 10). Without them, they would have to split *after* leaving a motorway. The prospect of negotiating roundabouts - or junctions - alongside one, as they leave the motorway, does not bear contemplation. Anyone intimidated by an ordinary juggernaut pulling out in front, must avoid motorways if these appear. If they are introduced, and *one* motorist complains of being directly or indirectly delayed, they should be removed at once from UK roads without compensation, since their advocates claim they will not cause delay.
Planning studies

Road traffic could be cut[6] by planning controls on the location of supermarket and retail distribution centres - forcing them to build near railways, and by enforcing distribution in vehicles more environmentally friendly than juggernauts. Delivery in towns should be in small units. If building slip roads, etc., to connect existing roads to converted railways could be 'financed' on the basis of time saved by motorists - there is no better way to save such time in the national interest, than by slip roads to rail-served distribution centres.

In its 1970 Report, the League called for an investigation into the best national use of railways, but ignored the converse - which would occur to an unbiased academic - that it should investigate roads to determine to what other use, they could be put. Statistics prepared by the author show that utilisation of roads[7] was much worse than railways, (see pages 88,173), and hence should be closely studied to effect an improvement by closing excess road mileage. The time has come to widen the debate, and look at the gains to be made from converting roads into railways. The conversion campaign has claimed that railways could be widened at little cost. They have been adamant that improved bridge headroom could be achieved - at low cost - by excavating formations or raising decks, and that some bridges could be closed. These changes could equally benefit rail transport, allowing wider and higher loads. This would include piggy-back carriage of juggernaut trailers. Getting these off roads would increase traffic flow, reduce road maintenance costs and slash accidents. Fewer accidents would cut costs of emergency services and

---

[6] RAC studies show that 25% of car mileage is to shops.
[7] These comparative statistics were based on data which inflates road transport volume (see page 153).

NHS, whose waiting lists would then fall. Contraflows would be reduced, leading to more constant car speeds and fewer accidents. Fuel consumption would fall. Lay-bys used as cost free overnight or weekend lorry parking could be closed, with modest savings.

Public Inquiries into road building

A policy change is required giving the public total freedom to object to new roads, a right to be given access to, and to dispute, traffic forecasts used to justify road building. This would be consistent with rights in respect of new railway routes and closures.

Transfer traffic to rail

'Heavy lorry mileage on journeys over 150 km represents 50% of all mileage and 20% of all goods. Transferring this to rail would cut total lorry mileage by a half.'[8] If trunk haulage was by rail, using smaller containers, haulage into towns and villages on shorter vehicles would slash congestion, reduce damage to buildings, and end damage to pavements and verges - some of which compare unfavourably with ploughed fields.

The Economist stated [April 1973]: government is sitting on a Report advocating switching road freight to rail. It will not be published by the DoE which commissioned the Report and should have laid all evidence for and against rail before deciding on the railways' future. From evidence of three studies covering large freight flows, the Report argues that the net benefit by switching to rail is about 2p for every mile travelled by HGVs. That is after calculating the rail subsidy and environmental costs of road and rail in terms of noise, pollution and accidents. A household survey suggests that those living beside a railway are less disturbed by traffic than those living next to a busy road. The Report is the work of Transport Consultants. The current minimum charge for using a heavy lorry is 25p per mile.[9] This Report (*The Economist*, 24.11.73), did not catch the eye of the Conversion League, when it trawled the pages of *The Economist* for 'expert views' in support of its campaign.

Converting road lanes to railways

In view of poor road utilisation, an option is to convert some roads to railways. The estimated annual goods vehicle km of 10.8bn on motorways[10] equates to only 185 vehicles per hour in each direction. Their average five ton load, is less than one train load, which would not tax one lane converted to a railway. Less oil and fewer lorries would be imported,[11] improving the balance of payments. Converting some roads to railways would not face the transitional problems caused by the converse. Random observations indicate that there is spare capacity on freightliner trains. Secondly, the under-utilisation of roads, which is referred to earlier, allows scope for re-routing road traffic during the changeover period. Much cross empty mileage would be eliminated by central control of containers. Motorway lanes converted to railways would not need widening, nor bridges need to be lifted. With freight trains thundering by at faster speed than cars, there would be an influence to steer straight and pay attention. Such trains would wake up tired motorists!

Build new railways with enhanced clearances

Three factors will compel the UK to re-ignite railway development, which can be based on electricity produced from nuclear fuel or non-fossil sources: global warming, the

---

[8] "*Goods without the Bads*", Transport 2000 Booklet.
[9] Economist 24.11.73.
[10] *Transport Statistics of Great Britain*, Table 4.9
[11] Only 5% of HGV operated by UK companies are made in UK.

escalating demand for petroleum, with countries like China boosting car sales, and a fall in oil reserves (e.g. Shell's revised estimation). Air travel will have to be curtailed because of its heavy consumption of oil, and its effect on global warming. Short haul air services within Europe will be the first to be hit, the beneficiary being rail. The price of oil will rise as a 'normal' market force to hold down demand to equate more nearly to supply. The effect will be to cut road transport - the beneficiary will again be rail. The countries that get onto the electric bandwagon first, will be in the forefront of selling materials and know-how to those that don't.

In view of the higher cost of privatised railways, which ought to be returned to the State sector, to cut the subsidy - but as politicians never seem to admit a mistake, have not been - any new railway built in place of motorways, should be run by the public sector.[12]

Using principles advocated by conversion theorists and practised by the DoT, the cost of a fast new railway could be offset by time savings expected to be achieved by motorists.

Other benefits from a reversion to rail transport

As 95% lorries are bought abroad - using a phrase beloved by the League - it may possibly give a shot in the arm to UK industry who may find it easier to compete in building smaller vehicles for town deliveries. This should improve the balance of payments

Environmental benefits would arise from replacing road by rail transport - using home produced electricity instead of imported oil, which has so many bad sude effects.

Provision of distribution depots at railway locations for transhipping containers to vehicles suitable for towns would cut damage to buildings, pavements, road furniture, water mains, gas mains, and sewers. They would cut hidden subsidies and reduce traffic delays arising from road works. Distribution into towns by small lorries would reduce traffic delays and congestion, as well as environmental and structural damage. They may even breathe new life into town centres by facilitating the re-opening of High Street shops. The whole subject needs a comprehensive study by independent consultants, which would look at the big picture and take account of reductions in road wear and tear, oil imports, savings from reduced damage and delay, and all other cost elements.

Rail-roads : joint use of formations

A new proposal is to convert railways to dual use of train and motor by infilling tracks with rubber. The common speed enforced by the braking distance of trains, the width of formations and the inability of road vehicles to overtake a train, renders it impractical.

An American reader wrote[13] to *The Economist* (26.8.74): 'a concrete and rubber tyre solution is costly and consumes vast quantities of land, is energy intensive, pollutes the air, creates the urban sprawl life style made famous by Southern California. It ultimately becomes so congested that consumer preferences switch back from car to train. I believe that is beginning to happen in the USA. Disillusioned Americans long for the day they can get from Boston to New York by train'. The conversion theorists overlooked this view in their references to the USA, and their selected quotations from *The Economist*.

---

[12] For evidence that railways were better managed under BR - see *Britain's Railways - The Reality.*

[13] Another view in the Economist overlooked by the League. It should be considered as an alternative to those who focus on the New York bus terminal.

Abbreviations

BA	British Airways
BR	British Railways
BRB	British Rail Board
BRF	British Road Federation
BRS	British Road Services
BTC	British Transport Commission
CBC	County Borough Council
CEA	Central Electricity Authority
cms.	centimetres
col.	column
CSO	Central Office of Statistics (now re-named ONS)
CTCC	Central Transport Users Consultative Committee
DCF	Discounted cash flow
DETR	Department of the Environment, Transport & the Regions
DoE	Department of the Environment
DfT	Department for Transport
DoT	Department of Transport
EEC	European Economic Community
EPT	Excess Profits Tax
ft	foot or feet; one = 30.48 cm
GC	Great Central Railway
GLC	Greater London Council
gvw	gross vehicle weight - the tare & load of a fully laden lorry
HGV	Heavy Goods Vehicle [later replaced by LGV]
HoL	House of Lords
ICE	Institition of Civil Engineers
HMRI	Her Majesty's Railway Inspectors [or Inspectorate]
H&SE	Health & Safety Executive
ins	inches (12 = 1 foot) 1inch = 2.5cm
LGV	Long Goods Vehicle
LNWR	London & North Western Railway [pre 1923]
LPTB	London Passenger Transport Board
LT	London Transport
LT&S	London-Tilbury-Southend line
MDC	Metropolitan District Council
Mg	Megagram = 1000 tonnes [used in Hall/Smith study]
M&GN	Midland & Great Northern Rly

MGR	'Merry-go-round' coal trains - 1000+ net tons, load & unload without stopping.
MoT	Minister/Ministry of Transport
mpg	miles per gallon
NBC	National Bus Company
NCB	National Coal Board
NER	North Eastern Railway
NFC	National Freight Corporation
NHS	National Health Service
NIMBY	Not in my back yard
NPV	Net present value
OLE	Overhead [electrification] line equipment
OMO	one-man operation (train or bus)
ONS	Office of National Statistics
PACTS	Parliamentary Advisory Council for Transport Safety
PSB	Power Signal Box
PEP	Political & Economic Planning
PCUs	Passenger car units (a DoT formula)
PRO	Public Record Office
PSV	Passenger Service Vehicle
RAC	Royal Automobile Club
RHA	Road Haulage Association
ROI	Return on investment
RRL	Road Research Laboratory, see TRL
RPI	Retail Price Index [indicator of inflation]
S&D	Somerset & Dorset line
SMMT	Society of Motor Manufacturers & Traders
SRA	Strategic Rail Authority
TRL	Transport Research Laboratory
TUCC	Transport Users Consultative Committee [Rail watchdog]
UKRAS	United Kingdom Railway Advisory Service
ulw	unladen weight of a road vehicle
vol.	volume

Notes

Most sources are shown as footnotes, or occasionally, in the text. An exception is *A new framework for freight transport* by Plowden & Buchan, which is referred to in the text or in footnotes by the names of the authors.

The views of the Stedeford Committee - officially, the Special Advisory Group - are mentioned. Their records can be found in the PRO under the following references:

MT124/361, /547,

MT132/80, /81, /82, /83, /84, /85, /86, /87, /88.

The author's previous books (see list after the Index), contain more detail. The file which contained their favourable views on professional railway managers was MT132/85. In that, they stated 'there was no real management of railways, and the Area Boards [created in 1953] were ineffective'. The Committee believed that the railways should be run by professionals. The Railway Executive - composed of professionals - had been abolished by the Tory government in 1953, to be replaced by a quasi-military style management introduced by the new chairman of the overlord body - the British Transport Commission - General Sir Brian Robertson. His replacement, Dr. Beeching - a member of the Committee - implemented changes to put professionals in control. Government failed to implement the Committee's recommendations on fares, closure and other freedoms.

The Countryside Commission Report (see chapter 13) is at the British Library F77/30732.

The information on the Pennsylvania Turnpike (chapter 12) is from the the 60th Anniversary history of the Commission., kindly supplied by Carl Defebo of the Commission.

Measurements

Length is expressed in sizes used in documents or books which are quoted. These include *Imperial* measurements, which were yards, foot (singular; plural = feet), and inches. Three feet equal one yard, 12 inches = one foot, and 36 inches = one yard. 1760 yards = one mile. A yard is 0.914 metres, one metre is 1.094 yards. A mile is 1.609 kilometres.

Weight is expressed in terms used in the documents or books quoted. These include the *Imperial* measurement tons which was slightly heavier than a metric tonne, one ton = 1.016 tonnes, one tonne being 1000 kg.

Diagrams

Diagrams in this book are to illustrate points made by this author, not to correct the lack of diagrams in other publications.

Hansard = Commons, HoL Hansard = Lords

page/chapter (lower case) refers to another page/chapter within this book.

Page/Chapter (upper case) refers to a Page/Chapter within the book quoted. In chapter 10, and Chapter 10 Part III, it refers - unless otherwise shown - to the Hall/Smith Report, in Chapter 10 Part II it refers to their *Rejoinders*, unless otherwise shown.

( ) Used to enclose a cross reference to another page or chapter in this book, or to show the Page or Chapter in a book from which an extract is included.

[ ] Used to enclose text which was within brackets in the text quoted, or is inserted by the author to clarify the meaning of the text.

Italics are the author's

Errata

page 22 note[19] March 1954 to be March 1955

page 167 note[8] 90 feet to be 90m

Index